REMO

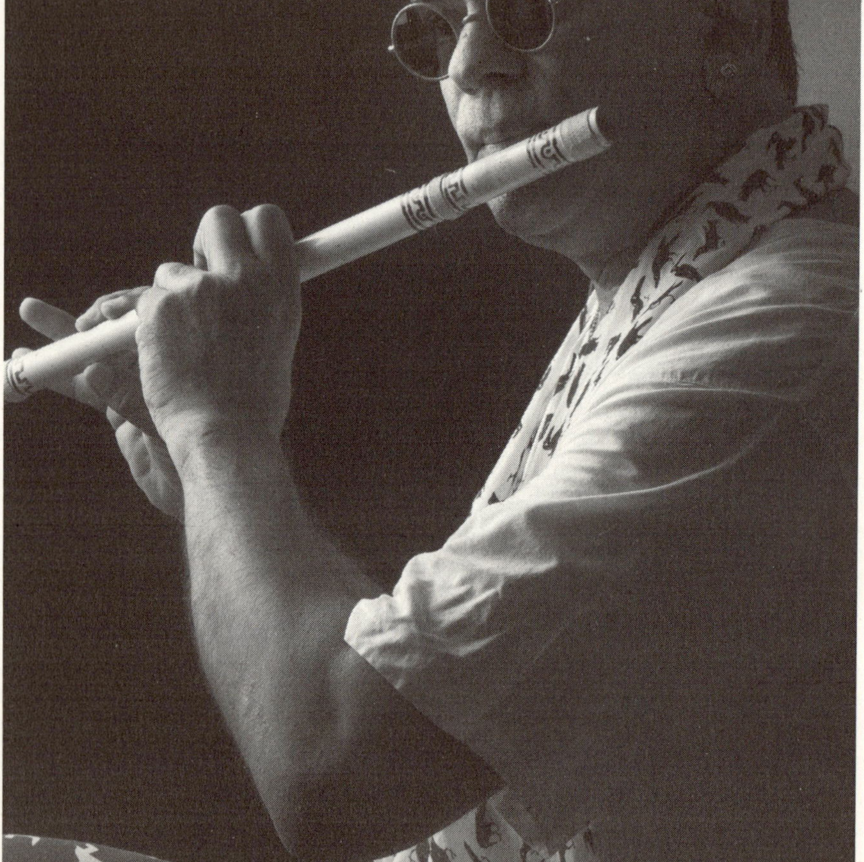

REMO

THE AUTOBIOGRAPHY OF
REMO FERNANDES

HarperCollins *Publishers* India

First published in hardback in India by
HarperCollins *Publishers* 2021
4th Floor, Tower A, Building No. 10, DLF Cyber City,
DLF Phase II, Gurugram, Haryana – 122002
www.harpercollins.co.in

This edition published in India by HarperCollins *Publishers* 2024

2 4 6 8 10 9 7 5 3 1

Copyright © Remo Fernandes 2021, 2024
Frontispiece photograph courtesy Alex Fernandes Portraits

P-ISBN: 978-93-6213-242-0
E-ISBN: 978-93-5489-341-4

Typeset in 11.5/16 Arno Pro at
Manipal Technologies Limited, Manipal

Printed and bound at
Thomson Press (India) Ltd

For Zenia

My life.

In words.

Contents

PART III: BACK TO ROOTS

PART IV: AFTER ALL

Prologue

'Bhai I'm telling you, soda water bijness is best bijness!'
'Why yaar?'

'*Arre, paani se paisa hota hai, bhai!* Water to money only! Just bubbles putting, and money becoming! *Ho gaya!*'

This conversation, overheard by my father in an Irani restaurant in Bombay soon after he threw his resignation letter on the table of his British boss at the censor's office, was a turning point. Not that Father believed the simplistic industrial theory of the man who was speaking, but it helped him make up his mind: he'd return to Goa and set up the best aerated water factory Goa had seen. And that's what mercifully made me a Goa Boy instead of a Bombay Boy. I have nothing against Bombay Boys; after all they're much more forward and savvy than us in everything, and Bombay would have been the place for me to rise and prosper tenfold more than I did in my chosen fields, music and showbiz.

But I wouldn't exchange the joys and pleasures of growing up in a quiet, blissful paradise like the Goa of those days for all the success, fame and money in the world.

PART I

GOA

1

And in the Beginning

Pangim, Goa, Estado da Índia Portuguesa

I knew the cracks on our old footpath by heart. They formed a formidable map of imaginary hurdles for a six-year-old zooming around in his red pedal-car called 'Thunderbolt'. I particularly loved the slightly broken mound where the footpath turned round the corner, right next to the old lamp post; there were two narrow cement strips on that little rise and fall, and in my world they were the wooden ramps leading up to the ferry boat to Betim. I zoomed off at full speed (a little over zero km/hour) from the other end of the footpath, dodging gorges and canyons on the way; and if I missed one of those cement strips, my vehicle and I would be wading in the Mandovi.

Footpaths, and even roads, were unofficial children's playgrounds in the Panjim I grew up in, for want of enough pedestrians or cars to be thus inconvenienced.

'*Remo, venha tomar chà!*' I heard my mother calling out from the window. Portuguese was my mother tongue, in that it was the first language I learnt from my mother (and father), and that was the only language I knew, besides of course a smattering of Konkani, the language of Goa. The evening call for tea was figurative. A six-year-old drank milk, usually reinforced with Horlicks or Ovomaltina.

3

The year was 1959. We lived in the corner house in a row of four, with a big compound on two sides and a narrow garden in the front, and with walls built of stone and wood. I particularly loved the two rooms made of wood. The house stood exactly where Sushila Building stands today, on 18th June Road.

LEFT: My first birthday, 8 May 1954. This was the footpath in front of our house, which was the first little row house on the right, not seen in the picture. RIGHT: My 'Thunderbolt'.

Panjim was a dream town. A doll town. Almost every house had a garden lush with tropical plants and flowers. Every moderate and large house was built of plastered laterite stone, adorned with arched doors and windows, fronted by verandas with intricate railings made out of wood or cast iron, and crowned with sloping tiled roofs. The humblest little house had a clean, colourful beauty, with cotton curtains and flowerpots on the window sills. Each structure had to be whitewashed or painted once a year, soon after the monsoons – or the owners were fined. Garbage had to be put out once a day at a certain time, within half an hour of the municipal truck's collection, in metal cans freshly painted a post-office red, with 'LIXO' (garbage) written in white letters of a uniform size. People had never heard of grills on windows; one slept with the shutters wide open, especially during the summer. My father sometimes forgot to put his car into the garage, and left it parked for the night in the street in front of our house, the windows rolled down, the key in the ignition. The possibility of robbery or theft didn't even cross people's minds.

Ours was a rather modest little house, the first one my father could afford to rent when he settled in middle-class Panjim. But as I sat in our dining room, dipping my English cream cracker biscuits sandwiched with Danish Blue Peter butter and Dutch Edam red-ball cheese into my hot milk and cocoa, I was in the greatest castle on the face of the earth.

Pai

The first photo Father sent Mother before marriage.

My father, José António Alfredo Bernardo Afonso Fernandes, or Bernardo as his friends knew him, or Pai ('Father' in Portuguese) as I knew him, had started the most modern aerated water factory of the day in Goa. Made on machines imported from England, his sodas and cold drinks featured impeccable hygiene and metal bottle caps with a cork lining, the type used even today, except that today the cork has been replaced with plastic. Until then aerated water bottles in Goa featured the old design with a round glass stopper – beautiful and quaint, they were however manually filled with inconsistent gas quantities, and were therefore dangerously prone to explode. The hygiene and safety features of my father's drinks soon ensured him an exclusive contract with the Portuguese Army and Navy, and that started him on his road to success – not the monumental success of mine-owners and big family business houses, but the success of an individual entrepreneur.

When you're six, your father can do no wrong. Mine was the most wonderful man in the world, and I just knew it the way one knows that chocolate tastes good.

Mãe

The first photo Mother sent Father before marriage.

And my mother, Luiza Maria Zuzarte e Fernandes, or Luiza as her friends knew her, or Mãe (Mother) as I knew her, was of course the most wonderful and the most beautiful woman in the world. Tailors would come and live in our house for a week or a month, and would impeccably recreate the latest European fashions from *Vogue* magazines which Father would buy her. The fabrics would be imported from England and France and Italy, and Mother's Singer sewing machine was temporarily shifted to the veranda for the duration of the tailor's stay.

Before you think that in-house tailors were a luxury, let me tell you that's the way clothes were stitched in most homes in Goa at the time. And before you think that 'imported from Europe' sounds grand, let me tell you that almost *everything* in Goa was imported from Europe those days – from cars to potatoes. Relations between Goa (still a Portuguese colony) and the rest of India were a no-no, and it was a lot easier, albeit more expensive, to go to Lisbon than to Bombay. The Portuguese had colonized Goa in 1510, though as a six-year-old I had no clue about any of that. In my little mind that's just who and what we were: both Goan and Portuguese. I don't think I'd even heard about this country called India until a couple of years later, when India liberated Goa from Portuguese domination. To me, as to most

Father liked Mother to dress well. And he loved to photograph her.

Goans, Goa was here and now, this tiny homely forgotten natural paradise lost somewhere in the back of beyond. Portugal was out there in the distance, at the very centre of the universe, the almost unattainable, golden, shining place where everything was perfect and everyone was beautifully fair-skinned, far, far away across wide, wide oceans. Everything else – Europe, the

Americas, Africa – was out there beyond even Portugal, in books and in occasional movies.

Grandfather Bailon

Grandfather Dr Bailon Fernandes 'The Strict'.

I didn't get to meet either of my grandfathers, so I know nothing of a grandfather's doting love. And I didn't get to experience any of that grandfather–grandson bonding, such as fishing or flying a kite together. Both my grandfathers had passed away well before I was born.

Despite the lavish gifts Father was to bestow upon me, he didn't start off in life as a rich man, or even a rich man's son. His father Dr Bailon Fernandes was a very highly respected doctor and an extremely strict man. Although most visitors to his house (the house where I now live) then found it – and still find it – large and impressive, he never owned or amassed a fortune. He was both doctor and apothecary to the people of his village. The properties he owned comprised rice fields and hills, but they didn't have a fraction of today's worth then. At best, they supplemented the rice and coconut stock needed to run his household and feed his brood of five sons and one daughter. In those days he charged a pittance for his consultations and medicines, that too only from those who could afford to pay. People were merrier, they worked harder, sang louder, walked longer, and were therefore healthier. And medicines for the more serious diseases hadn't yet been invented; so if you contracted one of those, you just quietly popped it and that was that. Therefore, apart from the occasional flu or cold or children's mumps and chickenpox, business couldn't have turned Dr Bailon into a millionaire. But he and his family lived well, their table was always hearty, and their doors were always open. He made one decision early in life: he would give all his children the finest education he could afford, but he would bequeath none of them a fortune. For starters, he had none to bequeath them. Secondly, he didn't think it his duty to do so. According to him, it was the education which was more important; something along the lines of the old proverb about gifting a man a fishing rod rather than a fish.

Dr Bailon was so seriously self-disciplined that he never ever drank a sip of alcohol or puffed on a cigarette all his life. Ironically, his wife turned out to be a dedicated smoker of roll-your-own cigarettes – thanks to him. The good doctor once prescribed his young bride a cigarette to help take her mind off a toothache, and she, who had never touched a cigarette before, didn't stop smoking since. She loved a tiny glass of port wine with every meal too. Just one tiny glass, mind you, never half a drop more. Today we love to think that all marriages in the old days were orthodox and male-dominated, and the women subjugated. I marvel to think that a hundred years ago I had a couple of ancestors in this very house of whom the wife drank and smoked, and the husband didn't.

But there was no escaping the fact that Grandfather Bailon was indeed strict, at least where his sons' upbringing was concerned. He forbade them to pursue extra-curricular activities which he deemed dangerous and/or a waste of time. Boxing came under his blacklist, and strangely enough, so did music.

Grandfather Levi

Grandfather Levi Zuzarte.

I don't know much about my maternal grandfather, Levi Zuzarte from Parrá. No one spoke much about him, but through the haze of my childhood memory I gathered that he had drowned when a canoe carrying him had capsized in the Chapora river in Siolim late one dark rainy evening. The boatman had survived, but had not managed to save my grandfather. One day Mother finally told me more about the incident, though very indirectly, and I was surprised at the vehemence and anger still pent up inside her. Well, what else can one expect when a topic is declared taboo and kept tightly bound and gagged, but well-nourished, inside one's heart for years and years…

It seems Grandfather Levi was himself a prosperous landlord's son. He had left Goa for Africa to pursue a higher education, having completed which he had decided to settle and work there.

'Goan *bhatkars* (landlords) would always insist on their sons returning home, even those who had good jobs and were doing well elsewhere in Bombay or Calcutta or abroad! Why did they have to drag them back?' Mother complained bitterly. She mimicked the doting parents: '*Meu Baba, volte para casa, sentimos tanto sua falta!*' (My Baba, come back home, we miss you so much!) Here Mother's voice would uncharacteristically rise by a few decibels and semi-quavers. 'And what did these highly educated Babas do when they returned? Nothing! Everything was served to them on a platter, there was nothing to do except to count the fish and lobsters and prawns and coconuts and mangoes and jackfruit and *khandis* of rice the *mundkars* (serfs) would bring in!'

Here Mother would actually tremble with fury. 'So the Babas took to playing cards and drinking. To while away their time. To forget their boredom. To efface from their memories the shameful waste of those years of study they had put in and the degrees they had earned.'

And probably to forget some blonde or brunette or black girl whose love they'd left behind, I thought, though Mother didn't mention those.

Eventually, as a last-ditch cure for their alcoholism, the parents would get their precious sons married, hoping their good new Goan wives would perform the miracle which the village patron saint couldn't. 'Cure, my foot!' exclaimed Mother. 'Soon after the honeymoon, the grooms were back with their old cronies, landlords' sons all, drinking and playing cards, playing cards and drinking. They made babies when they returned home at night all right, and then died young, often due to vices which too much leisure can breed, leaving young widows and toddlers in vales of tears in their wake.'

Mother never in so many words told me that this was her own father's story. I still don't know whether it was.

Grandmother Purçínia (Mamã de Parrá)

Luckily, I got to know both my grandmothers very well. My maternal grandmother, Levi's wife, was Dona Purçínia Zuzarte, whom my parents referred to as Mamã de Parrá (since she lived in Parrá, a village quite close to Mapusa), to differentiate her from my dad's mother, who lived in Siolim, and whom they simply called Mamã. Although she could easily afford taxis, Mamã de Parrá had a weakness for zooming around on pilot-motorcycles, to our great anxiety and much against all sworn promises to the contrary we managed to extract from her time and again. One Christmas noon, as the family started gathering for lunch at our home in Siolim, I drove out for some last-minute shopping. Returning home, I saw Mamã de Parrá, who was now past eighty, getting off a motorcycle a few houses before ours. She was going to walk in pretending she had come in a taxi, but this time she was caught red-handed. As she opened her parasol and paid off the motorcycle pilot, I cruised in from behind and called out, 'Want a lift, Dona Purçínia?' She giggled guiltily, and sheepishly got into my car. From then on my sister Belinda and I nicknamed her Miss Hot Wheels. She lived to see eight of her nine great-grandchildren, and died at the ripe old age of eighty-nine in her bed, not on a motorcycle. It was always wonderful having her and my parents at our home after our children were born, and to be aware that there were four living generations in the house at that given moment. Though very loving and caring, Mamã de Parrá

With my maternal grandmother Purçínia, or Mamã de Parrá, smiling wide to show off my newly toothless upper gums. Posing for a photograph was a rare occasion when I'd get to sit on her lap.

was not really the type prone to great physical demonstrations of affection. My mother inherited this trait, and was a bit of a touch-me-not, in spite of the tremendous love and affection she always showered upon both my sister and me all her life.

Grandmother Ida (Vovó)

My paternal grandmother more than made up for this shortage of physical cuddling. Dona Ida Afonso Fernandes, whom all younger neighbours and relatives called Tia Idinha and I called Vovó (children's affectionate variation of Avó or 'Grandmother'), was the quintessential grandmother from fairy tales, with silver hair tied in a bun, soft wrinkled skin, fresh starched cotton dresses, black velvet *chinelas* (Chinese home slippers) on her feet, and a squeaky clean smell of English lavender talcum powder. Added to that was the fascination of the little yellow metal box in which she kept her tobacco, rolling papers, matchbox, and the perfect, fine cigarettes she rolled. I loved the sweet aroma of her tobacco, which came in thick dark indigo packets. When she finished her quota too soon and had to send for more, she would justify it by telling us that Ramin the local grocer cheated and trafficked her packets (which would incidentally come tightly sealed all the way from Holland). I would watch her roll those perfect sticks in fascination, and would then insist on rolling a few cigarettes for her myself. She knew I would spoil them all, but would indulge me for a while. The first time my tongue came in contact with the tobacco while wetting the rolling paper, I stared at it in disbelief, wondering how such a dark brown, forbidding-looking substance could taste so good. That afternoon as she slept through her siesta I ate up half her packet of tobacco. That evening the local doctor had to flush out my stomach with a *clister* – an enema administered with a contraption made up of a white enamel container with warm water, hung from the poster of a bed, a long red snake-like rubber tube projecting from its bottom and ending up inside you through a frightening long black nozzle with a little tap. It miraculously cured us after every orgy of gluttony.

My paternal grandmother Ida, or Vovó. RIGHT: Vovó with my sister Belinda on her lap and me by her side.

Vovó called me Morgado (which literally means 'heir' or 'eldest son', but which is also used as a highly affectionate term for a beloved child), and I secretly loved to believe that I was her favourite grandchild. Since she had nine, that was a tough call, but I believed it anyway. Vovó loved hugging me, and I loved hugging her, snuggling into her lap as she sat in her easy chair, burying my face and nose in the heavenly-smelling soft and comfortable wrinkled crook of her neck, and begging her to tell me my favourite story.

She would feign exasperation, and complain to whoever was around: 'Now look at this *maroto* (naughty/saucy boy), I have told him the *História de Coló e Colí* a thousand times over, but he will still ask for the same one yet again!' It was my cue to plead, *'Só mais uma vez, Vovó! Ultima vez!* Just one last time, Vovó!' Then she would settle herself comfortably in her chair, adjust me in her lap, and artfully proceed to bring the old story of the lazy good-for-nothing fox and the hard-working foresighted vixen to life as though she'd never narrated it before. Each time a masterpiece.

I in turn would tell this simple story to my own sons dozens of times years later. I have a feeling they will tell it to theirs. Some things, however seemingly simple and insignificant, remain in families forever.

The uncles

My grandmother Vovó as a matriarch after her husband's death, with her grown but as yet unmarried children in front of the Siolim house. STANDING LEFT TO RIGHT: Fanchu (the boxer), Mariano (the elder), Angela (the terror), Renato (the surgeon), Bernardo (my father), Josito (the youngest).

I have mentioned how Grandfather Bailon abhorred activities such as music and boxing. My paternal Tio (uncle) Fanchu – pet name for Francisco – was a strapping young lad who had a great affinity and love for sport, and for boxing in particular. I don't know how he got himself a pair of boxing gloves without his father's knowledge, but he kept them hidden at a friend's house, from where he would secretly pick them up on his way to training or to a match. Being tough and strong, he usually returned home without a tell-tale scratch. But on the day he came back with a black eye, the beans were spilled; Grandfather got the whole story out of him, and was furious. He probably blackened poor Tio Fanchu's other eye for symmetry, and hung up his gloves for good.

My father showed a very strong inclination towards music right from childhood – but of course Grandfather decreed that all professional musicians ended up as paupers, drunkards, or both. And to be fair to him, in those days, most did. Father's love for music might have escalated from a hobby to a profession one day – and where would that get him? At the most, playing in Goa's top dance band, and being served dinner in the kitchen on par with the waiters and cooks when they performed at weddings and balls.

None of that nonsense for a son of Dr Bailon. Musical instruments were therefore forbidden in the house, in a land which danced and sang at every drop of the proverbial hat, and where almost every home boasted a piano and a violin, or at the very least a humble *gumott* (a Goan folk drum made out of an earthen pot with two openings, the larger one tightly covered with snakeskin).

My father took to visiting relatives and friends who had musical instruments in their homes, and there taught himself how to play the Portuguese guitar, the Spanish guitar, the flute, the piano, and several other instruments, all by ear. All this without Grandfather's knowledge, obviously. Musical instruments left no black eyes. Not unless you serenaded another man's wife, which my father apparently didn't.

When I was about four and showed the same inclination towards music, my father's joy knew no bounds. He would live out his musical dream through me. Whatever encouragement he had failed to get from his own father, he would bestow upon his son tenfold. Together with toys and gifts, he bought me every musical instrument I proclaimed a fancy to – and a child's fancy is fleeting indeed, changing every few months or so. And so it was that before I was ten, I had acquired and learnt how to play – in the following order – a mouth organ, a ukulele, a banjo, a piano accordion, and a Spanish guitar, all by ear like my father. I was also allowed to tinker around with Father's Portuguese guitar and Mother's mandolin.

Curiously, Grandfather Bailon didn't seem to worry that any of his children might take to art, towards which they all had leanings in various forms. He encouraged design in his brood without his usual hang-ups and restrictions, and whenever there were new curtain pelmets to be made, a new veranda railing to be built, or a new flooring to be laid, he would hold an in-house competition and prompt each of his six children to come up with a design. He would then judge and choose the best one, or combine the best features from several. Many items in the house have been designed by my father and uncles and aunt, which gives the home a very personal, familial touch which reaches out palpably through time. I particularly love the pelmets in the visiting room.

When my Tio Renato completed his studies in medicine in Lisbon and was scheduled to return to Goa in his glory as a full-fledged surgeon, his brothers knew there would be a marriage in the family soon. They decided to redecorate the visiting hall and ready it for the feast. I don't know who came up with the idea, but they cut out a cardboard stencil in the shape of clouds; for want of a spray gun or electricity in Goan villages, they adapted a Flit insecticide handpump with a nozzle broadened to allow oil paint to spray through; and, thus armed with these two sophisticated art tools, proceeded to cover the walls with a pattern most uncharacteristic and unusual for those days. It was simple but almost futuristic, a forerunner of the psychedelic culture which one of their descendants (I) would embrace so enthusiastically some decades later. Marmalade clouds of various pastel shades, each one with a metallic silver lining, covered half the height of the four walls, from the floor up to a good eight feet or more. They adorn the visiting hall's walls still, the tough old German metallic paint shining bright as ever. People who see the room today think that I painted the walls recently while smoking dubious herbs and listening to 'Lucy in the Sky with Diamonds'. I celebrated my marriage in the same hall about fifty years after Tio Renato did.

The visiting room in Siolim, with walls hand spray-painted with colourful clouds by my father, uncles and aunt in around 1935. Photo taken in 2007.

Incidentally, Tio Renato was my godfather, and I called him just that all my life – Padrinho. He turned out to be one of the most respected surgeons in the Hospital da Escola Médica e Cirúrgica de Goa, the erstwhile Panjim hospital which today houses offices of the Entertainment

Society of Goa and IFFI. That's where I was born. There was a move by the government of Goa to turn the grand old heritage hospital building into a commercial mall recently. I joined the august citizens who opposed it. We succeeded, and the mall idea was dropped. Thank god. I would have hated having to tell my grandchildren one day that I was born somewhere between McDonald's and KFC.

Tio Josito (diminutive for José) was the youngest of Father's brothers. He was the only one among them who remained unmarried. Based in Siolim with Vovó, he was exceptionally skilled with his hands, and a perfectionist at that. Being a confirmed bachelor who looked after his mother and the house when all his older siblings married and left one by one, and never having started a career of his own, he loved helping his brothers in whatever enterprise they undertook. I believe he was of invaluable help to Tio Fanchu when the latter set up his engineering concern in Bangalore, spending years there working alongside the ex-boxer. He did the same when Father set up his soda factory; he practically lived in our house in Panjim for weeks and months on end, supervising this, designing that, creating the other. I guess he was the paternal uncle I was closest to, mainly because he was the one I saw most of.

Father's eldest brother, Mariano, remained a total stranger to me until much later, when he finally returned from Uganda, Africa, where he had settled with his family since well before I was born.

While Father had five siblings, Mother only had one – my Tio Armando Zuzarte. However, he and his family lived in Bombay, and I therefore do not remember him or his family entering my consciousness until a little later in life, when his younger son Rex, exactly a couple of years minus a day older to

My mother's only sibling and his family. FROM LEFT TO RIGHT: Cousin Roy, Aunt Mariazita (my godmother), Uncle Armando Zuzarte and cousin Rex.

me, became my favourite cousin. Tio Armando's wife, Tia Mariazita, was my godmother. And their elder son Roy turned out to look like Elvis and dance like Travolta, to the great delight of all the young ladies who counted themselves lucky to know him.

Tia Angela

This may sound like a fib, but my mother adored her mother-in-law. And her reasons were simple: 'Mamã never ever took her sons' side against her daughters-in-law!' she would exclaim with admiration. 'Whenever there was a husband-and-wife quarrel, if at all she interfered, she would do just the opposite – side with the daughter-in-law and scold the son, saying "Enough now, you silly men always like to fight with your wives ... she is such a lovely person ... come on, kiss and make up!" She never made the mistake of getting into the details of an argument to try and judge who was right.' Mother took her example very seriously to heart, and when I got married, she would do exactly the same and take my wife's side under all circumstances, sometimes to my great exasperation. But I secretly admired and loved her for it.

When another daughter-in-law sometimes criticized Vovó for some reason or the other, however mildly, Mother simply could not bear to listen. Strangely, towards the end of Vovó's life, the woman who made the most fun of her was her only daughter Angela. Vovó had become increasingly distracted in her old age; her memory failed her, and she kept asking the same questions and repeating the same things over and over again, with rapidly increasing frequency. Her hearing kept deteriorating too, and shouting out the same answers at regular fifteen-minute intervals at the top of one's voice didn't really translate into scintillating conversation for those who visited her. Eventually she started failing to recognize her own sons. Angela would laugh at her derisively, exclaiming 'Mamã está tonta!' (Mama has gone nuts!) Mercifully Vovó's weak hearing ensured she was spared these remarks – though of course she would have forgotten them five minutes later. They however hurt Mother, a mere daughter-in-law, terribly. Mother was not at all the confrontational or argumentative type. Quite the contrary: at home she would think nothing of apologizing to Father in order to end an argument or quarrel – even when she knew she wasn't wrong, which used to exasperate my sister and me no end when we grew old enough to realize what was going on. Given this trait in her character, Mother obviously said nothing to her sister-in-law when she spoke thus about Vovó – in any case, no one ever dared say anything to Angela.

Tia Angela was an extremely elegant, well-dressed, well-informed, accomplished, talented, no-nonsense woman who instilled a deep sense of discomfort and inferiority in her sisters-in-law by her mere presence. One slightly critical appraising look from above her upturned nose and they would all turn to mumbling putty. Even her brothers treaded carefully around her, and Father, who usually bowed before no one, always spoke about her in a softer, more hushed tone than usual: Mana (elder sister) this and Mana that.

Tia Angela when younger, as a fashionable young Goan lady.

When she eventually married Marinho João Dias, a very rich, big and jolly man who had made his fortune in Africa, her already established position as the most authoritative figure in the Bailon household was firmly reinforced by virtue of her now also being the richest.

Mother remembers the first time Father officially took her out after they were engaged. It was to a grand formal ball in Panjim, and Mother was extremely excited at the prospect. The fact that social norms of the day demanded that Father bring along a female chaperone for the bride soon turned the excitement into petrification, as the chaperone turned out to be Tia Angela. Mother would playfully describe the underlying tension present throughout the evening years later. I used to hate it when she spoke of Tia Angela with near-fear and awe – a kid doesn't want his parents to be scared of anyone.

Tia Angela had just one son, Garçia dos Santos Dias, who went on to become one of the most famous architects in Goa, and who was indirectly responsible for my one-pointed obsession with becoming an architect myself, while I didn't yet fully know what architecture was. Her husband died very young, when Garçia was around twenty, and that left Tia Angela a very young widow. She always reminded me of a strict nun dressed in a very expensive and elegant Victorian black or grey dress. If Mamã de Parrá and Mother were a bit of touch-me-nots, Tia Angela was a confirmed don't-even-think-about-it-with-a-ten-foot-pole. I never received a real hug from her; her kisses were always given at least three inches away from the receiver's face; and when she came to visit ('*visitas*' lasted for days which sometimes turned into weeks), she would invariably come up with one or the other self-improvement scheme meant to enlighten my six-year-old soul or strengthen my rather skinny body. Often she would teach me difficult prayers in Portuguese – I knew all the ones a kid was expected to know, but she would come up with obscure incantations to obscure saints whose existence only she (and probably the old vicar of Siolim) were aware of. When I couldn't get the prayers right, she would tell me in a voice which carried to whichever room Mother might be in: '*O meu Garçia recita isto tão bem, sabes?*' (My Garçia recites this so well, you know?) At other times she decreed my chest too concave, and my arms and legs too spindly, all of which she again announced in full hearing of my mother, before proceeding to bestow upon me a miraculous set of *exerçícios respiratórios* (breathing exercises) which she made me practise under her watchful eye. Of course, this was always followed by '*O meu Garçia é tão forte, sabes?*' (My Garçia is so strong, you know?) Garçia continued to be this wonderfully perfect mystery cousin whom I had never seen, as he had been away studying architecture in England since before I was born. I wondered how she knew that he was reciting his prayers and doing his breathing exercises out there.

It was a good-natured and affectionate custom at the time to hide a guest's important pieces of travel clothing or footwear, or sometimes a whole suitcase, on the day the guest was intending to leave, thus forcing an additional day or days' stay. The guest's consternation – real or pretended – at the discovery that the items were missing provided raucous joy and laughter to the whole household, adults and children and domestic help alike, all of whom had contributed conspiratorial roles in the elaborate and well-planned coup. I loved playing such pranks on my grandmothers, on Tio Josito, and on most other visitors. But after just a couple of days of Tia Angela's prayers and exercises, I would ask her in my most polite voice, *'Tia Angela, quando vais para casa?'* (Aunt Angela, when are you going home?) My mother, horrified, would quickly change the subject, and Tia Angela would grandly pretend she hadn't heard me at all.

Ironically, as she reached old age, Tia Angela deteriorated into the exact same state which she had ridiculed in Vovó: she suffered from loss of memory and hearing. She would repeat the same questions every five minutes, and the same answers had to be shouted back at her. And finally, the one person who would laugh derisively and say *'Mãe está tonta!'* would be her only beloved son Garçia.

The aunt not known

Father had had another sister whom one never spoke about. The memory was too painful for everyone at first, and then it faded away with time – like smoke which fades away after a devastating fire dies. I remember being told when I was a child that she had been very beautiful, with very lovely long, long hair. When she was a child – perhaps ten – she happened to accidentally lean over an oil lamp in Siolim one evening (electricity came there about half a century later), and her long hair caught fire. The flames immediately leapt from her hair to her long cotton nightgown. By the time everyone rushed to her rescue, she had been burnt beyond salvation.

Vovó never spoke of her lost daughter. Just as Mother never spoke of her lost António. Mother-in-law and daughter-in-law shared their grief and consoled each other. Those lost little angels lived forever in the quiet recesses of their mothers' hearts.

My parents in British Bombay

Father and Mother were among a small minority of people in Goa who spoke English (besides Portuguese) in those days, and that was because they had gone out of Portuguese-ruled Goa into British-ruled India for their higher education. Most of those educated in Goa spoke only Portuguese, besides of course Konkani, which was the local language of Goa, and which *every* Goan spoke or at least knew and understood. But the Portuguese rulers together with some of the Goan Christian elite had decreed Konkani a language of servants, serfs and the illiterate – in other words, a second-class language in its own homeland. This was the status they allotted to most things Goan anyway, such as our now famous cashew and coconut feni, the potent and strong-smelling local drink which would never be served at functions or places of repute – it was supposedly drunk only by farmers and fishermen in tiny rustic village *tavernas*, and by poor men in shady city *tavernas*.

However, many cultured and even aristocratic Goans, despite affecting Portuguese customs and tastes in public, found it impossible to shed some of the deeper shades of their Goanness in private; so while they served and drank the finest scotches and wines in society, when alone, they would drink nothing but feni, the bottle carefully hidden in a cupboard in the storeroom. God help them if unexpected company should land up after they had imbibed some; disguising the strong smell was next to impossible. So they smiled and spoke to their guests like ventriloquists, their lips almost sealed, until they had washed out their mouths with fresh scotch.

Mother had been educated in a convent and finishing school in Belgaum, which is also where Father took his Bachelor's degree in Commerce. I think a BCom degree in those days was worth more than a doctorate is today. At least, the pride I heard in Father's voice when he mentioned his educational qualification certainly suggested so.

Of course, having been born and raised in Portuguese Goa, I didn't understand a single word of English – which my parents found extremely convenient sometimes, as young couples do. I remember it annoyed and frustrated me no end that they would on occasion switch to this strange language which to me began to signify conspiracy and connivance, and exchange those strange glances and smiles and plot and plan things which did not include me, their only begotten precious son.

After they got married they had decided to settle in Bombay, where Father got his first job with the British government's censor's office. I'm not sure whether it was due to World War II or Mahatma Gandhi's freedom movement, but every piece of news and every personal letter going out of and coming into India in the 1940s was heavily censored and searched for strategic information which might fall into the wrong hands.

Father's immediate boss was an Englishman. One day there was a problem in the office, and the Englishman spoke rudely to Father. There probably was a racist slur, very common in those days, involved. I have mentioned earlier that Father bowed to no one. He flung his resignation letter on his boss's table a few minutes later and walked out a proud but jobless man. He told me later that that was when he took a vow which he was to keep all his life: 'Never again shall I work under another.' Strangely, I never did, either.

Before heading home and breaking the news to Mother, he decided to have a last cup of tea at the Irani restaurant round the corner from the office where he and his office colleagues had hung out during breaks. Seated at the typical marble-top table and staring at the reflection of his furrowed brow in the mirrored wall, pondering his uncertain future, he overheard that funny but fateful conversation between two men seated at the next table, which ended with:

'*Arre, paani se paisa hota hai, bhai!* Water to money only! Just bubbles putting, and money becoming! *Ho gaya!*'

Not that Father believed the industrial theory of the man who was speaking, but the idea of a soda and cold drink factory appealed to him. He switched to his Bachelor of Commerce mode now, totally shedding his temporary avatar as a censor for the British government, and a seed was sown. By the time he had reached home, his pace quickening by the minute, it had germinated. He now had other news to give Mother apart from his resignation. They would pack their bags and move back to their beloved Goa! And there he would start the best soda factory the tiny territory had ever seen!

Mother, who was usually prone to exercise excessive caution before taking unknown steps and risks such as this, somehow didn't need much prodding to leave the crowded and noisy Bombay. They were lucky to be living in a large, airy and comfortable apartment in the then fashionable and central quarter of Marine Lines, they enjoyed the grand balls at the Catholic and Bandra gymkhanas, they loved to party and picnic with the wonderful lifelong friends they had made in Bombay – but Goa was Goa.

My elder brother who never was

Of course, there was another unspoken reason why she and Father were happy to leave the big city behind. The young couple had eagerly awaited their firstborn. Mother once told me about him, but just once; I was very young when she did, and I do not remember the details well. I think it happened like this: everything went perfectly during the pregnancy and during the delivery, but when the nurse lifted the bonny baby boy by his ankles to smack his bottom so that he could cry and bring out the remains of the placenta from his lungs, his body was still too slippery and he a bit too fidgety, the ankles slipped from the nurse's grip, and she dropped him on to the table on his soft newborn head.

The doctors in the hospital worked hard to save him. Some who had already gone home from their day shift were summoned back. One of my parents' friends, wealthy Prince Lobo (Prince was his name, not his title, but it fitted him well), struggled with them throughout those traumatic hours, driving sleeplessly all around Bombay, trying to gather as many of the city's top medical specialists as he possibly could. They all struggled all night long, but the baby died before day dawned.

When there wasn't much hope left, Mother had asked for a priest, who came in the middle of the night and baptized the baby, who was in a coma.

They named him António, after the patron saint of Siolim, with many vows and promises. Unfortunately this divine invocation failed too, and then their precious little newborn was no more. Months of joyful expectation were snuffed out in a night of tragedy.

Yes, Mother and Father were ready to leave Bombay and its sad memories behind them all right. The argument with the English boss had only been the last impetus needed to make the departure a reality.

I have always counted myself extremely lucky that my parents decided to return to Goa before I was born. 'I'm so glad I'm not a Bombay Boy!' I would think years later, when I went to study architecture in Bombay. There was nothing wrong with Bombay Boys really – they were hip, savvy, with-it, fast, smart, and everything a big-city boy is which a village boy isn't. And Goa was a large village in many ways when compared to Bombay – except for the suave Latin culture, tradition and finesse Goa had, which made most people from Bombay seem rather loud and crude in comparison.

Return to Goa: The birth of Industrias Benferds

On returning to Goa, my parents temporarily moved in with Vovó and Tio Josito into the old house at Siolim. Mother and Father were allocated the master bedroom, or the *'quarto dos noivos'* (room of the newly-weds), which had originally been my grandparents'. As each son had married, this room had been allocated to him and his new bride for the interim period before they left to set up their own home.

Father needed capital to put his dream in motion. As mentioned earlier, Grandfather Bailon had given him an education, but no fortune. The money came in the form of a loan from an old neighbour in Siolim, whom everyone in the neighbourhood referred to as Tio Joaquim. With the smaller part of that capital, Father rented out a factory premises and a row house in Panjim, to which he and Mother shifted from Siolim, lock, stock and barrel. The factory premises and the row house belonged to a Panjim landlord called Ananta B. Naik, who lived opposite the factory, a few metres down the road from today's Hotel Samrat which the same family owns. Their family residence, which was exquisitely Indian while simultaneously modern in its architectural style, still stands proudly. Sadly neither the factory nor the row house do.

With the bulk of the loan, Father imported three bottling machines from England, purchased a delivery pickup truck, hired workers, accountants and a driver, and commissioned several dozen wooden crates to store and transport the drinks. A small team of carpenters came and built the crates on site, by hand. Then they were spray-painted red and green. And then came the most exciting part of all: Father designed and cut out a stencil with the name of his new business, and this was spray-painted in white on the longer red side of each crate.

He took letters from his name Bernardo Fernandes and came up with the English-sounding acronym 'BENFERDS'. As his drinks grew in popularity, he started being referred to as Senhor Benférdes, the English Benferds taking on a Portuguese lilt. In the tiny Goa of those days, where everyone knew everyone else, one can easily understand how 'Benferds' soon became one of the best known names in the land.

In the evenings, Mother and Father would place two folding wood-and-canvas deck chairs in the back of the pickup truck, and drive off to deserted, wild Miramar Beach. No promenade, pergola or beach benches had been built or placed there yet. They would climb over the dunes where wild sand bushes grew, unfold their chairs, and sit there in the cool breeze holding hands, watching the sunset, sharing dreams about the future.

This outing to Miramar every evening just before sunset became a lifelong ritual with them. Father loved the spot so much, he vowed to Mother that someday, if and when he could afford it, he would build themselves a house on this beach. He eventually did about twenty years later, in 1971, and named it 'Benferds'.

Tio Joaquim would come from Siolim to Panjim on the first of every month early in the morning with the regularity and punctuality of a cuckoo springing out of a clock, for a cup of tea, and to collect the monthly instalment of his loan's repayment with interest. The friendship between him and my parents was great. That friendship and old connection continues to this day between his son Selvio (whom everyone knows as Babito) and me.

Inauguration of Industrias Benferds, Panjim circa 1950, by the Portuguese Governor General Fernando de Quintanilha e Mendonça Dias (third from right). Father is first from right, proudly explaining the wonders of his brand-new English soda-bottling machines.

My birth

And into this happy scenario of a new life in Goa and a new enterprise taking off, I was born on 8 May 1953 at about 11 p.m. at the Hospital da Escola Médica e Cirúrgica de Goa in Panjim. Almost exactly eight years after my parents had had and lost their firstborn.

I was baptized Luís Remo de Maria Bernardo Fernandes. A mouthful. But long names were the rage then, in Portugal, and therefore in Goa. I guess people weren't required to fill up immigration forms that often those days.

'Luís' was for my mother Luiza, 'Remo' because that's the main name they chose for me, 'de Maria' because I was born in May, the month of Mother Mary, and 'Bernardo' for my father.

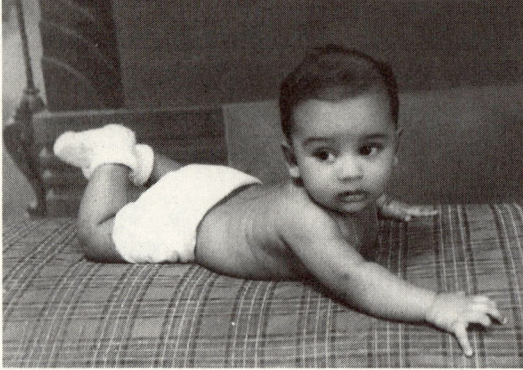

TOP: At four months. BOTTOM LEFT: In my baptism gown. BOTTOM RIGHT: With Father and Mother at seven months.

Today in Portugal it is customary to call everyone by the first given name – that's usually the only one to be filled in most forms, besides of course the surname. When I'm in Portugal, in all official and formal situations I am called 'Senhor Luís'. Which feels strange, because I certainly don't feel like a 'Luís'. I have always been Remo.

2

Growing Up in Goa Portuguesa

Ninho Infantil

We continued living in the old Ananta B. Naik house for exactly eight years after I was born. Those eight years were marked with the excitement and momentum of being a child, as well as the serenity and peace of growing up in a town as quiet, orderly and humane as the Panjim of those days.

The first school I attended, kindergarten, was heaven. And the teacher, Professora Eucária, an angel in her heaven. The school was situated on the outskirts of the minuscule town of Panjim, on the Rua de Ourem, by the pretty Ourem creek. It was officially called Ninho Infantil Doutor Oliveira Salazar after Portugal's dictator, but everyone knew it simply as 'Ninho Infantil', which means Infants' Nest.

Though I only knew her during the time when I was three or four years old, and never saw her after that, I can still see Professora Eucária's freckled, bespectacled face and short curly hair, and hear the exact deep tone of her voice. She was unmarried, and neither young nor old. She was the most loving and kind teacher any kid could be lucky to have; and to her, each one of us brats in her little school was the child she had never had.

I had just learnt how to wink, no mean feat for a three-year-old, after days of practice during which I could mostly only blink both eyes at once. At the big table in our classroom, a cute little girl called Suzete with hair in long falling ringlets sat in front of me. To show off my newly acquired skills, I winked at her one day. I was hoping to impress, but I got more: she burst out crying! I couldn't believe my wink had this unexpected superpower. From then on I quietly winked and made her cry every day, until the teacher caught on to what was happening four or five days later.

TOP LEFT: I was convinced that the whole building of the Ninho Infantil kindergarten was round. I was surprised when I went to photograph it in November 2008 to discover that it was not. The circular room in the corner, our classroom, is what had dictated the whole building's shape to a three-year-old's lifelong memory. RIGHT: An old Portuguese marble plaque at the entrance still carries the inscription 'Ninho Infantil Doutor Oliveira Salazar'. In Portugal, the plaque would have been removed and the name changed, as no one would want a reminder of the dreaded old dictator; but in Goa, it continues happily embedded in the wall, totally overlooked and forgotten. BOTTOM LEFT: I was amazed to come upon this photo on a website about a Portuguese lady photographer who had photographed Goa just before the Liberation. Curiously, the first thing I recognized was my school bag, which is lying on the table. That made me look again carefully, and I recognized myself sitting first from right.

Escola Primária de Massano de Amorim

After kindergarten, most kids in Panjim went to the Escola Massano de Amorim, which still stands today at the opposite corner from the National Cine Theatre in Panjim, and now houses Indian government offices of some sort. I visited it some months back on a pure impulse, and a government guard who merrily smelled of alcohol at four in the afternoon showed me around and even opened a locked storeroom – where I saw our old school benches. The very same old ones. They seemed so tiny… Made of a wood so solid and seasoned, they had withstood the abuse of hyperactive children for over fifty years. I caressed the elongated grooves where we had kept our pens and pencils; the square grooves where we had kept our inkpots; ran my hand in the narrow space beneath the desk where we had kept our rather slim but more than adequate school bags. Visiting the school was a treat, but finding those old benches was a treasure. I sat on one and stepped into a time machine.

Escola Primária de Massano de Amorim photographed in 1957, around the year when I joined the school. Don't miss the neatness of the lamp post and electric cables, compared to those in Goa today.

Moçidade Portuguesa

Once a week we wore uniforms of the Moçidade Portuguesa (Portuguese Youth), which was the Portuguese equivalent of the Boy Scouts, only more nationalistic and militaristic. I loved the uniform, simply because of its aesthetics: brown pants, olive green military shirt, a leather belt with a metal buckle which I think was in the form of the letter 'S' (could it have stood for Salazar?), a brown military cap with an insignia on the front, and the icing on the cake, the colourful and intricate Portuguese *emblema* on the left breast pocket.

Looking back today, I guess Moçidade Portuguesa was as different from the Boy Scouts as Hitler's Youth Army was. I don't remember camping, singing songs around a campfire, learning how to tie knots, trekking, or helping old ladies across the street. I only remember marching and chanting *'Viva Portugal! Aqui é Portugal!'* (Hail Portugal! This here is Portugal!) and singing *'Angola é nossa'* (Angola is ours). I think Angola, a Portuguese colony in Africa, was then beginning to emit grunts of rebellion and independence, and a nervous Portugal wished to remind itself and its colonies that it would never ever set any of them free. Therefore the song. A morale booster for the paranoid colonialist, composed for compulsory singing by every one of its colonized children around the globe.

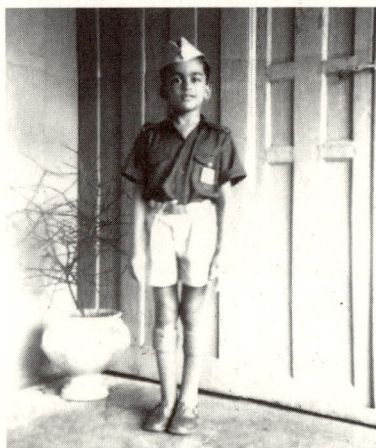

In the uniform of the Moçidade Portuguesa.

When I think of it now, we would have seemed very comical indeed to a visitor like say Jawaharlal Nehru – brownie kids in Asia singing that blackie kids in Africa belonged to whitey kids in Europe. Go figure. But ah, the innocence of childhood … we sang the song with such gusto, with such passion, because we believed we were singing for our own motherland. And I can't even begin to describe the breast-swelling we felt when the time came to sing '*Heróis do Mar*' (Heroes of the Sea), the Portuguese national anthem, which by default was ours ('*Aqui é Portugal*', remember?). I confess I still feel a stir of emotion when I hear it being sung by Portuguese football teams preceding a World Cup match. But this emotion today has nothing to do with political leanings or affiliations – it is the same emotion one feels when hearing a lullaby one's grandmother used to sing.

Professora Juja

Mango season in Goa is in April and May, our hot summer. New scholastic years – and the monsoons – start in June. June can therefore be representative of depressing things for schoolchildren: the end of playing outdoors, rain and grey skies, and worst of all, the end of holidays and a return to school. For my mid-morning snack at school that June, I often carried a sandwich filled with butter and *mangada*, a home-made jam made from all the abundance of uneaten mangoes left over from the just-concluded summer. The next year, I could not bear to smell or taste *mangada* – it reminded me of Professora Juja, the Portuguese lady class teacher I had that year, who was a terror to most children.

A classmate of mine nervously asked her permission to go to the toilet once. We were all around five to six years of age. The teacher refused. After about ten minutes he asked again. This time she scolded him severely and forbade him to leave his seat. A few minutes later, a foul smell filled the classroom. The poor little boy had not been able to hold it in any longer. Professora Juja rapped him with a ruler, and finally sent him off to the toilet to fend for himself. The meaner classmates teased him about it for weeks thereafter.

Another time, a boy who came from the weaker strata of society and was more at ease with Konkani than with Portuguese, was not able to recite a poem which had been assigned as homework. Professora Juja's reaction towards the little child was scathing: 'You son of a *padeiro* (baker), what do you want an education for? You should stay at home and learn how to bake bread with your father!' Social and economic boundaries were zealously guarded those days, and people were not expected or encouraged to have the audacity to rise above their lot. She instilled this unwritten rule early in her tiny tots.

This was the best and main school in the capital of Goa, and it amazes me today to think that some teachers there could be so insensitive and mean to little children. But not every teacher at Massano de Amorim was like Juja. Some were worse, like an older Goan lady who chastised and ridiculed her own little granddaughter before the full class, as the child happened to be a little slow.

It's a pity I had to form an association by taste for something as delicious as *mangada* with someone as nasty as Professora Juja. Thank god it didn't last long.

Professora Julieta Gomes da Costa

But most teachers were very, very nice indeed, my favourite being Professora Julieta Gomes da Costa. She was then a fashionable young Goan lady who had just returned after having finished her studies in Portugal – or perhaps she had been born and brought up in Portugal, as her Portuguese accent and command over the language was impeccable. I loved listening to her speak, and I hung on to her every word in class. Every lesson she taught seemed precious, too precious to be missed.

Besides which she was kind and gentle, the exact opposite of Juja. Whenever I saw her thereafter, as an adult myself, I have always called her Professora with an affection, respect and love which she has always reciprocated.

The junk treasures

On the way back from school, just round the corner, there was a printer called Tipografia Boa Sorte. The owner was a cranky old man with a bristling walrus moustache who worked at his machines in an undershirt stained with sweat and ink. Every few days I would stand at his door and ask, '*Dei-me papeis se faz favor …* Please give me some papers…' The objects of my desire were remnants of paper sheets which had been cut to size, in various colours and textures, and stacked in little bundles of various sizes. When the old man was in a good mood and gave me some, I returned home with a valuable treasure in my school bag, and on these pieces of coloured paper I would draw and write for days on end. Colours fascinated me, and so did all types of stationery material. They still do, and I can spend hours in a good stationery and art shop in Europe, enjoying the sights and smells of new paper, crayons, pencils, gouaches…

Another thing I collected and treasured at the time was scrap iron. There was a mechanical engineering school across the side street from our home, the Escola Técnica (today's Pharmacy College), where students worked on lathes. They threw out the most gorgeous scraps of metal of all shapes and sizes – perfectly square, rectangular, round, oval, the works. I went hunting for these once in a while, in the school's compound where they were sometimes discarded, and it is to my mother's great credit that she understood just how valuable that junk was to a kid. She allowed me to store it in tins and boxes in her storeroom, and once in a while I would take out all the pieces, arrange them in rows, admire them, and put them back again.

The tomato

There used to be a grocer in the lane where the famous landmark Café Tató (around the corner from Club Vasco da Gama) was and still is today. My parents took me shopping one day, and when we entered the grocer's I saw the most temptingly red, juicy tomatoes in a box placed just at my height.

As a child I hated vegetables and most fruits – but these tomatoes were a piece of art. Something made me covet one so badly, I stealthily put it in my pocket. I was all of three or four.

When we were about to leave the shop and I was out of earshot, the grocer confided in my father: 'Senhor Bernardo, your little boy has put a tomato in his pocket, thinking no one noticed. I'm sure it was "the lure of the forbidden fruit". Please do not embarrass him here, as it may scar him forever. But you might wish to speak to him at home, as one never knows which of our actions can grow into habits later in life. *Boa noite*, Senhor Bernardo.' My embarrassed but grateful father thanked him profusely, offered to pay for the tomato which the grocer refused, and we walked out to the car, me with my unsquashed trophy in my hip pocket.

The deep shame I felt when my parents gently brought up the subject at home is something I remember as though it happened yesterday. But the fact remains that after the incident and the gentle talk from my parents, I never ever stole again in all my life.

Luizinha

My parents had two good old friends who lived in Karachi, Marilyn and Pedro Abreu Lobo. Whenever they visited, the house resounded with irritatingly incomprehensible *Inglês* (English) for days on end. One time they came with a new little one-year-old daughter, Luizinha. As young mothers who are very good friends are wont to do, Mother and Marilyn made plans to marry off Luizinha and me when we grew up. I guess the prospect of waiting for about twenty-five years for the nuptials was to them but a minor trifle. Anyway, based on our mothers' decree, I dutifully recited 'Luizinha Abreu Lobo!' when asked *'Quem é a tua noiva?'* (Who is your fiancée?), though I couldn't understand the adults' amusement and laughter which followed. I took Luizinha for rides around the compound in my red 'Thunderbolt'.

With Luizinha Abreu Lobo, officially my first girlfriend. Our mothers, who were good friends, made playful plans to marry us off in the 'near' future.

The pampering

Most artists' stories are full of painful struggle, unhappy childhoods, perhaps abusive relatives, the works. I had the most ideal, happy, contented childhood I could ever wish for. Besides the unconditional and boundless love, attention and affection from my parents and everyone around me, every wish of mine was our household's command. The loss of their first child had devastated my parents, and when I finally came along eight long years later, one could understand and excuse their tendency to be overprotective, and to fuss over me a little more than would be considered normal.

I still remember my two wooden crates full of toys which would be brought out every morning to the veranda, where I would spend part of the day playing. Cars, guns, cowboys, Indians, horses, wagons and so on I would neatly arrange in rows. Dolls, if any had had the audacity to creep into my toy box, would be unceremoniously tossed out over the balcony.

I remember my two *veículos teleguiados* (remote-controlled vehicles). One was a magnificent silver-coloured car, and the other a huge silver-coloured bus. Wirelessly remote-controlled in the 1950s. Then there was a superbly detailed military police motorcycle with a headlight which lit up; the military man rode it, got off from one side, mounted and rode off again. For some reason, I was petrified of it in the beginning. I also remember my little Kodak camera with which I loved clicking pictures, some of which still feature in our family album. A View-Master with story discs in magical 3D images. Storybooks by the boxful. Father knew just how much I loved playing with sand on the beach, so along came two bullock carts one fine morning and unloaded fresh sand onto our compound, at a time when sandpits were not a common part of a child's play area. Of course our kittens thought Father had built them their very own poo-pit, so the sand had to be cleaned out every day, until it became too nasty-smelling to pass off for the beach.

LEFT: *Father clicked me clicking Mother.* RIGHT: *My sandpit. Behind me is one of the wooden walls which I loved so much. The diamond design of the wood made it easy for a child to climb in and out through the window, which was of course a much more convenient access to my sandpit than the doors were.*

Almost outgrowing my morphing tricycle in its bicycle avatar, in Dona Paula on a Sunday morning after Mass – therefore the bow and the Sunday clothes.

I also remember my first tricycle, of course my 'Thunderbolt', my first trottinette, and then my last tricycle. It was a huge one, with fat white tyres that had to be inflated like a real cycle's, which made it smooth and fast as a dream. It had this magical ability to morph – one removed the long back axle with two wheels, substituted it for a short one which had been provided, fixed one wheel on it, and voilà – a cycle was born. When I first discovered I could balance on two wheels, I felt a sense of thrill and excitement and freedom I hadn't felt before. It was almost as though I'd learnt how to fly.

A friend of my parents once said I was 'born with a silver spoon in my mouth'. I didn't know what that meant, and my parents seemed a bit embarrassed to explain when I asked. Tia Angela made her own version clear enough: *'Teus pais estragam ti completamente!'* (Your parents spoil you thoroughly!) You guessed it, the next minute I asked her when she was going home.

But although Father spoilt me with gifts, he instilled in me a great regard for honesty, especially for keeping one's word. To him, as to most old-school men of his generation, the spoken word or promise meant more than a written, stamped, signed, sealed and notarized contract. After all, a contract could be refuted in a court of law; whereas the only court that could judge a man's word was his own conscience. He was proud of the reputation he enjoyed in Panjim, and of the fact that every merchant and dealer in town would blindly trust him with credit if on a rare occasion he wasn't carrying money, and decided to buy anything, from an ice cream to jewellery. The local Mercedes Benz dealer once brought the latest Model 220, parked it in front of our house, handed my father the keys and said, 'Keep it and drive it for a week, Senhor Bernardo. If you don't like it, I'll come pick it up.' But Father had already set his eye on a British Vauxhall car, so he turned down the kind trial offer.

Even though I guess Mother secretly enjoyed watching me savour Father's gifts, she would never openly encourage extravagance. She had been educated in a nuns' convent, and was our in-house authority on morality, household economy and concern and respect for others, especially for those less fortunate. However, she practised all these tenets subtly and unobtrusively. Even though she'd never ever waste it, she never scrimped on food – our table was laid with the choicest prawns and fish and meats and vegetables and sweets, but always in just the right necessary quantities. She used to love to quote from a household economy book written by someone called Marden, which she considered her second Bible. At times we teased her about 'Senhor Marden' when we felt she went overboard with her economy thing. But to this day, I am not able to tear off a beautiful gift-wrapping paper and throw it away if it can be recycled; I squeeze a toothpaste tube till the very end, and sometimes cut it with scissors to squeeze the remnants out of their hiding places; I constantly turn off lights and fans in rooms which are empty, and shut dripping water taps, even in friends' houses or in public buildings – and I can't help doing several other things like this which I learnt from Mother, which she in turn learnt from her nuns, who in turn had referred to Marden's home economy handbook. If more homes and industries and governments had followed those tenets, the world would not have been facing the crisis it faces today, and we may not have found it necessary to coin terms such as 'ecological preservation' and 'global warming'.

Mother regularly gave to charities, quietly and unnoticed. She never asked my father for the money for her donations, though; she gave little, but she gave regularly, from her savings from the money Father gave her for household expenses. One thing which horrified her no end was ostentatious charity practised with show, pomp and publicity. A motto she drummed into my head was 'Never let the left hand know what the right hand gives'. It stayed embedded in my mind very deep, and would cause me some pain decades later.

The neighbours

I could do the semi-circular run, out of our gate, on to the footpath, and into the next gate, blindfolded. I did it a million times every day. Raju and Chandu next door were both around my age, and though they didn't speak Portuguese, we didn't need much communication for the games we played. I knew that they were Gujaratis, but I thought that just meant Goans of another kind, another religion, another set of customs and language. I had no idea that Gujarat was a place which their family originally came from. Their father, like many Gujaratis, was a trader and ran a shop.

He was always smiling. Their mother was a short, plump, friendly, but forever hassled-looking lady we called Babi.

Their row house was a double residence, the other half inhabited by a Goan Hindu family. There were no little boys there, only a little girl called Bharati, and so the house was of no interest to me whatsoever. Little girls were a hindrance who didn't know how to play cowboys and Indians, football, or any of those things which were the top priorities of life for any sensible human being.

There was one time, though, when the girl was of some interest to Raju, Chandu and me. We were all around five or six years of age, and Mother somehow coaxed us into allowing her into our games. We boys lured her under a bed on the pretext of playing hide and seek, and there lifted her little frock to find out what she had underneath which was so different from ours. She started bawling, Mother came running, and pulled our ears hard enough to make sure we didn't feel any such scholarly urges for scientific research in a hurry again.

The last row house was occupied by the Sardesai family, also Goan Hindu. I think the old man was no more, so the figurative head of the household was the old lady. Next in the hierarchy was the eldest son, a very respected professor at the Liceu, the revered educational institution up on Altinho Hill. I like everyone else called him Professor. His younger brother Auduth is today a well-known architect in Panjim. They had two sisters, Kumud and Suman. They were all much older to me, but I still ran in and out of their house. The sisters loved teasing me and called me Kiristão (Konkani for Christian). 'Chee,' they would say in mock disdain, 'you're a Kiristão and you eat meat!' 'Chee,' I would reply in the same vein, 'you're a Konknò and your god is an elephant!' And they would all laugh and tease me some more. This friendly ribbing about our differences was quite representative of how different communities got along in Goa then.

In front of our house, across the street, lived a Catholic couple, Senhor Evaristo and Dona Lucinda, whom I always thought of as elderly. They were indeed quite older to my parents, who therefore also addressed them with the respectful prefixes Senhor and Dona. They had a grown daughter, Maria do Çéu, which literally meant 'Mary from Heaven', whose name we pronounced as one word: 'Marid'çéu'. They also had a son who was away in Portugal, and whom I never met. Maria do Çéu was fair, had green eyes, and we secretly knew that she had admirers at the Liceu. They lived in a beautiful large house with a delicate lattice-worked veranda railing. I always remember it being painted light grey and white, even years after the Liberation, until it was finally broken down to give way to an ugly 'building'. (We in Goa call every office or apartment block a building – to differentiate them from houses and bungalows, which we for some reason do not consider buildings.)

Senhor Evaristo was retired, had white hair around his bald pate, and was passionate about philately. I remember him as always being dressed in his clean, long-sleeved, well-pressed striped pyjamas around the house. There was a sunny glass-shuttered room at one end of the front veranda where he had his study. There he pored over and worked on his precious stamp collection for hours on end. His desk was full of stamp boxes, stamp albums, thick almanacs with information about stamps of the world, pincers of different shapes and sizes, scissors, a water bowl, glue, and the most interesting item of all – a large magnifying glass. He would allow me to sit by his side, after extracting from me a solemn promise that I would touch nothing, and would show me his stamps and tell me stories about some of them. He spoke strange names of countries and currencies I'd never heard of before. I was fascinated by the odd triangular and circular shapes of some of the stamps he owned. The highlight of these sessions came when he would let me look through the magic of his magnifying glass. Of course I soon wanted to be a stamp collector too, so Father bought me a beginner's set: an album, an almanac, a magnifying glass, and a box of international stamps. I eagerly awaited every letter that arrived home from then on, and the ones that came from faraway places such as Europe, Africa and the Americas were obviously the prized ones. Of course, most philatelists aged six or seven find the hobby too passive after a short while, and I was no exception.

Senhor Evaristo also taught me how to play draughts, ludo, and snakes and ladders. I would run into their house once in a while, my boards under my arm, a seven-year-old kid, and ask this seventy-year-old gentleman, '*Senhor Evaristo, quer brincar?*' (Mr Evaristo, would you like to play?) He often did, and we spent hours at it. I guess he was the closest equivalent I've ever had to a grandfather. He was soft-spoken, kind and patient, and his world – especially his study with all those stamps – represented to me the quiet, clean, orderly world of the elderly, a world I was somehow as drawn to as I was to the raucous, noisy and energetic world I shared with Raju and Chandu.

His wife, Dona Lucinda, loved to talk as much as Senhor Evaristo liked being quiet, and had no qualms about making her opinion about everything and everyone known. She was very affectionate, and loved me like a mother and grandmother rolled into one. She was from Verna, Salcete, in south Goa, and the way she spoke Portuguese, spiked with colourful and choice (but never crude, she was too religious for that) Konkani expressions, complete with the Salcete sing-song lilt and pronunciation, was found to be extremely interesting and entertaining by my parents and their friends. She had a spicy sharp wit too, which added greatly to the popularity of her company and conversation.

As their official household mascot, I was once invited to a formal family lunch of some sort they were giving at home. Just me, mind you, not my parents. My first solo invitation into a home of adults. Mother dressed me in my best and, after a refresher course on table manners, which included saying 'No thank you' in case they offered me wine, sent me over. Crossing the road was as safe as strolling in one's own backyard. Dona Lucinda started by serving a little glass of port wine to everyone around her table. I said 'No thank you' when my turn came, and she passed on to the next guest. I pulled at her sleeve and hissed in a loud stage whisper,

'Please insist, Dona Lucinda. Please insist. Mother said I could have a drop, but only if you insisted.'

She narrated the incident for weeks afterwards to my parents and everyone who would listen, and sent them all into splits of laughter. It didn't take much to make people laugh then.

I'm not sure when Dona Lucinda's orphaned nephew and two nieces came to live with them. They were very kind and friendly, the extremely well-behaved, religiously brought up kind. Of course they seemed very sad too, wearing lost expressions and black or grey mourning clothes every day. The elder sister's name was Noelma, and the younger pair, who were quite older to me then (three years make a huge age difference when you're seven and your friends are ten), were Arlindo and Alcina. They gradually lightened up, their clothes went back to being colourful, or at least not black or grey, and by then we had become good friends. They took me under their wing, and treated me like a little brother.

Lar dos Damanenses

Across the street on our left was a house which was always painted a dark red, and which was known as the Lar dos Damanenses, a hostel which housed students from Daman and Diu. Daman and Diu were Portuguese colonies too, but they were in distant Gujarat, a connection which perhaps explained why Raju and Chandu's families had moved to Goa. Goa was the head of this Portuguese trinity in India, and the seat of the government and the Church which ruled and serviced all three. The Portuguese governor here was not just the governor of Goa, but the *'Governador Geral de Goa, Damão e Diu'*. Students from Daman and Diu desirous of pursuing a further education came to Goa for want of higher institutions there, and therefore the Lar (Home).

The young men (in their late teens and early twenties) who lived in the Lar spoke Portuguese with a very peculiar accent, which made them raise the pitch of every last word in a sentence or question, and of a few words in between too. They were particularly well-mannered, friendly and helpful. But the most beautiful thing about them was their music.

This was the street junction near our house in the 1950s when I grew up there. This is a photograph gifted to me out of the blue by our old neighbour when I bumped into him on the street just the other day. A rare photo, as hardly anyone thought of taking photographs of streets in those days. Unfortunately one cannot see our house, but on the extreme left one sees a bit of the compound wall of Dona Lucinda and Senhor Evaristo's house; across the street from it, also on the left, is the compound wall of our house; across the street from us on the right, hidden by the ambulance passing by, is the Lar dos Damanenses. I don't know to whom the house one sees most prominently on the right belonged; I think it was an office of some sort.

On the evenings when they felt homesick, they would sit on their veranda and sing songs from back home. They were beautiful songs, in a dialect of Portuguese of which we could not understand some words. Some were plaintive and melancholic, like '*Surumbai*'. And others were jolly and bouncy, like '*Barra de Damão*' and '*Maria Pita Che*'. I recorded a medley of these last two many years later, and it proved a big hit with people all over India, even those who had never heard of Daman or Diu or the Portuguese language, proving the universality of the appeal of their music.

Two or three of the Daman students became family friends; I remember Carlos and his brother Luís would drop in for a visit, and Mother would treat them to home-cooked delicacies, which she knew they, being so far away from their own mothers and homes, surely missed badly.

The Damanenses' was yet another house of grown-ups where I was welcome anytime. The neighbourhood felt very comfortable and homely and safe, with so many people taking me under their wing and treating me like their own child or kid brother.

Summers in Calangute

In the summer, Father would rent a house on Calangute Beach for a month or maybe two. Even though today the Calangute of old is unrecognizable, the house he would rent is the first one on the left as you get down the steps leading down from that big circle at the entrance of the beach – the one with a rounded veranda.

The house where we spent our summers in the 1950s and 1960s is the one in the background, facing the sea. That shack in the foreground didn't exist then; it's where Father used to park his car. This picture must have been taken in the 1970s.

As the house came without many of the comforts he was used to, he would get our factory workers to load our refrigerator and some other 'basic necessities' on to one of his factory trucks, in which the driver and the workers would follow his car.

Life in that beach house was idyllic, especially for a child; what could be better than having sand, that magical precious matter, just outside your door? And that too a whole unending beach of it, not just a sandpit?

I remember the long, sleepy, quiet summer days there; the never-ending sound of the sea forever lulling one; the afternoon sun making it impossible to step out; sitting in the veranda while all the adults had their afternoon siesta, looking out at the blindingly bright and shining empty beach and sea through squinting eyes; and then evening time when, after the customary high tea and biscuits and butter and cheese, we would all head to the cooled-down beach. There, some friends or relatives of my parents would join us, and there they'd sit or stroll for two or three hours, chatting away, while I'd be very busy with my pail and spade in the sand, and with other kids who might be around.

But perhaps the best fun of all was when Mamã de Parrá stayed a few days with us, perhaps with a grand-aunt or two. On those mornings, Mother and Mamã and the aunts would head for the sea for their yearly *banhos de mar*, sea-baths. These consisted of them sitting in the sand just where the smallest waves broke, dressed in their house gowns, Mother in her fashionable one-piece swimsuit, receiving those waves on their backs. Mamã was a great believer in the properties of water, and there was no summer when she would miss these sea-baths. During a certain season she would go for baths in the natural sweet-water fountain at hilly Oxel in Siolim. And in her own house, she would insist that we all bathe, even if we visited for just the day, extolling the virtues of her well water – which was indeed very rich in minerals, as the well was dug out in very rocky soil.

My first 'sexual sensations'

We somehow tend to think that one's first sexual experience is the first physical sexual contact with someone else, at an age when one is finally aware, however hazily, of what sex is about. I am no child psychologist, but I tend to think that our first sexual consciousness begins much before that. In fact, I believe our first sexual feelings and sensations begin when we are not even aware that they are sexual, when everyone around us sees us as innocent, harmless children, which in fact we are. I believe the first experiences are mental, in fact subconscious, not physical.

When I was around four or five, I often ran from our back gate into the back gate of our next-door Hindu neighbours. The back portion of their house had an open courtyard where the womenfolk bathed. No men were allowed here during their ablutions, but of course a five-year-old male child was not even considered a boy yet, leave alone a man. So other than talking and joking with me in a motherly or sisterly way while bathing, they saw me as no threat to their privacy. The women, who ranged in age from grandmothers to their daughters and granddaughters, bathed while dressed in sheer cotton saris, which after having a *kousó* (pot) of water poured over them became totally transparent. Their breasts, and particularly their dark, swollen nipples, became objects of deep wonderment and curiosity for me to gaze at. Often their saris' pallus would slip off their shoulders and expose a breast or both completely, but they in their natural innocence thought nothing of it. I, in spite of the innocence of my curiosity, somehow knew an unspoken rule: that however interesting, attractive and intriguing I might find these parts of their anatomy, I was not to touch them or talk about them. And I believe it was *this* knowledge, that they were forbidden and out of reach, that made the whole thing subconsciously sexual. I was filled with a strange primaeval longing which I was not even fully aware of.

Father clicks Mother getting ready for a night out with him. In the right-hand corner I'm playing with my favourite cars in bed.

I felt the same longing when I saw Mother and her friends dress up in their wonderful backless gowns on their way to grand balls in the Panjim clubs. Their behaviour and body language changed perceptibly once they were all decked up, and was to me representative of a world I knew existed but could not quite put my finger on. After Mother and Father gave me a million kisses and left for the ball, I went to sleep in my cosy bed in the comfortable darkness, with the sound of the fan whirring somewhere in the room. But as I fell asleep, I was subconsciously aware of being filled with this inexplicable longing.

I once told Mother that I would marry her when I grew up. She laughed and said that wasn't possible. When I, broken-hearted at the rejection, asked why, she said it was because she was already married to Father. Enough to awaken a full-blown Oedipus complex in a four-year-old!

The Goa that was

I have written about life in the Goa that I grew up in, especially in the villages, in a preface to Frenchman Emmanuel Chastang's excellent book titled *"Goa, ma belle…"* Rather than repeat myself in different words, I reproduce the preface below with his kind permission.

Most readers will not have known Goa while she was still an undiscovered, lost-in-time, forgotten and unfashionable pristine paradise. I consider myself extremely lucky to have been born and raised in that Goa, and I wish I could share that experience with you.

However, I am at a loss for words to try and make you feel the way time moved at a pace so slow and so relaxed in a place at once so Latin and so Indian. Words to make you see what I saw through the eyes of an eight-year-old child: devout Christian ladies in Portuguese lace gloves and parasols, carrying their high Hindu caste like an invisible armour hanging on an invisible string from their pale upturned noses; serious learned Hindu gentlemen in Indian dhotis, Nehru cloth caps, socks and shoes, and the latest European jacket (plus a solid black British brolly for good measure) to complete an unintended premature fusion fashion statement; the smell of sunshine and dry leaves floating through a lazy sleepy village summer afternoon so hot, not even a crow could be bothered to fly out from under the shade of an overladen mango tree; screaming children running to the front veranda to watch the only car which might pass by on a red dusty road in the course of a whole week; people who ordered a carved furniture set and wisely let years go by while the master carpenters calmly went at their craft with an abundance of a precious ingredient unaffordable to today's art: Time.

I remember the huge aristocratic mansions, the humble little huts and comfortable homely houses of all sizes in between, the ancient temples and whitewashed chapels and a few rare mosques, all safely hidden under millions of coconut trees … the allopathic and country and witch doctors, all eyeing each other with studied suspicion … the tamed rice fields and wild lush forests and virgin silver beaches spilling one into the other.

And above all, Goa's basically friendly people practising two main religions, speaking two main languages and abiding by two thousand unwritten social dictates, all co-existing in a harmony which stood firmly on one unshakeable philosophy: live and let live, and while we're at it, let's sing a song and share a drink to help the time go by.

No, I cannot accurately describe what it felt like growing up in such a place during such an epoch. I can, however, suggest you read Gabriel García Márquez. It doesn't matter that he writes about South America. The villages, the houses, the people, the states of mind, and above all the ghosts past, present and future he describes so poetically – that could well be the Goa I once knew and loved so well.

3

Music, a Sister, and War

My first musical instrument

When I was about four years old Father bought me a mouth organ. I guess it was the smallest, simplest musical instrument he could think of for a child. When he returned from the *Fábrica* (which is how we referred to his cold drink factory) that evening, he couldn't find me. Mother told him I'd been sitting under the bed and crying for the last half hour, and that she couldn't quite understand why. He found me there, the mouth organ in my lap.

'What's wrong, son?' he asked.

'I can't play this song!' I sobbed.

'Which one?' he asked, surprised.

I played the introduction to 'The Blue Tango', hit the wrong fourth note again, and sobbed louder in angry frustration.

Father understood immediately. His eyes shining with excitement, he told me to get dressed and get into the car. He drove me to Pedro Fernandes, who owned the one and only music shop that catered to the whole of musical Panjim and perhaps to the whole of north Goa, and asked for a professional chromatic Hohner mouth organ with a side button for sharps and flats. It came in a lovely box with red velvet lining inside.

Back home, Father explained how one attained the 'hidden notes' by pressing the all-important button, and I was overjoyed at finally being able to play the tune.

'What made you choose "The Blue Tango" as your first piece on the mouth organ?' he asked.

I didn't know. I just loved the melody. I love it still.

A few days into playing the mouth organ, I wanted to do something I'd seen someone do at a party: play it with one hand, while keeping rhythm with a maraca with the other. The maracas available were too big and heavy for me. Father improvised and found me a little metallic can; it was flat and circular, and he half-filled it with smooth green seeds of some sort. It made a great maraca-like sound, and I was in business.

I played for Mother and Father, who would be made to sit in the living room; I'd part the door curtains and come in as though I were stepping on to a stage; Mother and Father were prompted to clap, after which I would take a bow and sing and play. After that Mother and Father would clap again, I would take a final bow, part the curtains and walk out of the room/offstage.

I then played and sang at every family get-together and birthday party when asked to play, and I was always itching to be asked.

Music at home and in Goa

Father had bought a German Nordmende radiogram from the one and only Panjim dealer called Senhor Mungró. A radiogram was a handsome piece of highly polished teak or rosewood cabinet in which were housed, or almost concealed, several music-reproducing pieces of equipment. The one Father bought comprised a valve radio in the centre, driven by a powerful high-quality amplifier. Beneath this was a superb set of loudspeakers camouflaged behind a rich woven cloth fixed behind an intricate wooden grill. There were two loudspeakers on its sides too. On top there were two horizontal doors which opened upwards: one to reveal a four-speed Dual record changer, on which one could stack up to twelve records of all sizes, and the second door revealed a Telefunken spool tape recorder. In the front, on the left and right sides of the *meuble,* two handsome rounded doors opened to reveal compartments with vertical slots where one stored records.

The radiogram started off Father's record collection. It was an eclectic mix of big brass dance bands, western classical symphonies, Brazilian baiãos, forró, bossa novas and sambas, South American solo singers and harmony groups such as Trio los Panchos and Trio los Paraguayos, popular Italian singers such as Renato Carosone and Caterina Valente, English and American singers whose names I don't recall but whose songs I can still hear in my mind, a beautiful orchestral instrumental called 'Anastasia' which always made me feel sad, happy Portuguese folk songs, plaintive Portuguese fados of which Amália Rodrigues was the all-time reigning queen, and of course the few and rare 78 rpm records which had been then made of lovely Goan Konkani mandos and popular songs. Father loved Konkani songs, and I particularly remember one, '*Shivole, Sonar Khetti*', Father's favourite, as it was about Siolim, his beloved village; I was to re-record my version of it in 2021, as a tribute to Father and to its composer, Cruz Noronha. After the Goan mando and other folk songs, the fado came a close second in his personal chart list.

Between Mother and Father is the old Nordmende Radiogram which provided us with countless hours of music from the radio, records and tapes.

The first monsoon night that year, there was a particularly spectacular thunder and lightning storm. I was scared. Father decided to teach me how to appreciate the power of nature and not be frightened of it. He turned off all the lights, put on a classical symphony at a very loud volume, and sat me on his lap in the darkened veranda. We felt the powerful spray of the rain on our faces; the whole black street lit up with bright silvery flashes of lightning every few minutes, revealing familiar trees bent in two by the wind, the flashes punctuated by deep and loud rolling thunder fit to shake the house to its foundations; and providing musical background to all this was Beethoven's Fifth, since electricity hadn't failed yet due to a fallen tree or branch. Father kept whispering softly and soothingly into my ear, trying to explain to a five-year-old the beauty and power of this scene.

Today I love sitting out on my veranda on stormy monsoon nights, enjoying the surround sound of some of the most vibrant energy in nature, smelling the wet Goan earth, and sipping a glass of something straight from the heart of the Goan soil. But that night I burst out crying. Upon Mother's protests, Father gave up his very specialized lesson on music and nature appreciation, took me indoors and turned off the music. But the experience has stayed with me forever.

Every little party or gathering in Goa had music in those days. Not music playing out of a record player, but music played by the revellers themselves. Violins and mandolins would be brought out once the mood was right, the piano lid opened, and people coughed and tuned their voices which, smoothened by a few choice golden lubricants, rose in glorious song. Instruments exchanged hands, different people would be coaxed to sing 'their' songs, and by the third one, people got up to dance. The music, singing, dancing and drinking went on until the buffet was declared open – which was invariably delayed as much as possible, lest the guests think the host was being mean and miserly by bringing the festivities to a halt. And then everyone, now hungry but still not willing to stop singing and dancing, marched in time to a popular marching tune, the couples arm-in-arm, right into the dining room and around and around the dining table, the guitarists and violinists and mandolin players following with their instruments. The piano player was invariably left playing alone in the hall.

Once the music ended and everyone gathered around the table, the most eloquent speaker of the gathering was asked to raise the indispensable extempore *brinde* or toast. In my parents' circle, this task usually fell to Senhor Vasco Alvares, the large, portly, jolly but irreverent man who was one of the stalwarts of Panjim society, and a good friend and party buddy of Father's. His toasts were always a pleasure to listen to; they had just the right mixture of pathos, emotion, familial values, and most importantly, naughty humour which had everyone from us kids (whenever we understood it) to the oldest grandparents present in uncontrollable splits of laughter.

And then, before attacking the mandatory succulent piglet and turkey and giant kingfish and lobsters and fried rice, '*Parabens a voçê*' or 'Happy Birthday' was sung in harmony by one and all, their enthusiasm heightened by their gratitude to the gracious host for this great feast, he in turn thanking the gathering for decades and even generations of their tried and tested warmth, love and friendship.

Once dinner was done with, the feast invariably came to an abrupt halt, a custom which anyone but a Goan would see as impolite; and everyone left soon thereafter, but not before long-drawn-out goodbyes with much hugging and kissing on both cheeks. Pleasantly tired from the singing and dancing, still humming a tune and feeling content from the great buffet, families walked in the moonlight and yellow street lights to their cars, and drove back to their homes where cool and comfortable beds awaited them.

Moonlight was a very important part of evenings and nights. Even in the cities where they existed, the street lamps were so dim, one could see and feel the full power of moonlight and starlight. Much more so in villages, where there was no electricity at all.

Music played a very important role in people's daily lives. One didn't need to consider oneself a musician or a singer in order to know how to play an instrument or sing a song – why, everyone knew how to do these things, they were as natural as talking or writing without considering oneself an orator or an author.

Once, at such a party at Tio Renato's house on the way to Altinho, my cousin Jorge, who was then at least thirteen or fourteen years of age, got me drunk on champagne. I must have been all of six or seven. When he saw I was beginning to pass out, he panicked at the prospect of being found out by his parents and mine. He stealthily carried me down the stairs to our car, which was parked on the main road together with all the others, put me to sleep in the back seat, and left me there to sleep it off. His 'good deed of the day' was discovered a while later when Mother started looking for me. I believe he got more of a headache from his father's slap the next morning than I did from my very first hangover – which, coming from French champagne, probably shows that I started off in style.

The ukulele and the banjo

After the mouth organ, Father decided it was time he got me a stringed instrument. He bought me a little wooden ukulele, which was shaped like a miniature Spanish guitar, and which I still have.

He taught me my first simple basic chords, just the ones necessary to accompany myself as I sang popular songs of the day in Portuguese such as 'Cachaça' and 'Tiro Liro Liro'.

The ukulele had four metal strings, and Father tuned them to the first four strings of the Spanish guitar, the fourth one in a higher octave. I don't remember why, but soon after I learnt how to play it, Father bought me a little banjo. Perhaps the banjo was a richer-sounding instrument, and Father felt I could do with a better one now that I'd learnt the basics of chords and strumming. We tuned the banjo the same way we did the ukulele, so the transition was no problem at all.

The banjo became 'my' instrument for quite a while after that. I think I first performed on stage with it at a reçita at the Club Nacional in Panjim when I was five. These *reçitas* were very popular and frequent events at both Club Nacional and Club Vasco da Gama, the two stalwart centres of Panjim social and cultural life. Amateur performers – individuals, families, groups – would rehearse new songs for days on end. No one would dream of charging money to perform, and entry to all these shows was free to club members and their guests and often to whoever else wished to attend; but the enthusiasm and seriousness with which people prepared and performed could compete with that of Grammy nominees of today.

The song I sang on my first day on a stage was '*Minha Mãezinha Querida*' (My Dearest Mother), a beautiful old Portuguese waltz. I remembered it twenty-six years later as I was recording *Old Goan Gold*, and made sure I included it in the album as a personal souvenir.

With my faithful banjo, inseparable companion of many years. Photo clicked at the house of my cousin the architect Garçia dos Santos Dias.

When Father was driving me to the club for that performance, he asked, '*Remo, estás nervoso?*' (Remo, are you nervous?) I wasn't, but I guessed I ought to be, so I said, 'Yes.' Father's advice was: 'Remember that people in the audience can't play and sing like you. And those who can, probably couldn't when they were five as you are. Remember that and play and sing right on.'

I've never really followed that advice, and I've never thought that way about an audience. I guess I never needed to, because when I climbed on to the stage for the first time in my life a half hour later, I took to it like a fish to water.

Mina

The most important person in my early life, besides my parents, was Mina. She grew up with us as my elder sister and surrogate mother rolled into one. She was amazing in every way: a powerhouse of energy, loving and caring to the extreme, the most talented cook in the world, knowledgeable about music, armed with an elephantine memory for everything from song lyrics and tunes to incidents, a talent for accurately mimicking everyone from pompous priests to society ladies, all with a devilish sense of humour which would send Mother into unstoppable fits of laughter.

Mother always smiled easily, and she loved to laugh. Not only did she love to laugh, but if she found something really funny, she found it difficult to stop laughing – a trait amply inherited by my sister Belinda. Mother's own laughter provoked more laughter from her, and when she became conscious of the fact that she could not stop laughing, that would make her laugh still more, and when we would comment on how much she was laughing, that would only add to the avalanche of laughter, until it became an uncontrollable snowball growing in size and intensity as it kept rolling and rolling.

Mina made Mother laugh so much, cracking joke after joke after joke, that one day I noticed Mother had tears in her eyes. I had never ever seen tears in any adult's eyes, I only knew that tears in a child's eyes meant sadness and pain; and now I was seeing them in Mother's, and she was going on laughing and crying, crying and laughing... I started bawling, hitting out at Mina who I thought was 'torturing' Mother, screaming at her to stop ... and obviously this sent Mina and Mother into even worse fits of laughter and tears.

That day I learnt that not all tears mean pain; that adults can also cry due to silly reasons such as humour, happiness and joy.

Mina a couple of years after my primary school, when she tried to dress and look like her favourite
Bollywood actresses of the time, Nanda and Nutan, and got me to click her on Father's camera.

During the first few years of school, I was the most timid boy you could think of. Not only was I walked to school and back, but I couldn't even stay in school alone. Mina to the rescue. She stayed there through the whole duration of the classes. I was five years old, and Massano de Amorim (the junior school) seemed like 'hostile territory' after Ninho Infantil (the kindergarten). Many kids are known to cry when they see their mothers leave them in school on the first day; but having Mina stand by the classroom window where I could see her at any given time all morning long surely seems like an exaggerated solution to this timeless predicament. Well, I did say I was overprotected.

Since she 'attended' school with me, Mina was the perfect home tutor in the afternoons; she knew all my lessons, and all my poems and songs, by heart. Besides, she was an avid listener of the radio, and knew all the latest songs of the day, Portuguese and Brazilian, much better than either of my parents did. For the first few years of my life, she was the one who taught me the lyrics and tunes to my first songs.

Carnival

Between the ages of one and eight (that is, before I discovered my life's ambition, which was to be an American cowboy with a horse, revolver and rifle), I didn't have much say in how I dressed for Carnival. Mother and Father had fun thinking up costumes in which to dress me up, and off I went with them wherever they took me. During the day, it invariably was to friends' and cousins' houses; Father would stealthily take along coloured powders and water pistols, knock on their (always open) front doors, and colour and wet everyone as they came to see who had knocked. Their whole house suddenly filled up with excited screams and laughter, they ran in first for protection, and then to bring out colours and water of their own; and, after a good exchange of these carnivalesque ammunitions, everyone settled down to a glass of lemonade or beer. And then, joined by these newly drenched and coloured cousins/friends who were now in full Carnival spirit, we all proceeded to the house of the next victims.

While at home, the quiet of Panjim would suddenly be shattered with sounds of loud drums and shouts of 'Sheboi! Sheboi!' in the streets. We would all run out to the veranda to see five or six men, painted and dressed up outrageously in all kinds of raggedy disguises (never anything sophisticated or serious), passing by singing, dancing, playing drums which were often empty cans, and sipping strong feni from quarter pints sticking out of their pockets. Once in a while they would stop and put up an impromptu skit right there in the street. There wasn't enough traffic in Panjim to disturb the great dramatic troupe. The skits, mostly in Konkani but sometimes interspersed with hilariously broken Portuguese, were bawdy satires and spoofs. Their caustic wit would often be directed at authorities, whether religious or governmental. Even though Goa was under strict dictatorship and censorship from Portugal, on the three days of Carnival even Salazar's regime turned a blind eye to veiled spoof.

It is all-revealing that today, under our so-called freedom of democracy, the Goan government has declared a total ban on political insinuations in Carnival floats.

In the evenings there were children's fancy-dress competitions and parties at the two main Panjim clubs, the Nacional and the Vasco da Gama. Here Mother and Father's imagination took flight, and I was dressed up in whatever it took to satisfy their fantasy of the year.

Various costumes in which Mother and Father dressed me during Carnival between the ages of one year ten months and eight years. The last one, in the Nehru outfit, was soon after India re-took possession of Goa.

The Afonsos

Vovó came from the Afonso family, from Taleigão. A very large family, all very musical. There was the tall patriarch of the family, Ti Zé, and his tiny wife, Ti Luci. I think they had an all-male brood of children, who were Father's first cousins: Alberto, Mauro, António, Raul and Xavier. Most of them had only daughters, no sons, except for Mauro, who had only sons, and who lived in Bombay.

We and the cousins who lived in Goa were always in and out of each other's houses, but Raul and his wife Gracinda seemed to be closest to Father and Mother. They had four daughters, out of whom Lucia was the most musical. She played the piano and the accordion, and sang. We were the same age, and in the same class too. The parents instilled a friendly competitive spirit between us – about who learnt and sang more songs, and also about who knew the school lessons best.

I remember the parties at the Afonso household in Taleigão, a house so large it was eventually divided into three or four, each part being more than adequate to house a whole present-day family of 'only' three or four children each.

It was an undisputed fact that music came to me from Father, not Mother. And it came to Father from his mother's side, not his father's. Later I often heard Father's maternal cousins, the Afonsos, talking to Father about me: 'A musica veio para ele dos Afonsos, não dos Fernandes.' (Music came to him from the Afonsos, not from the Fernandes.) Out of all the music-filled parties of my youth, I remember the ones at the Afonsos' in Taleigão most vividly.

I didn't meet the brother who lived in Bombay, Mauro, or become aware of him, until some years later, unfortunately in a not-so-pleasant incident.

How to bully a twelve-year-old

When Primo (cousin) Mauro came down to Goa and attended one of the parties at the Afonsos', I got to see him at last. He ran a family band with his sons (and I think also his wife) in Bombay, and they played at the exclusive Rendezvous restaurant in the hallowed Taj Mahal Hotel, which in Goa was considered the height of heights, and which made him, to his brothers in Goa, a demigod. We too were all duly impressed.

I was quite in awe of his formidable reputation (within his family only, though I didn't know that then) and his big-city Bombay panache. As usual, in the middle of the party, musical instruments were brought out and a merry session of singsong started. Then we all watched with wonder as Mauro, urged on by his brothers, performed fast and difficult pieces, such as 'Czardas' and 'Flight of the Bumble Bee', on his violin.

And then for some strange reason, as if on cue, they all called me to accompany him on the guitar.

'Do you know "Stardust"?' Mauro asked.

No, I didn't. 'Don't worry, I'll call out the chords to you as I play it,' he said.

'Stardust' is a rather complicated jazz piece, with a whole lot of rare chord sequences, and would have been so especially for a twelve-year-old not at all into jazz, who played by ear without knowing chord names, and who was hearing the piece for the first time. But I accompanied Mauro correctly, and also managed to do so when he played it the second time around without calling out the chords to me.

I realized later that he and his brothers were quite disappointed that I hadn't faltered, so he raised the bar. He said, 'Ok, now I'm going to improvise on the melody. Just play the same sequence of chords.'

'I don't think I can do that, Primo Mauro; I don't even know this melody yet, so I surely won't be able to follow an improvisation in it.'

'Oh, come on, try. Let's see if you can,' urged Mauro and the other brothers, with provocative smiles. This started to seem strange. It was no longer about making music, it was turning into a duel of sorts.

Almost towards the end of the improvisation, I lost track of the sequence and missed out on a chord. As though this was the moment they had all been waiting for, Mauro stopped playing, and he and all his brothers – Raul, António and Xavier (except the eldest, Alberto) – jumped down my throat, laughing loudly and mocking me.

'Falhou! Falhou! You missed! You missed!'

'But … I'd never heard this tune bef…'

'Falhou! You made a mistake! You could not follow Mauro!' They gathered around me, teasing me and cackling gleefully.

I felt sick in my stomach. Father soon came to my side, trying to talk sense to them about me being totally unfamiliar with the tune; but the Afonsos had loud voices, and four of them drowned Father out.

The whole thing turned into an unpleasant scene. I remember Father leaving the party soon afterwards, taking Mother and me home with him.

I could never see the hitherto well-loved Afonso brothers in the same way ever again. They had displayed shades I hadn't been aware they possessed; unfair meanness and cruelty to a youth of twelve. From then on I disliked them all – except the eldest, Alberto, who had refused to take part in this farce. And I never went to their houses or parties ever again, except to Primo Alberto's. I couldn't believe that grown-ups could be so jealous, probably because someone from the Fernandes side of the family, and not an Afonso, was gaining popularity and fame in Goa. They must have planned that coup with their hero from Bombay well before the party started. Such bullying can mark a youth for life, even if subconsciously.

Years later, while I was studying in Bombay, one of the Afonso wives came over to invite my parents to a party. 'Remo is in Goa on holiday? Oh, how lovely, please bring him along!'

Mother, for a change, was very direct. '*Remo tem zanga dos Afonsos!*' (Remo detests the Afonsos!) she said, smiling.

The lady fell silent for a few seconds. She was not an Afonso, just married to one of them – she was António's wife. And then she said quietly, 'How the youth remember, no, Luiza? We think that when they're young we can say and do anything to them, but they have much more sensitivity and awareness than we give them credit for…'

Much later, when I was in the process of hitting it big, the Taj Mahal Hotel, Bombay, invited me to do a featured spot at their Rendezvous restaurant for a month. They put up big posters and cutouts of me all over the hotel, provided me with a suite in the magnificent old wing, and paid me a minor fortune for the duration. Primo Mauro and his family were still performing as the unnamed, unannounced house band at the restaurant. Contrary to what we were led to believe in Goa a couple of decades ago, I saw now that there was nothing exceptional about that; every restaurant worth its salt had a house band, but usually no one knew or remembered its name. And the bands ate in the staff canteens, while I had my choice of table in Rendezvous. Something tells me Mauro regretted the old 'Stardust' bullying when, night after night, I smiled at him politely but distantly as he sat in the dark wings, and I stepped on to the stage followed by the spotlight to loud applause, with the MC introducing me as the star performer.

I don't think I've ever been vengeful, and revenge is not commendable; but it does taste sweet, especially when it is not revenge at all. This was something that just played itself out without any doing or intention from my side.

Solfeggio

Around this time, Father decided to enrol me in piano and solfeggio classes. Down the road from our house there lived a piano teacher called Camila Peregrino da Costa, who gave private lessons in her beautiful home situated in one of the tree-lined streets of Campal. Campal is still very much the same, her house and street are today as they were then, and, except for a new concrete multi-storeyed eyesore in the form of a hotel, a walk through this area is a walk back in time.

Camila was a very gentle, kind and loving lady. Come to think of it, most people at that time seem to have been gentle, kind and loving. This couldn't be an illusion of my childhood memory now looking at those times and people through rose-tinted glasses; children are very prone to notice, and remember forever, unfriendly and mean adults. I guess it was the slow, natural pace of a contented and peaceful life, and the graceful norms of social behaviour and etiquette, which made most people so friendly and kind then.

Camila tried in vain to teach me how to read music. I found it drudgery. After she'd played a lesson from my piano book a couple of times, I knew it by heart, and would play it from memory, while pretending to read it from the book. She caught on to my trick soon enough, and tried harder – and with poorer results – to interest me in the wonders of reading solfeggio.

Whenever she left the room, I would start playing tunes of my favourite songs from the radio by ear. She would try to put on a stern voice when she returned to the room: 'Remo, now play your lessons, not those songs!' But her broad and bemused smile betrayed her.

After some weeks I told Father I'd had enough. However much I loved Camila, I just could not go through the exercise of turning beloved, natural music into a chore, which is how I viewed the deciphering of black and white dots imprisoned between five straight lines. The written, seen note was not music to me; the played, heard note was. Father mercifully understood and agreed to bring the lessons to a close.

But some time later Father made a last valiant effort at getting me to learn solfeggio. He enrolled me at the Academia de Música, that haloed music academy in Fontainhas, run by the equally haloed Maestro António Figueiredo, who also conducted the Goa Philharmonic Orchestra.

If I could not discover a love for solfeggio in the loving hands of Camila during our cosy one-on-one lessons in her beautiful living room, there was no way I was going to discover it here. This was a school where pupils came to study music with the same seriousness as the school where we studied Science and Mathematics. I wasn't going to allow my love for music to be reduced to such regimentation, even though I didn't formulate this thought in so many words at the time. I kept time and tune when I sang and played my songs on my banjo, and I did it with fun and joy. Here I was made to follow a cold, impersonal, dictatorial metronome which sat like an inquisitor on a throne. I was made to sing do-re-mi-fa to it with anything but fun and joy. The only instruments they taught were the violin and the piano, which I found boring, not the ones I found exciting, such as the banjo or the guitar. The teachers looked too serious and intimidating, as though they were teaching quantum physics and not music. Not the place for me.

Luckily, Father was wise enough to acquiesce yet again when I told him I wanted to leave the Academia pronto. I'm sure it wasn't an easy decision for him to take, but take it he did.

So I was 'free' again, to play my banjo and sing my favourite songs the way I loved best: by ear.

I must point out here that, at that time and until much later, 'playing by ear' was looked down upon in Goa by those who played and sang by reading music scores. *'Tó Décor Shett!'* (He's just a by-heart maestro!), they would pronounce dismissively and derisively of anyone who played by ear, especially if he played better than them. It was only when The Beatles finally proved what fantastic music (pop as well as orchestral) could be composed and performed without reading or writing a note of music, that these critics were silenced for good; and I realized then that it was *they* who were the musically deficient ones, who could not play a piece of music without reading from a score. They were like people without poetry in their souls, who could not write their own poetry, but could only read poems written by other poets. Whereas we, those who played by ear, were the true musicians. We played from the heart, from the soul and from the mind, not merely parroting and reproducing what someone else had written down.

Hats off to Father for resisting this kind of peer pressure, and for not forcing his son, for whom he had great musical ambitions, to learn how to read and write solfeggio which he dreaded so. I fear to think what a painful death my love for music might have died, had he forced me (with the best of intentions) to continue.

Eloy Gomes

I think the definitive end to father's efforts in finding me a music teacher came when he took me to Eloy Gomes. Eloy was the best guitarist that Goa knew, and he led the Tuna Academica, the best musical ensemble in Panjim, made up of students from the renowned and prestigious Escola Médica de Goa. And his perfect qualification, in my father's mind, to be the teacher to a kid who refused to learn solfeggio, might have been the fact that he played by ear and couldn't read solfeggio either. I was now outgrowing my little banjo, and Father wanted to buy me a guitar; and what better teacher than the best guitarist in Goa?

I still remember the visit most vividly. Eloy heard Father out, and then asked me to get my banjo out and play something. And then something else. And something else. He listened attentively. And then gave my father the best advice anyone could have given, in my opinion. He said, 'Don't find this boy a teacher. Just buy a guitar and put it in his hands. He will explore and learn it on his own.'

Perhaps that advice disappointed Father; but that's what he did, and that's what I did. That's how Eloy had learnt to play the guitar, and that's how I learnt too.

My first Holy Communion

People were highly religious in the Goa I grew up in. I did hear whispers, tinged with pity for their souls, about rare individuals who did not practise; these were invariably uneducated gone-case blasphemous alcoholics, or highly educated high-society intellectuals. Other than these few, most people were not just observers of popular morals, ethics and spiritual values, but serious and regular attendees of all kinds of religious ceremonies in churches, temples and mosques.

I grew up saying my morning prayers and my night prayers, and the whole family gathered before the home altar for the rosary every evening after their evening shower and before dinner. Well, the 'whole family' consisted of Mother, Mina, our maid Maria, and me. Father would conveniently be sitting at his desk in his study and working at his factory accounts at exactly this time, sipping a pre-dinner whisky and soda. Although he never missed Sunday Mass, Father wasn't too hot on the daily rosary. Once in a blue moon he cut in and recited his *decada* (a set of one Our Father followed by ten Hail Marys) from his study, though, and somehow this invariably sent us into a bout of giggles, which we tried hard to stifle and suppress, lest he hear us from the other room. After the rosary I went to Mother and Father with palms joined for their blessing and a kiss. From Father, besides a blessing and a kiss, I sometimes received a tiny sip of whisky – more of a touch of the liquid to my lips than a sip, actually.

Time came for my first Holy Communion. The prospect of my first full-length suit was now in sight, and so was a good Goan feast and party.

Excitement in the family. After this I would finally be one of the big boys who could go right up to the church altar during Mass and partake of the communion host, which was not allowed to me hitherto. I loved the taste of the host – I had already eaten plenty of ones which were unblessed, and which therefore did not miraculously contain the Body and Blood of Christ, courtesy Padre Roberto.

Padre Roberto was the friendly Siolim priest whom everyone in the village loved. As he rode his cycle around the village, his cassock tucked around his waist lest it got caught in his cycle wheels and chain, he waved, greeted, spoke to and smiled at so many people down the road, it was lucky there was no traffic whatsoever in the village those days. Today his popularity would have landed him in hospital.

Padre Roberto said Sunday Mass in the chapel in front of our Siolim house. The ever-laughing priest stammered and repeated every word five times, and often dropped in at Vovó's for her hot coffee and fresh cake and ginger biscuits after Mass. When he knew I was in Siolim visiting Vovó he would bring along a packet of surplus hosts wrapped in brown paper. That was a feast. I gorged on the whole packet the way one would gorge on grams or *chirmuleu*, the delicious roasted rice one found at feast fairs. I loved the taste of the hosts, and couldn't wait to discover the special taste the 'real' thing containing the Body and Blood of Christ would have, though I had been warned I had to let it melt in my mouth and swallow it without allowing it to come into any contact whatsoever with my teeth – I must not bite into Christ!

But the right to partake of Holy Communion had to be earned. So catechism lessons started in the evenings, and for these I went to a new place I'd never been to before: the Escola Dom Bosco just a couple of blocks away from home. Here, seated under a tree in the wide open spaces of the school premises, we learnt our Portuguese prayers and religious dogmas from Padre Saldanha, who was later to be my teacher of Portuguese in the same school.

I remember the first question in the book was 'Where is God?'. And the answer, which we had to learn by heart together with all the other answers to all the other questions, was 'God is everywhere'. I wondered why, if God was everywhere all the time, we had to go see Him in a particular chapel or church on Sundays.

But that was later. Now I was highly religious, fired by all the beautiful Bible stories, and as eager to learn my catechism as I was to learn the lyrics to my latest favourite songs.

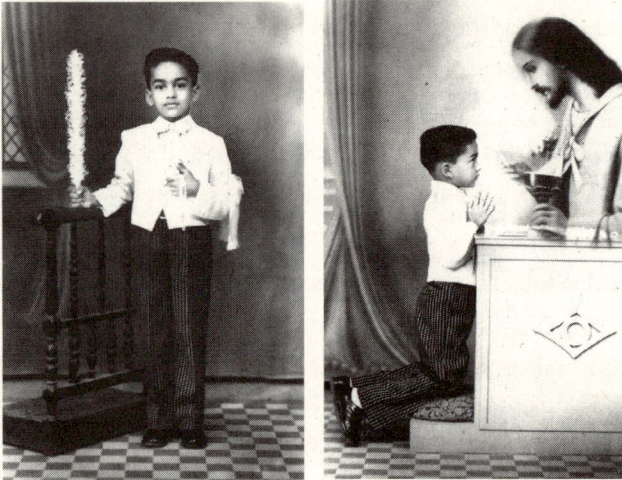

First Holy Communion, age six.

As the Big Day neared, catechism lessons and revisions were feverishly taken up at home by Mother, there were visits to the tailor for trials for the suit and shirt, and visits to Eugénio de Melo, the shop near the Jardim Municipal (municipal garden) in the centre of Panjim, which specialized in religious objects, accessories and artefacts, for the purchase of a beautiful rosary, a small silver Bible-shaped box to keep it in, and a prayer book with an ivory cover. There was also a long handmade wax candle which Mother and Mina proceeded to decorate with white paper which they finely cut, folded and stuck like lace. And there was the purchase of a white satin bow to go with my white silk shirt and white sharkskin jacket, a new pair of black shoes and white socks, and a white satin sash which was tied around the arm, not the waist. Little boys dress up in similar finery for their first Holy Communion in Goa even today.

One had to receive Holy Communion on an empty stomach; one couldn't possibly mix the Body and Blood of Christ with tea and toast. I had never stayed hungry till so late in the morning before, and the fact that from now on I would fast until 9 or 10 a.m. every Sunday was in itself a kind of rite of passage.

From the first Holy Communion Mass it was straight back home to the heartiest breakfast I'd ever eaten. That evening Father threw a big party at home, and everyone celebrated and sang and danced and drank and ate until well past midnight.

The next day, a Monday, it was back into the finery and accessories, which had been carefully preserved without crumpling, and off to a photographer's studio to immortalize the event for posterity. I was simply fascinated with the photo in which they superimposed the image of Christ giving me Communion. When a dozen or so copies of the photos were ready a few days later, Mother sat me down and made me write dedications on the back of each one in my best handwriting, and these were duly posted to the closest members of the family, and to close friends far away.

Mother learns to drive

Somewhere around this time, Mother learnt how to drive. Not many ladies drove in Panjim in those days, and although there was hardly any traffic worth the name, driving was not a joke – it was not just about changing gears smoothly, steering accurately and avoiding accidents; it was first and foremost about learning and following international driving rules. Those were the days when, in the near-empty streets of Panjim, one was fined for parking more than a certain number of inches away from the curb, or less than a certain number of feet away from a turn; for not dimming your headlights for another car in the night; for blowing your horn in a no-honking zone, such as near a hospital or educational institution. Things which seem natural in any civilized country in the world, but inconceivable in the Goa and India of today, where people are only arrested and fined for 'rash and negligent driving' *after* they have killed or maimed someone for life, never for the many dangerous or hazardous things they might do like cutting lanes, double and triple parking, driving down the wrong side of the road, or down the wrong direction in one-way streets.

But those were the days of law and order, and traffic law and order is just what Mother learnt day in and day out for weeks under the keen eye and tutelage of her driving instructor Senhor Cruz. There were special cars built for the purpose of instruction in Goa, mostly Volkswagen Beetles, with driver's controls on either side. The learner sat in the driver's seat, but the instructor who sat in the front passenger's seat had his own steering wheel and pedals, and could thus take full control of the car at any given moment of emergency.

No lady could be expected to go for these driving lessons alone with the invariably male instructor, of course. So Mina and I were appointed Mother's official chaperones, and we enjoyed countless *passeios* or rides in the process. We giggled in the back seat while Mother struggled to learn how to release the clutch smoothly but failed miserably each time due to her nervousness, making the car jerk and bounce up and down again and again, like in today's rappers' videos. We would describe Mother's travails and misadventures of the day in minute detail to Father in the evenings, to everyone's great amusement and laughter, most of all Mother's.

Even after Mother acquired her driving license, she never really enjoyed driving. But it was a great pleasure being driven to school and to other places by her, her knee-jerk take-offs included, in our Vauxhall which at the time seemed enormous to me.

The telephone

'*O telefone já veio! O telefone já veio!*' The telephone has arrived! Mina and I ran to Father's factory, where a brand-new massive black telephone now shone on his desk. There were just a handful of these in Panjim. It had a tiny handle which one whirred around after lifting the receiver. An operator came on line, and after the mandatory exchange of well-mannered and polite greetings, one gave her the name – yes, the name, not the number, because telephones in Goa didn't have numbers then – of the person or establishment you wished to be connected to. She connected you, because she knew all the subscribers by name, and that was that. The first few days I think I used the telephone the most, mainly calling up the house of my uncle Renato to talk to my cousins Jorge and Marilu, who had a telephone too, as their father was a surgeon.

Praying for a sister

It was at this time that Father and Mother asked me to include a new petition in my night prayers: *'Pai Jesus, dei-me uma irmāzinha, tá bem?'* (Father Jesus, give me a little sister, ok?) Once this idea was put into my head, I started to eagerly look forward to having a baby sister, who I was told would be like a little doll for me to play with and look after.

Perhaps Mother was expecting already, and this was their way of preparing me for the arrival of my new sibling; or maybe they now wished for a girl after having me, a boy. Or maybe they were having trouble conceiving (after all I was seven, and the first baby they'd lost had been born eight years before me – that's a long time between babies by any standards), and truly needed some divine intervention.

Mother's belly started growing in size until it was enormous, and on 20 February 1961, she was taken into hospital. Father returned home in the night, while Mina stayed and kept her company. As we went to sleep, Father told me I was going to have a little brother or sister, most probably the very next day.

After the initial excitement, I am embarrassed to say that my first sentiment was that of jealousy. I asked Father, 'But will you still love me as much after the new baby arrives?' I guess it's never easy for anyone to share the spotlight and centre stage with someone else after having been the only star of the household for all of seven long years.

Father came to my bed in the darkness and hugged me tight, assuaging all my insecurities. 'We will *always* love you as much! We will love you both just as much, both the same!' he said. I went to sleep with a smile on my lips, looking forward to this baby sister or brother that was coming.

The next day I was taken to the hospital, and there in Mother's room in the maternity ward, lying next to her in a little white cot, was the loveliest, fairest little baby I'd ever seen. I was the proudest brother on earth right from that moment, showing off my little sister to all who came to visit.

Mother, as usual, was keen to choose a very short name for her new baby. 'We parents rack our brains to find a beautiful name for our child, and then people shorten it to something silly. I wasn't going to allow that, so I named you Remo; you can't quite shorten that, can you?' she said. (I must point out here that 'Remo' is pronounced and called out as a single-syllable word in Portuguese, as the 'o' at the end is near silent.)

With the same logic, she chose Ruth as the name for her daughter. A lovely choice; both children with names starting with 'R', and both one-syllable long. But both Mother and Father also liked the name of a popular English actress of the day, Belinda Lee. Although it was three syllables long, and bound to be shortened to Bela or Billy or whatever, they decided to give my sister both the names, and to leave the decision of which would be the main name for later. So she was christened Luiza Maria Ruth Belinda Fernandes.

Everyone loved the name 'Belinda', a total novelty in Goa then, so Belinda she was called thereafter. At her christening party a few weeks later, her godfather Vasco Alvares, in his toast, could not help making a Portuguese play of words on the English name and saying: '*Ela chama-se Belinda, e é de facto bela e linda!*' (She is named Belinda, and she is in truth '*bela*' [Portuguese for 'beautiful'] and '*linda*' [another Portuguese word for 'beautiful'].)

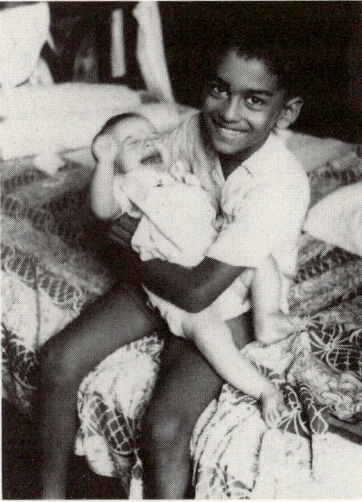

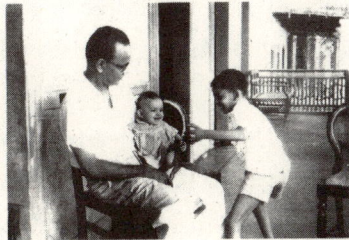

I must have been the worst baby-carrier in the world. My little sister bawled every time I proudly carried her. But as you can see from the two photos below, I could also make her smile and laugh – as long as I was not carrying her, I guess.

The rumbles of war

We settled into our new exciting life which was now centred around the novelty of a new baby in the house. A professional ayah (nanny) was temporarily engaged, and she moved in with us for a few months. The house was full of drying nappies, sweet-smelling Johnson's baby talcum powder and oils, baby toys, baby cries, baby laughter… I wanted to help in everything, from feeding my little sister to dressing her to carrying her. You can see from the photos how successful I was at this last endeavour.

In the middle of our newly enriched happiness, strange whispers started doing the rounds in Goa: *'Guerra! Guerra! Vai haver guerra com os Indianos!'* (War! War! There's going to be war with the Indians!)

I learnt about it by overhearing some visitors' whispered conversation in the house one evening. It was the camouflaged worry in their voices which caught my attention, and I asked Father about it after they had left. I was told that yes, there might be a *guerra* some time in the near future, but that I was not to talk about it outside the house under any circumstances.

I'm presuming today that, true to the dictatorial practices of the time, realities which were unpleasant to the regime were ordered to be ignored by the populace. While everyone privately knew that the Indian Army was going to advance into Goa soon, to liberate it from the Portuguese colonial rule which by now had lasted 451 long years, all Goans had to go around pretending that this was not so, and that everything was just the same as usual.

It was much later that I learnt about Goan and Indian freedom fighters (or *satiagras*, whom the Portuguese considered equivalent to terrorists) who had courageously held meetings in public squares in Margão and been mercilessly beaten up and imprisoned by the Portuguese military.

The rest of India had been liberated from the British way back in 1947. Even though this is not entirely so, I like to think that in the partition saga which followed her liberation, India had totally overlooked the fact that there were still three tiny colonizing fleas sitting on her body. The Gulliver-like giant, newly freed from British yoke, woke up one day fourteen years later, in 1961. And she noticed that colonials who had come from Portugal with Vasco da Gama still occupied and ruled over three of her tiny territories: Goa, Daman and Diu. And that some who had come from France still bossed it over Pondicherry and Mahe, though I was totally unaware of these last two then. To this giant who had driven the mighty British Empire from her shores, albeit non-violently, the prospect of forcefully evicting (if need be) the comparatively weak, almost non-existent, totally outnumbered Portuguese Army must have seemed like taking back the proverbial candy from a bullying child. So India politely asked the fascist dictator Salazar in Portugal to willingly and quietly leave Goa by a certain deadline, failing which she said she'd be happy to come and kick his ugly white ass out for him. Or words to that effect.

In the midst of this scenario, I remember repeating the pro-Portuguese bravado I had heard from some elder or the other to a Portuguese military man who was passing by in front of our house on one of those tense days. *'Goa sempre foi, é, e sempre será Portuguesa!'* (Goa always was, is, and always shall be Portuguese!) I shouted proudly in my eight-year-old voice. If I expected an appreciative smile and a pat on the back from the military man, I was mistaken. He stopped in his tracks, turned towards me with a very serious and worried expression, put his index finger to his lips, and said a soft 'Ssshhhhhh!' Then he turned and went on his way. I guess he knew that if a child repeated these slogans with an inadvertently wrong word in between, it could be construed as anti-Portuguese.

And even the utterances of a child could put his parents and family and perhaps neighbours in trouble with PIDE, the special secret Portuguese police force which was the main tool of repression used by Salazar. They had full authority to investigate, detain and arrest anyone who was thought to be plotting against the dictator or the state. Thousands of people were arrested and tortured in PIDE's prisons throughout Portugal and its overseas territories, which led to Goans hardly daring to utter the name. When they did, it was with the same dread with which Jews uttered the word 'Gestapo' in pre-War Germany.

Thanks to cowboy comic books and movies which I had lately begun to enjoy, imaginary gunfights and fistfights (in which I was obviously always the hero) had lately become part of my everyday fantasies. I was a cowboy in my mind, always fighting imaginary bandits and 'Indians'. But the cold probability of a real war with real Indians from India didn't seem as pleasant, and the dread which everyone around me seemed to be feeling rubbed off on me big time.

And then one day Father uncharacteristically returned from the *Fábrica* mid-morning and very seriously announced: 'Quick, let's pack some bags with clothes, food and valuables, lock up the house, and go spend a few days at Mamā's in Parrá. There is talk that the Indian Army is going to advance tomorrow.'

'Tomorrow?!' cried Mother.

'Yes,' he said. 'And the cities, especially Panjim being the capital, might be bombed. We should be safer in the village.'

So we crowded the car with ourselves, Mina, Maria, not forgetting Fifi the dog, and off we went. Would we come back to this house soon? Would this house still exist in a few days? Would Panjim? Would we?

4

Goa, India

The war that never was

A night at either of my grandmothers' houses was always magical, not the least due to the absence of electricity in Goan villages. One or two powerful petromaxes were lit in the main hall and dining room, and kerosene lamps all around the house, but usually not in the front veranda. When we sat there in the darkness at a certain time of year, *pirilampos* or fireflies would light up the night. Father would trap some and show them to me (without harming them in the least), in a white handkerchief rolled like a balloon until it looked like a flickering greenish electric light bulb. Of course, he would free them in the garden after a few illuminated minutes.

Tonight the oil lamps, and even the powerful ever-hissing petromaxes inside the house were not bright enough to dispel the gloom and anxiety everyone was feeling in the lampless veranda. *'Guerra!'* screamed the darkness. *'Guerra!'* screamed the sinister silhouettes of the coconut trees against the cold, starry December sky. *'Guerra!'* screamed the bats flying blindly around the fruit trees. But the soft worried whispers of the adults around me screamed the loudest of all.

The next morning we woke up to the sound of distant explosions. Somehow they were more bearable, but still ominous, in the bright daylight of the village than they would have been the night before. The explosions were few and far between. There was no means of knowing what exactly they signified; I think the one and only local Portuguese radio station, Emissora de Goa, had been silenced by the Indian Army. Telephones only existed in the cities, and might have been silenced too. Here in Parrá one banked on someone passing by on his way back from Mapusa for news. But on this day there was no one outdoors. We could only imagine the fierce, bloody fighting that was going on far away between the Portuguese and Indian armies. Who was winning? Who was losing?

I think it was in the late afternoon that the explosions stopped.

We learnt later that the bombs were not signs of fighting at all. That the Portuguese, totally outnumbered, had fled at the very first sight of the immense and well-equipped Indian Army. The explosions we heard were the Portuguese blowing up bridges behind them as they retreated, to try and prevent the Indian Army from catching up.

Legend goes that Salazar, who was rumoured never to have set foot outside Portugal, and therefore never to have had personal contact with (or love for) any of its numerous colonies, had ordered the then Portuguese Governor General of Goa, Manuel António Vassalo e Silva, to follow a 'scorched earth policy' and raze Goa to the ground, and to fight to the death rather than surrender. 'What a mean, treacherous man!' said indignant Goans who had hitherto been loyal to the Portuguese. 'Like a spoilt brat who can't play with a toy, and would rather smash it than return it to the owner!'

Vassalo e Silva, who had developed a great love and fondness for Goa and Goans during his years of governance here, for once disobeyed his dictatorial master and saved Goa from fire and damnation. And so, upon his repatriation to Portugal, Salazar promptly court-martialled and jailed him.

When the Salazar regime finally fell twelve long years later, and diplomatic relations between Portugal and India were resumed, one of the first things the freshly-released Vassalo e Silva did was to return to his beloved Goa as a state guest of the Government of India. Besides a warm welcoming committee, made up of people who knew what he had stood up against for the sake of Goa, a few politically misguided elements received the old man of eighty with black banners and protests at the airport. If they only knew that he had saved Goa from total destruction, and had paid for it with twelve years in jail... But ignorance is always at the root of all hatred and intolerance.

Driving back to Panjim from Parrá a few days after the 'war' was a lesson in relief. If we had feared we would see the city war-ravaged, or even transformed a bit because it was now under Indian rule, we had feared in vain: there was no change whatsoever. I, who had secretly hoped that our school had been bombed, was most disappointed to find out it hadn't.

However, there was something to be awed by and to marvel at after all: the huge tanks, guns and war vehicles which the Indian Army paraded regularly around the capital, making our houses tremble with their rumble. And my first sighting of a Sikh soldier. I had never seen men so big, long-bearded and turbaned. They fascinated me, even though they caused apprehension in the beginning. They were after all the 'enemy' whom we had dreaded for so long before D-Day.

After the first one smiled at me and my worries were laid to rest, I joined the rest of the kids in my neighbourhood in competing for who would shake hands with the biggest number of Indian soldiers in a day as they patrolled in front of our houses.

The change to English medium

Even though I was disappointed that my school had not been bombed, I loved Massano de Amorim, my Portuguese primary. Just as I had Ninho Infantil, the kindergarten. I found a copy of the old reader we had used in Massano in an antique bookshop in Coimbra a couple of years ago, grabbed it like a long-lost friend, and spent a few near-teary-eyed hours with it at home, looking at all the beautiful old familiar colourful illustrations and reading the artistic text. My fantasy about the school's bombing was just a schoolkid's universal desire for extended holidays, that's all.

But meanwhile Father had decided it best that I change to the English medium. He, having lived for a while in other Indian cities, knew first-hand that the Portuguese language would only serve me within tiny Goa and, should I choose to go there, in Portugal or Brazil. So he took me to the best all-round English medium school in Panjim, Don Bosco, in which he enrolled me. Since the Portuguese standard of education was so much higher, I and other students from Portuguese schools were automatically upgraded by a year. So, right from mid-term in Standard Three, I was promoted to Standard Five.

My excitement at joining a new school and learning a new language was short-lived. When I discovered the idiosyncrasies of the English language, I cried tears of frustration and anger. I was used to being one of the best students in my class, and I just couldn't understand why I was getting such low marks here, simply because English was so full of useless letters that one didn't even pronounce, like the 'gh' in words such as light, tight, fight, and so on. Portuguese is a Latinate language where you mostly pronounce what you write, and write what you pronounce. Compared to English and French, Portuguese spellings and pronunciations are very logical and practical.

When I complained about this to Father, he tried to encourage me in his usual way. He quoted the old Portuguese proverb: *'Inglês é a língua dos cavalos!'* (English is the language of horses!), and made me laugh imagining a whole country full of horses who spoke English.

I soon warmed up to it, though. But it must have been tough learning subjects such as Science, Maths, Geography, etc. in a strange and weirdly spelt new language in the beginning. Or maybe the school took it a bit easy in the first year after the liberation of Goa, to facilitate the children who had shifted from the Portuguese medium.

Moving house

One of those days, our neighbour from the next block, Senhor Eugénio de Melo of the religious articles shop, came over to have a very confidential discussion with Father. His house had an identical twin attached to it, divided by a common wall in between, in which lived the well-known Dr Pacheco. The good doctor was moving to Portugal that very night – all this was divulged in great secrecy and hushed whispers. Perhaps the fear of exposing one's plans was an old residue of the Portuguese dictatorship. Goans tend to be unduly secretive about the silliest things even today, like serious illnesses; they won't stop boring you with details of their indigestions or flus, though. Anyway, would we be interested in moving into the soon-to-be-empty house? They would love to have us as tenants.

The house was at least three times the size of our present one, and the rent probably three times as much. Father took a decision on the spot. Yes, we would start to move tomorrow itself.

What excitement for an eight-year-old! I had to make sure no toys and storybooks and View-Master discs were left behind outside my toy boxes, behind doors and elsewhere.

Ah, the novelty of being in a new house! It had four bedrooms, and I could have had one for myself. But I was deemed too young for that, so the distribution was made thus: Mother and baby Belinda in one bedroom, Father and I in another; a third one was kept as a guest bedroom, and the fourth one, closest to the entrance, was transformed into Father's office/study.

The greatest bonus of this move was that Senhor Eugénio and Dona Pia, his wife, had a son exactly my age called John. Not João in Portuguese, mind you, but John, a very rare English version of the name in those days. We immediately became inseparable friends, and spent every moment away from school and homework playing games, until our mothers shouted and forced us back into our own homes. Well – his mother shouted, mine never did.

And at last – my first guitar!

A year or so earlier, at my grandmother's in Parrá, I had heard a guitar being played in a style which was neither Portuguese nor Latin nor Goan for the first time in my life. My cousin Roy had come down from Bombay with a couple of pals, and they all spoke in English and sang English songs.

They were sitting around a table in the veranda in the afternoon, having a cold beer, and one of them picked up a guitar and shattered the village silence with a kind of voice I'd never heard before. He sang Fats Domino's 'Blueberry Hill'. But he sang Louis Armstrong's version, and was reproducing (pretty well) the great master's famous growl.

I couldn't understand that voice, so I whispered to Mother asking whether he was drunk. She said, 'No, that's the way this song is.' But it wasn't the singing that left a mark; it was the guitar playing, the first time I heard someone strumming out a hard blues rhythm. Of course I loved the sound of guitars already, in the soothing melodic songs we were used to listening to in Goa, but this was something else. A bit like what I felt when I first heard rock 'n' roll, though this tempo was half-time.

And I first heard rock 'n' roll when my cousin Garçia, Tia Angela's hallowed son, returned on holiday from London, where he was studying architecture. When we went to visit them, he and a female cousin, who had also returned from London on holiday, decided to demonstrate to us a new dance which was the rage there.

They played a record they'd brought with them called 'Rock Around the Clock' by Bill Hayley, and danced an amazing new dance which we today call the jive. We'd never seen a dance so full of energy, where the couple didn't stay holding each other from beginning to the end, like in foxtrots and waltzes, but where they flung each other right across the floor and up in the air and between their legs! The music, more than the dance, changed life as I knew it forever. The sheer excitement, the sheer thrill, the sheer energy of rock 'n' roll was something else altogether, though I would forever love, cherish and play the lovely Latin and Goan music I'd grown up with in Goa.

After these first two encounters with American music, and in the middle of the slow introduction of the English language into Goa (and with it of course the insertion of English and American music into our radio programmes), my father surprised me with my first guitar.

It was a beautiful second-hand acoustic, ebony coloured, with a cutaway on the bottom, which made it very stylish. And, following Eloy Gomes's advice, Father 'just bought it and put it in my hands', without a tutor.

Now I was an eight- or nine-year-old boy with a full-sized instrument, proudly experiencing the first stinging and bleeding cuts on my fingertips from the guitar's steel strings, happily stuck indoors with it during many joyful hours of discovery.

The prizes too good

The admirable thing about my new school, Don Bosco, was the importance it accorded extra-curricular activities – particularly sports. Today the richest school in Panjim has covered its open ground with school buildings and classrooms, milking every rupee possible out of every square metre of its property. But Don Bosco High School, despite being far from elitist, and despite being situated in one of the most commercially prime properties in the city, between the city market and a prestigious cine multiplex, keeps enough land open for not one but several football and basketball grounds even today. However, I wasn't much into sports, not seriously.

Don Bosco wasn't deeply involved in music, that is, it offered no music classes, but every year the school held an eagerly-awaited singing competition. As we paraded into the auditorium (which on other days was the boarders' refectory), we saw the prizes spread out tantalizingly on a table in front of the stage. They comprised mainly books of adventure which appealed to boys, life stories of saints which appealed to boys who already suffered from early priestly symptoms, and a few religious artefacts such as statuettes, rosaries and shining medals to be pinned on shirt fronts, the latter appealing to us all.

In 1964 when I was called to the table to have the first pick of the loot, as I'd won my customary first prize, I noticed a huge fat book which was prominently displayed. It was titled *SHAKESPEARE: The Complete Works*. Of course I had vaguely heard of Shakespeare as being

Shakespeare's Complete Works, which I won as the school singing competition first prize; I still have the well-worn-out copy of the book more than fifty years later, as I do the dictionary.

the world's greatest poet, and I knew this book was big-time stuff, though I'd never had the occasion or reason to read even a line of his until then; but the book itself was physically the thickest, heaviest, most impressive-looking book I'd ever seen at the time, and so I coveted it, and chose it as my prize.

The school principal, Father Dennis Duarte, himself a marvellous and beloved orator and teacher of the English language, was caught by surprise. Tactfully turning his back to the audience, he tried subtly but firmly to dissuade me from my choice in soft stage whispers.

'Do you think you will be able to read and understand this book, Remo?'

'I don't know, Father.'

'Look at all the other books on the table; look at that lovely hardbound copy of *Tom Sawyer*, and that one of *Robin Hood*, and *Huckleberry Finn* and *The Count of Monte Cristo* – why don't you take one of those instead?'

'I want this one, Father,' I said with a sheepish smile.

'Shakespeare?'

'Yes, Father.'

'But you won't understand it, Remo.'

'I'll try to, Father.'

'Are you sure?'

'Yes, Father.'

'Well, then, here you go. Do bring it back to school to my office tomorrow so I can write the prize quotation on it.'

'Yes, Father. Thank you, Father.'

The next day, without further attempt at dissuasion in his office, the principal wrote some beautiful lines on the first blank page, finally letting go of this precious school possession.

The next year they had a Pocket Oxford Dictionary on that table – though I couldn't imagine someone with pockets so large. Its thickness and red cover (a faded dark brown today) appealed to me, and I picked it as my first prize. I used it right until the time when computers and online dictionaries came along. I still have both the books.

Henceforth I don't think they ever risked keeping such expensive books on the prize table just to impress the parents present, thinking that no schoolboy would choose them. They must have awarded storybooks only, which I promptly lent and lost.

Cowboys & Indians

In spite of the craze for music, my obsession with being a cowboy did not abate. But how could an Indian be a cowboy, you may well ask. Especially if he was from India? However, the reach of Americana was such that, even in remote Goa, we all grew up on cowboy heroes such as Kit Carson, Buffalo Bill, Billy the Kid, Buck Jones, the Lone Ranger and many others, who peopled our fantasies day and night. And of course characters such as Walt Disney's Mickey Mouse, Donald Duck, Uncle Scrooge, Goofy and more. Not that we knew that all these characters came from America; we read the illustrated books in Portuguese. We didn't know that they had been translated and published in Brazil either. American characters using Brazilian/Portuguese expressions such as *'Puxa!'*, *'Maldição!'*, *'Oba!'*, etc. seemed the most natural thing in the world. We devoured them, exchanged them, lent them and borrowed them and lost them and fought over them.

When my parents went to Bombay for a short trip, I kept begging them to bring me a real horse. They must have known what a ridiculous and impossible request it was, but in my mind, all I could think of was riding it to school. And tying it to the school cycle stand. And how happy he'd be to see me when school was over and we rode home in glory.

By this time I must've grown into a ten-year-old, and naturally gravitated towards new friends from the block across ours. They were mostly of Portu–Goan descent. I remember an old Goan lady, their neighbour, quietly and secretly coming and warning Mother not to allow me to mix or play with them, as they were too 'wild' for us pure Goans – they learnt how to party, smoke, drink and romance much earlier than 'us'. But they were just the kind of exciting friends I could never give up, and so we formed friendships and connections which were meant to be for life, even if we drifted down different paths later.

In the evenings we got into the habit of playing a game we called 'Pólen' – don't ask me where that name came from, or what it had to do with cowboys or even the Portuguese language, but that's what all the youth in Panjim called it. It consisted of dividing ourselves into two gangs, both made up of cowboys, or one of Indians and one of cowboys. One group hid in ambush and the other one hunted it down. The whole neighbourhood (two whole blocks of houses) was our playground as we jumped over compound walls, climbed trees, and found exciting places to hide in, from where to 'shoot' at the enemy. We shot each other with a loud cry of 'Pólen!' while pointing our hands shaped as imaginary revolvers. The rule was that the other was dead only if he had been clearly sighted from the head till the waist when the cry was uttered. As you can imagine, this resulted in constant cheating and vociferous arguments and quarrels: 'No, he couldn't see my waist, I was crouching behind the compound wall!' and 'Oh no he wasn't! He was running across the open compound in full sight!' and so on and so forth. It was all part of the game.

I was so much into this imaginary world that I got myself a cowboy outfit. They weren't available ready-made, so I put one together. A shirt made by a tailor, especially fashioned after cowboys, with different-coloured chest and cuffs, tassels and all; jeans; a handkerchief tied around the neck; for want of a leather waistcoat, I had a woollen one which had been bought for the Goan 'cold' of the Christmas season; a sheriff's star cut out of cardboard and covered with silver paper; and, the highlight of it all, heavy awkward rubber gumboots meant for the monsoon, instead of slick leather riding boots. There was also a black straw cowboy hat (with 'Sheriff' emblazoned on it), a wonderful revolver which actually shot out plastic bullets which happened to be silver-coloured (like the Lone Ranger's, who made his out of pure silver from his secret private silver mine), and a gun belt with cartridge loops and gun holster. My old friends tease me till this day for dressing the part to a T then, since they never did; they were cowboys in their minds only, during the Pólen games. But I've always been that way about my fantasies; either live them out to the fullest possible, and dress the part, or what is the use of having them?

When my wonderful plastic gun belt and holster finally gave way due to too much use, Father got me another one made at the best cobbler's in Panjim (under the Club Vasco da Gama) – this one of real leather. It had two holsters for two guns, one on each side! These guns were made of metal, and were authentic replicas of the Colt .45. Ah, I spent hours in cowboy heaven, playing with them, posing with them, and admiring them...

How could I help wanting to be one of them myself?

Although we must have overdone it quite a bit quite often, jumping in and out of people's compounds and gardens screaming 'Pólen!' at the top of our young lungs, I don't remember the neighbours ever telling us to shut up, to get out, to stop our rowdy game, or whatever. I guess people were infused with an attitude of 'live and let live, children will be children, you're only young once and we were young once too'.

'Billy the Kid & His Rangers'

No wonder that both my passion and my fantasy, my music and my cowboy persona, soon fused together. By that time I had become pretty good on the guitar, and could sing quite a few songs and accompany myself on it, and play some lead too.

Around this time Father decided that I ought to form a musical group made up of kids. Or, rather, that he ought to form this group for me. I didn't know it at that time, but he was living his musical dream through me – all those things he hadn't been allowed to do by my over-strict grandfather, he encouraged in me tenfold.

Much later I realized that Grandfather's forbidding strictness could have turned Father into a bitter man who forbade the same things in his son. It is to Father's credit that he reacted in a positive way instead.

Father shortlisted half a dozen kids from Panjim who played various instruments: guitars, accordion, mouth organ, piano, and a bass box. After obtaining approval from their parents, he drove to their houses and picked them up for rehearsals, which took place at our house in the evenings – and then dropped them back home, of course after a high tea prepared by Mother and Mina.

I wanted this group of mine to be a group of cowboys and cowgirls, so we decided we would dress accordingly on stage. My favourite song at the time was 'Pancho Lopez'. It was about a child cowboy who 'could hit the eye of a mosquito without aiming when he was two, had killed two men when he was three, married when he was four, and valiantly died in a gun battle when he was five'. It became our signature opening song.

Billy the Kid & His Rangers at our first performance in Club Vasco da Gama, Panjim. LEFT TO RIGHT, BACK ROW (HIDDEN): Caetano Abreu (guitar); Manuel 'Manecas' Alvares (bass box). LEFT TO RIGHT (NOT HIDDEN): Tomás Menezes (guitar); Manuel Abreu (mouth organ); Remo Fernandes dressed in black as Billy the Kid (guitar and vocals); Ruth Valadares (vocals).

The name of the group? I wanted to be Billy the Kid, my favourite cowboy of the moment, all dressed in black, so the group was called 'Billy the Kid & His Rangers'. After a while the name proved too long, so it was shortened to 'Billy Rangers' – which didn't make much sense, but it was catchy, and it stuck.

The average age of the group members must have been eleven or twelve. We played at a few *reçitas*, concerts organized for members at the two social clubs in Panjim. I can remember the excitement of those evenings even today. Both clubs possessed one microphone each, which was used by whoever was singing or playing the lead part. Everybody else was heard unplugged. And that worked perfectly for the packed-hall audiences who stayed silent and attentive throughout. Music volume requirements, for listening and even for dancing merrily all night long, were very different then – no amplification required. Today we don't seem to be able to move a limb unless our ears are bombarded and brains numbed. Perhaps our music and musical tastes have become like modern colas, which can't be enjoyed unless our taste buds are desensitized with a mountain of ice cubes.

The Billy Rangers carried on steadily for quite a while, rehearsing and performing whenever we weren't too busy with exams or studies or playing football or Pólen.

In football I had started to hero-worship a player called Basílio who played for Sta. Inês, a team from a neighbouring ward by the same name. He was sturdy, had unkempt curly hair and a beard, and bulldog eyes and eyelids. A handsome brute of a macho man, the kind you didn't want to meet in a dark Panjim alley with a street bulb missing, if you were on his wrong side. Decades later an actor called Bud Spencer would resemble him. But Basílio was the original, and he was a goalkeeper. And what a magnificent goalkeeper he was. A save by Basílio was applauded by his supporters with deafening whistles and shouts and claps, and by supporters of the opposing team with loud groans of grudging admiration. He flew and dove fearlessly to all corners between the goalposts, and in between players' feet though they wore tough leather boots with wooden spikes – all this on a hard ground of mud and pebbles. We never imagined that in Europe football was being played on smooth flat pitches covered in soft green grass. Matches in most of Goa were held on rough rice fields when it wasn't rice-growing season; and in Panjim, on the hallowed parade ground inside the police station, at the two ends of which stood immense wooden goalposts. I stood in line, paid a few paise for a ticket, and spent two fascinating hours watching arch-rivals Sta. Inês and Academica battle it out.

After watching Basílio, of course I wanted to be a goalkeeper in our football games on the streets in front of our houses. So I got myself a long-sleeved sweatshirt and padded kneecaps to protect my elbows and knees from the rough tarmac of the road as I tried to dive Basílio-style for the ball between the two large stones which were our goalposts.

The same old friends, who were also my Pólen mates on days the general consensus so decreed, tease me to this day because I dressed that way to play football. But hey, like I said earlier, what's the use of having a fantasy if you don't dress the part?

The Mando Festival

Around this time Father, together with Bab Moraes, started the Mando Festival, reviving the old Goan folk song which was all but extinct. Bab Moraes was a staunch Konkani scholar who also spoke excellent Portuguese. He gradually stopped speaking Portuguese altogether, and answered only in Konkani. His Konkani was so scholarly and of such high standard, though, that even elitist Goans who considered it a 'language of the servants' had to strain to understand him.

My father was no Konkani scholar, but he was a Konkani- and Goa-lover all right. And, very specially, a Mando- and Goan folk song-lover. And, most importantly, he was then the president of the Club Nacional of Panjim, which put him in an excellent position to launch and organize an all-Goa-scale Mando Festival.

The mando is a beautiful form of Goan folk song, originated and developed by the aristocratic and learned strata of the Goan Catholic community, mainly from south Goa, where Konkani was spoken proudly even in the grandest houses. It is slow and soulful like the fado, though in a 6/8 rhythm which established its Goan roots. In the best mandos, the melodies are unforgettable jewels, and the lyrics sheer poetry which evoke the imagery and feelings of true and eternal love, forbidden love, unreturned love, broken hearts and lives, speaking of a time when love, honour and respect all went hand in hand. Mandos were mostly written and composed by musically inclined gentlemen of leisure, to be sung for the first time at the upcoming wedding ceremony of a beloved daughter or son or niece or nephew. If a mando struck a strong chord with all those present, it would be sung again and again at various functions, until it became what is known as an immortal hit – being passed down from mouth to ear, and perhaps through the odd handwritten music sheet, at a time when electricity was almost unheard of, leave alone a tape recorder.

The solemn pathos of the mando was invariably followed by shorter and faster-paced couplets known as dulpods. These were thematically unrelated to each other, each one created by a different composer at different times, but strung together in random order by the guests at the wedding according to which one came to whose mind after which drink. Just like the mandos, the best and most unforgettable dulpods are still sung today, and their melodies and lyrics are treasures of creativity, a rich record of life as it was, especially in Goan villages. Whether describing a girl's graceful movements and bounce as she draws water from a well, or warning that the monsoon is nigh and the roof needs to be retiled, or telling of a young girl's excited cries to her mother as a handsome stranger parks his bicycle against the front gate and proceeds towards their front door, or how two neighbours are fighting over their poultry's antics, or how a woman keeps delivering baby after baby while her husband is away at sea, or whether they are veiled and witty satires on figures of religious or governmental authority who were otherwise impossible to criticize, they filled up the whole gathering with mirth and joy and a musical and rhythmic build-up until, running out of any more dulpods for the evening, everyone entered into a grand finale with the solemn and plaintive '*Ya, ya, maya ya*'. And if someone remembered yet another dulpod before the grand finale was over, well why not, there they'd go again.

Since the mando was mostly sung and danced at society weddings, the correct attire for its stage performances today is considered to be what guests wore at those events: a full suit with tailcoat for the men, and a *bazu torop* or *pano baju* for the ladies. Curiously the latter costume arguably comes from Macau, and resembles a Chinese dress rather than an Indian or European one, complete with white socks worn under open sandals, and with the lady carrying a fan and fanning herself to rhythm while dancing.

A very important part of the attire for men is a spotless white handkerchief, which he removes from his pocket with a flourish at the right moment when the mando turns to dulpods. He then unfolds and holds the handkerchief with the fingertips of both hands, forming a white triangle which he gracefully sways before the lady he's dancing with, like a well-mannered red-flagged matador wooing a beloved bull. Oops ... if an old-school mando aficionado read this irreverent and inelegant description he would probably throw a fit.

Family legend has it that a certain cousin of my father's (I shall not name him; though he has expired, his children, my cousins, are still around), during a well-attended society wedding at a club in Panjim, danced the mando with happy abandon waving his white handkerchief which, unbeknown to him, had a large hole in its centre, noticed by all except himself. It had undoubtedly been made by his overzealous *mainato* or dhobi. He was forever teased by his brothers and cousins, who exaggeratedly inspected his kerchief before he got up to dance a mando at every party thereafter.

This precious form of Goan song and dance was in its death throes in the mid-1960s, the way all things considered old-fashioned are if they're not rediscovered as 'heritage' just in time. It was in this scenario that Bab Moraes met my father, and they drew up their ambitious plans. Their festival would offer different categories: polyphonic, symphonic, and so on. And, so that it didn't only revive the old mandos, Father decided to institute a special award for Best Original Mando, thus ensuring new ones would continue being written and composed. And, giving in to vanity and a desire for immortality, he established and donated a prize which he called 'The Bernardo Award' in this category. The statuette was modelled after the Oscar. There was also a category for youngsters, or the under-18s, to ensure that the new generation would gain an interest and carry on with the tradition.

The festival awakened incredible excitement. Goa, which used to sing mandos casually but probably didn't have any established troupes of mando singers, saw the birth of several being formed for the occasion, in its villages and its cities. Every group was most cordial to each other as per the strictest etiquette of the day, but underneath the good manners, the competition was fierce; every troupe rehearsed, performed and danced to their very best capabilities, and vied for the best costumes. Spies were employed to find out which mando the rival troupes were singing by eavesdropping on their rehearsals, unseen, from a safe distance away from their mansions.

Father, never one to do things on a small scale, invited Maestro Victor Paranjoti, the leader and conductor of Bombay's famed Paranjoti Choir, to be the head of the jury.

Father also decided that the Billy Rangers, who were fine at singing the modern popular songs of the day, ought to get into the mando. So he gathered a number of teenage singers to add to our group and form a choir, which I led while playing the bass on an electric guitar. And thus our name changed from 'Billy Rangers' to 'Billy Rangers and Adepts' for the occasion. Our lead singers were the velvet-voiced Silveira sisters, Yvette and Ceuzita (Maria do Céu).

Father kept it a total secret from Mr Paranjoti that the Billy Rangers was his son's group, so that the maestro might not be influenced in any way whatsoever. And so it came to pass that, based solely upon his musical judgement, Mr Paranjoti awarded us the first prize in the teenage category.

The Billy Rangers and Adepts at the Mando Festival in 1967. On the extreme left is me, playing the bass and leading the group. Centre stage in front is little Belinda, our mascot.

Decades later, after I had attained fame and awards around India and abroad, Luís Abreu from St. Tomé, Panjim, accosted me in the street one day and spoke thus: 'You know, Remo, when you were young and won that prize at the Mando Festival, many Goans spoke behind your back and said you achieved what you did due to your father's influence. I confess I did too. Today you have achieved success and fame where your father has no reach whatsoever, and have proved us all wrong.'

I had no idea that people had thought that way, but I should have known better – Goans will always be Goans. I was touched beyond words by Luís's confession. Of all the malicious gossiping Goans he spoke of, he was the only one who had had the grace and courage to come out of his way and tell me what he had done. He didn't really have to. *Obrigado*, Luís.

My first girlfriend

It was at about this time that I started going steady, and had my first girlfriend. But let me explain what going steady meant then, at least to me. It consisted of sending a handwritten message to the girl you fancied, usually through her best friend, saying something like, *'Eu gosto de ti; tu gostas de mim?'* (I like you; do you like me?) If she sent back a written note or verbal message saying *'Sim'* or Yes, that was it. You were in seventh heaven, and the next step was asking her to write something in your autograph book, and you wrote something in hers.

Autograph books were a huge thing with us then. The secret meanings of messages a girl and boy wrote on each other's pages, hidden between the lines, could only be deciphered by the initiated. Most of them, however, were silly templates which appealed to neo-adolescents, such as:

Tulips in the field
Tulips in the park
But the best tulips I see
Are four lips in the dark.

Or perhaps:

Some love three
Some love two
But I love one
And that is you.

In the middle pages we created *Paredes de Amizade,* or Walls of Friendship. In these, we drew columns which everyone was expected to fill, where we asked for details such as Name, Birthday, Favourite Boy, Favourite Girl, Best Singer, Best Film, Best Actor, Best Actress, and whatever else the book's owner's curiosity might demand. The columns for Favourite Boy and Favourite Girl gave free reign to creativity in secrecy, especially to those who were dying

*The secret diagram through which I
wrote my first girlfriend's name.*

to shout out their latest flame's name from the rooftops but didn't have the guts to. I had devised a way to write my girlfriend's name so that all the letters, when written in capitals one on top of the other in a certain way, formed a mysterious geometric pattern.

If the column for Best Boy and Best Girl created great amusement and interest, the ones for Best Singer created an India–Pakistan kind of conflict. Everyone was divided into two camps: you either liked Elvis or you liked Cliff. You could not, at any cost, like both. At almost every birthday party there would be spirited (but good-natured) discussions and arguments for and against each unsuspecting superstar. If they were to give us a cent for every minute we argued their cases, we'd be millionaires.

I liked Cliff. But I must shamefully confess here that, in order to impress my girlfriend who was an Elvis fan, I turned coat one day. I was derided by my old fellow Cliff-supporters to such an extent at the next party that, the very next day, I switched right back. And well – after all, Cliff was Cliff. And he had The Shadows to back him.

How we tried to achieve Hank B. Marvin's electric lead guitar sound – on our acoustic guitars. If we wanted to achieve his echo, we replayed that note softer and softer until fade out. Until we saw The Shadows in the film *The Young Ones*, we didn't know about tremolo arms; we thought they detuned and retuned the string by the tuning peg, and that's what we did. Quick tremolo action was reproduced by twitching the finger strongly on the string, or by grabbing the guitar neck by its head and jerking it violently, hoping it wouldn't break. No mean feats, these. Certainly ought to go down in guitar playing manuals.

I am blessed I still have my autograph book. Most of my friends have lost theirs. It is full of memories of a time in life too precious to forget.

A few excerpts from my old autograph book. One of the Walls of Friendship; and a few entries from a friend my age, older friends who drew well, and a few favourite teachers.

Anyway – after the ritual of autograph signing, you then asked your girl to go to a movie with you. The darkness of a movie theatre, where you were surrounded by people, was all the privacy you could hope for during the next few years. But a movie date was easier said than done. I had to enlist the services of her first cousin, my best friend. I bought three tickets in the back row at Cine Teatro Nacional. He, being her cousin, walked in with her first, without raising eyebrows in the auditorium where everyone knew each other on a first-name basis in the Panjim of those days. I waited outside until I was sure the main feature had started, and therefore the hall lights were dimmed. I then snuck in, trying to telepathically discourage the usher who showed me to my place from sadistically shining his powerful torch right up to her face for him and all to see. The back rows were mercifully empty, except for the odd couple of like-minded lovebirds who nodded knowingly and encouragingly in the flickering reflected light of the moving images on the screen as they made way for me to pass.

I then found my seat next to hers and we shyly and nervously exchanged a few pleasantries. After the appropriate time had elapsed, I 'accidentally' brushed my fingertips against her wrist. She didn't slap my hand away, so after a few minutes I kept my fingers firmly on her wrist. And we eventually spent the rest of the film holding hands, which felt like they were on fire. Or maybe they were just sweaty. And that's all. There was no talk, no joking, no conversation, no exchanging of ideas (whatever ideas two neo-teens might have), nothing. I realized later that if I were to name the two predominant qualities of that first relationship, they would be awe and shyness. I guess the third and fourth would be awkwardness and silence. I couldn't truly say that she was ever really my friend. I can almost safely say I didn't really know her at all. Except that she fascinated me because, in my mind, she looked a bit like Saira Banu, pearly white skin and all.

Alas, it must have been my Catholic upbringing, all those Masses I attended from the front row, my Don Bosco school and its Salesian priests, and of course my mother's casual but well-studied comments, which made me believe that the girl I went steady with was someone to be treated almost like how I would treat Mother Mary herself, were she to descend from heaven. I thought sex and sexual thoughts were impure, not at all to be inflicted upon a hallowed girlfriend.

Besides, don't forget I started dating young; perhaps too young. I was twelve, and it was impossible to find a girl younger to me to go steady with.

How could I take out a baby of ten or eleven? So right from the start, I started going out and going steady with girls who were a year or two older to me – that is, girls who were old enough to go out with a boy. In retrospect, some of them were surely more experienced than me, and therefore might have expected bolder advances. However, I didn't hear them complaining. Perhaps they enjoyed being treated like Mother Mary.

A couple of films later, though, the purity of my thoughts was slowly diluting. I took courage into my hands, folded my arm in the darkness of the theatre and lifted it as though I needed a stretch, and casually brought it down on the back of her seat. Ah, now my arm was almost around her shoulders! I leaned my head towards her, and the sweet girly smell of her hair drove me breathless and giddy. I then slowly took my arm down from the back of her seat and actually rested it on her arm. And after another film reel or so, I gathered the courage to take my hand down and start feeling her breast.

I heard her cousin giggling from his seat next to hers. I stretched my head to see why. My inexperienced hand had miscalculated distances and was groping his shoulder instead. By now she was giggling too. And I wished I could have crawled under my seat and died.

Mando Festival to the rescue

Mercifully, the Mando Festival was educational in more ways than one.

After the success of the first show in Panjim, there were repeat shows in Margão and Vasco. In those days when little Goa was our whole universe, that almost felt like a world tour. Every troupe travelled to and from the shows in special buses assigned to each one of them.

The additional singers who were attached to my group included a girl who was very forward and fearless in matters of romance and male–female relations. She was very easy to talk to and joke with, and made this unusually shy guy feel right at ease. Besides, she was at least three to four years older than me, and therefore there was no expectation or demand that we go steady, and especially not, god forbid, that we get married. I was too young to want to be saddled with such commitments, which I thought were de rigueur if you got intimate with a girl. A lot of close whispering and 'accidental' rubbing of body parts went on with her in the darkness of the backstage while other troupes were performing, keeping my teenage hormones in a constant state of effervescence.

After the show, she hurriedly whispered to me that she would keep the seat next to hers reserved right at the back of the bus, and that I was to come straight there when I boarded. Which of course I did, fully conscious that everyone else might be watching where I was headed. But everyone was too busy singing 'bus songs' to notice.

And there, in the darkness at the rear of the bus, behind a horde of teenagers loudly yelling rowdy and bawdy songs of the time (like 'If I were a single man and if I were to marry'), I first felt the softness and firmness of a female thigh as she pressed against me. And felt her hand on my thigh. And, however bumpy and shaky the old bus might have rendered the experience, I felt female lips against mine. And the crowning glory – that forbidden but most coveted, most tempting fruit of all – I felt a female breast for the first time in my life, when she guided my inexperienced hand to it.

Who said the mando was an old-fashioned dying song-form for the old? This was rock 'n' roll!

5

From Billy Rangers to The Beat 4

Alexandre do Rosario

When John Lennon first met Paul McCartney, John was leading a teenage group called The Quarrymen. When he heard Paul, he knew that the latter would be a great asset to his group. But he also instinctively foresaw there would be a clash of egos, a tussle for the alpha position. Should he, shouldn't he ask Paul to join? John permitted his desire for the betterment of the group to overpower his personal concerns, and Paul was in. It is curious that, in the end, it was the huge clashes between these two giants within The Beatles which led to the group's dissolution.

No comparison, but I was faced with the task of taking a similar decision when I heard of this boy called Alexandre do Rosario in the early 1960s, and heard him play. His family had moved to Goa from Daman, as his father, who worked for the post office there, had been transferred to the post office in Panjim. Since Goa, Daman and Diu were Portuguese colonies, they had a common government while under the Portuguese, and the head of the government was in Goa, the biggest and most important of the three. It must have been quite a feat governing them from one place, especially with the communication facilities available at the time, as Daman was over 700 km away, and Diu 1,400 km, both in the state of Gujarat. This trend of governing them jointly under one head based in Goa continued after the Portuguese left all three in 1961, as the Indian government administered them jointly too, right until 1987 when Goa attained statehood and Daman and Diu were declared a separate Union Territory.

Perhaps the first time I heard Alexandre was when he sang at a selection held by Radio Ceylon for their musical programme called *Cadbury Amateur Hour*, which was very popular in Goa. The selection was held at a function at the Club Gaspar Dias on Miramar Beach. I think he sang a Portuguese song together with his sister Maria do Céu, who sang the harmonies. I was ten, and I sang 'Be-Bop-A-Lula', the 1956 hit by Gene Vincent which had just become known in Goa. At the time, records and films and most other things took not days, not months, but years to reach here. Films often arrived mutilated by the censors, sometimes so badly that it was impossible to make head or tail of the plot. And records were seldom released in their entirety; for example, only two or three of the biggest hits out of a Beatles' album would be released as singles in India. When I finally got hold of the entire albums decades later, I was able to discover the other jewels in them for the first time, as though they'd been concealed in a time capsule.

Anyway – I felt an unprecedented excitement for my 'Be-Bop-A-Lula' number. For the first time in my life, I'd worked out a routine for my item. I'd sing it in our usual position at the time, i.e. sitting on a chair with my new (second-hand) guitar, which looked bigger than me. But just before the last chorus, I'd do my great moment of showmanship: I'd start swaying to the music and slowly change from a sitting to a standing position! Whoever had heard of that!

Cadbury Amateur Hour *for Radio Ceylon in 1963, age ten.*

From sitting to standing in the middle of a song! And swaying for the rest of it too! How daring could I be! Wearing my new cream shoes with laces on the side (not the middle, how fashionable could that be!) which I'd bought during my recent first-ever trip to Bombay, a zip-up rocker's jacket, and with a hairstyle held up by shiny pomade, not even the fact that I still wore shorts on stage could dampen my bravado – though off stage I was still the shyest schoolboy on earth.

My performance was selected to be featured in the radio programme, and I'm sure Alexandre's was too.

Thanks to Mina's passion for music, we had been following Radio Ceylon's exciting Sunday programmes which featured the latest hits from the West which we were deprived of in India, glued to the transistor and moving it and its antenna to maximize reception. I can't describe how exciting it was to hear myself on that haloed favourite programme of ours, hosted by Ameen Sayani, whose voice was more loved and recognizable to us than even Jawaharlal Nehru's.

Not only were we deprived of the music and films and comic books we were used to during the Portuguese days in this India, which was a socialist state, but as a child of eight I used to sob out of frustration at the taste of Indian butter (more like glorified margarine) at the breakfast table, missing my usual Blue Peter, and at the taste of Indian chocolate which tasted like anything but chocolate. When I read the biography of Chairman Mao written by his doctor decades later, I shuddered to think how closely India had resembled that kind of communism, with all its deprivations and queues and rations and a strict ban on importation, minus mercifully the persecutions and purges.

Indian dealers descended upon Goa and offered prices which were slightly higher than the original for our foreign cars, and many Goans thought they'd done very smart business selling off theirs. Until they learnt that those foreign cars were worth ten times the Goa prices in the rest of India, where importation had been made impossible with red tape and prohibitive taxes, and where the newly-launched Indian car industry was a joke.

I remember a neighbour booking an Indian Fiat and receiving it after years of being on the infamous 'waiting list'. He had opted for sky blue, but got black; it was 'take it or leave it and wait a few more years'. While driving the brand-new black car from the dealer to his house, the steering wheel came off in his hands. And he wasn't even in the circus.

Imagine undergoing such experiences after having been pampered by salesmen of the best car manufacturers in the world, from Mercedes Benz to the populist Volkswagen. I don't wish to knock our new country, but it was not easy getting used to it and its restrictions, after having been part of the open international community during the 451 years under Portuguese rule. That's a long time, about fifteen to twenty generations, more than enough to make a people totally unaware of what life was like earlier. The rest of India was under the British for 'only' 150 years or so, and perhaps that is the reason why it remained more 'Indian', while Goa kind of developed a culture of its own. Other reasons could be that the Portuguese mixed, mingled and even intermarried more freely, while the British were racist as hell, affixing placards which said 'DOGS AND INDIANS NOT ALLOWED' on first-class compartments of the Indian Railways. To my knowledge, we were never subjected to such insults and segregation in Goa.

It was in this scenario that Alexandre started frequenting our neighbourhood and circle of friends.

The love gurus I almost had

But there was also another scenario happening simultaneously and tumultuously in my life, albeit one which was very personal. Not even my best friends were told about this. Call me old-world, but I've always considered anything that happened between a girl and me as something very private, more so for her sake. I could not, and still cannot, understand guys who brag about female 'conquests', especially in cheap locker-room lingo.

Anyway, I think one of the most beautiful things that can happen to a yearning adolescent boy is to be taken by the hand by a slightly older, more experienced girl or woman who, besides other things, has an affection for him; and to be led by her up that mysterious path of physical love with care. Especially when he's too young to approach a girl himself, and when girls his own age are much too young to go up that path themselves.

It's curious that in a reversal of roles, if a willing adolescent girl is taken under such tender guidance by an older boy or man, it is looked upon in a totally different light, and the man might end up lynched or in jail.

To me, this beautiful shepherding *almost* happened twice when I was around twelve or thirteen years of age, i.e. in the seventh or eighth standard of school.

Our next-door neighbours, John's parents, kept boarders. About eight or ten young women in all, most of them studying in college, and a few working, averaging about twenty-one years in age. They were all Mina's friends, and they all treated me like a well-loved younger brother.

Well, almost all. One of them was a young woman from somewhere in south India. We weren't exposed to many people from out of state at that time. This one was fair-skinned, wore glasses, and dressed in saris. She was very recently married, and her husband was back home, while she was in Goa to pursue some advanced course or the other. Father and Mother engaged her to give me Maths tuitions in the evenings, and the timing was fixed from 6 to 7 p.m., after I had supposedly finished my games. It also happened to be the time when my parents went to Miramar Beach to relax and meet their friends. The tuitions took place in my bedroom – I now had a room to myself.

The house was empty at that time of the evening, as Mina too was usually out, visiting her own friends. Maria, our maid, was usually ensconced in her bedroom at the back of the house. The tutor and I had to sit close to each other at my study desk in the darkening evening, with just the desk lamp on. I noticed after a while that, as she tried to instruct me in the ways of mathematics, her hand would gently rest on my bare thigh just below my shorts. And, as she tried to make mathematical points, her hand would tighten and loosen, sometimes moving gently up and down my thigh. And she would lean right down next to the books on the desk, allowing her pallu to slip off her shoulder, bending forward so that her already low-cut blouse exposed more than it ought to.

My eyes would involuntarily move to that beautiful cleavage. Although well aware of that, she didn't make the least effort to readjust her pallu or her leaning position, or to lift her hand off my thigh. But at that time I betrayed no reaction whatsoever. Why not? I guess there were many reasons. I didn't like her much, and that itself had many reasons: the timing of her tuitions took me away from the best part of our football or Pólen games, just when they were about to end; I didn't like the fact that she was teaching me Maths, the subject I liked the least; I didn't like her glasses, which had a light-coloured shell frame which made her look very strict. She was quite pretty without them, and had a very svelte body. But she wore a sari, which to me then represented an older woman of authority, which she was. I was too young to know that a young married woman might also be prone to trying to seduce a schoolboy, and therefore perceived her advances with great confusion. What if her actions were merely standard methods of Maths instruction, and I, misunderstanding her, put my hand on her thigh in return? She might scream blue murder and tell my parents!

When I grew older and my mind somehow travelled back to that tuition teacher one day, I realized that she too must have been confused by my inaction, and must have been petrified that I might tell my parents if she went any further. And I saw that I had missed my chance of turning my Maths tuitions into an adolescent boy's nirvana. And I kicked myself in the ass. Hard, real hard.

The other girl was incidentally also a boarder in the same house. I've described the corner where our verandas touched and were separated by a common wall which came right up to the veranda parapet, around which

John and I jumped into each other's houses. It was also the corner where Mina leaned and chatted with her friends from among the boarders, some of whom remain Mina's good friends until today.

Well, this girl and I got into the habit of leaning against the parapet and chatting with each other too. Innocently at first, as good friends, despite our age difference; but eventually we felt a genuine liking and great attraction for each other, and would make plans to meet and chat there when there would be nobody else around, like after dinner.

Amongst all the boarders she was the youngest, just about twenty. She had big expressive eyes, a short bob-cut of curly hair, and a lovely smile. Our chats started turning more and more intimate and private. And soon we started exchanging notes or letters, which we slipped stealthily into each other's hands.

We wrote about how we liked, and even loved, each other. And we did, though I was thirteen and she twenty. Not love each other as there being the remotest possibility of us ever being a couple of course, but love as a very genuine feeling for each other. A feeling of strong affection coupled with very strong physical desire. We wrote about how we were both tempted to lean a little further across that wall and kiss each other's lips. And in the last letter we promised that we soon would, the next time we met at that parapet.

But just before that could happen, Mother found the three or four letters from her which I had stashed as secret treasures in the bottom drawer of my study desk.

She came into my room looking extremely serious, holding up the letters in her hand. And she gave me a talking-to. About some mysterious *doença* or disease which happened with girls, which of course I didn't understand, but also about how I ought to be concentrating on my studies at this age, about how this shameless girl was leading an innocent schoolboy astray... It pained me no end to hear her being thus spoken about.

Mina was very angry with her as well, and she was given the task of telling the girl that if she didn't stop communicating with me straightaway, her landlady would be informed, and she would surely be thrown out in shame.

To say that I was heartbroken is an understatement. Two people breaking up is always a sad affair for at least one of them. But when the break-up is forced upon both by a third person or external circumstance, while they still love and desire each other madly, it is sheer torture. The letters were of course confiscated and destroyed, so I didn't even have the comfort of reading and rereading them as I had been doing hitherto. I think the girl soon left the boarding house at the earliest opportunity, without my knowledge, as all communication between us had been abruptly put an end to. Today, cell phones and computers and cybercafes render such censorship of youngsters' communications near impossible without the use of iron bars.

A year or two later, a drummer who had just returned from Africa joined our band. He was older to me – a college-going young man, while I was still in school. One day he mentioned the girl's name and told me, rather callously, 'Oh, I slept with someone you know the other night; she was a virgin, and I had a wonderful time.'

I felt terrible pangs of sadness and jealousy.

He added, 'I'm telling you this because she said, "There was a time when I wanted Remo inside me very badly," or else I wouldn't have told you anything about it at all.'

One can imagine what an effect the words 'inside me' had on me; I had never envisaged going that far with her. Although this last statement brought great comfort and a wistful smile, it only added a feeling of deep regret and loss to my sadness and jealousy.

Like I've said earlier, it was in the midst of this scenario that Alexandre came into our circle of friends. At the age of twelve or thirteen no one questioned how a new kid landed up in your circle, especially in a tiny city like Panjim where everyone ended up knowing each other anyway. Besides, he played the guitar and sang like a god, so he was more than welcome.

In addition to singing, Alexandre yodelled, something none of us had ever heard done before. It was fascinating, and all of us must have secretly tried it out in our respective bathrooms later, to disastrous results mercifully camouflaged by the sound of running water.

I could strongly sense that our personalities would clash. Although we had similar amounts of passion for music, we were different in other ways which at that age I could not quite decipher. I knew that he would be great for my group, though, and when I asked him to join the Billy Rangers, he readily agreed. And although we later formed a unique combination on stage, I realize that I cannot say that we ever became close friends or confidantes.

'Remo e Alexandre Labambaram!'

Alexandre and I might have performed together in the Billy Rangers at other shows earlier, but the first one which stands out in my memory is a concert at Instituto Menezes Bragança in Panjim. Trini Lopez's fiery modern version of 'La Bamba' had just started driving us crazy, and we decided to sing it.

We had never heard of the word 'improvisation'. We didn't know what improvisation was; no one in Goa did. We didn't know it was possible to change a song, which existed on record, as per our whims and fancies. We learnt songs verbatim, tried to sound as much as possible like the original within our limited means (e.g. acoustic guitars instead of electric, no bass or organ, etc.), and followed the song's structure of verse/chorus/verse to a T, including the solo in the middle which we'd reproduce note by note – the more faithfully you reproduced the piece the better you were supposed to be, like a good-quality photocopying machine. A formula the best Goan bands follow to this day.

I don't know what happened to us as we got into 'La Bamba' that evening, sharing a mic, our feet up on the same chair, balancing our guitars on our raised knees. Without planning to, we slowly drove ourselves into a frenzy, and simply could not stop singing the song. In the last chorus, one of us sang the 'Bamba, Bamba' part while the other improvised on top, and then we interchanged roles. And on and on we went. We dipped down in volume until it seemed like we were fading the song out, only to have one of us build it up again with the 'Aaaa, aaaa, aaaa, aaaa, aaaa…' section which rose and took the song to another bursting climax.

The packed hall was going wild. Not just the youth occupying the back half, but also the usually staid suited and booted adults who occupied the front half. While the youth were yelling and singing along, the adults were clapping to the beat with incredulous grins on their faces. What was happening here this evening?!

The next morning, the headline in *O Heraldo* screamed '*Remo e Alexandre Labambaram!*' It was an article by Senhor Carmo Azavedo, who usually wrote very serious philosophical, political and sociopolitical articles, and was older than even my father. He had created a verb out of the song title 'La Bamba', and made up a phrase which defied English translation. 'Remo and Alexandre Labambaed' doesn't quite sound the same.

Alexandre and I had done something bigger than ourselves, and it took us a long time to come down from that high. We now became known as a duo to be reckoned with. And henceforth we carried a similar excitement into almost every Beatles and Rolling Stones song we sang, especially 'Satisfaction'.

The Beat 4

After another year or so of carrying on with our acoustic guitars, the time came for me to want to form my first beat group. 'Beat group' was the name given to the new popular formation of the time, which soon became a classic: all-electric lead, rhythm and bass guitars, and drums. The Beatles and The Shadows had adopted this formula, and therefore the rest of the world was doing so too. Out with mandolins, accordions, pianos and violins. A new sound had dawned, and it was electric.

Ah, a beat group sounded like a great idea. But could I go around turning it into reality? Nobody I knew in Goa owned an electric guitar. I knew Father would buy me one, but no guitar-playing youth I knew in Goa would be willing to acquire one at my suggestion or request, to form Goa's first beat group. Certainly not Alexandre.

Father to the rescue. Once he saw how obsessed I was with this idea, he decided to order all three electric guitars for the whole group.

He did his research. I have no idea how one researched things before computers and Google, but he found an electric guitar manufacturing company in Kerala. Remember, nothing foreign was available in India any more. The name of that company, Manuel Industries, was later imprinted in my mind with dread.

He wrote to them asking for their catalogue. When it arrived a couple of weeks later, I was highly excited to see the photographs and descriptions of all kinds of guitars. I zeroed in on the best lead guitar; it had four pickups, not three as the top foreign guitars had. Wow! And it had a tremolo arm too, that new invention of a magic wand with which you could create an exciting bend or tremolo of the strings.

I also chose the best four-string bass guitar they had to offer, as well as the best rhythm guitar. And the best guitar amplifier–speaker combo, with connections for two guitars.

Father made the payment and placed the order.

Then started the period of eager waiting. I had this habit of continuously making sketches of my fantasies, thus bringing them to life on paper. If earlier I couldn't stop sketching cowboys on the back pages of my school notebooks, now I was sketching electric guitars and beat groups.

Until one day I returned from school to see four heavy wooden crates lying in our veranda. Could they be ... ? I rushed into the house, and Father said, 'Yes, your guitars and amplifier have arrived!'

Oh my god, the excitement ... Father got one of his factory employees to come and open the heavy crates by removing the huge nails which held them together. Inside, under a packing of hay, were three massive, heavy wooden rectangular guitar cases covered in rexine. And inside these, three shining, colourful, brand-new guitars! And in the fourth one, a white Formica-covered guitar amplifier!

If they didn't quite look like the equipment used by The Shadows in the film *The Young Ones*, they certainly didn't feel the same once I lifted them out of their boxes either. My excitement soon turned to the greatest disappointment I had known in my young life until then.

The distance between the strings and the arm of my guitar was way too much, making it hard to press them. The arms of all three guitars were rough, and the frets much too high. The audio level of each string was uneven. The cables provided were thin, flimsy and short. And the tremolo arms, those eagerly awaited magical things, were unusable; if you pressed them, they didn't quite come back to the original position, and the whole guitar was detuned.

If my lead guitar, the best and most expensive one in the catalogue, suffered from all these anomalies, the worst was the rhythm guitar. Firstly the colours: the rhythm guitar was a gaudy parrot green, and the cheap plastic plate covering the electronics was an ugly bright orange.

The bass guitar seemed to be the least bad of the lot.

The amplifier had connections for two guitars, but it couldn't even handle the load of one adequately.

And the connectors! The guitars and the amplifier had those screw-on connectors, which one found on the Ahuja microphones of the time. A crude, ugly, bulky, unreliable system.

The excited dreams of all those months turned into a nightmare. If I used to sob over Indian butter and chocolate, I was ready to howl over Indian electric guitars.

But well, what could we do? We marched valiantly on. I trained my fingers to handle these barbed wires which passed off as strings, and learnt how to pull the tremolo arm back to a near-original position every time I used it.

Now I needed the right guys in my beat group. I asked Alexandre to take over the bass. I was a much better lead guitarist, so that position was mine. There weren't any bass guitarists in Goa, as there simply were no bass guitars either.

But Alexandre was an excellent rhythm guitarist, with a great sense of chords and harmonies, so that made him very eligible to play the bass – a talent which would have been wasted playing mere rhythm.

As rhythm guitarist I chose Caetano Abreu who, again, was excellent with chords and harmonies. Besides, he was tall and lanky and wore glasses, which reminded me of Hank B. Marvin, the lead guitarist of The Shadows. So I rechristened him Hank Abreu, and the name stuck.

We already had a drummer in the Billy Rangers during the last few years. Tony Godinho lived not far away, and he had a real drum kit – or at least three quarters of it. He was much older, and we listened fascinated as he shared his great knowledge of sex and girls with us. Like for example his dictum that we adolescents ought not to masturbate, but to fuck. This was because, according to him, one masturbation expended as much energy as precisely nine fucks, which was a sheer waste. Which was all very well for him, for he was old enough to know willing girls who would visit him in the isolated room that he rented at the back of Cristo Rei. But where were we schoolboys supposed to find girls willing to help us conserve our energy?

One of the first Indian cigarettes to come into Goa, way back when I was eight years old, was called Cavanders. It was a green packet with a sailor's image as its logo. One morning I had woken up to the commotion of seeing four super-tall men comfortably walking down our road, dressed as sailors, reaching up to the lamp post cables and lower branches of trees, with legs as tall as giraffes'. How could they be that tall?! My parents told me they were walking on wooden stilts hidden underneath those enormously long trousers; I would have never guessed. They were advertising for Cavanders cigarettes. They were super tall. Tony was extra tall. So he had become known as Tony Cavanders in Panjim.

Anyway, the line-up was ready. Now all we needed was a name. My cousin Rex from Bombay had told me about the fabulous beat groups there, called The Combustibles, The Phantoms, The Reaction, The Beat 4… This last name fascinated me. It had the magic word of the moment, 'beat'. And it had the magic number of the moment, '4' – The Beatles and The Shadows were both made up of four guys. It wasn't very original of us to copy it, I know; but I was a schoolboy, Bombay was a distant land, and surely no one there would ever hear of a group of youngsters in little Goa bearing the same name. And no one in Goa would hear of our Bombay counterparts either, unless they had a cousin like Rex. So 'The Beat 4' we were.

Now I spent my daydreaming time in school sketching and designing our name in logo form, so that it fit on the round bass drum. I got it painted on thick cloth by a signboard painter, Tony fixed it against the skin of his bass drum, and we were in business.

The Beat 4 (original line-up). LEFT TO RIGHT: Caetano 'Hank' Abreu (rhythm guitar); Remo (lead guitar and lead vocals); Tony Godinho (drums); Alexandre Rosario (bass guitar and lead vocals). Photo clicked in Estúdio Lisboa, Panjim, opposite the Church of Immaculate Conception, circa 1966.

Rehearsals started in earnest, as always at my house. I asked Father to get us an amplifier for the bass guitar, and we got a carpenter to make a cabinet for its twelve-inch speaker, which was considered jumbo size – we'd never heard of bigger speakers in Goa. Without following any rules of acoustics whatsoever, all we knew was that the cabinet for bass had to be big, and so it was.

Ah, now we were playing 'our' music, the kind we liked as new teenagers. Our repertoire comprised mostly The Beatles and The Shadows, and eventually Herman's Hermits, odd one-hit-wonders like Los Bravos' 'Black Is Black', Tommy James and The Shondells' 'Mony Mony', The Archies' 'Sugar Sugar', culminating in a vast selection from The Rolling Stones.

Father walked into the room after about an hour of our first rehearsal, and told us we ought to include his favourite 'La Paloma' in our repertoire. I made a face and said, 'No, we don't want to play those kinds of songs any more.' He tried persuading me for a while, saying we ought to be able to play for every age group in the audience, but I won the debate.

After a while, as we were rehearsing a Beatles song, he walked in again and said a chord was wrong. The Beatles made some chord progressions which were strange and weird for those days, but the youth of the world took to them like fish to water. If a song was on A, they would go to a G or an F before an E. While I knew the chords were right, Father and his generation took a while to accept them. So when he insisted the chords were wrong, I crossed my arms and defiantly said, 'Well, you tell us what they are then.'

He looked at me for a while, and then silently left the room.

I felt extremely remorseful about my behaviour afterwards, but I guess that's the moment when I broke away on my own musically. No more playing Father's repertoire, no more having him as my band's de facto leader from behind the scenes. I was all of thirteen now, and this was *my* group, and we were going to play what *we* wanted to play. There was no confrontation or argument; our love, respect and affection for each other was not compromised at all, but I think Father understood it at that moment, and so did I – I had come of age.

The first public performance

It was on the stage at Miramar Beach one summer Sunday. Miramar Beach was frequented by people from Panjim in the hot months of April and May, which were also school holidays, and Sundays were the highlights, with local singers and musicians performing on a stage specially built for the purpose on one end of the beach, against a backdrop of sweet-smelling pines (of which we cut off branches for our Christmas trees every December).

The evening started with a technical disaster of sorts. One of our flimsy new guitar cables snapped, and we learnt the hard way that we ought to carry extra cables with us always. I think it was the cable of the bass guitar.

That called for a quick decision-making tête-à-tête between Alexandre and me right there on stage, even while we were setting up in front of the full audience; we could not play without the lead guitar, and we could not play without the bass guitar; perhaps we could do without the rhythm guitar? So we quietly exchanged Caetano's and Alexandre's cables, without the former's knowledge. And Caetano happily strummed and sang through the show, without realizing that his guitar was giving out no sound. Solid-body electric guitars gave out no sound on their own, and he presumed the sound must have been coming out of some speaker somewhere. Our panache and enthusiasm, and my doing some 'extra-curricular activity' playing rhythm in between my lead parts, carried the show through, and no one was wiser about the 'disaster'.

My first composition

I don't know what made me feel like composing my first song when I was fourteen. Could it be the fact that my new heroes, The Beatles, weren't just pretty boys with pretty voices like Elvis and Cliff who sang songs composed by others, but wrote their own lyrics and music? They surely must have been an inspiration. But that alone cannot make one start composing. Alexandre, for example, wrote just one song as far as I know. I must have had that bug dormant in me, and The Beatles woke it up. I didn't stop composing since.

There was a sofa which we kept in the veranda, and I remember sitting there with my guitar one morning when the bug bit me. The first song I wrote was for my first girlfriend of course, the film-going one. When you're fourteen and you're in love, you know it's going to last forever. So my song was called 'Till I Die', and the lyrics went:

I'll love you till I die, my baby, yeah
True love just can't die, my baby, yeah
Someday we will be in heaven's clover
Someday when we're gone and love will start all over
Ooooh, ooooh, ooooh, ooooh.

I was so thrilled about having my very own song for the first time, I wrote it down very neatly in a notebook, with the legend *'Lyrics & Music by Remo Fernandes'* beneath the title. The song was on A, and I devised a slurred bass guitar line for it, slurring from G to A, and then from C to D. When I rehearsed it with The Beat 4 it sounded like music to our ears, if you'll forgive the expression. There was also a one-note harmony which I'd worked out for the verses, which either Alexandre or Caetano sang. The beat too was a bit special for this song, and Tony handled it beautifully. I've never ever recorded those early songs, and I've been toying with the idea of recording two albums called *School Days* and *College Days* for quite a while now.

To this day I don't know what I meant by 'heaven's clover'. An impressive rhyme indeed for 'start all over'. When you write about everlasting love at fourteen, you need to use words which will make people realize just how knowledgeable and experienced you are on the subject.

After 'Till I Die' I wrote quite a few more, most of them in school. I've found pages of old notebooks on which I scribbled lyrics, and attempted to write some musical notes my way, so that I might remember the tune later (remember, I knew no solfeggio).

Pages from old notebooks on which I wrote some of my earliest songs in school.

Father had bought Belinda a lovely acoustic piano, the traditional choice of instrument for girls. She loved it, and of course I started plonking away on it too, and ended up composing an instrumental which I named 'Dreamland' due to its ethereal, romantic nature. I played it on guitar with The Beat 4, and there are still people in Panjim (especially a guy called Paiva) who remember it fondly, as it was invariably played towards the end of a ball, when everyone danced cheek-to-cheek with their sweethearts in the darkened club halls.

Ravindra Roplekar and Poona

One day, we received either a letter or a visit from someone called Ravindra Roplekar. He was from Poona (as it was then called), he had heard about us and about this new music called 'beat music', and he wanted to organize two or three shows of ours there.

We were excited right out of our school pants. They had heard of us outside Goa? We were being invited to perform in the *União Indiana*, the great Indian Union beyond Goa? Wow!

Mr Roplekar was what one might call a very traditional and vernacular man, someone who apparently knew his Marathi but not much English, and therefore was an unlikely candidate to organize beat shows of western music at that time. But Poona was known to have a thriving western music scene, with pretty good beat groups of its own, and we were excited to travel and perform there. Although he wanted his show to be on 1 January 1968, there was no way a self-respecting Goan could be found away from Goa on Christmas and New Year's days, so he agreed to have it on 7 January instead.

We were to take a bus which left from Betim (across the Mandovi river from Panjim) very early in the morning. There was no bridge across the Mandovi yet, and I think the bus left too early for us to risk the first ferry, so it was decided that we would spend the night in Betim. Mina to the rescue: she arranged for us to spend the night at the house of one of her wide circle of friends, who lived right in front of the ferry wharf, where the Poona bus left from. She would chaperone us until she saw us safely on the bus. Our journey started after dinner, when we all met and crossed the ferry with our luggage and instruments.

In the middle of the night Mina heard some noises. Caetano had woken up and, not finding his thick glasses in the darkness, was groping his way around. Not finding the light switches either, he mistook the kitchen for the toilet and, standing at its door, was about to start relieving himself into it.

Mina grabbed him by the elbow and Caetano, his apparatus in hand, was dragged to the real toilet just in time, thus saving us from acute embarrassment towards our kind hosts the next morning.

She saw us on the bus at the break of dawn, and we waved goodbye as we took off on our exciting 'concert tour'.

There were five of us now: The Beat 4 had a manager, Tomás Botelho, also from St. Tomé like Caetano. Why we needed a manager is beyond me, but it sounded good when we introduced him as such. He was smart and able, and looked and sounded very professional – at least to us, if not to the organizers of our shows. I guess the comforting news that he had a sister and brother-in-law in Poona had influenced my parents into allowing this whole odyssey.

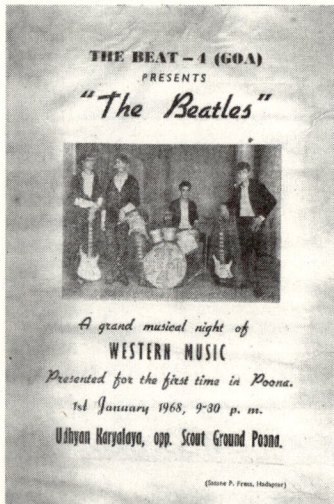

A flyer and ticket for our Poona concert which never was.

Ravindra Roplekar was there to receive us at the Poona bus station, and he took us to a lodge where he put us up. True to his word, he had printed flyers advertising our show with our photograph and all, and we were thrilled to be handed a few of these proofs of our new-found superstardom, though we couldn't understand how we could be presenting The Beatles; perhaps he thought that was a type of music.

That was the last we saw of Mr Roplekar for days. He was simply not contactable thereafter. We were five hungry boys from Goa left high and dry in a little lodge in Poona.

The lodge didn't provide meals, but it did provide 'free unlimited breakfast', which consisted of coffee and butter sandwiches. Coffee and butter sandwiches never tasted better, and the next morning we had at least five coffees and twenty sandwiches each – which the lodge, true to their promise, thankfully delivered unlimitedly up in our rooms.

Tomás marched us off to his sister's house for meals. Our stomachs full, he shyly showed us the lyrics to a song called 'On the Highway' which he had scribbled on a cigarette packet in the bus. We liked them, and Alexandre and I set them to music. So the whole trip wasn't a total bummer after all.

After a couple of days of Roplekar's abscondence (and after feeding five hungry boys for two whole days), Tomás's brother-in-law decided to take matters into his own hands. He paraded us all to the local police station to lodge a complaint.

The police inspector, a kind but stern man, studied the situation and, before setting out to look for Ravindra Roplekar, gave us a piece of his mind. 'You are five schoolboys from Goa, and you come to Poona on the mere promises of an unknown man?' he asked. 'What if he were part of a gang that had kidnapped you all and held you to ransom? This is the kind of naive and careless behaviour from people which gives us policemen unnecessary headaches!'

Such thoughts had never struck us before; kidnappings only happened in films, never in Goa. We hung our heads, contrite and repentant. Despite their stint in Bombay years ago, my parents must have been too softened by the honesty and trustworthiness of the people of little Goa to mistrust Roplekar.

'And look at this press release your Mr Roplekar has issued! He calls y'all playboys!' the inspector bellowed, pointing to a local newspaper. We didn't know what a playboy was, and I'm sure neither did Roplekar. We played, we were boys, so we quite accepted that we were playboys. That there was a deeper, darker meaning to the word was beyond us Portuguese-speaking Goans.

A very dishevelled and dazed Ravindra Roplekar was brought into the station in a police jeep later in the day. He looked over at us very sheepishly, and we felt sorry for him. He had meant no harm or evil; the whole exercise of organizing our 'grand show' had proved totally out of his league and, other than printing flyers and tickets, he hadn't been able to do much more to turn it into a reality.

The police inspector made him pay for our return tickets and the stay at the lodge, and to Goa we retreated crestfallen, with proverbial tails between our legs. As they say, such experiences are rich lessons for the future, and we learnt that we couldn't smell coffee or butter sandwiches for quite a while thereafter.

The first car

Like most boys, I was obsessed with driving. Father had been letting me take the wheel while we drove on empty roads for a while now. When I turned fourteen he started giving me serious driving lessons. A little later he would also send me out driving with one of his factory drivers sitting by my side.

I've said it before, I was pampered. And that trend did not abate. When I completed the ninth standard Father bought me a car – a fifteen-going-on-sixteen-year-old schoolboy with his own car! Unheard of at the time, and pretty rare even today. It was a Standard Herald. I promptly got the roof taken off and turned it into a convertible red beauty with a black stripe running along its side (was I recreating my old Thunderbolt?). I still had two years to go before I could reach the magical age of eighteen and acquire a driving license. But drive I did, every single day of those two years, when it was still illegal for me to do so – for Goa and Panjim were small, quiet and deserted enough for one to get away with it. Ironically, I was finally found out and fined by the notoriously feared, lame traffic inspector Cruz on the way to Calangute Beach on the hot summer evening of 7 May 1971 – a few hours before I turned eighteen.

In retrospect, I guess one of the reasons why my father fulfilled most of my desires and wishes so easily was that, besides following my musical passion head-on, I was also good at my studies, though I haven't told you this before. Once I got over my initial problem with the English language, I regularly ranked among the top three in class in all tests and exams. This exasperated my friends, whose parents held me up as an example to them: 'Look, not only has he made a name in music, he also studies well!'

So, before you judge me as an over-spoilt rich man's kid, let me try and convince you that I earned at least some of that spoiling. And I do like to think that if Father gave me gifts, Mother made sure they didn't turn me into a rotten spoilt brat. Father's success as an industrialist gave him a natural tendency for living well and giving a materially good life to his family; and Mother's convent upbringing, which I've spoken about before, kept her grounded, thrifty and humble – and us too, as far as she could manage.

Good foreign electric guitars!

And I guess that was the spirit which made it impossible for my father to watch me and my bandmates suffer with those horrible Manuel Industries guitars. He did further research, and found out that a cousin of his was returning from Africa. He had plenty of space in one of his containers, and as it was a permanent shift, he was allowed to bring in personal stuff without the infamously prohibitive Indian custom duty (I think it was over 300 per cent at the time).

The German brand Höfner was *the* thing in electric guitars then, mainly because The Beatles used them. So Höfners it was for us. Once The Beat 4 disbanded, the bass and rhythm guitars were sold, but I still have my lead guitar, which was again a top model, and had an innovative little lever called 'organ effect'. Half a century later it still plays perfectly, the tremolo descends and rises back in perfect pitch, and the arm hasn't warped one bit. All this without any maintenance or servicing whatsoever.

Another time, Father got a friend who was returning from Africa for good to bring me a five-speed Raleigh racing cycle. It was a beautiful metallic green. Eventually it couldn't be used any more because the tyres wore out and no replacements were available in India. That was often the fate of foreign items here, even of foreign cars. Indian mechanics had become expert artisans at repairing, improvising and even recreating perfect spare parts out of scraps of metal and junk, but some things just couldn't be fabricated or duplicated, and I guess thin professional racing-cycle tyres was one of them.

We played those wonderful Höfners until the end of The Beat 4, and I played mine well beyond.

Just out of curiosity, I did a Google search for good old Manuel Industries, Kerala, after writing this chapter in 2020. Somehow I wasn't too surprised to see they've thrived and grown into a multi-showroom chain of good-quality musical instruments. Their website, though full of photographs of their outlets, doesn't seem to have specific information about their instruments, so I'm not sure they still manufacture their own brand; they do seem to be selling good international brands like Fender and Gibson and Yamaha today, though. Just about half a century too late for The Beat 4.

6

Goodbye Goa

The *kuttus* before the show

At a show on Miramar Beach, just before we were to go on stage, I saw Alexandre running off somewhere. I asked him where, and he signalled to me to come along. The excited look on his face intrigued me, and I followed him. He ran into the old (by then dilapidated) Hotel Miramar which lay just beyond the pines behind the stage, me at his heels. There he headed straight for the reception counter, which now also served as a bar counter, and ordered a rum and coke. And he extended his expert advice to his pal who was two years younger than him: 'You must always have one quick drink before going up on stage. It makes you play and sing much better. Try it out today.'

By that time my friends and I did have a drink at birthday parties and at dances. Our first drink, in keeping with the sweet tooth of youth, was rum and coke. My mother had drilled it into my young head that I must not have more than one, and I didn't. Of course there were those of us who always outsmarted the elders who kept an eye on the bar, and managed to have more – sometimes many more – than one. Many of them aren't alive today.

But anyway, having a drink at a party was one thing, and having one just before going on stage, another. An exciting, naughty thing to do. And I did it, ordering a rum and coke for myself. *Kuttus* is a fun Konkani term for a quick neat one, the kind farmers and fishermen usually down at the local tavern in one gulp before heading for home after a hard day's work. We gulped ours down that way and ran straight back up on stage. It was a little before sunset.

Truly, at that evening's performance I felt and exuded an energy and an exuberance that was new to me. My parents noticed it too, and mentioned it at home with appreciation. When I told them what Alexandre and I had done, they were aghast, and warned me never to make that a habit. I'm happy to say I didn't, at least not for many, many years. It did become a habit towards the height of my career, but I soon broke it, replacing the drink with a few yogic '*Surya Namaskars*' just before climbing up the stage. The energy they gave me was incredible.

The near-blinding turn

Some time after this we were rehearsing in our living room for an all-Goa beat contest which was going to take place on the happening Calangute Beach, also on a Sunday in summer. Calangute was more happening than Miramar because it attracted larger crowds comprising Goans from Bombay who returned for the holidays to their villages in and around the Bardez belt. The Bombay youth was always more hip than us Goans, as they came from a big city with British and American influences, while the Portuguese influence on Goa was more traditional in a Latin way. The Bombay chicks in their tight bell-bottoms and miniskirts and skin-fitting t-shirts, and the guys in their equally tight bell-bottoms and broad belts and high collars and longish hair, could be spotted from a mile away. And heard too, as they all spoke in loud English, with fashionable expressions and expletives colouring their language. Everyone was 'this bleddy bugger' or 'that bleddy bugger, men'.

We were rehearsing The Rolling Stones' '(I Can't Get No) Satisfaction', and we decided to add a little stage action to the song for the contest. At the first 'no no no', we three guitarists would jump and execute a 180-degree turn, and stay the two-bar drum break with our backs to the audience, our right legs bending and unbending at the knee in time with the beat. At the end of the drum break we'd do another 180-degree jump, and face the microphones just in time for the 'a-hey hey hey'.

These jumps and turns had to be executed with full strength, our guitars swinging hard together with us. Unbeknown to us, Belinda, my little sister who was by now about five years of age, came running across the room from behind us. We were executing our turn when one of our guitar heads hit her hard on the forehead as she ran straight into it. She collapsed on the floor unconscious. Shocked shouts from the band. The music ground to an abrupt halt, and I, almost fainting myself, knelt down to inspect the damage; had she lost an eye?! My parents had come rushing into the room. Luckily the guitar had hit her just above the eye, missing it by half a centimetre or so. But it was still her forehead; the bone could have cracked, or some permanent internal damage could have been caused.

But a few minutes later, after the application of ice, she came to, and apart from crying for five minutes from the pain, showed no signs of having been affected by the clash at all.

But to this day, when she acts a little irritatingly, I tell her that that guitar must have left some damage behind after all.

My sister Belinda at the age of five,
around which time she got hit
by that hard revolving guitar.

The first Simla Beat Contest

Our rehearsals paid off, and that year we won all the prizes in all categories. The Beat 4 won the first prize for the Best Beat Group; I won the prizes for Best Lead Guitarist, Best Vocalist and Best Original Composition (we had played 'Love at First Sight', a song with a time-signature change which I had just written; more about its inspiration later); Alexandre won the prize for Best Bass Guitarist; Caetano for Best Rhythm Guitarist; and Tony for Best Drummer, which he had won with a rabble-rousing drum solo.

Together with our cups and shields, we were gifted countless cartons of cigarettes. The Beat Contest was organized by the extremely popular Simla cigarettes, a product which shouldn't have been organizing events for youth, much less distributing its killing sticks to them. But anti-smoking awareness was below zero then, and all that the elders would tell us was 'You're too young to smoke', as in, after a few years it would be ok to do so. So we hung out on the beach after the show, feeling all grown up with the heady knowledge of being successful beat boys with cigarette packets in our pockets, and – we smoked. Cinema heroes smoked fashionably on the silver screen, and this evening we did too.

I must add here, not without some pride, that thereafter we won the first prize at every beat contest in Goa.

Earlier that summer – or was it the previous one? – my cousin Rex from Bombay had come down and told me about this 'hot chick' he had met on the boat to Goa. He had made plans to meet her on the Calangute Beach that evening. How did youngsters find and meet each other on a crowded beach without the help of mobiles in the 1960s? By radar. I was already fascinated hearing about her, and when she turned up in her olive green hipster miniskirt, her long hair blowing in the breeze, something happened to me. Not just to me, but to her as well. I was to learn later that it was called 'chemistry'.

We all went together to a village dance in Parrá a few evenings later, she as my cousin's date. She ended the dance as my date instead, as we danced the last slow set of songs in the darkened hall glued to each other and glued to one spot.

And, even though we never discussed it or even spoke about it, my cousin took it very well, with an 'Oh, there's plenty of fish in the sea' attitude. He was a great dancer of twist and jerk and shake, the dance crazes of the time, he was tall and handsome and a smooth operator, and fish swam to him like to a gourmet bait. So he was indeed fine. And, in an unspoken way, it was understood that she was now with me.

I had never experienced chemistry like this before; she had a way of looking at me from under her eyelids, while biting her upper lip with her lower teeth, even while agreeing to my suggestion of a midnight drive during a dance or party, which drove me crazy. Chemistry soon turned to physics.

I had written 'Love at First Sight' for her, with pompously grown-up lyrics like:

I saw, I loved, and I wanted her
I knew it was love at first sight
I was told she belonged to another man
But I didn't care for anything right then.

Ha! She belonged to another *man*?! All three of us, she, my cousin and I were mere teenagers. Just adolescents with hormones raging.

Anyway, she was in the audience, she knew the song was for her, and she was my most valuable award that evening, not the shields and cups.

After the beat contest there was a ball which followed at the Tourist Hotel just down the beach. She and I left it somewhere in the middle of the night, and walked along the deserted moonlit beach until we found a suitable place to lose ourselves in among the dunes which lined it. The dunes were then full of wild bushes; anyone who remembers those bushes will remember their strong sweet and spicy heady scent. We spent the rest of the night in a small white sandy clearing among those bushes, the soft moonlight lighting us up, the loud sound of waves crashing a few metres away. Goa and its beaches were totally safe then, and totally empty in the night, except for stray lovers, as beaches ought to be. Without a worrying thought in our heads, we spent the rest of the night in heaven. No heavy sex, mind you, but mainly kissing. Her lips were very malleable, and they folded and bent every which way like soft sugary jujubes. Besides kissing there was also caressing and hugging (I guess what the Americans call petting and necking) like there was no tomorrow.

But tomorrow did arrive totally unannounced. When we eventually looked up for air, we saw that the day was dawning. We had walked to the dunes covered in darkness, but we walked back to 'civilization' fully revealed by the light of the rising sun. And I was mortified to see my mother looking straight down at us from the balcony of our room at the Tourist Hotel, which my parents had booked for a few nights.

After the girl and I said our goodbyes I climbed up and tiptoed into our room where Father was still asleep, but there was no reprimand from Mother. I guess she accepted the fact that I had reached that age when nothing and no one was going to keep me away from girls any more. And, apart from her by now usual warnings about possible *doença* (she never did have the courage to explain herself any further on the subject), she and especially Mina actually teased me about the way I emerged from the darkness holding a girl's hand that morning.

I was relieved and happy that I was now being accepted as having come of age in more ways than musically.

Changes in The Beat 4:
Kenneth Mascarenhas on drums

I don't remember when or why exactly, but Tony was replaced by Kenneth Mascarenhas on the drums. Perhaps Tony was moving to Bombay, where he (and eventually Alexandre, incidentally) joined Emeliano da Cruz's The Gay Caballeros, which was the house band at Hotel Heritage in Byculla. (Gay only meant 'cheerful' and 'jolly' at the time.)

Kenneth had just returned from somewhere abroad, probably an African country. Lots of Goans were returning from Africa at that time, mainly due to political turmoil there. I was too young to know or care what the turmoil was all about, and the youth who had returned didn't seem too keen to talk about it, or about all that their families had lost or left behind. But I do remember the colourful *kitenges* the Africa-returned guys and girls wore as shirts and dresses; the thick black elephant-tail-hair bracelets they wore around their wrists; and the beautiful songs they brought down with them, such as '*Malaika*' and '*Pata Pata*'.

Anyway Kenneth was a drummer with the kind of speed which hadn't been heard in Goa before. He did great drum solos, and we were finally able to play The Shadows' 'Little B' – *the* drum solo of the time, and still a masterpiece today.

When we watched *The Gene Krupa Story*, the film about the legendary American drummer, we realized that Kenneth even looked quite like Sal Mineo, the actor who played Krupa, with his curly hair and Latino features. But that was not a criterion; looks never were, not even for Caetano who looked like Hank B. Marvin – they were just bonuses.

And The Beat 4 rocked and rolled happily from success to success; we were getting better and better at our craft.

With Kenneth Mascarenhas, our new drummer, third from left. Others (left to right): Caetano Abreu, rhythm; Alexandre Rosario, bass; Remo, lead.

Steve Sequeira on drums

Again, I don't remember the reason, but over time Kenneth was replaced by Steve Sequeira, a drummer who had also returned with his parents from Africa. He was and looked much older to us all, although in a hip kind of way: long curly hair, a short beard, and very, very thick spectacles which made his already beady eyes look deadlier when he stared at you sardonically. He liked jazz and Jimi Hendrix. Until then I had thought that James Last was the epitome of jazz. And when I heard the Hendrix album he lent me, I didn't like or understand much of what was going on. I was a schoolboy in love with The Beatles' comparatively clean, neat and exciting sound, not yet ready for Hendrix's heavy distortion and long undecipherable guitar solos. But Steve was a great drummer, and his smooth subtle jazz touch brought a new finesse to our pop and rock.

He's the guy who, a while later, told me he had 'had' the letter-writing girl I had been so obsessed with, thus breaking my heart. But we got along fine.

Emy Gomes on vocals

After a reign of all-boy bands, solo female singers were now beginning to have beautiful hits again. Mary Hopkin with 'Those Were the Days', Nancy Sinatra with 'These Boots Are Made for Walking', Jeannie C. Riley with 'Harper Valley PTA', and of course Lulu with a whole string of them like 'I'm a Tiger', 'To Sir with Love', 'Boom Bang-a-Bang', and so on.

So I decided to ask a girl called Emily Gomes to join the band. She and her family were newcomers in town, if I'm not mistaken returned from Kuwait, quite rare at a time when the great Goan exodus to the Gulf hadn't even started. She sang beautifully. It was a delicate thing, asking a girl to join an all-male group. But she and her family were cool about it, and soon she was 'one of the boys'.

I didn't want to change the name of the group to The Beat 5, so sometimes we called ourselves 'The Beat 4 + 1', and sometimes 'The Beat 4 with Emy'.

LEFT TO RIGHT: Remo, Steve Sequeira, Emily (Emy) Gomes, Edwin Saldanha, Nandinho Lobato Faria.

Edwin Saldanha on rhythm

By now a whole beat group of Goan guys from Africa had come down to Goa. They were called The Beethovens, and thanks to the transfer-of-residence customs allowances, were able to bring a lot of foreign equipment with them, which was cheap in Africa – certainly cheaper than in India. They had come down with not one but three Vox amplifiers! The ones The Beatles used! And they had with them an electric organ. I never much liked the sound of this old-fashioned church instrument in beat groups, like in The Dave Clark Five. There's no denying it added a very smoothening, full sound to a group, but I guess that's exactly what I didn't like about it: its smoothness took away the bite which I felt pop and rock ought to have. It was only Deep Purple's Jon Lord who, a few years later, produced a screaming raspy sound and style of playing the electric organ, which in my mind made it a truly worthy rock 'n' roll instrument.

Anyway, now we had tough competition – not musically, as we were second to none in that department, but from equipment. And we had no way of acquiring better equipment in India.

Around this time news came that the father of a boy called Edwin Saldanha had imported a powerful big Eko guitar amplifier from Italy. It possessed an ethereal new effect called reverb. They lived in Campal, pretty close to our house. I dropped by and asked to see and try out the amplifier, and promptly fell in love with it. Ah, the tone and sound of my Höfner guitar through a real guitar amplifier with reverb! I realized at last that half of that fascinating Shadows sound came from their equipment itself.

By now I was fifteen, a bit too mature to ask or even expect Father to keep buying things for me or my group. However, I felt very embarrassed and guilty about replacing Caetano as rhythm guitarist; sacrificing a human being for an amplifier seemed immoral. But fond as I was of him as an old friend and founder member, it was high time we had people in the group who brought something to it in terms of equipment, without it being Father who provided everything single-handedly. And that Eko and its sound were much too tempting. So finally I did speak to Caetano about it and, true to his accommodating nature, he readily agreed and said he understood perfectly.

So Caetano was out, and Edwin was in. I'm sure he knew that his amplifier was the primary reason for his inclusion, but we never ever said so in so many words; and it had been agreed that my lead guitar would now go through his amplifier's reverb channel, and his rhythm guitar through the normal one.

Soon our vocal mic went through the reverb channel too, and his rhythm guitar was shifted to my amplifier, but he didn't mind or complain once.

Troubles with Alexandre

After Alexandre had a few glorious years with the Billy Rangers and then with The Beat 4, his father was transferred to the post office in Ponda, quite a few hours away from Panjim. That was a blow to us all, especially to him, as all the action and all his friends were in Panjim. We agreed that he would come for all the shows anyway, and that for a few days before the show, he would stay at our home for the rehearsals.

That worked fine for a while. My father would phone his father at the post office and inform him about a show and rehearsal dates, and a happy

Alexandre would be back in Panjim for the duration. And everything went on smoothly. Alexandre enjoyed staying at our house where he shared the second bed in my room, and food was cooked especially to his liking. In short, he was treated like an honoured guest, which was the only way one treated guests in Goa those days – and even today in most households.

Until one day Alexandre didn't turn up on the promised day. The whole group waited in vain, ready to rehearse. When my father called, his father said he had missed the bus and would be there the next day. But again, he wasn't. Finally he turned up on the day of the show, and we had to perform without having rehearsed with him. Which meant we could not do any of the new songs I had planned on. Alexandre didn't seem contrite about his late arrival at all – in fact he was sullen and distant. We all found it strange, but thought it was a one-off thing.

LEFT TO RIGHT: Alexandre on bass and lead vocals, Edwin on rhythm, Steve Sequeira on drums, Emy Gomes on lead vocals, Remo on lead guitar and lead vocals. This was one of Alexandre's last shows with us. He was already showing signs of being aloof. The amplifier in the foreground is Edwin's precious Italian Eko with reverb.

At the next show the same saga repeated itself, though. Thereafter we never knew whether Alexandre would turn up or not, and having him in the group started causing tensions. We had to rehearse without him, hoping that he would learn the bass to the new songs on his own. While he and I had shared the lead vocals in the past by singing an equal number of songs each, I now had to sing most of them, simply because he wasn't there to rehearse them.

His attitude became less and less friendly. The strange thing was that there was no reason whatsoever for this transformation; there had been no quarrel, no argument, no misunderstanding. However, he was drinking more and more, especially for a teenager. And his irregularity and bad vibes went on worsening until it all erupted at a dance we were playing at in Club Vasco da Gama.

Towards the end of the dance it had fallen upon our group to play the last set, always a romantic one comprising slow songs, and people were waiting. I went looking for Alexandre, whom I found sitting drinking at the club bar with a couple of his buddies. When I told him it was time for us to play, he dismissively told me that he'd join us soon. The rest of us went on stage and turned on our instruments, but there was still no Alexandre. I put my guitar down and went to call him again, and this time he was downright rude, saying something like, 'Can't you see I'm having a drink? I said I'll come, and I'll come when I'm good and ready.' I must specify here that every time I called him I was very polite and friendly. I still didn't know how to act hard with someone who deserved it; today the second time would have been a firm warning, not a request.

With the audience waiting and calling out for the music by now, I had to find a solution. I took Alexandre's bass guitar (remember all the guitars were provided by Father), and I started the last set with a soft romantic song. Somewhere in the middle of it a drunk Alexandre, probably upset at seeing he wasn't indispensable, stumbled upon the stage and asked for the bass guitar. I didn't want to stop the song midway, so I signalled that I'd give it to him for the next song. Enraged at not having his way at once, he tried to take the guitar from me, stopping me from playing it by grabbing the strings; and when I resisted, he caught me by the neck and started choking me, to stop me from singing.

Those were the days when parents and teenagers all went to these dances together. Father, who couldn't believe what he was seeing from the dance floor, felt his blood boil. He asked Mother, with whom he was dancing, to wait right there. He was young and strong, and climbed up on stage and slapped Alexandre hard across the face. Since the lights in the clubs were drastically dimmed for the last dance, perhaps not many noticed the drama unfolding on stage.

However drunk or ill-mannered, in those days a Goan youth never, but never retaliated or hit back at an adult. Alexandre let go of my neck, shamefacedly walked off the stage and back to the bar. The rest of us completed the set in peace, and Alexandre came home with me in my car in silence, as he was staying at our house.

The next day, badly hung-over and still smelling of alcohol, he packed his bag and left, and I was happy to see him walk out of our house, out of my group, and out of my life.

He eventually died at the untimely age of fifty. And he wasn't the only one. I lost too many ex-bandmates to see much glamour in a wrongly glorified aspect of 'the rock 'n' roll way of life'.

I had the opportunity to come into contact with quite a few alcoholics and to hear their inside stories a few decades later. Through them I learnt that some of the characteristics of an alcoholic are a bloated idea of self-worth, of biting the hand that feeds him, and of believing that he is the reason for the success of his benefactor.

When a teenager is provided with a wonderful imported guitar, an amplifier, and a warm and welcoming place to stay and rehearse, when he can literally come barehanded, bringing nothing in the form of equipment to the band, not even for his own personal use, and go back with the glory of a successful performance and show money in his pocket, and when his ego is constantly stoked by his admirers, perhaps it is easy for him to attribute the success of the whole band to himself. Unfortunately people stop feeling gratitude when too much is given too easily.

Nandinho Lobato Faria on the bass

With the exit of Alexandre, I asked Fernando Lobato Faria ('Nandinho' to all Panjim) to join us as bass guitarist. He was an easy-going, ever-smiling and joking guy from St. Tomé, Panjim, and we had very similar Panjim backgrounds of cowboys and music. He was a great singer too, and did great renditions of 'Black Is Black', 'Save the Last Dance for Me', and other hits of the day. And he yodelled perfectly too. We were even schoolmates for a few years.

The Beat 4 with its last-ever line-up. LEFT TO RIGHT: Nandinho Lobato Faria on bass, Remo on lead guitar and lead vocals, Edwin Saldanha on rhythm, Steve Sequeira on drums, Emy Gomes on lead vocals.

The first joint

It was at around this time that we started hearing about this new thing called marijuana and hashish. The Beatles were reportedly smoking it (no, we never heard about LSD at that time; marijuana to us was supposed to be the height of 'drugs'), and their music had reportedly gained so much in depth and insight and complexity as a result... I couldn't wait to hear their new record, and when *Sgt. Pepper's Lonely Hearts Club Band* became available in Goa, I bought the first copy.

Oh my god … I could not believe what I was hearing! The music put me on a high even though I was dry, sending me tripping between marmalade skies and the Isle of Wight, smiling at stern meter maids and Billy Shears, and fixing a hole with Mr Kite. If the music could do that even without marijuana, I simply had to smoke it.

There was this college student who came from Bombay who bragged that he had 'stuff', and in fact had already offered to 'turn us on', saying that musicians ought to. Before you get the wrong impression, no, he wasn't a dealer or pusher. He just loved the stuff and wanted to share it with us. Before I heard *Sgt. Pepper's* I'd said no, but now I simply couldn't wait to experience it. At the next movie I saw him sitting a few rows in front of me, and I loudly and innocently asked him, 'Hey Joe, do you have some stuff?' He slowly turned around and put his finger to his lips, signalling me to shut the heck up. Nobody in Panjim would know what 'stuff' meant of course, but I was being too naive here.

During the interval he came and whispered that he could give me some. But could I inhale smoke? No, I could not, in spite of the Simla cigarettes after the contest, which I'd puffed on without inhaling. He said it would be useless then. So I was given the homework of learning how to inhale, and I was to get back to him when I did. Finally one day, after I'd passed my initiation, he gave me a small packet folded out of newspaper, in which he said was enough marijuana for one. I was not to show it to anyone, and he explained how I was to roll a joint.

The word 'drugs' didn't exist then, marijuana didn't have the reputation of being bad or dangerous, in fact no one knew about it at all; so I went home and told my parents about it. You can imagine how innocently and naively I viewed it myself. They, in their total ignorance, were very curious. I opened my magical packet, we all smelled the dry marijuana twigs in it, and I told them this was something which, when smoked in a cigarette, made you 'hear colours and see sounds', like The Beatles did. We decided to puff on it together.

I'm sure you, dear reader, might have tried a joint or two if you belong to my generation and disposition. But how many of you can truthfully say you've tried to turn your parents on?

On my study desk I carefully and more or less successfully rolled the joint, with my parents standing next to me, watching and commenting curiously every now and then. Then I lit it, and after inhaling a puff or two like a boss, passed it around. Father had been a smoker of fifty Du Maurier cigarettes a day years ago, but had quit totally after he had collapsed in a faint one day on his short walk to the factory. He broke his long hiatus to try marijuana that day. Mother, of course, could hardly puff, leave alone inhale – I went into giggles watching her efforts, surely aided by the fumes which were now slowly rising to my brain. Father said it made him feel relaxed.

After they left the room I closed the curtains, turned on my psychedelic lamp to illuminate the huge oil painting I had made on one wall to symbolize all of The Beatles, and I put on *Sgt. Pepper's Lonely Hearts Club Band*. And if 'Rock Around the Clock' had changed my life forever with rock 'n' roll about a decade earlier, this album changed my life forever with psychedelia and the hippie way, which was to be the new major influence in my life – musical, graphic, and philosophical.

Typing

My school life was going fine. Goan students who were nearing the SSC (the exam after the eleventh and final school year at the time) were happily exempted from Hindi. We didn't have a solid enough background in the 'official language' of India, having been totally ignorant of it until the Portuguese left Goa, by which time we were already in mid-school, and were allowed to take shorthand or typing instead of Hindi. It became a trend for all the girls to go in for shorthand (since I guess it was presumed they were more prone to opt for a secretarial career), and for the boys to go in for typing.

These two subjects were not taught in school, and my classmates and I all went for typing classes to a place called 'Kamat's Typing Institute'. This was down today's 18th June Road, and was situated on the first floor of the old building which still houses Farmácia Ananta on the ground floor today, next to Café Central.

Mr Kamat who ran these classes was a sour, ill-tempered, unsmiling middle-aged man. He chain-smoked Simla cigarettes all day long, right in the classroom, and resembled a cigarette himself, very thin and very dry, skin dark like tobacco. The classroom was a long hall lined with rows of rickety desks holding ancient typewriters, all of which had some problem or the other. He had a rasping voice which he never employed to answer a 'Good evening sir' or 'Goodbye sir' from a student, but to loudly and derisively criticize the slightest mistake in any assignment. Blaming one of his faulty typewriters to explain a mistake only earned his ire, and we learnt to accept all blame early on. Perfect assignments were received with total silence, as in 'How dare you deprive me of the pleasure of being unpleasant to you?'

Today I have come to the conclusion that typing is the most practically useful thing I learnt in my eleven years of schooling and five years of architecture. No one knew then that computers would one day be invented and rule our lives from morn till night, and every time I see someone clicking at the computer keyboard with two fingers, however dexterously, I send up a silent thanks to sour Mr Kamat in whichever heaven or hell he might be polluting with cigarette smoke right now, for helping me learn to type with all ten.

The end of schooldays

We now started discussing my future. Father asked me whether I wanted to take over his aerated water factory. One is still too young to know what one wants to do in life when one is sixteen, but somehow I knew that wasn't my trip. So with a grimace that came involuntarily to my face, I said no. When he asked me what I wanted to do, I said I wanted to be an architect.

You see, it was always drummed into my head that music, while a very graceful and gratifying hobby, was not to be considered as a profession. As a professional you became something respectable like a doctor, an engineer or a lawyer, who also played and sang in the evenings when the mood took him, at home or at social gatherings, as a genteel pastime.

But the thing which had clinched it for me years earlier, while I was still a child, was when I saw the whole family making such a fuss over Garçia, Tia Angela's son, when he returned from London with his degree. *'Ele é arquiecto!'* I heard them saying admiringly. 'He's an architect!' When I asked Father what an architect did, I was told that he designed houses and buildings. Design? That meant drawing! And I just loved drawing, almost as much as I did music. If I could earn all that respect and fuss and a comfortable living from drawing, architecture it was for me, since music couldn't be it. The decision I took that day as a child remained stuck in my head beyond reason. Blissfully unaware that Architecture also comprised advanced Mathematics and Calculus and Physics and Chemistry, I had then brought my childish fantasy to life in my usual way: I had rushed to my drawing book and 'designed' a building. There, of course I could be an architect!

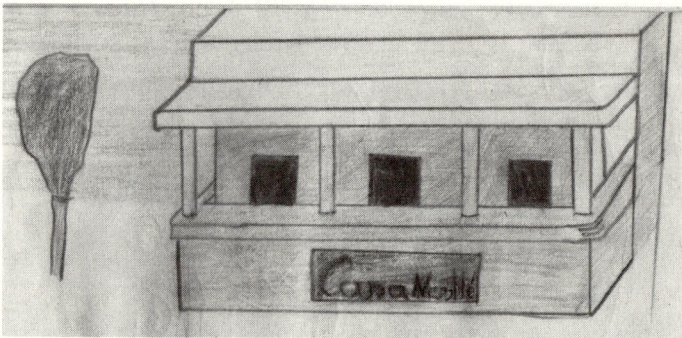

Father, who was a very keen amateur artist and musician, taught me the first principle of perspective (evident in this drawing I did at the age of around seven) and shading.

Father got down to his research, and from among schools in the near-equidistant metros of Bangalore and Bombay, the Sir J.J. College of Architecture in the latter city was deemed the better one. Letters were written, a syllabus obtained, and I was on my way to being a singing architect. Of course, one had to await my SSC results before actually applying for a seat.

SSC stood for the Secondary School Certificate exam. For the first time, we were going to answer examination papers set not by class teachers from our own school, but by a board which operated impersonally from far away – was it from Poona or from Bombay? Bookshops were rampant with paperbacks such as 'SSC Guides', 'SSC Exam Papers of the Last 10 Years', 'Most Likely SSC Questions This Year', and so on, which all of us bought and solved at home. There was a nervousness and a seriousness about this 'final year' which was palpable in all parents, and which obviously contaminated all the students in turn. Our school teachers had been warning and preparing us for it right from the ninth standard.

This just goes to show to what extent we were disconnected from the way things ran in the rest of India those days, but at the very last minute, we found out that a course in Intermediate Drawing was essential to render one eligible for the Architecture course at the J.J. College. This drawing course was so simple and easy, I could well have done it simultaneously with my SSC and typing classes. But now it presented me with a good reason to remain in Goa and at home one more year, and Mother and Father were pretty happy about it too; no one lamented the 'loss' of one year of my life.

And then, finally, in the summer of 1971, it was time for me to leave Goa.

Farewell to The Beat 4 and ... to music?

What repercussions was this going to have on my beat boy days? On my music? On The Beat 4? Drastic ones, to put it mildly.

Firstly, it was decided that we would disband The Beat 4. Goa was sad about it, especially our friends and fans, and we decided to organize a dance at the Club Nacional in Panjim, which we would name The Beat 4 Farewell Show. Steve, our dirty old man, would tell anyone who'd listen that we were breaking up because 'Remo was going for an architecture course, Emy was going for a higher course, and he was going for intercourse'.

It was also decided that after the farewell show I would hang up my guitar, so to speak. The family consensus was that the Architecture course was no playing matter, and I would have to give it my full and undivided attention for its duration. I cannot imagine that I full-heartedly agreed to that, but I did. If I had followed it through and totally suppressed music for five years though, my life might have taken a very different turn – architecture could have brainwashed me by then. But if I may leave humility aside, I'll say that, knowing my temperament, I would have achieved in architecture (or any other profession of my choice) more or less what I have achieved in music.

The Beat 4 Farewell Show at Club Nacional a few days before I left for Bombay to study Architecture. LEFT TO RIGHT: Steve Sequeira on drums, Remo on lead guitar and lead vocals, Emy Gomes on lead vocals, Edwin Saldanha on rhythm, Nandinho Lobato Faria on bass.

Farewell to my first real girlfriend

Leaving for Bombay, for the unknown, for the bright lights of the big bad city of India, going into a mysterious future, was very exciting, of course. But at that time I had my first steady girlfriend in Goa. She was the first girl I 'went public' with – no more hiding and entering cinema halls incognito, for example. Even though we normally went out with our group of friends, the two of us danced cheek to cheek at public functions, we went out for drives together, and the whole of Panjim knew we were going steady. And you guessed it, she was a couple of years older than me. But again, with her, what I now call my 'Mother Mary Complex' still persisted, and that's how I treated her: with affection and love, but no sex.

Perhaps that's what made me do what I did at my birthday party that summer, about a month before leaving for Bombay. After my girlfriend went home, I danced with the Bombay girl from the Calangute Beach bushes; she had come back to Goa this summer too. You can be sure she was no Mother Mary to me. Ours was a sizzling chemical and physical relationship which burned like a devastating flame, destroying all semblance of reason and loyalty along its path, and by the end of the dance I was ready to ask her to come for a drive with me. We went and parked on the deserted roads of La Marvel Colony in Dona Paula which had no constructions yet, and there I had my first hardcore sexual experience. No, far from all the way yet, but the furthest I had been.

When, after unbuttoning her blouse fully, I was struggling and unable to open the first bra I was confronting in my life, she reached behind herself and unclasped it for me. I can't explain how exciting that was. To most girls from Goa, at least the ones I had hitherto known, being sexy and sexual meant 'allowing' a guy to do things to them; they hardly ever took matters into their hands. But this girl opening her own bra was such an honest declaration that she wanted to offer her gifts to me, it was the most erotic thing ever to happen in my life until then, though that record was about to be broken less than half an hour later. For now, seeing and feeling the first pair of naked breasts took all my attention, all my consciousness, and all my oxygen. I was in a place which was surely beyond heaven, because I couldn't imagine naked breasts in heaven.

The record for 'the most erotic moment ever' was broken when she unbuttoned and opened my trousers. Never ever before had I been touched. If I was beyond heaven earlier, I didn't even know where I was now.

The next morning I remember feeling happy and proud at finding burning nail marks on myself, because they proved that it hadn't all been a dream.

A friend later described such experiences as being 'A to Y'. Z would come later.

Somehow I could not live with this unfaithfulness I had committed towards my girlfriend. Besides, I was going to Bombay for five years, and was sure I would see this girl there again. And I was going into a co-ed college after a boys-only school, and I was sure I'd meet girls there too. So I did the only noble thing I could think of. I broke off with my girlfriend in the friendliest way possible, setting her and myself free. We're good friends still.

Changing the rules of Bombay University

An unexpected problem cropped up at the last minute. The architecture college could not accept me, as I had not taken Hindi in my SSC exams as required by Bombay University. Of course due to India's disjointed system, the university had not taken into account that they themselves had exempted students in Goa from taking Hindi that year, and refused to budge and accept their own conflicting rules.

Father to the rescue. His old friend, Olympio Rodrigues, was a senior professor in Bombay University. After a few urgent telephonic conferences (one had to book a trunk call and wait for an hour or so before one got through from Panjim to Bombay), Father left for Bombay armed with the required documents and certificates. With Professor Rodrigues's help, he shook the staid old university's foundations, and finally managed to change the rule for Goan students and procure an exemption for me just in time. And, thanks to him, a few more Goan students besides me who had passed the SSC without Hindi managed to join courses in Bombay University that year.

And so, one emotional morning in June 1971, I left for Bombay with Mother, who was going to see me settled in there.

I was leaving my beloved Goa behind. I was leaving all my friends behind. I was leaving my car behind. I would have to travel by the infamously overcrowded Bombay B.E.S.T. buses and local trains now; how I wished I could take along my red beauty. And let's not even talk about leaving my parents and little sister behind. We were a very small family, and a very

The Goa airport, as built by the Portuguese, from which I left for Bombay with Mother in 1971.

close-knit one. It was very brave of my parents to 'let their only son go', but I am eternally grateful they did. At home I had not even learnt how to make my own bed, how to make a cup of tea, or how to boil an egg. And, if I'd stayed on in Goa, that's the way I would be when I married, like most guys in Goa, in fact in India.

Bombay forged and toughened me. And prepared me for what was to come after those five years.

PART II

BOMBAY AND EUROPE

7

Bombay City!

The first days of architecture college

I walked into the empty first-year classroom. I'd never been in a classroom this big; it was built like an amphitheatre. I was a front-bencher in Don Bosco, but here I chose a row somewhere in the middle and settled down. Minutes later a second student walked in; he was fair-complexioned, had an impressive nose, curly hair, and was jovial and friendly. 'Hi!' he said with a huge smile, and settled in a row in front of me. Turning around, he started a conversation.

'Where are you from?'

'Goa.'

'Oh, so you're a Macapao!'

I was bewildered.

'I'm not a Macapao. What's a Macapao?'

'Yes you are. People from Goa are Macapaos. People from Gujarat are Gujjus. People from Punjab are Punjus. Muslims are Miyas. Sikhs are Surds. I'm a Parsi, so I'm a Bawa. Hi again! Rohinton Balsara.' He extended his hand, rattling on merrily, giving me my first lesson in Bombay ethnography.

Mother had dropped me to college that morning, and she would return to Goa later that afternoon. Our farewell in the campus reminded me of my first days of school, except that I wasn't going to see her when I returned home that evening. In fact I wasn't going to see her for months. And, however excited I might have been to start this long-awaited course, and at the prospect of the freedom that Bombay promised, that goodbye choked me up.

After Mother left I walked around the huge campus, which housed not just the architecture but also the commercial arts and the fine arts schools. Majestic ancient trees, open grounds with natural unkempt lawns and beautiful old grey stone buildings from the British days made it a haven of peace in one of the busiest areas of Bombay, right between Crawford Market and Victoria Terminus (VT for short).

A walk around the Sir J.J. College of Architecture campus.

As I walked back towards my building, a boy who appeared to be my age collapsed on the ground near the entrance, frothing at the mouth, his whole body convulsing. I'd never seen something like this before, and before I could even react, a couple who appeared to be his parents rushed up. I thought they would pick him up and carry him to a hospital – but they put a leather slipper into his mouth instead. This was becoming more and more surreal. I learnt later that the boy was a fresher like me, my classmate-to-be, and that we were to insert a leather slipper between his teeth if and when a seizure like this recurred. The slipper prevented him from biting his own tongue right off.

I don't remember his name, but I can still see his perennially sad, serious face. He was a loner, and always seemed to have something pessimistic to say about everything.

After two or three days we were all itching for the first lecture in Design – that was the raison d'être of architecture, and we Frank Lloyd Wrights-to-be were impatient to show off our skills and imagination in the very first project.

The great day arrived; we sauntered into the big design hall with its huge metal desks and slanting wooden drawing boards, fixed our drafting sheets on to them with clips or pins, and, our brand-new T-squares quivering, awaited our first assignment. Would it be a fancy bungalow? Or an auditorium, or an office/apartment building?

The professor walked in, and asked us to design – a bus stop. *A bus stop?!* What did he think we had signed up for, the Bombay Municipality?! We were here to revolutionize the world! And, unwilling to let go of the great fire with which we had marched into the design hall, each of us designed the fanciest bus stop the world had never known, made out of reinforced concrete combined with bricks, wood, glass and stainless steel, some with domed roofs, some with cantilevered roofs protruding every which way … only to get big fat zeroes at the end.

And that was our first hard lesson: that the main requirement of a structure was utility, not fancy shapes and looks. And that an equally important aspect to be taken into account was its cost.

Love Lane, Mazagon

Father had already sought out three young men from Panjim who were studying architecture at the J.J. College. They were in their fourth year, with one more year to go. They were renting and sharing an ancient apartment in Mazagon, just bordering Byculla, on a street called Love Lane – a misnomer if ever there was one. During the monsoon the lane flooded, and we had to wade through black murky water, with unidentified floating objects coming at us – dead or swimming rats, or worse? At the beginning of the lane was the Byculla police station, and if we walked by at night we sometimes heard horrible screams emanating from there. I recently read *Byculla to Bangkok*, a book about the 1970s mafia dons and gangs of Bombay, by S. Hussain Zaidi. And I was amazed to discover what had transpired almost in our neighbourhood – gang wars, knifings, shootings, bombings and murders. Thank goodness we had remained blissfully ignorant about it all. Love Lane indeed.

Yes, the Goan students had place for one more. And that's how I met Fernando Ribeiro (the tallest and leanest of all, nicknamed Pinum), Roque Godinho (the joker and prankster who loved playing matka, nicknamed Babush), and Agnelo Martins. This last was the oldest, as he had completed the full seven-year course in the Portuguese Liceu in Goa before opting for architecture. He was also the wisest, and was going to influence me very significantly.

They knew all about me as a musician in Goa, but that didn't stop them from ragging me when they saw I didn't know how to make my bed or a cup of tea the first morning. But it was all good-natured, and they were great teachers of all such essential survival tactics of life.

When they had accepted me as a flatmate they had expected many musical evenings, including guitar lessons, and when they learnt I had hung up my guitar for five years, they were dumbfounded and disappointed – but they deemed my resolution wise.

Never having been to a boarding school, this was the first time I was sharing a roof with strangers, though they soon became close friends. More importantly, this was the first time I was living without a house help.

Agnelo Martins

One evening when we were chatting about Goa, talk turned to the latest escapade of a famous 'adventurer' from Panjim. About a year earlier, after a night of drinking, he had crashed his car into a lamp post while driving on the wide deserted Campal avenue. He told everyone at his habitual tavern the next evening, 'Of course I saw the lamp post. I said, *"Ó poste, afaste-se! Ó poste, afaste-se!"* (Lamp post, move! Lamp post, move!), but the bastard didn't move.' He was the only son from a rich and respected old Panjim family, but he notoriously drank every night (and every day) with people from all walks of life, mainly those way below his family's social and financial status. Heartbroken and unable to put up with the sheer hell he created at home, his family had purchased him an apartment. There, he had started living in with the young woman they had hired as his maid.

This evening we were discussing his latest exploit. After a whole day of drinking in Goa he had decided to drive to Bombay, to carry on partying with friends in the city. On the Western Ghats (or Sahyadri mountains) he had driven off the road, and was found in the morning fast asleep in his car which was hanging from a tree. In the course of our chatter I happened to say, 'What a pity he turned out this way, coming as he does from such a good family,' which was something everyone in Panjim said about him.

Agnelo didn't quite snap at me, but in a good-natured but firm way, he asked, 'And what is a good family?'

Taken aback, I tried to explain the obvious. 'Well, you know, it's an old family, they are well known, well respected, they live in a huge beautiful ancestral house…' I was finding myself at a loss for words. I couldn't bring myself to say that they were rich, and I was beginning to see what Agnelo was getting at.

'And does that make them good?' insisted Agnelo quietly.

I kept silent, and for the first time in my seventeen-year-long life, I pondered a very common and widely used expression: *ele vem de boas famílias,* he comes from a good family. And I realized it all finally depended upon caste and wealth, and to a great extent, external behaviour and etiquette. Did all that really make them *good* people?

I noticed that although Agnelo seemed like a lazy guy who spent time lying in bed reading newspapers and novels instead of working, Pinum and Babush often turned to him for help and guidance in studies. After the seventh year of Liceu, architectural mathematics, Calculus, Physics, Chemistry and structural design were a cinch to him. And soon I noticed that his other classmates from college would turn up at our apartment for his help too. Helping others seemed to be Agnelo's purpose in life.

However comfortable he might seem in bed, he would immediately jump up and explain the most complex and difficult problems when asked.

I never ever heard Agnelo speak ill of anyone. Not once. In all areas, I was slowly discovering that he was one of the most morally upright persons I knew. And yet, Agnelo was the first Christian I met who didn't go to church. He never talked about it, he never tried to influence others, and he never ever made fun of churchgoers such as the rest of us. I myself was reaching an age when I started questioning my youthful beliefs, and was coming to the conclusion that god was way beyond man-made religions. And though I loved Jesus and all he stood for, my belief in the church itself was all but dead.

But on that first Sunday when I did not attend Mass, I half-expected the ground under my feet to open up and swallow me into a fiery pit before the midnight hour struck. Years of conditioning and superstition don't let go of you overnight. But midnight came and went, and the next morning I did wake up alive. And in the best of health and spirits as ever.

When I visited Agnelo's house in Panjim, I realized that he came from a very tiny and humble home, but that he had good friends from among some of Goa's best-known families – I had learnt from him not to call them 'good' families – who all treated him with the utmost respect and affection. He had lost his father, but was brought up by a mother, now aged, who never came out and met people. Perhaps it was his own humble roots which made him clearly see the difference between a 'good' family and a 'rich' family.

He never married. I had seen with my own eyes what a genius he was in architecture. And I know that if he had had the desire and the gift of the gab, he could have been one of the top architects in Goa. But he had neither, and he died prematurely, not too differently from the way he lived: quietly, self-effacingly, unsung by the public in general, but deeply mourned by his good and true friends from all walks of life.

It was years later that I realized that Agnelo Martins had been one of the informal teachers life had brought into my path. I was asked to speak a few words in church at his funeral (whether as per his wishes or not, he was buried in a church he didn't attend or believe in). From what I spoke,

I remember having named him one of my gurus. Later, after the priest had recited the last rites over his grave in the cemetery, he made it a point to come up to me and ask, with ill-concealed sarcasm and censure, 'So Agnelo was your guru, was he?' He certainly knew Agnelo was an agnostic who did not attend church. 'Yes, he was,' I answered proudly.

The Savages

During the five years when I studied architecture in Bombay, I lived in eight different places. The first few days, before I moved to Love Lane, were spent at my Tio Armando and Tia Mariazita's (Mother's brother and sister-in-law's) apartment in Dadar. They had two sons, Roy who was quite a few years older to me, and Rex who was just a year older and my favourite of all my cousins – the guy who introduced me to the girl in the Calangute sand dunes, remember?

Now I usually spent weekends at their place. On the very second or third weekend, Rex took me along to a friend's birthday party. A guitar was brought out, and someone asked me to sing and play. I probably sang a composition of mine, and on request, sang a couple more, surely a Portuguese song thrown in as well.

A dandy young man came up and said, 'Hi! I'm Russell Pereira.'

'He's the lead singer of The Savages,' Rex introduced him. I was dumbstruck. Out of all the records we grooved to at our parties in Goa, there were two by Indian bands: the romantic 'Love is a Mango' by The Cavaliers from Calcutta, and the highly danceable 'Simple Simon Says' by The Savages from Bombay. The very fact that they made records put them right up there in Heaven, seated at the right hand of God the Father, totally unreachable to us mere mortals. And now here was a real live Savage, standing in front of me, extending his hand to me.

Russell continued, 'I'm not with The Savages any more, I've just left them to join a dance and wedding band – I needed a steady income, man. I loved your singing and your acoustic guitar-plucking just now. And Rex says you're the hottest electric lead guitarist in Goa. The Savages' lead guitarist

Hemant Rao has left for the Gulf, and they're looking for a replacement, and I'm sure would prefer someone who plays lead as well as sings. Why don't you audition?'

Me, audition for The Savages?! I must be dreaming! But as it happened, Rex knew Ralph, their bass guitarist who also lived in Dadar, and spoke to him about me. 'Sure, bring him over to Prabhakar's house next week; we're rehearsing there and would be happy to audition him. He can play Prab's guitar if he doesn't have his own here in Bombay,' Ralph said.

On the appointed day there I was, feeling pretty nervous about meeting them all after seeing them on album covers and magazines: Bashir Sheikh the drummer and leader with his drooping moustache and drooping eyelids, Prabhakar Mundkur the square-faced bespectacled organist, and Ralph Paes the tall and angular bassist.

Friendly introductions done, we got down to business. 'Ok, let's start with a song we all know; how about "Suzie Q"?' asked Bashir. 'It's on "E"', said Ralph. 'Which chord is "E"?' asked I, and they all gaped at me.

That was in 1970. Today, exactly fifty years later, I spoke to Ralph in order to refresh my memory about that first day, and he said, 'We were shocked you didn't know the names of chords and keys, but soon realized that you were a natural who could play any song on any key. And that you didn't know the names of chords in English because you knew them in Portuguese.'

As indeed I did. I must have played and sung ok, because by the end of that evening I was officially welcomed into the band as one of The Savages.

I didn't walk home from the audition, I floated. I didn't sleep all night, and I rushed to the post office first thing next morning. My five-year resolution totally forgotten, I telegraphed Father: 'JOINING SAVAGES STOP PLEASE SEND ELECTRIC GUITAR URGENTLY STOP LOVE REMO.'

Father called, and after a long conversation where I explained to him what and who The Savages were, and how much this meant to me, and after a solemn promise that I would not allow the playing to interfere with my studies, he agreed. And a few days later my beautiful Höfner guitar was once again in my hands.

Armed with it I marched straight to my first rehearsal with The Savages, which was at Bashir's residence in Mazagon – which, as luck would have it, was just a few minutes away from where I was living in Love Lane. They played on three brilliant amplifiers built by Bashir's nephew Fazal, and six square cabinets containing a twelve-inch JBL speaker each – the sound was powerful, deep and clear. Ralph says he played on that same superb home-built amplifier for years on end.

My first record!

Soon, news came that we were expected to cut a record with Polydor. I was going to be on a record, that prestigious, priceless piece of vinyl! But the news got better. Out of the four songs, two were to be our original compositions, and the two selected were my latest ones, recently written in Bombay: 'Ode to the Messiah', reflecting my recent inner conflict with religion, and 'The Girl with Kaleidoscope Eyes', the latter obviously a take on The Beatles' 'Lucy in the Sky with Diamonds', but far from a copy. Being my compositions, these would obviously be sung by me. And though that seemed impossible, the news got better still: out of the remaining two tracks which were decided by Polydor, one was 'Julie, Do You Love Me', to be sung by Bashir; and I was to sing the title track of the record, 'Old Turkey Buzzard'! The film *McKenna's Gold* had just been released in India. The song 'Old Turkey Buzzard' sung in it by Jose Feliciano was a big hit, but Polydor couldn't release the original here due to Indian copyright or foreign exchange restrictions of some sort. Indian artists were sometimes asked to record covers of such problematic songs locally, and The Savages were asked to record this one, just as they had been assigned to record 'Simple Simon Says'.

On the much-awaited day we walked excitedly into the recording studio assigned to us. The recording engineer was a middle-aged white-haired gentleman in a dhoti and kurta who looked at our electric instruments and amplifiers with suspicion, exuding a great disappointment that they were not sitars, harmoniums and tablas. He looked at our long hair and tight jeans and love beads with even more distaste, and not even Bashir's diplomatic sweet talk in chaste, respectful Hindi laced with Urdu could erase one line from his frown.

He placed one huge ancient microphone to record both the bass and the full drum set. Another similar one for both my lead guitar and Prabhakar's organ. And whoever sang the song got one dedicated mic for voice. All in the same huge room.

When we marched into the recording cabin and tried to tell him that the drum set alone required not one but several mics, and each of the other instruments at least one mic each, he lost his temper.

'I have been recording Shankar–Jaikishan for twenty-five years, and you youngsters are trying to teach me my job?!' he yelled, spitting out his paan accurately into his personal spittoon next to the mixer.

No amount of coaxing that Shankar–Jaikishan's was Bollywood film music (then famous for its strident, tinny sound and loud distorting volume, not its recording quality), and that ours was Western-style rock music requiring different recording techniques, could make him budge.

We resignedly let him record our four songs. The record sounded so bad, I broke my copy when I went to Goa, before I could even play it for my friends, which I had so eagerly and proudly looked forward to doing.

Recently a Savage ex-bandmate sent me MP3s of that recording, and I can stand it even less today than I could then. Today even home recordings on a phone sound a hundred times better. On writing this passage I've re-recorded 'Ode to the Messiah' in my studio, for the sheer pleasure of listening to it as it ought to be.

Boom Shambu!

I was highly attracted to the hippie scene (music, art, thought, philosophy, dress, sexual freedom, etc.), and after that first hearing of *Sgt. Pepper's* I was fascinated with marijuana and hashish. At the time, I justified myself by saying that they were totally natural substances which had been smoked by our holy men, rishis and sadhus for thousands of years. We weren't calling them drug addicts, were we now? Drugs were chemicals, created in laboratories, they were hallucinogenic, highly addictive, and could cause great harm and even death in excessive quantities. Meanwhile the world today has begun to legalize marijuana. Lecture over.

In Bombay, where hashish was available freely (albeit not officially) and cheaply at every street corner, I had all the freedom in the world to indulge. I will never say that 'company' led me to it; it was I who sought like-minded company and, out of the hundreds of students of architecture (all of whom I considered 'straight' and unexciting), I found a handful who shared my tastes. Most of these guys were staying in the college hostel.

Me in the room of one of the hostels in which I stayed while studying architecture, clicked by Poony, my Thai classmate, a photography aficionado (right).

The authorities concerned, in all their wisdom, had built our hostel in the other end of the city – the college as I explained was near VT, and the hostel in Bandra East, then a foul-smelling swamp infested with mosquitoes, with hardly any construction on it yet. Its location caused the hostelites the untold hardship of travelling for hours every day in crowded buses and trains, and of exposing themselves to malaria and every other mosquito-borne disease.

The complaint in the all-male hostel was that you couldn't take a pee without getting a mosquito bite on your pee-wee.

All this notwithstanding, when my three wholesome Goan mates completed the course a year later and returned to Goa, the prospect of the company of my new like-minded friends enticed me to move into this hostel-in-the-swamp.

I moved into the room of one of my best friends in college, who was a foreign student called Poonsak Hotrapavanon, or Poony for short, from Bangkok, Thailand. He happened to own the first stereo set I had ever heard, an unthinkable luxury in a student's hostel room. And he had albums like James Taylor's *Mud Slide Slim and the Blue Horizon*. Ah, the clarity and sound quality of that stereo! I'd never heard acoustic guitars sound so good. And that guitar picking was right up my alley.

And then he went and bought *Jesus Christ Superstar*. It was another game changer in my life. If Agnelo had confirmed my belief that churchgoing was redundant, this album made me see Jesus very differently – as a man, and a most misunderstood one at that. We listened to the brilliant rock opera until all hours of the night, with lights dimmed and candles burning. Who knew that, decades later, I would receive indirect praise from Sir Tim Rice himself.

Breaking the news at home

Besides rushing to Goa for the big holidays, I would also make use of every long weekend to grab the boat or bus home, and add a couple of extra holidays of my own to extend my stay as much as possible.

The delicate matter of me not going to church any more had to be brought up with my parents on the next Sunday home. One great thing about our relationship was that I never hid anything from them. We sat and thrashed out all issues head-on, whether it be religion and rituals, social matters, my long hair and beard and clothes, male–female relationships and freedoms, whatever. This sometimes gave rise to heated arguments and raised voices – like it did this time – but it kept us firmly in communication and together. I knew friends who didn't go to church, but told their parents they did, and headed for the movies on the quiet instead. In my opinion, a certain vital link to their parents was broken.

However drastically my views may have differed from my parents', and however rigidly they might have been preconditioned to theirs since generations, in the end they very often saw things my way. They had simply never questioned their beliefs, and when I questioned them and argued their answers, they often accepted that they had no logical explanations or reasons.

But the fact that my parents always knew what I was thinking, and in which direction I was growing or going, kept us firmly together. And I am eternally grateful to them for having had an exceptionally broad mind at a time when most parents in India simply dictated 'You will do so because I say so'. I know many who do still.

The first time

There was a groovy girl from Nagaland in my class. She was hip, wore cool clothes, and shared all of my tastes and beliefs. She was very talkative and full of life, and this quiet guy and she hit it off famously from day one. We hung out and went out in a group to movies and restaurants with common friends, and soon we were a couple. My hair slowly grew to shoulder length, I had a beard to be reckoned with, wore kurtas and loose trousers, blue round sunglasses and beads around my neck, and carried an embroidered cloth bag slung across my shoulders in which I had everything from architecture books to smoking paraphernalia. She was petite, wore glasses with octagonal frames and brown lenses, and dressed practically in the same style as me, cloth shoulder bag and all – except that her clothes were much tighter, accentuating her beautiful figure. As we all know, North-Eastern people have lovely East Asian features, and this prompted friends to sometimes call the two of us John and Yoko – which I must confess tickled and pleased us not a little.

After we'd got to know each other better we discovered that we were both virgins, and decided it was time to set that right. But she lived in an all-female hostel, and I in an all-male one. No members of the opposite sex were allowed into either. So *where* to do it was the question.

A friend in the know told me about a shady hotel on Colaba Causeway which rented out rooms by the hour. It was aptly called '007 James Bond'. After discussing the pros and cons of going to such an establishment, we unanimously agreed that it was the only solution open to us. While she waited nearby, I ventured up the rickety wooden staircase to the hotel reception on the first floor. I felt awkward asking for a room for three hours, but the blasé and bored receptionist rattled off the rate, took the money, gave me the key, and returned to his matka calculations. I went back downstairs to fetch her and, moving as stealthily as two undercover agents of whom Ian Fleming would have been proud, we hurried into our room and locked the door.

Despite both of us being architecture students, we somehow simply couldn't get our foundations and elevations in sync, though both of our young bodies and minds were every bit as ready and willing and able as required. We spent three very pleasant hours trying, though, but walked out of '007' as virginal as ever.

A week later we were visiting a friend who happened to tell us how her Alsatian had mated with her Pomeranian. My girlfriend and I stared at each other in silence. 'An Alsatian and a Pomeranian could do it, but we couldn't?!'

The next weekend we marched back to 'James Bond' with renewed resolve.

And this time we discovered why the universe had placed us on this earth.

Woodstock, Blow Up and another war

I did quite a lot of gigs with The Savages, but some stand out more than others in my memory. *Woodstock* the movie had finally hit Bombay at Eros theatre which was within walking distance from J.J. College, and I saw it almost every day of its run. Those were the days before TV, and before any foreign bands had performed in the new socialist India. We had heard the music, but never seen these artists perform it, not even on screen; we just didn't know what they were like on stage. Seeing so many of the world's best in one long film was a revelation beyond description. The things they did! Besides performing that amazing music impeccably, they moved and projected an energy, emotion and showmanship of a kind I'd never seen before. Ten Years After, Santana, The Who, Joe Cocker & The Grease Band, Sly and the Family Stone … they all drove me dizzy one after the other. Crosby, Stills, Nash and Young with their acoustic guitars and harmonies floored me completely. And so did solo artists like Richie Havens, Joan Baez, Country Joe McDonald. And an equally important 'performance' was being lived out by the audience itself. The love, the peace, the clothes (or lack of them), the brotherhood in the face of the storm, the interviews, that nun showing the peace sign – all these were precious food and drink for a youth hungry and thirsty for that culture.

But for us Indians, 'going abroad' was almost as impossible as going to the moon. A passport took years to be issued, if at all, foreign exchange allowance was a meagre $100 after much official rigmarole, air tickets prohibitively expensive, and visas almost impossible to obtain on a $100 allowance. So those of us who liked Western culture lived in a make-believe, substitute, parallel world which existed mostly in our minds.

The Savages were asked to perform before a special showing of *Woodstock* at the Eros theatre. Cool t-shirts were unheard of in India, but my flatmate Pinum had painted a peace sign on a white-sleeved banyan, and he generously lent it to me for that day.

Lined up in front of the movie screen, we performed for a hall full of youngsters who, just like us, were living this parallel life in a parallel make-believe world. We were Santana while we performed 'Soul Sacrifice', we were Richie Havens while performing 'Freedom', we were whoever we wished to be. And the audience was not in Eros theatre, Bombay, but on Max Yasgur's farm, in Bethel, New York. The air in the theatre was sweet and heavy with hashish, people were dancing in the aisles and on their seats, and though no girls took off a single piece of their clothing, some guys took off their shirts and carried their girls on their shoulders. This remains among my most memorable gigs with The Savages.

The Savages: Remo, lead guitar and vocals; Ralph Paes, bass; Bashir Sheikh, drums; Prabhakar, organ.

We also took up month-long (or longer) contracts at happening joints in the city, such as the discotheques Blow Up at the Taj Mahal Hotel at Gateway and Hell in Hotel Hilltop in Worli. These, although exciting in the beginning, were starting to turn into routine. And they were beginning to affect my college life. We usually performed until about 1 a.m., and by the time I got to bed it was usually at least 3 a.m. Which made it very difficult, if not impossible, to attend college the next morning. And I was approaching the third year, when the course started getting tougher.

One of the last long-term contracts we took up was at Talk of the Town at Marine Lines. We had performed there on Sunday afternoons for a while, but now we were performing nightly. Usha Iyer (now Uthup) and Ajit Singh, excellent singers of cover versions, performed there too. Christmas was approaching, and this year, for the first time in my life, I was to spend it away from home, stuck in Bombay due to this commitment – a most depressing thought.

One night that December as we walked out into the street after our gig, we heard sirens cutting through the air, searchlights scanning the black skies, tiny black shapes of Pakistani bombers, and anti-aircraft mortar shells exploding. I wasn't overly scared, as the bombers couldn't descend to the height required to drop their bombs, thanks to the city's defences which were very much in place. But that experience left me feeling even more depressed and melancholic, and drove home the question: 'What the hell am I doing here instead of in Goa?!'

The next day I explained my position to The Savages. Bashir was obviously unhappy about it, but eventually they all understood the attachment I had for my family, for Goa, and for my friends there. And so I packed my bag, was back in peaceful Goa for Christmas and the New Year, and The Savages found a substitute for the duration.

Going solo and sitar on guitar

By that time I had started writing a lot of solo songs, accompanying myself on the acoustic guitar. My new acoustic was a superb twelve-string built by the budding Bombay luthier from Thane, Peter Pereira. One needed to wait for months after ordering one of this guitars. My friend Darryl Mendonsa had just received his, and when I heard and played his guitar it was another 'love-at-first-sight' experience, and I was never able to resist those. Through gentle but persistent persuasion, I managed to coax and bully Darryl into selling me his, and into waiting a few months more for a new one for himself. Being the gentle and friendly soul he was and still is, Darryl acquiesced. I felt embarrassed and guilty at having got that guitar out of him that way, and fifty years later I sent him an apology. But just as I knew he would, he smiled and said there was nothing for me to apologize for.

Writing a song in the hostel, clicked by Poony.

By that time the acoustic folk musicians from America and England like James Taylor, CSNY, Cat Stevens, and balladeers like John Phillips were beginning to appeal to me more than heavy bands like Black Sabbath and Deep Purple, though I enjoyed these too.

Woodstock the film had marked me very deeply, and Joe Cocker's 'With a Little Help from My Friends' in more ways than one. I had never heard a Beatles' cover I had liked (how dare anyone mess with perfection!), but I adored this one. Rather than merely copying it, though, it made me feel like looking deeply into my roots and composing an Indian version of the song. So one day as I sat in my hostel room with my guitar, I started experimenting with the tuning, trying to make it sound like a sitar or sarod. Of course I had not studied any music at all, least of all Indian, but I instinctively knew that I wanted to avoid a third note which would determine and restrict the tuning to a major or a minor key. Now my two-note twelve-string guitar sounded very Indian, and I started developing a way of bending the strings which made it sound more sitar-like. And I inserted Indian-stylized vocals of 'With a Little Help from My Friends' in the middle of it all.

I was gaining quite a reputation in the college and university circuit as a solo singer/songwriter, perhaps because I was almost exclusively doing my originals, and not trying to be an 'Indian Bob Dylan' or an 'Indian Joan Baez', while most local singers took pride in being tagged as such bootleggers. Except for a very few like Ronnie Desai, who spoke in his unadulterated Bombay accent and wrote hilarious spoofs about everything; and Ronnie Mistry, who wrote at least one very beautiful and memorable love song called 'Little Girl' for his petite girlfriend. I was being invited to perform at almost every college social and concert (I think all those gigs paid nothing, perhaps just taxi fare, but as a non-professional amateur student it was a thrill performing). My new guitar–sitar composition was bringing the house down, especially as it accelerated up to dizzying speeds towards the end. No one I knew of had attempted, or thought of attempting, making a guitar sound like a sitar before. And that 'wannabe American' streak in the Bombay youth, which I've spoken about earlier, was finding an Indian voice and a reason for Indian pride here.

I couldn't help thinking at the time, and I think still, that if I'd managed to go to Europe or the US with that guitar–sitar composition of mine in the '70s, I might have hit the international scene big time. The West was crazy for all things Indian then, and like I said earlier, something like that had never been attempted or thought of in the folk/rock genre I belonged to, or in any genre for that matter. (A few years later John McLaughlin did, in fusion/jazz style.) Talk about being in the wrong country at the wrong time.

Shiraz Rahimtoola

A burly young student approached me after one such gig, and besides saying how much he'd enjoyed my playing and singing, invited me to perform at some important event at his college, St. Xavier's, then perhaps the most happening college in Bombay. He was the president or secretary of some art-related youth organization there. His name was Shiraz Rahimtoola. Not just a great talker, he was an efficient doer too. We became friends, hung out together, and he offered to be my manager. As I've said, I earned nothing from these gigs, so our arrangement could not have been commercial or financial at all, as any percentage of zero is still zero. He wanted to do it for the same reason that I was performing: out of passion. And it felt great having him in charge.

Shiraz was like an efficient bulldozer who ran his way through Indian inefficiency and lethargy and got things done from gig organizers. I was a very bad talker, even on stage, at that time: I just took my guitar and sat on a chair or stool and played and sang my songs. No showmanship, no stage chatter. You had to appreciate my music for itself, I would never talk you into it. Off-stage I was equally quiet. If you didn't see my worth that was your problem, not mine. Quite a bit of that attitude still resides in me. But that's where Shiraz completed and complemented me.

And he was protective as hell. My girlfriend and I felt safe with him taking us around for shows within and outside Bombay, and the three of us hit it off famously, sharing smokes and jokes and chatter. And, just as I did in Goa right since school, he had his own car in college, a Fiat gifted by his mother who was a successful lawyer. He was going to study to be a lawyer too.

When the time came, Shiraz came along with me, in the capacity of 'manager', to speak to The Savages about me leaving the band and going on a solo career – if you can call an unpaid passion a career at all. I loved playing with The Savages, but playing solo would not affect my college and studies. I wouldn't have to spend evenings at rehearsals, wouldn't take up long-term contracts which required late nights, and, most importantly, would not take up anything at all which might come in between me and my frequent trips to Goa. I could, in short, be my own boss.

Shiraz's and mine was a youthful students' friendship and association, and we gradually lost touch after we both finished college. I wish he were my manager and/or agent today, a de facto one with a proper percentage of high fees. I feel we could have scaled great heights together.

The flute

My Naga girlfriend lived in the Government Girls' Hostel on Marine Drive, right next to the Taraporewala Aquarium (it's amazing how all these names flood back). Her hostel had stricter visiting hours than mine, and once when I went there too early I was told to come back in an hour. So I decided to spend the hour at the Chowpatti Beach nearby.

Among the vendors of balloons, children's toys and so on at the entrance to the beach, I saw a flute seller, with flutes sticking out like little branches from a long stick he held upright. I had fallen in love with the sound of the instrument from hearing records by Traffic, Blood Sweat & Tears, and of course the daddy of them all, Ian Anderson of Jethro Tull. And with our own Indian classical flute played by Pannalal Ghosh. I'd never thought of playing the instrument myself, but ... why not try it out for fun? I paid a rupee for a flute and decided to pass the time discovering it from scratch, sitting in front of the sea. Half an hour later as I was walking back to the hostel I stopped at the vendor's and told him it played wrong notes, could I have a better one? He gave me a curious look and said, 'Wah wah, just now you couldn't even blow a sound out of it.' He had sold me one of the toy flutes meant for children. Now he reached into a bag he kept on the ground, where he had his 'serious' instruments. He selected one and handed it to me, without charging me extra for the exchange.

And that is how my lifelong love affair with the flute began. I felt it complemented the guitar perfectly. If I saw the guitar as male, the flute was the female that completed it. Much easier to carry than a guitar, it became a permanent addition to my cloth bag, whether I was going to college or elsewhere.

Eric and Hubert

One evening in Panjim, my friends and I ran out of hashish. So we drove to Calangute Beach hoping to pick up some. We couldn't find any, so we settled in a restaurant for dinner, my faithful guitar leaning at my side.

A very long-haired Indian-looking guy with a foreign accent came up and asked if he could borrow and play my guitar. I said sure, and asked if he had something to smoke. He said sure, and invited us all to the room he had rented in a fisherman's house on the beach. There, after a smoke, he asked me to play something. And after that he played something. And we kept alternating songs. And after each one he kept asking me a question about myself, such as 'What was your first instrument?', 'When did you first start playing the guitar?' and so on. And his remark to every answer of mine was 'You too? Me too!' in his funny accent with the soft t's. We had so much in common, we could not believe it.

Except that he was a classical guitarist, and I didn't even know that a method for playing classical music on the guitar existed; it totally fascinated me. It turned out he was French, lived in Paris and, together with his Parisian buddy Hubert, had hitch-hiked all the way from Paris to Goa. I had hardly noticed Hubert, because both Eric and I had eyes and ears only for each other's guitaring. We spent the whole night playing. Right until sunrise. Playing, smoking, and going 'You too? Me too!'

I don't remember meeting them again in Goa, but they gave me their address in Bombay, where they were going soon; it was Sheel Hotel, and as luck would have it, it was right next to VT, walking distance from my college.

We met again in Bombay as soon as I returned there – and again and again and again. Every day. It was a tiny, cheap hotel, but in their room I discovered the magic of Bach, Beethoven and Villa-Lobos being played on the guitar.

Eric turned out to be Indian-looking because he was from Réunion Island, France's ex-colony near Madagascar, where four races lived, thrived and mixed: African, Indian, Chinese and European. He told me how it was not uncommon to see families where each member was of a different colour walking down the street in Réunion. Hubert was a proper white, blond Frenchman from Paris. He let out many years later that his parents were rich aristocrats with whom he did not see eye to eye.

Listening to the classical guitar, I felt as though I had been totally ignorant of my instrument until then. I was fascinated by the fact that all five fingers of the right hand were used to pluck out the melody, the bass and the accompaniment simultaneously. Without knowing how to read music, I learnt to play quite a few pieces from Eric, mainly by Villa-Lobos, but also the simpler Bach 'Minuet' which I loved, and the 'anthem' of every French classical guitarist, 'Jeux Interdits'. I just knew my father was going to love this stuff.

I'd forgotten that Eric and I had performed on stage somewhere, probably at some college concert. He played a classical piece, while I improvised on the flute over it. The photographer certainly clicked this from the wrong side if one wants to see Eric's face – but it's the only photograph I seem to have of his in India.

One day I declared to Eric and Hubert that I was going to totally give up my kind of music and become a classical guitar player exclusively. Eric was happy and proud, but Hubert was not. 'You are going to totally give up this very unique style of playing which you have developed on your own?' he asked. 'You pluck with only your thumb and your index, but I've never heard someone do what you do with those two. You play melodies, bass and accompaniments too.

In France and in Europe there are plenty of classical guitarists, all playing the same pieces the same way, but I've never seen someone who plays like you.' I tacitly saw sense in what he said, and at least temporarily gave up giving up my style. I continued learning as many classical pieces from Eric as possible, though.

The more I got to know quiet Hubert, whom I had almost totally bypassed until now, the more I realized how much I had in common with him too. He loved drawing in a surrealistic style, just as I did, and loved writing poetry and prose, just as I did. We now spent many hours talking and showing each other our drawings and writings. He was a very sensitive and almost shy kind of guy, while Eric was always self-assured and earthy.

At that time, adults in Goa (and we youngsters too) thought that hippies were all sponsored by their parents. We simply could not conceive that any youth could afford to travel abroad on their own resources, and live doing nothing on Goan beaches. Eric and Hubert laughed when they heard this. No one had sponsored them. They had worked at temporary jobs for a few months, until they had the budget they'd estimated for this journey, and then had simply taken off.

These things were hard for us to grasp: you could work at a casual job for a few months, and earn enough to travel abroad? People in India worked all their lives in respectable steady jobs and could never ever hope to visit a foreign country. And, after earning enough to travel, these guys had chucked up those jobs? In India, if you were lucky enough to find a job, you held on to it for dear life. And what would they do when they returned to Paris? 'Find another job!' they answered, smiling. Phew! The West was truly beyond our comprehension. Here, finding a job was tougher than finding nirvana.

But right now they were broke, not a little depressed, and they were at the end of their journey – with no money for their return air ticket.

I don't remember the details, but I remember that Father came to the rescue and wired them some money from Goa. And I remember that, true to their word, they sent it right back almost as soon as they returned to France.

These are the drawings I loved doing at the time – they're dated 1971 and 1972, i.e. at age eighteen and nineteen. The last one is by Hubert, and he did it for me in 1973, when we met in Goa and Bombay. He loved drawing and writing poetry and prose, three things I loved doing too. And Eric loved playing the classical guitar, which fascinated me. I was now twenty years old, and these two became very close soul brothers to me.

I was heartbroken and lonely when my new friends and soul brothers left. We corresponded and kept in touch for a while through letters, the only avenue available for communication at the time. But the letters gradually dwindled away, and then stopped completely when the duo was drafted into the military service compulsory in France then.

Nightmare City

I hated Bombay. Every single day of the five years that I lived there as a student. I'm sorry, Bombay City, and I'm sorry, my friends in Mumbai, but I do hope you try to understand where I was coming from: a young man just about twenty, who was terribly missing the natural paradise that Goa was at the time.

Father's first-hand knowledge of Bombay dated back from the British days, but the British had left in 1947, and the Bombay of the '70s was another kettle of fish altogether – and a rotten, stinking one at that. The British had left rural India impoverished and opportunity-less, developing only the metros for their own profit and convenience. So poor, destitute Indians from all over the countryside had been pouring in large droves into the cities, overcrowding them, creating some of the world's largest and filthiest slums, the fledgling but doddering Indian administration totally unable to cope, until the cities themselves became putrefied heaps of garbage and uncaring humanity. Corruption and crime were rampant, openly practised with impunity on the streets as much as in government offices.

If Father had personally visited Love Lane, I'm certain he would have found me accommodation in a much better locality. But in retrospect I'm not complaining, because shifting from my comfortable home in Goa to Love Lane and then Bandra East was a trial by fire which no prep school could have provided me.

Right now I was in the middle of my architecture course, and saw clearly that I did not wish to ever work as an architect in my life. There were a few reasons which led me to this conclusion; there's seldom one single one. A youth is much too young to know what he really wants to do in life when he walks out of high school straight into a professional college in India – on an average, barely sixteen. There's a certain reason why eighteen is declared the official age of adulthood. Well, I was twenty now, and I could see things clearly.

Meeting Eric and Hubert had opened my eyes to the fact that doing what one loves in life is much more important than doing what fetches most money and respect. Eric was studying classical guitar at the Conservatoire de Paris, and Hubert was studying Fine Arts at the École des Beaux-Arts, both following their personal passions. Yet they had temporarily chucked up their courses, and worked at odd jobs until they had enough money to go waltzing halfway around the world.

The third year was known to be the year when the architecture course started getting really tough. Not that I was chickening out, but having decided that I would not work as an architect, it seemed like such a waste to make all this effort for nothing.

I went about my student life perfunctorily, attending classes and doing my assignments like a soulless robot, my passion reserved for writing songs like 'Nightmare City' and 'I Just Keep Walkin' On'; writing a short book called 'The Sunshine People' or something similar, extolling the virtues of rural life against big-city life; writing a two-hour answer in an architectural exam, about the need to be connected with Infinity and Creation, that is with Nature, and about the fallacy of building a layer of tar and concrete to isolate us from it. At that time the famous avant-garde architects who advocated local building materials and architecture which blended with nature still hadn't made their theories known, though, and I was given bare passing marks in that exam. In my architectural thesis the next year, I wrote an in-depth treatise on Divar Island, Goa, explaining why I would not build a bridge and connect it with the mainland, ending with how and why I would not allow it to deteriorate into another city, but develop all the arts, crafts, farming and fishing already existent in the village into state-of-the-art rural occupations.

And I wrote The Letter to Father.

In the letter I explained exactly why I had decided that the most important thing in life was to make a living doing something one loved. How it was important to make one's passion one's profession (no, I had not heard that phrase before). How I had seen clearly that all I wanted to make was music, and that I didn't care how much money it fetched or didn't fetch me. And mainly, that I wanted to chuck up this course which I would never ever use, and return to Goa and dive headlong into composing and performing.

Father gave me the wisest advice ever. He wrote back, 'Son, you have almost completed your third year. After this there are only two more to go. I suggest you complete the course. So that if someday a musical career does not work out to your liking, you will always have architecture to fall back upon. But if you give it up now, you will always feel like an incomplete man. And that might cause you a very deep regret someday. After you complete the course, by all means do whatever your heart tells you to.'

Besides seeing great wisdom in his advice, I was overwhelmed by the fact that it was a suggestion, and not an order. If it had been the latter I might have rebelled.

To fully understand Father's magnanimity in taking the above stand, one must take the following into consideration: After I told him I didn't want to take over his aerated water business but wanted to be an architect, he quietly sold his factory (which by then had the Gold Spot franchise in Goa) and went into land development and construction. He formed a partnership with a friend, the well-established and respected engineer Eufemiano Dias, and bought a large parcel of land in Miramar. He divided it into plots, forming the St. Mary's Colony, and built intermediate roads and facilities like drainage and electricity. His plan? That, by the time I completed studying architecture, I would have a whole lot of bungalows ready to be designed for these clients.

I didn't know it then, as he never ever said so to me, but in retrospect I see that Father had changed his whole profession from aerated water to estate development based on my whim to be an architect. And then I broke the news to him that I didn't want to work as an architect after all, but to be a full-time musician. That must have been a major setback, but it is a sign of his big-heartedness that he never ever made me feel guilty about it. Why, he didn't even tell me about it. He quietly subdivided and sold the plots.

He also bought one closest to the beach for himself, on the other side of the road, and there started building his dream bungalow. The one he had promised Mother he would one day build, way back when he used to take her to the beach with a couple of folding chairs thrown in the back of the factory pickup truck.

8

Goodbye Bombay
(And Thanks for the Awakenings)

An overcrowded, stinking, cheating, noisy, loud, putrid city. The last place where someone from paradisiacal Goa would find a bit of self-discovery, preparation for life, and maybe even a little spirituality. Right?

Wrong. These things usually come in places where – and at times when – you least expect them. At the minimum, such places toughen you up. And prepare you for what's to come.

Noel Godin

My solo performances and songwriting were going on as passionately as ever, taking preference over college and classes. I was asked to perform at an important concert at Birla Auditorium in Marine Lines, featuring the top solo artists of Bombay at the time. I don't remember whether the concert featured bands as well, but I do remember that, as usual, everyone played and sang copies of their favourite western songs. I sang a few of my originals, including my guitar–sitar favourite. And then I did a cover version too of a new song I liked a lot and, if I may so myself, sang and played rather well: 'American Pie' by Don McLean. It brought the house down.

The next day there was a review of the concert in one of the city's leading dailies. It was very astute, very witty, and not a little bitchy. It said of another singer, 'He should go far; the further the better.' In all honesty the singer in question had not been very good. The article was by one Noel Godin. It went on to sing praises in all keys about my performance.

I had now shifted to the St. Xavier's Academy Hostel. This was in a short tree-lined road perpendicular to Churchgate station, walking distance from my college, and very close to the Birla Auditorium where the concert had taken place. It had a strict curfew for coming in at night which I wasn't used to – perhaps 10 or 11 p.m., which actually wasn't too bad on normal days. But if you went out for a late-night movie or party, there was this old, very cranky and grumpy watchman who needed to be coaxed to wake up and open the gate, with pleading entreaties and a red two-rupee note.

While at breakfast a few mornings after that concert, I was told there was a phone call for me. It turned out to be from the music critic, Noel Godin. He worked for Lintas, the city's premier advertising agency, and he was recording a jingle the next day at Western Outdoor, the leading non-film recording studio in the city; would I like to sing it?

Would I? Singing jingles was a much-coveted line, perhaps right after singing film songs, and here I was being offered one on a platter. They paid a mini-fortune too. My backing musicians were going to be the guys from The Human Bondage, the amazing hot new band in town, here all the way from Madras – Suresh the guitarist, Ramesh his brother the drummer, Xerxes Gobai the bassist, with their vocalist playing the flute. Would I? You bet I would, Mr Godin.

The next day I was at Western Outdoor early, and met Noel Godin. He was a handsome and elegant man in his late thirties, spoke impeccable English with a rich deep baritone voice (I learnt later that he was an amazing singer himself, besides being an amazing theatre actor too), his intelligent Wodehouse-like wit leaping and dancing in every sentence. He dressed immaculately, in a straight corporate way.

The jingle turned out to be much more than a thirty-seconder extolling the virtues of a soap. It was a beautiful full-fledged song with sensitive lyrics about life. It was called 'New Beginnings', and I think it was written by Noel himself. The session went off fabulously, and I'd never been involved in such an excellent-sounding recording. After that Noel invited me to coffee and a snack.

We took a taxi to the new five-star Oberoi Hotel at Nariman Point. We settled into the plush and lush seats of its coffee shop overlooking the spectacular sunset against

A sketch I made of Noel Godin when he acted as Job in The Book of Job *in Bombay in the 1970s.*

the Arabian Sea. The luscious club sandwich and huge coffee with ice cream were far above the fare dished out by the cook at my hostel. I was slightly ill at ease in this smooth world of luxury, which I had not yet visited in Bombay. It seemed totally removed from the stark realities of the city I walked around in and took crowded buses and trains in every day. In fact, as a newly confirmed hippie, I kind of looked down upon this glitz and glamour. The décor just didn't seem to go with my well-worn kurta, beads, faded jeans, wild long hair, beard and Kolhapuri chappals. I saw that Noel was totally at ease here, though, and I started seeing him as someone from a world I didn't belong to.

As we stepped out after the hearty meal, which I as a perennially broke student thoroughly enjoyed, I fished out my bundle of beedies from my cloth bag and was about to light one, when Noel said, 'Why don't you have one of mine?' pushing an open packet of Rothmans, an expensive foreign cigarette, towards me. I said, 'No thanks, I prefer my beedies.' He insisted, 'Do try one of these. I think you'll like it.' I couldn't believe he was being such a snob, and was about to tell him I had tried expensive cigarettes before, thank you very much, but genuinely preferred the earthy taste of beedies, when I noticed the mischievous glint in his eyes. I looked at his cigarettes more closely. He had taken one out of the packet and was handing it to me. It was crumpled, and its end was rolled up into a sharp point. It was a joint.

If my rather strained expression broke into a wide, happy smile of recognition towards a 'brother', he returned a wide smile of self-revelation. So his straight formal clothes were a front for a hippie at heart! We then spent a lovely hour walking along the sea and chatting about various things, mostly about Goa. Yes, his family was originally from Goa, though he had been born in Quetta, Baluchistan in 1933. When he was barely a year old, an earthquake had destroyed Quetta and his family's fortunes. They came as refugees to Delhi, where he was raised through school and college, until he started working in Calcutta, and then in Bombay.

When I told Noel the songs I loved singing most were Portuguese, Brazilian and of course Goan, he said, 'Oh my god! You must come over for a weekend then. Preferably with your guitar, though I do have one.'

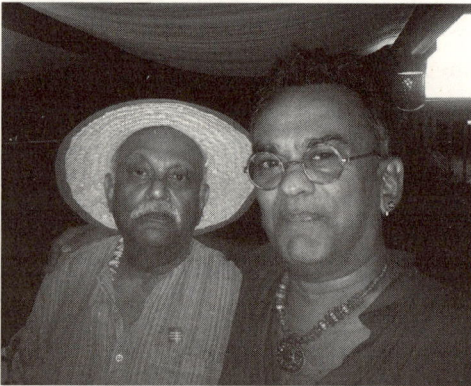

Noel and I in Goa in 2012. I tried to keep a face as straight as his – but couldn't.

A student living in a hostel is always happy to spend time in someone's home, but this was more than that. Noel quickly turned into one of my best friends ever, and into another (and arguably the most important) of my life's gurus. Today, almost half a century later, he is one of my best friends still.

Family rooms

Bombay had a very curious institution called 'family rooms' in some of its restaurants and Irani tea houses. They originally started off as large rooms where a family of four to six could gather and eat a meal in comfortable privacy. But in a city where holding hands in public attracted stares and disapproval, and sometimes even attacks, someone soon hit upon the idea of creating 'family rooms' for needy couples. These were tiny cubicles containing a very narrow table against one wall (which was actually a wooden partition separating it from the next cubicle), and a narrower bench against the partition opposite, which could seat two. Couples disappeared into these and, even though there was no lockable door, spent an uninterrupted hour or so of bliss assured by the fact that the cafe charged about three times the price for colas and snacks in these rooms in exchange for precisely this privacy; and also thanks to a tacit understanding that the waiter would be receiving a handsome tip in the end. Waiters never forgot the faces of poor tippers, and were in the habit of barging in abruptly and noisily just as such couples were beginning to steam up their cubicle.

I was introduced to these rooms by a young big-breasted apprentice nurse from Bombay Hospital who walked into the college campus one morning looking for me. My reputation as singer and musician was beginning to yield bountiful fruit. The cafe she invited me to was in Colaba, opposite Regal Cinema – the cubicles were up a narrow staircase on the mezzanine floor. She loved being a tease, and would hide her large breasts and nipples with her very long straight hair until she drove me crazy with desire. We saw each other regularly for quite a while, until the waiters at this cafe all knew us well and gave us 'extra time'.

Another girl I frequented these 'family rooms' with, soon after her, was someone from the Commercial Arts section in my college. She was beautiful, had large doe eyes, a heart-shaped mouth, tended to wear long ghaghra-like printed cotton skirts and embroidered Indian tops, and sported a Rajneesh (as Osho was then known) mala. And she smiled. Ours was a very special relationship, mainly because she hardly ever talked. She just smiled all the time, and much more beautifully and mysteriously than Mona Lisa ever did – I never could understand the fuss over that painting, especially when I stood before it at the Louvre a few years later.

She and I tended to visit family rooms at an Irani restaurant in Fountain. There she taught me, for the first time in my life, to what physical and spiritual heights a slow, sensuous mouth was able to take a man. Especially, perhaps,

She smiled her way through
crumbling hearts
without really meaning to hurt.
She wasn't really a flirt.

She just smiled away
her guilt-free way
and say
she wasn't furniture nailed to the ground.

And they tried to have her tied
to their lives
like a horse to a cart.

She neighed and flayed and raised
her hoofs and kicked behind
[actually, she just smiled]
and galloped a w a y
to freer lands.

* * *

And she crossed the green green fields
and across the high high hills
she saw someone new. She said oh, he'll do.

So she met him, he met her,
and they met each other and were happy.

And then she went weary
all tensed like a rabbit
[just a force of habit]
waiting for him to start tightening his grip
on her soul.

But he did no such thing.
He smiled and
she smiled and
they smiled and
lived free as jail birds after release.

* * *

So she said you're my man;
you're as cool as I am;
I'll stay and be your woman.

* * *

I neighed and flayed and raised
my hoofs and kicked behind
[actually, I just smiled]
and galloped a w a y
across the high high hills
I crossed the green green fields
on to freer lands...

*A poem I wrote for the beautiful,
silent, smiling Rajneesh follower from
Commercial Arts.*

a mouth that didn't talk and chatter in vain. We saw each other regularly and for quite a while too.

There was something noteworthy about some of these relationships from the student days; there was no commitment, we did not even go steady. There was just a pure joy at the 'here and now' of being together when we were, no questions asked and no promises asked for. But I wrote her a poem which I'm afraid shows that towards the end she did tend to shed a bit of her non-attachment. Anyway, once we finished college we completely lost touch.

More than a couple of decades later, when my marriage was beginning to go on the rocks, she suddenly turned up at my home out of the blue. I remember her saying that she was now living abroad – perhaps in England. I was extremely happy to see her, but nervous as hell, as the last thing I wanted was more trouble with my wife due to a visit from an ex-lover from the distant past. She gave me her telephone number, but I either lost it, or it was secretly discovered and destroyed. I have regretted that greatly, as I would have really liked to meet her (though not necessarily in a 'family room') and catch up on where life had taken us.

The Butterfly

I spent long weekends in Goa more and more often now that my heart was growing less and less enamoured of architecture. Back home my Standard Herald was replaced with an even more used car – but this one was my favourite brand and model, a precious German Volkswagen Beetle, famous for being indestructible and everlasting. When the seller, a retired police officer and avid hunter, came to show it to us, he drove it up and down from the road onto the footpath and back, bumping it violently on the steep step of the rain drain between the two, to show us how tough it was, while we stood on the veranda watching, our hearts in our mouths. Father had to shout out, 'Stop, stop, we're taking it!'

The car was a military olive green, and I painted a tiger face on the back bonnet, and tiger stripes on all the four wheel guards. Around that time I fell in love with a young girl just out of school while dancing with her to the record 'Butterfly' by Danyel Gérard; her favourite colour was purple; so (you guessed it) I got the car painted purple, and then I painted a lovely colourful butterfly on its back bonnet. I wish we had just a fraction of today's photo-clicking addiction those days, I would have had at least one photo of my Butterfly (the car). I have a few of my Butterfly (the girl), but those are for my eyes only.

'Butterfly' was part of the two pairs of sisters who, together with me and three of my buddies, formed an inseparable group that met up every evening. The two elder sisters were just out of high school and in their first years of college, while the two younger sisters were still in school. None of the girls had had boyfriends before, while we guys were well 'experienced'. We felt totally protective towards them, however, and it was a fresh, beautiful experience for us to have this purely platonic relationship with these 'kids'. Surprisingly, their parents even allowed them to go out camping with us over weekends, to empty family country houses or farms – such was their trust in us, and we totally lived up to that trust.

Everyone had expected me to eventually go steady with the girl among them who had established contact by visiting me at my home the next day after I had first met her at another party. She was what everyone (and especially she herself) considered an intellectual who read 'heavy' authors like Ayn Rand and Aldous Huxley; she played the classical piano; she was tall and beautiful; and she had leadership qualities which made her the ringleader among the girls, as I was among the guys. We were similar in so many ways, and were considered highly compatible. However, what turned me off her was the fact that she seemed to think that all these qualities made her superior to other people in general; and what turned me off even more was that she seemed to think that mine made me superior to others as well, and sometimes said so in not-so-indirect ways.

Everyone was surprised when I started going steady with Butterfly, who they might have seen as the most unlikely of all; she had a very simple and ever-smiling temperament, displayed no intellectual or musical airs, was nice and friendly to people of all walks of life, especially those from humbler backgrounds who adored her in return, and had an earthy wisdom which to me is more valuable than the highest intelligence.

Once I had made my usual 'disclaimer' clear, that we were too young to make a permanent commitment which might lead to expectations of eventual marriage, we happily went steady for a few years. She was the girl I missed during my later years in Bombay, and though she never wore sexual freedom on her sleeve, she offered me her most precious and beautiful gift of all: her virginity. For her I wrote songs like 'I Just Keep Walkin' On', with lines such as:

> I wanna sit hand in hand with my Butterfly
> But I don't want my heart to rule over my mind
> So I have nobody to run to
> And I have nobody to run away from
> So I just keep walkin' on.

And 'Lay My Head on You', with lines such as:

> I just wanna lay my head on you
> And I wanna close my eyes on everything that's wrong
> There's a time when even a song seems so difficult to sing
> That's when I wanna lay my head on you.

However, I was a firm and genuine believer in romantic freedom, and in the fact that it was perfectly possible to love more than one person at a time, in different ways and for different reasons. So part of my 'disclaimer' had been that we were both free to go out with others if we felt like it. A disclaimer which Butterfly fully agreed with.

I wanted to explore what a relationship with the 'intellectual' might be like, so I asked her out in Goa once. Though she was beautiful and there definitely was strong and tense chemistry at work there, we didn't go very far. We also met once in Bombay, and went out and hung out in the cosy darkness of a discotheque, but didn't go far then either. I guess the apprehensions I listed earlier kept me at bay. But that didn't stop me from writing one of my most beautiful songs of the time for her, one among the most loved by my friends and audiences then. Since she played the classical piano, I wrote a Bach-like piano or harpsichord passage in the middle of the song. I called it 'You', and its opening lines were:

Sing your song to me, let me hear your voice out loud
I think we've got lots to give to each other.
I'm not saying that I love you, or that I want you to be true
I'd just like you to know about the times when I miss you.

After Butterfly and I started going steady, one by one the other guys tried to go steady with the three remaining girls in our group. Those connections didn't work out though, and the group slowly and gradually disintegrated, though Butterfly and I stayed a couple for a couple of years.

That magical mystery college tour

Our college was organizing a study tour visiting places of architectural interest in the north of India. I and a couple of friends from the International Students' Hostel, where I was now staying as a 'parasite' in the room of a classmate from Fiji, signed up. My knowledge of and travel in India was hitherto restricted to Bombay, with a car trip to Bangalore and Mysore with my parents as a kid, and I was looking forward to seeing more of my awesome, mysterious country.

Our train was scheduled to leave at 4 a.m., and we had decided to buy the indispensable hashish for the journey on the way to the station. We directed our taxi to our usual supplier, but he was shut at that early hour. We went to another, and he was shut too. Frantic and desperate, we went to two more, but they were both shut as well. Now it was a choice between making the train or going on searching. We rushed to the station hashish-less and just about boarded the train as it started pulling out. How were we going to enjoy this fascinating trip without a high?

A full train carriage had been exclusively reserved for us for the entire tour. Most of the students grouped together in the centre of the bogie and started playing and singing noisy games and songs as Indian students (and adults) are wont to do while on holiday, thus totally missing the sights along the way. That made it easy for me to find a window seat in a relatively quiet corner, and I made it my own for the entire tour.

Bombay and its suburbs were a sprawling mass of ugly, messy construction and garbage, and we traversed all of it in darkness. But just as dawn was breaking, we had travelled beyond the city ugliness, and the fairy-tale Indian countryside began coming into sight; vast open expanses, tiny villages with their perfect thatched mud houses where life was beginning to show as smoke through the roof, ruins of tiny centuries-old temples, and silhouettes of majestic banyan and coconut trees could be distinguished in the slowly brightening morning. As the sun rose, I could see farmers and shepherds in white clothes and turbans setting out with their cattle, who raised a thin layer of red dust which turned golden against the sun. I had never seen this India before, and my mind started travelling far, far away. I was not in the train any more. I was out there in those fields, and then beyond the fields and into the horizon, and then beyond the horizon with the sunrise, and then beyond the sun with the cosmos … and then everything was perfect, not just in the cosmos, but even inside our carriage. The noisy students didn't and couldn't disturb me; they soon exhausted themselves into sleep, and I was the only person awake. I could not drag my eyes away from the window, which was a window into infinity.

The tour continued like a magical trip unfolding. The absence of hashish was long forgotten. Every changing view of the countryside, every station we passed or stopped at, every cup of piping hot Indian tea I was handed, everything was a perfection to be celebrated and thankful for. And when we visited the Dilwara Temples at Mt Abu, I collapsed on my haunches at their sheer beauty, and my eyes moistened. The exteriors and interiors were nothing but fine, intricate lacework made out of white marble. The very flooring was carved. The Taj Mahal, which we visited much later, paled in comparison.

At Chittorgarh our bogie was 'camped' at the railway station, from where we had a spectacular view of its famous fort.

LEFT: The potter at Mt Abu who made earthen cups in which I bought tea at the station. When I tried to return the empty cup, I was told I ought to drop it on the floor and smash it; it was for one-time use only. I carried mine all over the tour and brought it back to Bombay and then to Goa. RIGHT: A small cafe in Manali where I had a coffee and a snack with a magnificent view on my trek up to Vashisht.

LEFT: *Sketches made at the Chandigarh railway platform. RIGHT: A corner of the upper berth where I slept at night on the train. During the day I sat at my window under it.*

Every place we visited was magical: Jaipur, Udaipur, the Chittorgarh Fort, even the Jantar Mantar in Delhi. I was travelling in another dimension simultaneously, the other one being far, far back in India's past. Places with contemporary architecture didn't excite me much, though my mates were all going into ecstasies at Le Corbusier's Chandigarh. Chandigarh was my Butterfly's hometown, though, and she had spoken so much about it,

Our train carriage was sometimes parked at a railway station and we spent the night there – for all practical purposes, the carriage was our mobile hotel, and the station platform our backyard when deserted. Those days saw me get my guitar out and sing. My college mates, who were brought up on Marathi and Hindi music, would gather round and listen to my English compositions.

I missed her being there when I finally visited it. I was not into photography, but I loved sitting and making sketches of things which struck me. While clicking a photo was over in a second, making a sketch required you to absorb a scene, go into it in depth, and then record as much as possible – which made you consciously go into every detail in front of you. Unfortunately, during the tour, I never had enough time to complete my sketches with the shading and detailing which I so loved. I hoped I'd do that 'later', but of course never did.

Anyway, since we had left Bombay, I had been living with this 'connection with the cosmos' I spoke about – which rendered everything perfect: the good, the bad and the ugly sides of life. In fact I felt there was no good, bad or ugly – it all just *was*, and it was all fascinating.

When we reached a certain station more than halfway into the tour, two professors strolled up to me and said, 'Remo, you are the most mature and peaceful person on this tour.' This surprised and almost shocked me. I chose not to read too much into their comment though, as I didn't want it to make me self-conscious and lose my 'beautiful state of mind'.

Vashisht

When we reached Manali, that mythical place so fondly spoken about by young foreign travellers who came to Goa, I found out to my disappointment that we were being put up in an ugly concrete structure in a boring 'new' part of town at the foot of what was the legendary Vashisht hill. I was almost certain no student would be allowed to go on an overnight hike, alone, away from the group, up into the hills and mountains; but I took a chance and asked the professors who had told me they found me 'mature', and to my surprise, after not too much persuasion, they agreed.

So I packed my backpack with bare overnight necessities including some food and water, and set out soon after breakfast early next morning. The walk through the fields, and then up the hill, was sheer beauty and peace. Up and up I climbed on a narrow villagers' path, and stopped every now and then to watch the ever-widening view.

Perhaps I spent a little too long appreciating the nature, because I reached Vashisht after darkness had fallen. I could make out the beautiful village houses built out of tree logs and rough grey local stones, but they were all in darkness already. Of course there was no electricity here at all, but as I walked around I saw lantern light peeping out of one window. I knocked on the door and asked if there was any place in the village where I might spend the night, and they directed me to a temple nearby.

It was a rudimentary but beautiful ancient structure also made up of rough logs and stones. I stepped into the courtyard and, in the moonlight, noticed an ancient pool on one side. I chose a corner away from it to keep as far from the cold of the water as I could, snuggled into my sleeping bag, and slept like a log after the day-long climb.

I woke before dawn to the soft sound of voices. In the early mountain light I could make out two sadhus with long beards and matted hair sitting on their haunches not far from me, smoking a chillum. Seeing me stir, they extended the pipe to me. I thanked them warmly but declined; then I heard two other sadhus, whom I hadn't yet noticed, calling out to me from the pool. 'Come into the water!' they said. 'It's a great way to start the day!' I thought they must be crazy to think I could control my body temperature like they could, to bear the freezing cold natural mountain water at dawn. Seeing my hesitation, they laughed. 'Come feel the water,' they said. And I noticed the steam rising out of it. I had forgotten that Vashisht was known for its hot springs! Slipping out of my sleeping bag into the cold mountain air, and stripping myself as naked as they were, I climbed down four steep ancient stone steps into the most comfortable, hottest bath I've ever had in my life.

After soaking there forever, I walked around the beautiful untouched village and saw it stirring to life; found a house which served piping hot local breakfast and tea; sat and sketched at a few places, always surrounded by excited children; and, my exploration done, started on my beautiful trek downhill.

On the way down I met a couple of kids who wanted to sell me hashish. I saw them rolling the wild marijuana leaves which grew by the path into hashish with their bare hands. I couldn't leave Manali without tasting its famed, sweet hashish, now could I? Especially when offered to me in such an innocent, pure form, for next to nothing, while Manali hash sold at a premium in Bombay and Goa? I bought a little piece.

Up in smoke

Once down at our guest house, I smoked after weeks with my friends from the hostel, and promptly lost that state of mind. The self-consciousness, self-doubt and guilt returned.

And it was upon losing that state of mind that I became aware that I had possessed it. Nothing was perfect as it was any more. Beautiful and pleasant things made me happy, but unpleasant ones made me unhappy and even irritable as they always used to. I was conscious that I had dropped back down to a very mundane, ordinary level of existence. I sat at the same window the rest of the journey, but now my time was spent trying to understand what that state of mind I'd been in and had lost had been.

And finally I came to the conclusion that it had been what the Christian religion called the state of grace. Perhaps other religions spoke about it too. I decided that I would go looking into religions, hoping that they would help me find it again.

When back in Bombay, I visited churches, I visited traditional temples, and even the Hare Krishna temple in Juhu. I spoke to the 'Children of God', then rampant on the streets of Bombay, who wanted to give me pamphlets and lecture me, but would not listen to what I had to ask or say. One night I walked alone in the deserted Crawford Market streets strewn with the day's refuse and garbage. Suddenly I noticed a small narrow door which was ajar. Inside I saw the most unlikely, unimaginably beautiful and clean courtyard covered in white marble, with a white colonnade, and a pool of clear water in the middle. It seemed to be lit by moonlight, which meant it was open to the sky. I looked in for a long time, and called out softly, but no one answered – the place was deserted. It beckoned to me strongly, so I took off my Kolhapuris and stepped barefoot on to the cool floor, and sat cross-legged under the colonnade facing the pool. The silence, the beauty and the peace engulfed me, and I don't know for how long I had sat there before two silent shadows came up and stood on either side of me.

'What are you doing here?' one of them asked. He spoke softly, but the voice was threatening and suspicious.

'Nothing.' I was totally calm and at peace, and my voice showed so. 'I saw this place and found it beautiful and peaceful, and felt like stepping in.'

'What religion do you belong to?'

'None,' I said. 'Well … my parents are Christian, but I'm not. To me, God is One.'

I think by now they had sensed that I was not a fanatic from a conflicting religion who had come to desecrate their spot, and their voices relaxed a bit.

'Please go from here, you are not supposed to be here.'

'Ok, I will go. But could you please tell me why I cannot be here? I have had a really good feeling here, like a divine peace,' I said.

In the darkness, I could see their mouths relaxing into faint smiles. 'This is a mosque. It is meant for Muslims only.' They added softly, 'Now please go.'

'Of course,' I said, and got on my feet. I bowed to them, walked out, put on my Kolhapuri chappals, and slowly headed back to my hostel.

I also went looking in holy books and scriptures. Bombay was blessed with footpath book vendors selling used books, spread out on large mats or cloths on the floor, very cheap. I picked up as many as I thought might be interesting. Of course I knew that Christianity gave me the Ten Commandments, which were good guidelines for proper behaviour in one's life. However, no blueprint was given on how to achieve that state of mind which automatically resulted in that behaviour. No such guidelines were given in any of the other religious books I read either.

Until I came across the Bhagawad Gita. After I got over the initial part about the preparation for war, and about how it was all right to kill your own family members in an opposing army because their bodies were only manifestations of illusion, I hit gold. The rest of the book was nothing but a scientific, psychological and philosophical discussion on the nature of that 'perfect state of mind', and on how to achieve it. I couldn't believe such a 'religious' book existed, and that achieving that state of mind had been made into a religion thousands of years ago. This was exactly what I felt a religion ought to be – a lifelong pursuit of that state of mind, and not a blind 'my god is the only true god' doctrine. I felt proud of my ancestors, and despondent that today their philosophies had been reduced to mere ritualistic adorations of idols and noisy celebrations of festivals with ugly displays of wealth, totally bypassing the ancient wisdom.

I saw posters advertising free talks and lectures on the Bhagawad Gita at the Azad Maidan, or was it the Oval Maidan, by one Chinmayananda – his title, H.H. (for His Holiness), did not impress or interest me, whether it was self-bestowed or otherwise; more information on the Bhagawad Gita did. I attended the talks, and I bought his thick version of the Bhagawad Gita, beautifully bound in red and gold.

The Bhagawad Gita became my favourite book, and at the Nalanda Bookshop at the Taj I found a small and thin paperback edition which became another welcome addition to the contents of my cloth bag. I have it still, well worn and thumbed.

It was wonderful to read that a whole ancient civilization had discovered and analysed and endorsed this state of mind or awareness, because that showed me that it truly existed and was meant to be my goal in life, and that it was not something I had imagined or which was simply caused by the absence of hashish. Another wonderful result of this experience was that it greatly reduced, and gradually altogether stopped, my indulgence in this substance.

And this – the accidental attainment and loss, and eventual recognition of this state of mind – remains my most memorable experience of the last two years or so in architecture college, though it didn't have much to do with either architecture or the college.

From CSN copies to 'Street'

After The Savages I had played as a freelancer for the duration of a contract at Blow Up, the discotheque at the Taj Mahal Hotel, with a kind of splinter group where The Savages and The Brief Encounter had merged to form The Savage Encounter. This had brought two new guys into the band, Nandu Bhende on vocals and Darryl Mendonsa on bass. The three of us had a passion for songs with three-voice harmony, which Crosby, Stills and Nash was making so popular. So, outside The Savage Encounter, we formed an acoustic group of our own, for our own sheer pleasure. Nandu of course sang the lead vocals; I sang the seconds and played acoustic lead; and Darryl sang high-pitched or falsetto thirds and played acoustic rhythm. I remember the three of us sitting in a park near Churchgate in the middle of the night, after our gig at Blow Up, and singing. Or maybe we were rehearsing for our first public performance, which I think took place at a festival at St. Xavier's College. Besides CSN, we also sang some harmony-oriented songs by Procol Harum, Chicago, and so on. No originals, but our harmonies and guitaring were novel enough in Bombay.

While travelling on the Bombay local trains those days I couldn't help being totally impressed by young beggar kids who came into the compartments and played as they passed a can around for coins. One of them might have possessed a real instrument such as a battered harmonium or a dholak; the rest mostly used big deep cans as drums, smaller cans as temple bells, and cans with a few tiny pebbles in them as shakers. The effect they achieved was dynamite; they had punch in their veins and fire in their voices; and the beats they drummed up always got my feet tapping, and imaginary flute improvisations and melodies kept running in my head. The classical percussionists I'd heard had amazing technique and knowledge, but their playing was very structured and disciplined, and simply didn't have this combustion.

And one day it struck me: why not form a band with some of these guys? I spoke to Darryl (bass) and Steve Sequeira (my old drummer from Goa who now played with us in The Brief Encounter), and they were game. I was staying in a hostel with a room-mate, and Steve in a tiny one-room accommodation, so rehearsals would be at Darryl's family house in Dadar. When I came across the next group of such slum ruffians belting out fiery music somewhere, I approached them. And of course they were game too. We fixed the rehearsal for the next day.

The first rehearsal went off fabulously, the fusion of these guys' folksy fire and our rock created magic. After the rehearsal Darryl, Steve and I were sitting excitedly discussing our course of action, when Darryl's mother came into the room looking very worried.

'I'm sorry, Remo, but I'm scared!' she said.

'What of, Mrs Mendonsa?' I asked.

'Of the way these boys were eyeing everything in the house! I won't sleep well today, worrying that they'll return in the middle of the night and strip it bare!'

She did have a point. We had been too busy with the music to notice. These poor slum boys had probably felt like they'd stepped into Buckingham Palace (minus the royal security guards) here. And when we realized that, together with Mrs Mendonsa's crockery and silverware, our guitars and drums might disappear too, we quietly acquiesced. Back to square one.

But the fusion bug had bitten us now, and there was no stopping it. We put our heads together and decided to go looking for more respectable musicians at the Doordarshan television studios in Worli. There we came across a jolly tabla player called Babi Laad. He was brilliant, and we decided to make do with just one good tabla player instead of a whole lot of fiery but undisciplined guys.

At the rehearsal the next day, there was an Indian beat Steve just couldn't figure out on the drums.

'It is easy, Steve!' said Babi. 'Just think of chicken biriyani.'

'What?!'

'Yes,' said Babi, and started clicking his fingers and singing to the beat:

Chickenna, chickenna, chickenna,
Bi-ri-ya-ni
Chickenna, chickenna, chickenna,
Bi-ri-ya-ni…

That did the trick for Steve. After the rehearsal we were so famished, we headed straight for the closest Muslim joint for good spicy biriyani.

I had named the band 'Street' as it was going to be made up of street musicians. Now there weren't any, but the name stuck. I wrote a few songs especially for this configuration: a song called 'God' with time-signature changes, an instrumental in 7/4 I named 'Seven-Up', and a simple flute folk-tune I had heard my hostelmate from Nepal play and which I totally rearranged. I also adapted a couple of my solo guitar and voice compositions for this band.

We performed only one gig, at a rock show at the Birla Auditorium. And we made a rather wonderful recording in the house of my friend Roger Drego, who was just venturing out into sound at the time. If I may say so myself, this kind of fusion was way ahead of its time back in 1975.

And then the time came for me to leave Bombay, and eventually India.

Back to Goa

I answered the last exam of my fifth and final year of architecture and, my bags already packed days in advance, set out for Goa as soon as possible, with no regrets whatsoever in leaving Bombay behind. I wished and hoped with all my heart that I would pass, for no other reason than that I might not have to return. In due course my results came, and I was thrilled not that I was now an architect, but that I was done with architecture college and Bombay. I found my moth-eaten degree the other day, and I reproduce it here for whomsoever it may concern.

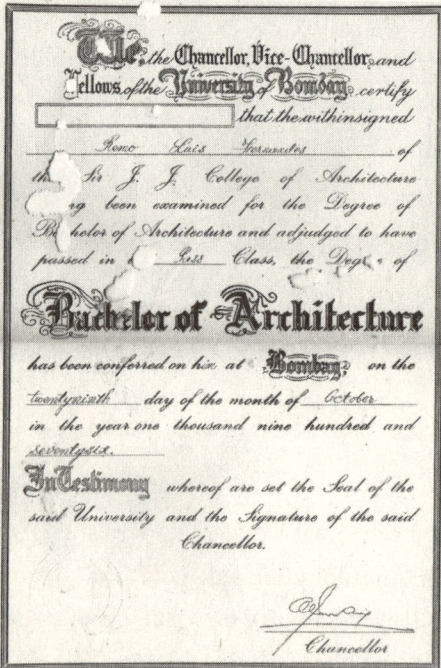

My moth-eaten architecture degree. For whatever it's worth.

Now I could bask for an unlimited while and enjoy the warmth of being back home with my parents and little sister, without the dread that I'd have to return to Bombay in a few short weeks. My sister was still a kid to me. Eight years is a huge difference when you're twenty-two and your sister is fourteen.

But she was growing up, and there were more and more things we could talk about, which was wonderful.

The last few times I'd come to Goa it was to our new bungalow on Miramar Beach, which Father had named 'Benferds'. It was wonderful, it was modern, it had four bedrooms and large living and dining rooms, large verandas and a terrace for parties (he loved throwing them), a study, servants' quarters, a truly large compound and garden at the back and the side away from the road, the works. But somehow I never felt fully at home in it. Perhaps because I never did spend enough time there.

Father's dream bungalow on Miramar Beach.

Most in my group of friends in Goa had completed or were completing their studies too. Goa's first five-star hotel, the Taj Fort Aguada, had just opened, and many of them started their professional lives there, including Butterfly.

Butterfly and I amicably broke off at around this time. I don't remember what the actual reason was, but there was certainly no unpleasantness involved. There almost never was, with any of my past girlfriends. We're almost all still good friends, or at least friends.

I had no specific plans for what I was going to do next. But having observed the young Europeans and Americans who flocked to Goa, having read books like *The Drifters* by James Michener, culminating in having met and shared so much and so much time with Eric and Hubert, my first option was to travel.

When I spoke about it to my parents, Father said, 'Excellent idea! I'll buy you a three-month round-the-world all-inclusive ticket. And then you can come back and start your career as an architect. The travels will surely open up and enrich your mind about what's happening around the world.'

When I explained that that's not how I wished to do it, that I wanted to go without planning which country I was going to proceed to next, that I wanted to work and earn my way around the world, picking grapes here and washing dishes there, and that I wished to go for much longer than three months, without knowing when I would return, he could not understand it at first. But eventually he did. And I started to daydream about and loosely plan for my trip.

Charlie Brown

It was at some party that I met her. She was a young student from New York, in Goa on a Rotary Club exchange programme, to learn about our way of life and culture. The party was at someone's house by the sea, and while it went on noisily indoors, we spent most of the evening chatting on two easy chairs on the lawn facing the moon and its reflections on the waves.

She had been here for about a month. What had she seen of Goa? She had seen the Rotary Club at meetings and dinners, the Dhempe College at lectures (I think she had been put into the second year, Science), and the homes of Rotary Club members. She had been shifted to a few different ones already. All of the above in Panjim, Goa's capital city – more a town really.

Had she visited a Goan village and walked around in it? Had she walked around rice fields and smelled the red Goan soil? Had she walked on a Goan beach at sunrise or sunset? Had she learnt a phrase or sentence in Goa's language, Konkani? She said she loved to play the guitar and sing; had she learnt a Goan folk song?

The answer to all of the above was no.

So how was she expected to learn about Goan life and culture? In a lecture room? She said she was beginning to feel very frustrated, that she couldn't understand the lectures due to the alienness of the professors' accents, that the Goan Rotary families were always telling her who to mix with and who not to, and that the cooler people she wished to go out with always seemed to be on their blacklists.

I asked if she wished to drive around the Goan countryside the next day, and she jumped at the opportunity. The next day was magical. I loved my Goa, of course, and I think I transmitted not a little of that love on to her. We drove through beautiful villages and hills and fields, getting down and walking and absorbing the smells and sounds wherever and whenever we felt like it. In the afternoon we visited Mamã de Parrá at her village home; she met my grandmother and we had tea and my favourite *merenda*, a tea-time rural snack. We drove around some more, saw the sunset from the steps of a lonely whitewashed chapel on a hill overlooking the sea, and then I dropped her home. But not before we had both made plans to meet again, this time for dinner. She was very easy to talk to, we had so many interesting things to discuss, and we hit it off beautifully.

We met a couple of days later for that dinner, after which we drove to Dona Paula and parked there. It was one of my all-time favourite spots: a big tall rock in the sea, to which one could drive on a broad old cement ramp built by the Portuguese, and then climb up the steps to the top of the rock, where they had built a romantic whitewashed pergola. From there one saw the distant lights of Vasco da Gama, Goa's port city, across the very wide bay where two important Goan rivers, the Mandovi and the Zuari, met each other and the sea. Dona Paula was then almost empty during the day, and totally deserted (and safe, like all Goa used to be) at night. It was Father's favourite short drive destination, sometimes after Sunday Mass in the mornings, and sometimes at sunset time.

But we never got to climb that rock that night. Almost as soon as I had turned the ignition off, we fell into each other's arms in a passionate embrace and never-ending kiss. The attraction was mutual and had been spontaneous from the very moment we had met at that party, and after yesterday's sightseeing and tonight's dinner, it could be restrained no more. And I learnt that with an American girl, restraint was not quite necessary.

As our kissing turned more passionate, her hand slid into my shirt and started caressing my nipples.

I got the shock of my life; perhaps the greatest sexual surprise I had experienced until then, though also the most pleasant one. I had highly erogenous nipples, but had always thought it was an aberration, perhaps a freak fact resulting from my having more female hormones than I ought to. I had treated it as a shameful secret to be kept from everyone, my own dark secret to be explored only when I was alone, because I believed that nipples were meant to be erogenous only in women. I expressed my surprised to her, and now it was her turn to be surprised at my surprise. 'But of course,' she said, 'all or most guys have erogenous nipples! Didn't you know that?'

No, I didn't. I heaved a huge sigh of relief, and was very happy to discover that I was normal after all. I wouldn't be surprised if many male readers, especially Indian, are still going around feeling ashamed of and hiding the fact that their nipples are sources of pleasure; and if many female readers, especially Indian, have never even thought of caressing their male partners' nipples. If this passage helps liberate you in this area, it alone ought to make the price of this book worthwhile to you, though sexual liberation was never this book's intention. Go for them, ladies!

From then on we met every single day. We fell in love, more and more deeply the more we met. This was not a chick to simply go out on dates with and make love to; we discussed books, we discussed movies, we exposed each other to our favourite music, we read our poems and prose to each other, we shared our thoughts and dreams, we shared our troubles when we had them. I taught her Goan and Portuguese songs, and she introduced me to her favourite American singers/songwriters such as Jim Croce and Gordon Lightfoot. I composed a classical guitar piece for her which I called 'For Charlie'. She wanted to attend one of the great universities back home, and I helped her write out her applications to Harvard, Cornell and Princeton where she described the details of her experiences in Goa. We were too young to plan something definite for the far future, but we certainly didn't see our relationship ending when her stint with the Rotary Club was over and she returned to the US, and when I went off on my tour. Though she was going to America and I to Europe, we figured we would surely meet somewhere.

She had short brown curly hair. She wore baggy jeans and tight t-shirts. And I called her Charlie Brown. She called me Charlie too, for Charles Manson. I hadn't heard of him, and wasn't too flattered when she explained he was the leader of a cult hippie commune in America which ended up murdering nine people including actress Sharon Tate. But she assured me he was a handsome, charismatic devil who charmed people – mainly young women – into doing his bidding, and that it was my 'beautiful long black hair and beard and piercing black eyes' that made me resemble him, not any 'murderous streak'. So Charlie I was, and Charlie she was. And we still call each other by these names, though she's married with two grown kids, and I have two grown kids of my own too.

My parents loved her, and she was over at our home almost every day. We sneaked into my room and locked the door during my parents' mandatory two-hour daily siesta; the rest of the day we hung out in my room with the door wide open, in the living and dining rooms, or went out.

She was being shunted from one Rotary family's house to another every week, which was making her life very messy and unstable. While with a Hindu Rotarian family, she was warned not to mix too freely with the Catholics, and while with a Catholic Rotarian family, she was warned of the opposite.

Eventually, the half-expected threat came from the Rotary president himself: she had not been attending enough classes, she had been hanging out too much with a non-Rotarian long-haired hippie musician like me. She went and met the Rotary committee armed with well-documented evidence of all that she had learnt about Goa outside the classrooms: her photographs and writings about Goan arts and crafts, Goan literature she had read, about the places she had visited and learnt about, she even took her guitar and sang them the Goan Konkani folk songs she had learnt, together with a couple of Portuguese ones.

But all this had no value or significance for them. She was here on their exchange programme, and had to adhere to their strict curriculum: only college classes and Rotary meetings counted.

She kept her parents abreast of what was transpiring here. They understood her, but asked her to try and conform and compromise. So she tried to attend more of those boring, useless Inter-Science classes, and in between we went on exploring Goa as much as we could. Until, one fateful day, they dropped the bomb: the Rotary Club was sending her back to the US before she had finished her term in Goa.

Of all the separations I had gone through until now, this was the hardest. I wrote Charlie a song, which I wrenched from my tearful heart, called 'You're Going'. When the day came I dropped her at the airport in a daze, and shed tears of sorrow for the first time in my adult life. We held each other for as long as we could.

After she left I was empty. She had become a part of my life: not just my lover, but my best friend. I had never hated anyone the way I did the Rotary committee.

I let out my frustration through a drawing and a scathing poem about the Rotary Club and their exchange programme, which was published in *Goa Today*, Goa's monthly magazine. I set it to music reminiscent of the Rotary Anthem. Of course I knew that none of this would bring my Charlie back, but I had to vent.

I drew the Rotarian trinity (president, secretary and treasurer) holding up the Rotary symbol, to which is attached a cage. In this cage they have jailed Charlie, and it is the only place from which she is allowed to view Goa.

Goodbye, Little Goa!

By now preparations had started in full swing for my first foray into foreign lands. Father set about putting together names and addresses of relations and friends around the world whom I ought to meet, and I wished and wished that I had those of the two people I wished to meet most – Eric and Hubert.

The plan was for me to start my journey in Portugal, as my parents had most of their friends, as well as some distant relations, there. But there was no direct flight to Portugal from India, so under 'good' advice from the manager of Air India, Father bought me a ticket to Paris, where I could stop for a few days before taking another flight or a train to Lisbon. (I found out later he had sold us the most expensive ticket possible.)

I was going to Paris! How that made me wish yet again that I had Eric and Hubert's current address.

As Father took me around to say my goodbyes to close family and friends, that heart-wrenching tear-jerking farewell mando 'Adeus Korcho Vellu Pauló' started playing in my mind, and I felt like weeping at my own departure.

9

Paris, Je T'Adore!

Love at first sight

Everyone remembers their very first day, or even moment, in a foreign land. Especially if it happens to be in a country or a city made legendary through books and films and songs. The first thing that hit me when I walked out my door into the fashionable Rue du Bac on my first morning in Paris was – the silence.

I had no preconceived idea about what a European city would be like, but in my unthinking subconscious, I guess it was a matter of scale. Paris was one of the greatest cities on earth, and I guess I expected it to be greater than Bombay in everything – including traffic, crowds, and therefore, sound. Nothing had prepared me for this silence. No horns, no voices. I watched vehicles pass by in silence – I couldn't even hear their motors. Silent buses stopped at bus stops, passengers alighted and boarded without clamouring or pushing. Was it a special day today, a holiday when the city was deserted?

I stood on the footpath and watched. A very fashionable lady in a lovely winter fur coat was being led by a beautiful poodle – in a sweater. It was the month of October and it was getting cold. I watched on. Another fashionable young lady in very tight jeans, knee-high black leather boots and a short tight black leather jacket followed her eighteen-month-old child, who walked

208

ahead of her dressed like her miniature – on a leash. I blinked. Had I just seen a dog in a sweater and a child on a leash?

After I'd stood there a while, being amazed and already beginning to fall in love with this city, I started walking without caring where I was going. Everything here was beautiful, clean and magical. If you loved your dog and didn't want to leave him alone at home just because it was too cold for him outside, well of course you bought him a doggy sweater. And if you loved your child who had just started walking, and didn't want to hold him prisoner in your arms when you took him out, well of course you fixed a short baby leash around his waist so he could walk safe and not wander into the street or into unwanted things. I stood at a curb wanting to cross the street, and got my third shock of the morning: a car stopped for me. It didn't try to run me down. The driver smiled and waved me across. I crossed the street still looking back at him, my mouth slightly open.

I walked on in a dream, looking and marvelling at everything which to Parisians was commonplace, the way foreigners look and marvel at cows on Indian roads, until I came across the fabled Seine river. More standing and gazing. Finally I crossed the Pont Royal and was standing there looking at the legendary Louvre which I had reached most unexpectedly, when a Frenchwoman came up and asked if she could take my photo. 'Ah,' said I to myself, 'my exotic long black hair, black eyes, thigh-length George Harrison-like Indian leather coat with the embroidered front and fur collar are attracting admiration from the locals already!' I gladly, and not a little vainly, posed for my admirer with the Louvre in the background – until she pulled the photo out of her Polaroid and told me it cost five francs. My vanity smashed to pieces, I explained to her as best as I could that I had no French money on me whatsoever, only the $100 bill which the Indian government had generously allowed me, and which I hadn't yet encashed. She muttered something, waved an ok, and went looking for other tourists on this autumn morning.

The previous evening, Tatiana Mendes, our new neighbour in Miramar who had just shifted to Paris, had come to pick me up from

Charles de Gaulle airport as planned. I stayed with her the first day or two at Rue du Bac.

She showed me the initial ropes of Paris: how to use the metro being perhaps the most important and useful one, and how to eat a filling and cheap meal at McDonald's where she took me for lunch being the other. The metro and bus issued a Carte Orange, which was a weekly or monthly card for unlimited use. I chose a weekly one, as I was then scheduled to go to Lisbon and 'officially' start my travels there.

After a couple of days at Tatiana's, for which I was extremely grateful, she unceremoniously dumped me at the apartment of someone who I think worked at the Indian Embassy with her. I seem to remember that his name was Gupta, and he was one of those Good Samaritans one hardly sees any more.

That saintly man said, 'No, you don't have to pay me anything. Every Indian who first comes to France and doesn't have a place to stay is welcome here until he finds a job. After that the only thing I ask of him is that he help a new arrival from India find one too.'

Feeling very grateful but low and depressed, as though I had landed at the Salvation Army, I placed my suitcase and guitar next to an empty bedding in the crowded room, and got ready to spend the five most awkward, uncomfortable days of my life until I left for Lisbon.

Meanwhile, I decided to sightsee as much as I could in this city I loved more each day, and to spend as little time as possible in this charitable dormitory. I prayed that I would find my suitcase and guitar in place each night, and I did.

Armed with my Carte Orange, I first went to places suggested by guide books: the Champs-Élysées and the Arc de Triomphe, Saint-Michel in the Latin Quarter, Montmartre, and so on. After these spectacular tourist attractions, my new method of sightseeing was to choose a random metro station whose name intrigued me, get off there and walk around. I didn't speak a word of French; the French were very reluctant to speak English. But I got by.

One day I was sightseeing in a very posh area, and I needed directions. I saw a rare sight: an old-world middle-aged gentleman with an upturned grey moustache, in a dark three-piece suit, wearing a hat and carrying a neatly rolled up umbrella like a walking stick. I approached him and, armed with my translation book and map, asked in very halting French: *'Excusez-moi Monsieur, où est la Rue du Machin s'il vous plait?'* He guessed my predicament and gave me prolonged directions in impeccable English laced with the faintest trace of a French accent. I realized then that the French people's reluctance to speak English was not due to old politics and wars as was claimed, but more due to an inferiority complex at not knowing a foreign language. That, if a Frenchman knew English well, you couldn't stop him once he got started.

As I walked around the city, every time I saw a girl from the back with short brown curly hair and a build like Charlie's, my heart raced for a while. How I missed you, Charlie Brown. And of course, just being in Paris and hearing French all around me made me miss Eric and Hubert like crazy.

On my second last day in the city I decided to take the metro to the furthest station I could, which turned out to be Porte de Pantin. I walked out of the metro, saw that this suburb seemed vast and desolate, and was about to walk back in when I noticed two huge billboards; they advertised Santana and Weather Report. They stood at the entrance of an extensive open ground as big as a football field, at the end of which stood a gigantic hall or pavilion which bore the legend PAVILLON DE PARIS in gigantic font. I stopped in my tracks and went back to the billboards. With the help of my Portuguese, I deciphered that they advertised concerts at the pavilion in front of me. So this was the hallowed place where international greats performed in Paris! After going through the smaller posters of concerts which were scheduled for months later, like The Rolling Stones, Joan Baez, Eric Clapton and so on, I stepped aside and gazed at the holy hall where my gods left their footmarks, fingerprints and sounds. It was mid-morning and of course the hall was empty, and so was the mammoth ground before it which I presumed was used as parking space at concert time. Well, not quite fully empty; there was a solitary figure walking halfway across the ground away from me towards the Pavillon.

I don't know what made me stare at him, but I stood there doing just that. I know what made him feel my stare at the back of his head, though. He stopped walking, turned around, and stood there staring back at me. We stood motionless, staring at each other for what could have been anything from two to twenty seconds, and then he slowly raised his arm, pointed at me, and shouted, 'Remo?!' in that voice and French 'r' which I knew so well. And I raised my arm, pointed at him, and shouted back, 'Eric?!'

All's well with Paris!

We couldn't believe our eyes. We couldn't believe our ears. We couldn't believe our brains. But there we were, meeting in Paris by chance four years later, defying all laws of probability. But perhaps obeying all laws of synchronicity. After all, all my longing of the last few days – months – years – could not have gone unnoticed by the universe.

What had made me stare at him? I had only known him in loose white kurta pyjamas, long hair till well below his shoulders, wearing Indian chappals. What had made me sense something about this guy in a leather jacket, leather boots, tight jeans and short hair? He was going to meet some buddies at the Pavillon de Paris, where he used to work as a lighting engineer for all these big concerts until recently. But that could wait for another day! After a long, warm, tight hug, we headed for the nearest cafe, which was right across the street, for a beer. By the time we finished the beer I had told him roughly what I was doing in Paris, where I was staying, and that I was heading for Lisbon in two days' time. He said, 'What nonsense! Lisbon? We've just met! Let's go pick up your suitcase and guitar; you're coming and staying with me!'

He now lived with (another surprise!) Hubert's half-sister, Elisabeth or Babette as they called her. He walked to the cafe's coin phone to call and inform her they were going to have another flatmate in an hour or so. 'Guess who I've just met!' he asked her excitedly. Of course she couldn't, so he said, 'Remo!' When she said 'Who?' he was almost upset. 'I've been speaking about him for years! You don't know who Remo is?' he almost shouted into the phone. 'Oh, I do now! You caught me unawares,' she answered. All this in French, of course, which he translated to me in his inimitable accent.

I don't have to explain to you the excitement and wonder and happiness and relief I was feeling. Was Hubert in Paris too? Yes, he was. We would call him later, once I was settled in Eric's apartment, and invite him over for dinner, without telling him I was here, and surprise the daylights out of him.

I had found Eric and Hubert in Paris – the only people I was truly dying to meet, not just in Paris, but in the whole of Europe – within my first week here, two days before almost leaving. Now I was going to stay on in the city I had fallen head over heels in love with. They were like-minded, and would show me my kind of ropes – where I could find work as a musician, places to stay. My trip was off to a good start, the greatest start I could ever have hoped for. All was indeed well not just with Paris, but with the world.

Eric and Babette had cooked up a nice dinner and opened a couple of bottles of wine to allow them to breathe, when Hubert rang the doorbell. After about five minutes of blabbering things like 'How? When? Where? Why?' on seeing me open it, he settled on the sofa with a glass of wine, and we clinked to each other and to our renewed togetherness, and once again went through the improbability of what had happened today.

Eric told us why he had gone to Porte de Pantin, where he usually never went any more: a girl to whom he had lent money during the journey to Goa four years ago

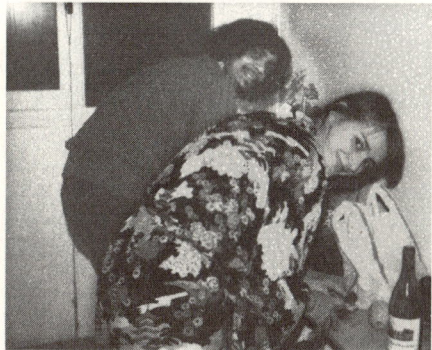

Eric and Babette cooking in their little apartment.

lived there, and still hadn't paid him back. She had no phone, and so he had gone to try his luck at retrieving his money once again – alas, as usual, she wasn't home. So he had decided to take the opportunity to visit his buddies at the Pavillon de Paris nearby. It was therefore a Goa connection which had made him walk towards a Goan who was lurking in the vicinity.

This story made me realize the significance of what had just happened in Goa, and I narrated it to them. 'A week before I left Goa,' I said, 'a "wrong number" call came in at about lunch time. It was an unknown girl with a seductive voice, and we joked and chatted for a while. Surprisingly, the next day she called again at around the same time. This time it was obviously intentional, and our joking and chatting turned flirtatious. When she called again the third day, I told her I was leaving for Europe soon, so why didn't we meet? We did, and she was beautiful. We went out, and ... well, the inevitable happened. As we chatted afterwards, she told me how she had seen me, but not met me, about four years earlier. When I asked where, she asked if I remembered a night I had spent in a hippie's room in Calangute, playing the guitar until dawn, with a small group of people sitting around listening. Well, she had been in that group, together with her boyfriend, sitting and listening.'

I continued, 'Tonight I realize that four years ago our stars (that girl's, yours, Eric and Hubert's, and mine) crossed in the skies and we happened to be together in Goa. Well, four years later our stars appear to have crossed in the skies again: she and I met through an accidental (or perhaps intentional) phone call, and, a week later, I meet you, Eric, by chance in a city of eight million; and then of course Hubert. Call it stars crossing, call it destiny, call it synchronicity, or call it mere coincidence – but happened it has.'

Eric's apartment was small and crowded, and they were a couple. Hubert's was larger, and he lived alone, so after a few days it was decided that I move in with him. And thus started my long sojourn at 7, Rue de la Collégiale, Les Gobelins, Paris – a place I would call home. The locality was wonderful; there was the Avenue d'Italie with its cafes and shops, the folkloric Marché Mouffetard with all its colour and rural foodstuff two blocks away, and the Place d'Italie with its multiple metro connections a couple of blocks away in the other direction. On good days I often walked all the way from home

Our table at Hubert's in Gobelins wasn't pretty, but it was certainly good; don't miss the champagne bottle among other goodies on some occasion. This was when my hair had grown longer.

to Place Saint-Michel in the Latin Quarter through the most beautiful old neighbourhood with ancient monuments, and even across the Seine and beyond.

The big leather boots I'd bought in India started letting icy cold water in as winter progressed. My feet and socks were wet and freezing, and I was quite uncomfortable.

'Uncomfortable? You're going to fall sick at this rate, man!' exclaimed Hubert when he noticed it one day. 'Come, we're going shopping right now, before you catch pneumonia. And bring along a fresh dry pair of socks in your pocket,' he said.

He took me to a shoe shop – I still remember it was in Châtelet. And there he bought me a pair of warm, soft, sturdy, comfortable Clarks shoes. Walking out of the shop, I threw my pair of Indian boots (the soles of which were opening: must have been cheap

Hubert and I.

leather and cardboard combined) into the first dustbin I came across. Together with the fresh dry socks, my new Clarks felt like central heating had hit my feet.

People who know me well swear I've told them this story at least ten times. That's how much Hubert's act of kindness (together with many others) meant to me. I was now living on my own, being independent, totally avoiding taking any money from my father. But I swore to myself that when I had enough money someday, I would repay Hubert and Eric multifold.

Eric visiting Hubert and me in Gobelins with his boss's dog.

Eric introduced me to a cafe he knew at the Gare de l'Est, and it was arranged that I would sing there in the evenings, in exchange for the money that the customers put into the 'jar for the musician' which was kept on the bar counter. Eric accompanied me the first few nights, until I learnt the ropes. I sang a repertoire of Brazilian songs which the Parisians loved, Beatles songs which they loved to sing along to, other hits of the '70s like James Taylor, Cat Stevens, etc. and also some compositions of mine. The guitar–sitar piece of course was something they all enjoyed and which got a huge ovation each night. I now wove a French children's song, 'Frère Jacques', into it. Within a couple of weeks I started having a following, and the jar was getting fuller and fuller every night.

I'd gone to Paris in October, and it was slowly getting colder, wetter, the days were getting shorter; in fact what the Europeans consider the most depressing time of year was creeping in. But to me it was all wonderland.

This season was something I'd never experienced before: I'd only heard about autumn and winter, but here I was seeing how beautiful (albeit melancholic) the falling autumn leaves and trees going bare against dark grey skies could be. However, I was lonely with no female companion, especially when I was seeing so many beautiful girls everywhere every day, seeing couples hugging and kissing so romantically all around me without raising eyebrows or inviting stares. I realized that while I had been used to being approached by girls within circles where I was known for my music in Goa and in Bombay, here, for the first time, I was finding myself in a place where I was a total unknown. And that I had never ever approached a girl who didn't know who I was. So I decided to recruit the experience and wisdom of Hubert and Eric.

'Guys, France and especially Paris are known for the ease of relations between men and women,' I said. 'But how does a total stranger approach a totally unknown girl here?'

'Oh, it's very natural and easy, man!' they offered. 'If you see a girl you like – whether in the metro, in a cafe, wherever – you just go up to her and tell her she's got beautiful eyes, for example, or whatever you do find beautiful about her.'

'Just like that?' I asked, surprised. 'And she won't scream harassment, and slap me for acting fresh?'

'What?!' they asked, amazed. 'Why would a girl do that for being complimented?!'

'Well, she'd do it in India, and the people around her would probably lynch you and throw you out of the cafe or the moving train.'

'Ah, we remember seeing all those Indian beauties and going crazy, but you and other local acquaintances warned us against approaching them unless we had common friends who introduced us first. Rather difficult for two unkempt foreign hippies, and it was most frustrating … but luckily for you this is Paris, man!' They smiled. 'After you compliment her, gauge her reaction. She'll probably say "Thank you". If she seems interested, you can always ask if she'll have a coffee with you. If she says yes, you're on your way, and from there on it'll all depend on how your mutual vibe vibrates at the cafe. If she says "No thanks" to your invitation to coffee, she probably has a steady boyfriend, or you're simply not her type of guy. In this case I'd just say, "No problem, you've got lovely eyes anyway", smile and walk away.'

Hmmmm … a very useful and edifying lesson.

One day soon I found myself in the metro sitting opposite a girl with amazingly beautiful, straight, long blonde hair. I was still nervous about following my friends' advice, so I hesitated until I neared my station. As the train started slowing down, I stood, took the two steps between us and said, 'Excuse me, I just want to tell you that you have incredibly beautiful hair.' In English, of course.

She looked up from her book, surprised, and said, '*Merci bien!*'

I said, 'You're welcome,' and walked out of the train which had stopped and opened its doors. As the doors closed and the train pulled out I looked back. She was looking at me smiling, and waved out and mouthed 'Bye!'

I smiled and waved back happily, glad that I had probably made her day. And happy to know that I was in a place civil enough not to have broken into a mini riot involving the burning of a train or two.

Some days after that I found myself in a cafe having a coffee and sandwich, and at a table near the wall I noticed a very striking young woman. She was dressed all in black and had short black hair – a look which had been made classic by the 1920s' artists in Paris, and which I loved. She was sketching in a big drawing book laid across her table.

Emboldened by the pleasant experience with the girl on the metro, I approached her and asked, 'Would I be disturbing you if I sat at your table with a coffee and quietly watched you sketch?'

She seemed amused and answered with a half-smile, 'Ok, sure, if you like.'

'And while I'm at it may I get you another coffee too?' I noticed her cup was empty.

'Sure, thanks.'

And thus started my first affair in Paris. But it didn't last very long because besides sketching we really didn't have much in common. And I really could not get used to her habit of lighting a strong, filterless Gitanes and drinking an equally strong, bitter, milkless, sugarless coffee as soon as she woke up in the morning, while still in bed, before she even brushed her teeth.

But I'd seen the way. *Et vive Paris!*

Why travel?

A lot of people back home thought I had gone to the West to try and 'make it' in music, or perhaps to find a 'foreign job' as an architect. That's what everyone from back home went to the West for anyway. But I really went there to travel. To see a bit of the world. To watch, to

A photo I clicked of myself in a photo machine in a metro station in Paris.

observe, to learn, to listen, to taste, to smell, to feel life and people and music and food and art and culture and thought in other places. Hippies were fond of saying they came to India to 'find themselves'. I didn't go looking, but I did eventually find a big chunk of myself during my travels. But that came to fruition later.

Come Christmas, I was wondering what I could gift my friends with my new-found wealth from playing at the cafe. I wasn't a believer since you know when, but I certainly did enjoy the tradition of making a crib, putting up a pine tree and some illuminations at Christmas time. I knew they weren't going to put up any, so I went out and bought the whole set with my limited finances. They were out for the day, so I came home and put it all up rather beautifully. It was at Eric and Babette's new apartment, where I was spending Christmas. And then I waited for them to come home in the early darkness of winter, and for their 'aaahs' and 'ooohs' of wonderment when they saw their beautifully illuminated living room. When they got home, all I heard was derisive laughter.

Of course they too had seen through religion long ago, in fact had probably never grown up in it, but they could not even appreciate a crib and a tree as tradition and folklore. That made me sad. For them.

My first snow

That New Year's Eve I was driven by Eric and a bunch of friends to someone's country house in a beautiful village. It was freezing, but that night there was a warm fire in the fireplace, and there was a feast where, besides other delicacies, I tasted my first cheese fondue. An electric pot kept the communal melting cheese warm at the centre of the table, and all of us dipped pieces of bread stuck on long-stemmed forks into it, rolled up the cheese, and … wow! Good French baguette dipped into Swiss cheese tasted heavenly.

My friends had invented a rule wherein whoever lost their bread in the pot had to empty their glass of chilled white wine bottoms up, and have it immediately refilled. I, being the most inexperienced in matters fondue, lost it most often, and I suspect my friends' skilful manipulations of their forks under the molten cheese had quite a lot to do with it; but the superb white wine was nothing to complain about.

I went to sleep well covered in multiple blankets on this cold night. I was the first to wake up, with the mother of all headaches and hangovers. But as I bravely parted the curtains I saw that it had snowed during the night – and now the sky was blue and the sun was shining bright.

I dressed quickly and went out into this magical morning. The whole village was fast asleep, and as I walked around the wonderland, my headache and hangover miraculously disappeared. The white virginal snow in the bright sunshine was the first snow I was seeing and touching and walking on in my life, and I'll never forget it. I marvelled at each little stalactite formed under each tree branch and even under some leaves, and each stalagmite formed on the wooden fences and mailboxes of people's homes, each with sunrays passing through it forming little dancing rainbows.

The hour or so I spent walking in and around that village all alone in white snowy sunny glory made for the most memorable New Year of my life, and I remember it still on every 1st January morning.

The only seasons I had known until then were summer and monsoon. Watching winter turn into spring was in itself a revelation. Those tall bare trees, which had looked almost forbidding during all the dark freezing months, were sprouting bright fresh green leaves, and some already had their first flowers. And best of all, the people looked happier and smiled more and their clothes became lighter and more colourful. I never understood why these countries with dark dreary winters chose blacks, greys and dark blues for their winter collections. You would think that those grey months required the brightest colours of all. But no – the designers (and the people) felt their clothes ought to reflect the darkness of the season. But the inborn style of the Parisians, especially the more tastefully dressed ones, made those dark colours something to see. A lesson in autumnal, wintery aesthetics.

Although my following was growing at the cafe, and I could see from where I was singing that the 'jar for the musician' on the counter was getting fuller and fuller, by the time I'd had dinner and was handed my cache by the husband-and-wife team of owners, the sum just wasn't growing. One night I went straight from the stage to the bar counter, sat at a stool and asked for a beer, and with a sweet smile at the owners, emptied the jar on the counter and started counting the money myself. And why shouldn't I? The jar was exclusively for the musician, and there was no reason why the owners should be the ones counting and handing over the money to me. They seemed shocked at what I was doing. I wasn't surprised to find out the amount that night was a little over double what I was given on other nights – and they didn't seem too happy that I'd found out. That was the last night I sang there. I didn't want to play and sing, something I loved doing with all my heart, with a bad vibe hovering around me.

I spoke to Eric about it, and we soon found a better and much bigger cafe for me to sing at. More clients, a better stage and sound system, and … more money.

I wasn't able to honour my promise to Mr Gupta though. The first cafe certainly didn't require another employee – they were a self-sufficient husband-and-wife team who did everything themselves. And very frankly,

I am embarrassed to say that by the time I started at the other cafe, I had forgotten all about it.

While gathering my memories for this book now, more than forty years later, the incident with Mr Gupta came floating back. I managed to trace Tatiana, to try and contact Mr Gupta and repay him somehow. But she said she didn't remember any of it – neither shifting me to his apartment, nor the existence of the man.

One evening there was a particularly appreciative group of young professionals in the new cafe. A pretty girl from among them came over after I'd finished singing and invited me to their table. She had a cute impish upturned nose, freckles, and long straight light brown hair. She spoke English rather well, quite a rarity in Paris in the '70s. Turned out she had just returned from Canada, where she had lived and worked for some time. She and her friends dropped me home in one of their cars afterwards, and as we all stood on the footpath chatting a while, I asked if I could see her again. She said sure, she'd love that, and gave me her telephone number. Her name was Isa.

10

Travels in Europe

Learn French? Find French lover

I called Isa a day or two later, she invited me over for dinner, and after that I discovered why Parisians had acquired the reputation of being the greatest lovers on earth. A generalization, of course; the whole world has its share of fabulous and lousy lovers, as I was to learn in future. But somehow the French seemed to have earned an exclusive reputation in this department – and with reason.

And we met again – and again and again and again. She asked me to move in with her, but I wasn't sure I wanted to do that, so I kept going back to Hubert's apartment in between.

Most of my friends in Paris wanted to practise the English they knew with me – with the result that I didn't get to learn French. But Isa was something else. 'What, you've been here six months, and you still don't speak any French?!' she asked. 'Well, I'm going to teach it to you. And I'm going to speak to you exclusively in French.' And from then on she kept to her word.

Thanks to her patience and enthusiasm I soon started picking up words and sentences, and I realized that, just as France was somewhere in between England and Portugal geographically, the French language was somewhere between English and Portuguese too. So if I couldn't translate a French word from English, I usually could from Portuguese. And of course there were those which were rooted in neither, and these I learnt.

Isa worked in the day, and our routine went something like this: I returned from the cafe late at night. We made love, and she went back to sleep and so did I. She woke up early in the morning; we made love, and she got ready and left for office while I went back to sleep. She called me during her lunch break, which was when I got up. Then I spent the afternoon and early evening on my own, until she got back at about 6 p.m., when we probably made love again.

I got into the habit of reading French signboards and advertisements, pronouncing words in the most atrocious way I could think of, and I turned out right seven times out of ten. With that and other homemade methods I assigned myself, with my little pocket English–French dictionary I always carried in my bag, with the English–Portuguese connections I saw in French, and of course with Isa's enthusiastic efforts, I picked up French quite quickly and effortlessly. And of course, learning it from a French person and hearing it all around me in Paris, I couldn't help but pick up the right accent too.

And in a few months, Isa, who was sharing her sister's apartment, moved to a place literally two street corners from Hubert and me. Now it was even easier for me to shuttle between the two places.

A visit from Mother and Belinda

In my early days in Paris, I had a very realistic dream. In it, now that I was well settled, I went back home to Goa to tell my parents so, and to say that they needn't worry about me. We were all very happy and busy rejoicing about it, until I realized that I had used up my return ticket just to give them this news. I was now stuck back home without being able to return. Wondering how I could have been so stupid, I woke up kicking myself up my backside, and was extremely relieved to find out that I was still in Paris after all.

My second dream came quite a bit later, and was quite troubling. Again, I dreamt that I had gone back to Goa to see my family. I entered a large hall where they were waiting for me. The hall was deserted, all the furniture bore white sheets like in empty houses, and there were cobwebs here and there. In the dim light coming in through the drawn curtains I saw three large ancient revolving chairs with their backs towards me. Though I could not see them, I knew my father, mother and sister were sitting on them, and I called out. The chairs slowly turned, my family smiling at me. Their faces were skeletal, and they were dead.

I woke up in a sweat and in a panic. I could not sleep any more, and as soon as Hubert emerged from his room in the morning, I narrated my dream to him. I wanted to rush to the closest post office and call home. But Hubert, who had studied dreams and Freud's interpretations of the same, reassured me that my dream only meant that I had broken free of my youthful attachment to my family, and had now grown into an independent man ready to live on his own, though continuing to love them as always. And so it was, and I was reassured, and I marvelled at this new-found independence and progression in life.

All this 'independence' notwithstanding, I was overjoyed when Mother announced that she and Belinda were coming on a visit to Europe in March, and would be visiting me in Paris. And maybe I'd accompany them to Portugal and Spain? But of course!

I was excited that I was going to see them again, to show off my knowledge of Paris and French, and preparations to receive them started. Isa offered that we all stay in her new apartment, as it was much better organized than the bachelors' pad Hubert and I ran.

Isa remembers today that my mother seemed a bit embarrassed to see her 'little boy' sharing a bedroom with a girl for the first time, but I didn't notice.

Although I showed them all the sights of Paris, my mother could sit at the huge French window in our second-floor apartment just watching the street and people and horn-less silent cars below for hours. In a couple of days I was surprised that they were able to go to the boulangerie downstairs before

I woke up and buy baguettes and croissants for breakfast on their own, from the ladies who spoke no English.

After a couple of weeks in Paris we went to Portugal, and finally got to see this country in whose awe we had lived in Goa. And I was disillusioned to see that it was in shambles – after Paris it seemed poor, dirty, and the people sad and forlorn. Was this the land of milk and honey, our great *Mãe Pátria*, our all-powerful ruler for whom we had shouted 'Viva Portugal' for four centuries and a half?

The fascist and elitist rule by Salazar had wreaked havoc on the country's economy, which collapsed as all their colonies attained independence one by one due greatly to his stubborn policies. He knew he could not win the wars being waged against his rule by resistance armies and movements in Africa, but his ego simply wouldn't allow him to let go of those colonies in peace and goodwill. So he mercilessly sent hardly trained Portuguese youth on compulsory military service to fight and inevitably die in the wars. His successors continued this practice for a while after his death, until the Portuguese Army revolted in Portugal. The Portuguese people themselves, normally peaceful and accepting, unexpectedly joined the army and staged a revolution. Together they overthrew the fascist government (including the PIDE, their dreaded secret police, responsible for the imprisonment, torture and death of thousands of innocent Portuguese citizens arbitrarily declared enemies of the state) on the historic 25th day of April, 1974. This day is celebrated today as *Dia da Liberdade*, or Day of Freedom. But more poetically and popularly, the revolution was known as *Revolução dos Cravos*, or the Carnation Revolution.

I love this name and the story behind it. Legend has it that a florist in Lisbon, a lady called Celeste Caeiro, was stuck with boxes of carnations in her shop, which was closed due to the upheavals in the city. Not willing to let her beloved flowers die alone in the darkness of her shut-down shop, she went around on the 25th distributing them to the people who came out in the streets to celebrate the end of the revolution, as well as to the soldiers.

Other demonstrators took up the cue, and carnations were placed all over the city and the country in the muzzles of guns and on soldiers' uniforms, to celebrate this victory over dictatorship where almost no shots had been fired by the sympathetic army.

Portugal's peaceful Revolução dos Cravos *(*Carnation Revolution*) of 1974, so named because citizens went around inserting carnations into the muzzles of the soldiers' guns.*

All this had happened just four short years before we had landed in Portugal. Initially the Portuguese people were overjoyed at their new-found freedom, but now the country was reeling under its after-effects – rebuilding a country's economy is not easy. Luckily, unlike the Germans, they didn't have to rebuild the country's houses and buildings and roads, as nothing had been bombed and destroyed.

While the revolution took place in Portugal I was studying architecture in Bombay, and was quite disinterested in what was happening in Europe. And now I was twenty-five, totally enamoured with Paris, and all I saw was sad depression in Portugal.

Going through its beautiful countryside today, I see the well-preserved and perfectly restored historic villages, the wonderful highways, and the prosperous people living in good houses and driving good cars. And I do wish I had had the maturity, time and foresight to travel inland and visit the Portugal of the '70s. It wouldn't have been easy. I would have had to take country buses mostly, share space with village people and their chickens – yes, Salazar had left the interiors of the country undeveloped – but there's such beauty in that old authentic rural life. I would have got to see these villages as they were in their original form before restoration – people in their traditional clothes, farmers in caps riding on or leading donkeys with their burdens on interior trails, not roads; and though there wouldn't have been any hotels in those interiors, I'm sure I would have experienced those simple folks' hospitality and friendliness.

But I didn't. Yes, I often do regret it today as I drive around present-day Portugal. But I do admit that at the time I had eyes mostly for Paris.

Anyway, our trip was fun, and it was great being with Mother and Belinda after half a year, and receiving first-hand news about Father. He didn't come of course; his phobia of flying had resulted in him hardly ever travelling in his life, except to places close to Goa, that too only by road or ship: Bombay, Poona and Belgaum as a young student and working man; Bangalore, Mysore and Ooty when we drove to these places as a family to 'visit India' after Goa's liberation; and such.

LEFT: *Mother and Belinda in Europe.*
Belinda hardly wore saris in Goa, but our
Indianness is usually awakened when abroad.
ABOVE: *Belinda on a train.*

In Lisbon we met up with my old architecture college mate with whom I had shared the apartment in Bombay, Fernando Ribeiro – or Pinum, as we all knew him. He was now successfully working as an architect here, had a car, and showed us the sights of the city. And then he offered to take us right down south to Algarve. I remember crossing Alentejo on its then single-lane road, still totally non-touristic, and seeing the older men and women typically dressed in black, the men wearing black caps and the women wrapped in black shawls, mostly sitting outside their houses or the odd cafe, chatting.

Other old friends of my parents that we visited or called up, who had enjoyed so much of our hospitality and friendship in Goa, were very casual and distant here in Lisbon. One particular couple, who used to spend weeks as my parents' guests in Goa, didn't even invite us for a meal – I think we were asked to tea as an 'obligation'. And, as I said, were treated quite distantly. Another family which I found distant and indifferent comprised relatives who were also very close and intimate in Goa. Well, people do change, and the European air certainly does give some people misguided superiority complexes towards people from back home. Here we were seeing their true colours.

In Portugal my mother fell in love with its ceramic creations, and bought a beautiful large vase, and a water dispenser and basin to be hung on the wall – decorative pieces in dark blue and gold ceramic with lovely designs on them. And who might you think was in charge of carrying the large, heavy pieces by hand, as we gallivanted around the country and Spain and back to Paris, in trains which we sometimes had to change in the middle of the night due to different railway track gauges in different countries at the time? Yours truly. It is but fitting that the pieces now adorn my house in Siolim, Goa.

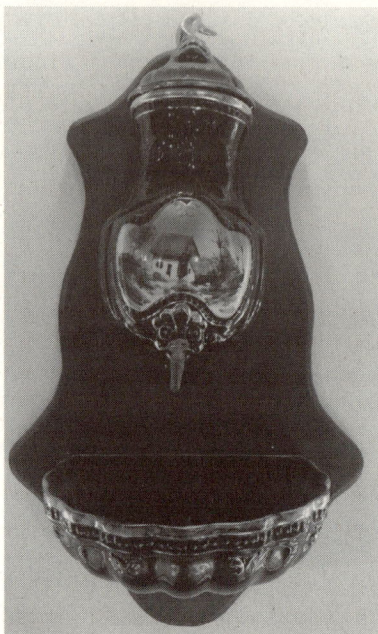

The huge water dispenser and basin, and vase, which I carried all the way from Portugal to Spain to France. Ah, the things one does for love!

Though travelling and spending time with Mother and Belinda was wonderful, this was not my ideal way of seeing countries, i.e. just visiting the capitals and one or two other main cities. I wanted to hitch-hike slowly, cover each one east to west and north to south. I would do that later on my own. Right now it was my time with them which I savoured.

After Spain we returned to Paris, where they spent some more days. But like all good things, their visit ended, and now I was going to drop them to London. They had chosen to take their return flight from there, as they wished to visit that city and relatives in England.

Reverse racism at English immigration

We took the night train to London, which included the ferry crossing from Calais to Dover, on which we would get our 'visas on arrival'. Mother and Belinda easily got theirs.

My immigration officer happened to be of Indian origin. He eyed my air ticket, which was valid for a year.

'This is an expensive ticket!' he remarked, as though he didn't think I ought to be able to afford it.

'My father is a rich man,' I replied, not liking his attitude very much.

'How can I be sure that you will not settle in the UK?' I was amazed at this question.

'I don't like fog and rain, and certainly not English food,' I said.

He wasn't liking my replies. I guess he expected an Indian from India to be meek and mild and submissive, but my months in France, the capital of bluntness, had given me cheek.

'You know that people from Goa are entitled to Portuguese nationality, right? And that once you have one, you could come and live in England? How do I know you will not do that?'

'Listen mister, I know that many of my countrymen have found ways of settling in the UK by hook or by crook, but I have no intention of doing so. If at all I do settle in Europe, it will be in Portugal. Or in France. So do rest assured your UK is safe from my invasion.'

He was liking me less and less. He himself was my countryman who had come and settled in the UK, though I had genuinely not intended my remark to be about him. He sent me into a cabin where a few other passengers (notably Africans) were kept in detention for the rest of the journey, and took my private diary and letters to read.

Towards the end of the ferry crossing we were summoned back to his desk.

To me he said, 'Your diary and letters indicate that you love Europe a lot, especially European girls, and there is therefore every possibility that you might try to settle in the UK. Your entry here is therefore denied.' So saying, he put a stamp saying 'Entry Denied' or words to that effect on my passport, and crossed the page with a ball pen and ruler, running the pen over the cross several times until the paper almost tore – perhaps he thought I might have got a forger to erase it.

Luckily I had met Geraldine, a friend from Paris who now lived in London, on the ferry, and introduced Mother and Belinda to her before we were called to line up for our visas. As I now said my sad farewells, Geraldine assured me she would look after Mother and Belinda, and that I had nothing to worry about on their account. I was happy they were in safe hands, and I was happy that the French authorities were obliged to take me back, even though my French visa had expired.

I learnt later that Geraldine had taken Mother and Belinda straight to her house, and looked after them very well. After a couple of days they shifted to a cousin's house in Wembley, where they were very well looked after as well. I was relieved.

I got off the boat in the early morning light, and stood at the quay a bit dazed at what had happened. I was wondering what to do and where to go next, when a car stopped by me. The middle-aged gentleman at the wheel asked in French: 'Son, you look lost. Where are you going?' I noticed a tiny cross on his shirt pocket and realized he was a priest.

'I'm going back to Paris, Father. I have been denied a visa to England by a racist immigration officer.'

'Oh that's sad … I'll give you a lift to the railway station from where you'll get trains to Paris.'

I thanked him and got into his car.

'Perhaps you could use some breakfast? Let us stop at my sister's house and grab some.'

The cafes around were all still closed at this early hour, so I gladly accepted. His sister was a middle-aged spinster, who was happy to see her brother, and made some coffee and brought out some baguettes and warm croissants for us.

The priest narrated my story to her, and I got the feeling he was showing off his 'deed of charity for the day'. Anyway, they were both very hospitable, the warm breakfast was indeed welcome after a sleepless and unpleasant night on the ferry, and I was grateful. He dropped me off at the station.

Back 'home sweet home'

Well, now I was safely in Paris, and my friends were happy to see me back. It was a pleasure being among French people again, who, unlike the English, showed no racism whatsoever towards Indians.

I told Isa about my dream of hitch-hiking around Europe in the summer. She loved the idea. 'I've hitch-hiked a lot in America,' she said, 'but never in Europe, and I'd love to. Would you like us to go together?' Oh yes, would I! Besides being the greatest lover I'd had until then, she was great company too: easy to get along with, with a ready laugh and sense of humour, happy and interesting conversation, and a good sport. And most importantly, my very good friend. In short, the perfect travelling companion.

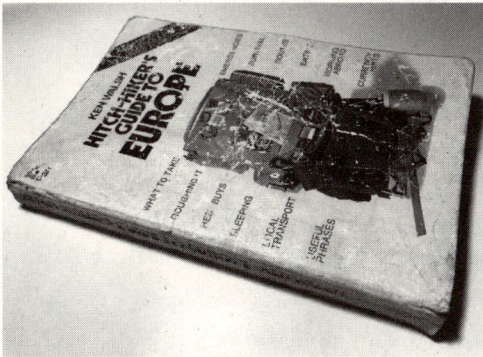

My old trusted companion on my hitch-hiking trip and other travels in Europe and North Africa. I preserve and treasure it still.

As summer drew close we went shopping for a good haversack and sleeping bag for me (she already had hers), a good tent and travelling cooking range for ourselves, and we were in business. The travel guide I had bought in a Bombay bookshop, *Hitch-hiker's Guide to Europe*, was truly excellent, and it was now finally going to come in handy in the way it was intended – that is, for hitch-hikers. I have and preserve it still as a well-thumbed souvenir of the most adventurous travels of my life. Isa had suspended her job and allotted herself a budget for the three to four months during which we planned to hitch-hike. And I carried my guitar with which I was going to busk on pedestrian streets and at restaurant terraces and whichever place I could sing at, to pay my share.

And guess what, by the time we left on the journey, I knew enough French to dare carry with me *Le Père Goriot*, a thick classic novel by

Honoré de Balzac, as reading material for travelling. I loved it, and Isa explained whatever I couldn't understand.

After we said our goodbyes to Eric, Hubert and Babette with a nice dinner, we set out from Paris full of enthusiasm, almost before summer started. The first day was a bummer; we hardly got lifts, and didn't even manage to get out of Paris. By evening it started raining, and we had to pitch our tent in what looked like an abandoned factory yard under very wet and uncomfortable conditions. The next morning was sunny, though, and we got a lift from someone who had been an experienced hitch-hiker. He told us that the place to start out from Paris was not within the city itself, but at one of the city's four *portes*, the old historic city gates, from where the old medieval roads, and now the highways, left in all four directions. From there, he said, we would get the really long hauls: cars and trucks which were leaving Paris for distant cities and even countries. Luckily for us he was going towards the south gate, and dropped us there.

On the road at last!

And sure enough, once we positioned ourselves correctly, i.e. at the entrance to the highway going south, we were quite promptly picked up by a car going halfway to the southern coast of France. Our adventure had started.

The idea was to head for Italy. And I was keen to start with a visit to my famous namesake city, San Remo. A wrong choice: the inhabitants were some of the richest, snobbiest bunch of people in Europe, who considered hitch-hikers as debris that the storm had blown into the city during the night. If I'd thought I'd mint money singing on pedestrian streets here, I was sadly mistaken. After half an hour of singing my heart out, not a single lira had been dropped into my guitar box.

It was the citizens' way of telling us, 'You don't belong here. This is not a city for the likes of you. This is a city for us folks who have our yachts moored down at the harbour, who are paying a small fortune for every meal, and another small fortune for our dogs' pedicures, and we want to keep it that way. So move on.'

We were very happy to leave – except that none of the Rolls Royces and Lamborghinis were picking us up. We finally got a lift from a jolly truck driver who had brought supplies into the city. It didn't matter where he was going, as long as he was going out of here.

Incidentally, some of the best lifts we got were from truck drivers. Their cabins were large and comfortable, and it was curious to see that they had cosy sleeping areas behind the seats. The drivers themselves were by and large good-humoured, hard-working men who were happy for some company. And they stopped in the best eating places: special restaurants for truckers, run by families, with fixed menus of economical but wonderful wholesome home-cooked meals. In France this chain was known as Les Routiers. The drivers mostly knew each other and the restaurant owners by name, so there was great conversation and camaraderie all around. Before stopping for lunch the drivers usually made it politely clear that we'd have to pay for ours – I guess some hitch-hikers had been too broke to pay for their own meals, and the drivers had ended up having to pay their bills.

One driver pointed out a middle-aged couple to us. The man was going to retire the next year, and his wife had been riding with him every day since they had got married about forty years ago. On the way out he pointed out their truck. Their cabin had flowering plants growing inside, and curtains on the windows.

Another driver revealed, once we were well on our way, that his cargo was explosives. He asked if we preferred to get off. I said no, it would be a mind-blowing way to go.

Oh, how I loved taking lifts from truckers!

La dolce Italia

It was good to breathe free once we were out of San Remo; now we were in *la vera dolce Italia*. We headed for Rome, and we were very lucky: we were picked up by a young Roman who was driving back home, right into the heart of the city. It was a lovely journey, and we got to know each other pretty well along the way. He said he lived alone in his parents' big apartment, and he invited us to stay in the guest room for as long as we were in Rome. Was that hospitality, or was that hospitality? It was just what the dentist ordered for rinsing away the taste of San Remo.

One could literally see the layers upon which Rome's history was built. On the upper layers was today's Rome. On some layers below one saw churches and cathedrals built in the Middle Ages. And on one of the lowest layers stood the magnificent Colosseum. In the middle of today's busy and noisy traffic one could switch off and hear the ancient Romans' horses and chariots driving up. Inside, one could smell the fear and the bloodbaths of the slaves, gladiators and animals down in the arena as they faced or dealt out death. And one could hear the cheers and shouts of Roman citizens hungry to watch humans and animals die for their entertainment.

Though I carried a camera, I preferred sitting and sketching while travelling. It took more time, but it made me truly absorb the scene I wanted to preserve.

Now I was having a lot of success as a busker. Rome had a lot of lovely piazzas or pedestrian squares where one could open a guitar case and start a mini concert. Most of the time I was soon surrounded by a crowd, and money kept dropping into the guitar case. One of those days as I was singing with my eyes closed as usual, I heard myself being accompanied by a beautiful bongo beat. I opened my eyes and saw a smiling bongo player sitting and playing right next to me. He accompanied every song with ease, and after a few he got up and passed his hat around the audience. I'd learnt to be careful on the road, and worried that he might be barging into my busking to take my money and run. But no, he returned to my guitar case and poured it all in. He did that after every few songs, and I found that this way there was much more in my guitar case than when I waited for the people to come up themselves. I offered him half the earnings, but he refused. So I invited him for a beer or two. Isa, he and I spent a lovely time chatting and laughing. He said he was Sicilian, a jazz drummer, his name was Fabrizio, he lived with his parents, and that we must call him when we got to Palermo (which wouldn't happen for another month or more), and come over for a meal. I wondered whether he would remember us by the time we got there, but took down his number, grateful for his good intentions.

By that time I had started reading *The Agony and the Ecstasy*, Irving Stone's novel about Michelangelo. It was like a multilayered dream, travelling all over Italy seeing his sculptures and paintings everywhere, from the Sistine Chapel ceiling to *David* to *Moses* to *Bacchus* and so on, and reading about his life simultaneously. It was also magical that we were travelling through Carrara, where he got his favourite marble from, just as I read that passage.

I carried a camera, but my favourite method of putting down memories was to sketch them. We spent hours in museums and cathedrals and beautiful spots in cities, and if we had collected a couple of yen each as toll from the hundreds of Japanese tourists who came, clicked, glanced and left by the time I finished a single sketch, we'd have been millionaires.

Venezia and more

Venice was nothing but pure magic. Those mammoth cruise boats which dwarf the delicate city with their presence today hadn't invaded it in 1978; and though there were rather large package tour groups of tourists already, we soon discovered that, just like cattle, they stuck together at the more famous squares, streets and canals. A short walk away from those, and you had the soul of Venice all to yourself. There was beauty at every step, in the smallest of houses and the oldest of bridges and footpaths and boat-tying posts.

You stepped away from the main famous places, and you had beautiful Venice to yourself, in peace and tranquillity while you sat there and sketched – or just sat.

I remember having particularly good audiences for my busking sessions in Venice. I discovered that I was able to sing only when I felt like it, or when I needed money, say for an hour or two at a time. And with that I was able to comfortably share 50 per cent of all our travel expenses with Isa.

The most economical accommodation we had found here was the Youth Hostel, but it had separate wings for males and females. For a couple like Isa and me, this was torture. The other young travellers told us to not even try smuggling each other into our rooms – they had all tried it, but the Italian hostel keepers were much too vigilant and smart. By the third day Isa and I were suffering from serious withdrawal symptoms, if you'll forgive the analogy, and we roamed aimlessly along the streets of Venice.

We walked to the end of the city where we found a very quiet, sleepy, deserted little street. We sat on the steps of a shaded old closed front door, flung our jackets on our laps using them as (what else?) Venetian blinds, expertly and strategically placed our hands under each other's jackets, and proceeded to slowly and lovingly make up for the unbearable deprivation imposed upon us by our hostels. The pasta and wine that afternoon must have been particularly good, because the neighbourhood didn't wake up. We never stayed in separate accommodations after that, but we remembered that doorstep with a good laugh for years thereafter.

Ah, gli Italiani!

Wherever we went, we could hear and see Italian men passing comments and hurling proposals at young women in the streets. Strangely, we never saw any irritation in the women. One day we got to sit and talk to some of these guys, and I asked them why they did this, and why to each and every woman who passed by. They appeared shocked. 'But if we do not compliment them they will think they are not beautiful!' they exclaimed, horrified at the possibility.

Most Italians we struck up casual conversations with would end up asking 'Ti piace l'Italia?' (Do you like Italy?) and I would answer 'Sì, molto!' (Yes, very much!) And they would invariably end with 'L'Italia è il paese più bello del mondo!' (Italy is the most beautiful country in the world!) After a while I started innocently asking them, 'Have you ever been out of Italy? Have you travelled all over the world?' to which they would answer sheepishly, 'No, not really…'

My Portuguese and my new-found French were helping me navigate my way through Italian, and with a mixture of the three, and by dramatically waving my hands around like the Italians, I could make myself understood enough to get by. Italy was the only country in which I appreciated the men perhaps more than I did the women. No, I'm not gay or bisexual, but Italian men are exceptionally elegant, well dressed and handsome. The only problem is that they know it, and strut around like Roman gods.

In Italy we were loaded with money. Except that it was worth about 1/100th its bulk. They still had their lira then, and the currency was amusing. One had to pay tens of thousands for an entrance to a museum, and all that loot was worth just a few French francs. You can imagine the astronomical figures which were dropped into my open guitar case everywhere I busked.

I had never heard my name better pronounced than in Italy. They sang it – like they sing most of what they speak anyway. It is after all an Italian name, of one of the two mythical founders of Rome, Remo and Romulo (Remus and Romulus in the original Latin). Isa just adored the way they called out to me.

As we watched package tourists being herded in and out of museums and restaurants and coaches, we couldn't help feeling fortunate (and a little superior) at being hitch-hikers who could spend as many hours in a museum as we wished, who could just sit schedule-less in squares and laze the whole day imbibing the city atmosphere, and who could buy a bottle of wine in a shop and great local street food, and enjoy it all under the shade of a cool tree on a park bench.

My hair and beard had grown quite a bit by now, and there were bunches of kids following me, pointing out and shouting 'Sandokan! Sandokan!' This word surely meant something mean in Italian, I thought, and these rascals were teasing me. I ignored them royally and walked on with my nose in the air, muttering choice Konkani curses under my breath such as *'Sandokan tuzó pai!'* (Sandokan your dad!) Until it started happening more and more often, in different cities, always that same word. Finally someone explained that *Sandokan* was the name of a new TV serial which was growing extremely popular in Italy at that moment, especially with kids, and that its hero, whose name was Sandokan of course, was a brown-skinned pirate who had long black hair and a beard. I was relieved and not a little flattered, and even more so when I learnt that the pirate hero on Italian TV was our own Kabir Bedi. I was a thin, lean hippie then, but I guess my long kurtas, my bag strapped around my shoulders and chest, the hair and beard, and of course the Indian features, set the kids' imagination racing. When I met Kabir a few years later I told him about it, and we had a good laugh.

LEFT: *The loyal tent, our beloved home sweet home of many months. RIGHT: And I guess that's why the kids called me 'Sandokan', though I see no resemblance to the handsome and well-built Kabir Bedi at all.*

I won't dwell much on the places we visited, I won't even list them all, as this is not a travel book, and as today you can see any place you wish to at the click of a mouse. Suffice it to say that I was thrilled and enchanted to visit my first country 'abroad' from France on our own. The golden Tuscan countryside… The ruins and fossilized bodies in Pompeii… The leaning tower which leaned more than I had thought it did… The amazing streets in ancient medieval cities and towns, especially Florence, where even the ancient lamp posts on the footpaths were like museum pieces to be admired… And the Italians themselves, who were truly nice, good people.

And we had our moments of magic too. When we landed in Siena, we headed for the camping ground which was on a hill overlooking the old city. I woke up early and sat outside the tent looking down at the empty medieval city square. It was so perfect, so untouched, I started fantasizing about medieval horsemen riding in it once upon a time. When, suddenly, two medieval horsemen rode out, blowing ancient horns. I rubbed my eyes –

The only photo I can seem to find from that famous Palio morning, of a local girl dressed in medieval clothes for the occasion.

was I still in my sleeping bag, dreaming? As though in answer, more horsemen rode out and blew their horns too. Each one dressed in impeccable medieval clothes. I woke Isa up. We had landed in Siena the evening before the Palio, their popular yearly medieval festival – and we'd made it just by chance. And, unknowingly, had chosen a ringside viewpoint in the camping ground. Young girls, young boys, older men and women, all rode out on horses or marched in line, dressed as though they were extras in *Romeo and Juliet*, with the ancient Siena itself as their film set. We witnessed the spectacle of our lives, and then went down to the city to mingle and have fun with the revellers.

A similar magical coincidence happened in New York many years later, when I walked around the Village in the '80s, wishing I'd known it during the hippie heyday – when suddenly I saw a bunch of late '60s hippies coming out of a street corner brandishing signs saying 'Make Love, Not War' and such. It happened to be a Cheech and Chong film shoot.

Cheech and Chong shooting a hippie episode in the Village in the 1980s.

Sicilia

In Sicily I imagined the mafia, but luckily they didn't turn up like the horsemen or the hippies. We landed in Agrigento. The camping ground was right on the beach. It had a large open dining shack, and the ambience was such in the evening that I felt like taking my guitar and singing – just for fun. Camping grounds were mostly frequented by young budget travellers like us – not places where you could collect much money in your hat, even though there were a few car owners too. We all had a lovely time drinking wine and singing along, and a pretty young Italian girl with curly hair who was giving me the eye came to chat – notwithstanding Isa's presence.

That night in the tent Isa said, 'She's cute, huh?'

'Who?' I asked, feigning ignorance.

Isa laughed. 'Oh my poor innocent baby!' she teased. 'Remember our first conversations in Paris, how you told me that you'd like our relationship to be free and open? How life in India wasn't as sexually liberated as in Europe, and that quite simply, you didn't grow up having as much sex as we did? I bet you need to make up for it at least a bit. Go for it; I'm incapacitated these days anyway.'

I couldn't believe my ears. 'Are you serious?' I asked. 'And even if so, how can I go up to her, when I'm with you?'

'Tomorrow morning I'll go off somewhere with a book. You go and see her. I think she's just a few tents down from ours. I'm sure she'll be very happy to see you. And yes, I'm serious.'

'Well,' I said, 'that's a Parisian girl for you.'

'No, not all!' said Isa. 'I'm just feeling particularly generous today, so go for it.'

The next morning after breakfast and a kiss, Isa did indeed take her book and go to the beach to read. I went up to the girl's tent, and she was very surprised to see me.

'Where is Isa?' she asked. I had introduced them the previous evening.

'She's gone to the beach. She told me I should come and see you,' I smiled.

She could not believe her ears. 'That's so grand of her! You mean you can come and spend some time with me? In my tent?'

'Yes, that's what Isa means!'

'Wow! I'm sharing my tent with a girlfriend. I'll request her to go to the beach as well.' She leaned into the tent and there followed some rapid-fire Italian with a female voice inside. Then a girl stepped out in her swimming suit, smiled and said 'Ciao!' to me, and continued, 'My friend has kept me awake half the night talking about you. Have fun!'

'My girlfriend and I have been talking about her half the night too,' I smiled back. 'I think we will have fun!'

The cute curly-haired girl and I stepped into the tent, zipped up its flap, and spent all morning strengthening Indo–Italian relations.

Isa was absolutely fine after this, and asked me how it had been. I've narrated this little incident here just for an indication of how different life in some youth circles in Europe could be from India.

Sicily with its dazzling green countryside and brilliant turquoise sea was like some anteroom to heaven. We finally hit Palermo, the town where Fabrizio, the bongo player who had jammed up with me in Rome, and who had invited us for a meal, lived. We got off at the train station in the late morning, and I decided to take a chance calling him – maybe he could suggest a suitable hotel.

'Hotel?' he exclaimed. 'No way! You're going to stay in my house! Remo and Isa, I'm so happy to hear from you at last! I spoke so much about you to my parents! You are at the station, no? Wait right there, don't move, I'm coming to pick you up.'

A few minutes later his little Fiat screeched to a halt before us, and after hugs and after we'd somehow fitted our haversacks into the tiny boot, he drove us (like a true Italian madman, of course) home.

His Mama and Papa were as friendly and warm and welcoming as him. They showed us to our room and told us to freshen up and come down for lunch, which was almost ready. We were happy to be in a family after long, and proceeded to have the greatest lunch we had had in a while. Real Italian home cooking. The Papa kept refilling our wine glasses, and the Mama our food plates. After that lunch we were good for one and only one thing: a good Italian siesta.

After three days of relaxing in Fabrizio's house with him and his wonderful parents, sightseeing in Palermo, and after a warm farewell dinner during which the Papa sang like an Italian opera star while Fabrizio played the bongos and I the guitar, Isa and I did what we had come to Palermo for: we took the long twelve-hour ferry to Tunisia. I was going to see a totally different country in a totally different continent. North Africa ahoy!

11

Dropping in on the Last Century

Tunisia: Shades of India

After more than half a year in Europe, stepping onto Tunisian soil was a flashback to India. It all started with the boat to Tunisia itself: it left from Palermo eight whole hours late. Reminded me of our monopoly-holding Indian Airlines back home, whose flights were often late by eight hours and more, and sometimes unceremoniously cancelled altogether after a whole day's wait at the airport.

I put this sticker on a page in my sketchbook the day we arrived in Tunisia. And towards the end of our stay and many sketches later, jotted down some impressions.

Besides the delay, the Oriental culture, the sounds, the smells of spices, the people and clothes, the poverty and lack of perfect hygiene – all of these instantly transported one back to India, even though this was North Africa and an unequivocally Muslim country.

I felt Tunisia's contrast with Europe and its similarity with India most starkly when I saw a bunch of poor kids playing at an oasis we visited. They had made toys out of sticks, strings and stones, they were ragged or half-naked, but their joy, merriment and shouts of glee contrasted sharply with the serious, bored, rather aggressive attitudes of the French kids of the same age back in Paris who played with branded sports equipment, clothing, shoes and protective gear that cost a fortune. Poorer kids always seemed to have more fun than rich ones. In India, one didn't have to travel to another country to witness this truth – we could watch the kids in posh bungalows and buildings, and then turn our eyes just a few degrees towards the kids in the slums behind them.

Matmata, Tunisia. ABOVE: A desert dweller relaxing/ praying just outside his 'courtyard'. MIDDLE: A housewife posing with a traveller. BELOW: Rooms accessible from the courtyard. Don't miss the room on the first floor in the middle with the most adventurous steps. Perhaps a kids' room.

The places we visited in Tunisia, and then in Algeria, somehow blend into a haze in my mind, and

many of my photographs and sketches seem to have been lost or misplaced. I do remember visiting a desert where traditional homes were 'built' in a most ingenious way: there were huge round holes dug into the ground, and these acted as courtyards. From these courtyards doors were dug which led to underground dwellings. These houses were amazingly cool in the summer and warm in the winter. We visited one in the sweltering summer heat, and witnessed this miracle of natural air-conditioning first-hand.

LEFT: Ancient troglodyte houses in Medenine, Tunisia. RIGHT: That's me in the photo.

Sketches made sitting in a tea-house in Kairouan, Tunisia. Of course, the women were passing by on the street outside. One never saw them in coffee- or tea-houses.

We visited Medenine, also bearing ancient houses, these built above ground. Beautiful white troglodyte dwellings with rounded roofs.

Perhaps the greatest pleasure we enjoyed in Tunisia was drinking their mint tea. Men could be seen sitting in tea-houses drinking it at all times of the day, and we soon became aficionados of this great sweet, cooling drink in the desert heat. A little before sunset it was a pleasure seeing some men stepping out freshly bathed, wearing a fresh clean white *jelaba*, a fresh jasmine stuck behind one ear, for their pre-sundown dose of mint tea.

Sexual harassment: More shades of India

Sadly, what stand out most from our short foray into North Africa are the incidents of sexual near-aggressions which Isa, and even I, encountered.

The first and perhaps the mildest one was when we were hitch-hiking in the middle of the desert. It's not that there were no lifts; there were no cars. But when the first vehicle came along after almost an hour's gap, the driver screeched to a halt, happy to pick us up. He was a farmer, carrying ancient rusty farming equipment at the back. As per the courtesy I had got used to in Europe, I let Isa enter first and sit in the middle between the driver and me, and I entered next.

The long wait in the desert heat and the monotonous road with nothing but hot burning sand on both sides made me drowsy, and I was soon nodding and then fast asleep. Luckily Isa didn't wake me up to tell me what was happening, or it might have led to an ugly scene; as it was, she handled it well enough on her own. The driver had tried to feel her thigh. She had pushed his hand away angrily a couple of times, and when she finally slapped it rather hard, he had taken out money from his pocket and offered it to her. One devastating look and a raising of her voice had put him in his place. Luckily for us, the local North Africans were still in awe of the French, their erstwhile masters and colonizers.

One day we landed up in a pretty little town rather late in the evening, and, still carrying our haversacks and guitar, stepped into a bakery to buy bread. The owner was a very mild-mannered and soft-spoken young man who spoke pretty good French, and we got chatting. We asked him to suggest a hotel or guest house, and he kindly invited us to stay in his house. He told us he lived with his whole family: his mother, his wife and children. And he invited us to dinner at the best North African restaurant in town. His name was Ahmed. I'll never forget it, because I had to call it out in anger and frustration during half the night.

After a wonderful dinner he drove us to his house, which was a new construction on top of a hillock. He opened the outside gate, and we stepped into the open courtyard which was lit by the moon but otherwise in darkness. We asked about his family, and he said it was late, they must have gone to sleep.

He showed us a room on one side of the courtyard, and told us it was the guest room, ours for the night. It was nice and comfortable, with an attached bathroom. He said he was going to go to sleep, and wished us good night.

We showered, got into bed, and turned off the lights.

After a while there was a soft knocking on the door. Ahmed, more soft-spoken than ever, was whispering from outside: 'I have forgotten to carry my house keys, and I don't seem to be able to wake up my wife. If I bang on the door any louder I'll wake up my aged mother, and she is a heart patient for whom sleep is most important. May I please sleep in the guest room too?'

Isa and I looked at each other. This was turning fishy. We decided there was no way we could let him sleep in the room with us, and we told him so. He kept knocking every five minutes, pleading and begging, and this went on for over an hour, but we refused to open the door.

Finally he said ok, I shall sleep on the hard ground here in the courtyard. We said fine.

After fifteen minutes the soft knocking and pleading started again. 'Please!' he kept saying. 'It is very cold here! I cannot sleep! I'll get pneumonia before the day dawns. Please allow me to sleep on the floor in the room.'

We kept refusing for another hour, while his gentle knocking and soft, plaintive pleading went on and on. But here was a man, politely begging to be allowed into a room in his own house, that too to sleep on the hard floor. Were we being too suspicious? Finally we started to relent. 'What if this is all true?' Isa and I asked ourselves. 'What if we find him totally sick, or worse, dead in the morning, lying outdoors in his cold courtyard, his family accusing us of having been ungrateful wretches? Should we let him sleep on the floor in one corner of the room?'

It was past three in the morning. His voice was now shivering with the cold. Taking pity, and giving him the benefit of the doubt – it was his house, he could have turned aggressive if he wanted to, but hadn't – we finally opened the door and let him in.

He thanked us profusely, took a bed cover and pillow from one of the cupboards, spread it on the floor, and went to sleep. We heaved a sigh of relief; he had been genuine, and we had done the right thing after all.

But we had hardly dozed off when we were awoken by his moans. He was tossing and turning, and his moans just wouldn't allow us to sleep. 'What is wrong, Ahmed?' I asked.

'Oh, the ground is very hard! I am not used to sleeping on the floor. I can't sleep, my whole body is aching, and I have to get to work, open the bakery and start baking bread in an hour or so from now. Can I please rest a while on one corner of the mattress on your bed? I promise I will not disturb you.'

We said no, but his moaning and groaning and tossing and turning went on anyway, making it impossible for us to sleep. What if this too was genuine? We had seen him in his bakery, and it was true that bakeries needed to open before dawn. Let the poor guy get an hour's decent sleep in his own house, we thought.

And thus, finally, by hook and by crook, Ahmed had reached where he wanted to be: in our bed. Isa slept against the wall in one corner, I slept in the middle against her, and he was given a small corner of his own. He thanked us profusely as though we had offered him shelter in our house, and that made us feel guiltier. In a few minutes he was snoring softly. Relieved, we finally fell asleep.

Only to wake up with his leg swung urgently over me, his snoring still continuing softly. 'Ahmed!' I shouted, shaking him awake. He appeared to wake up in a stupor, and I told him to go back to his corner. He did, and we almost fell asleep again.

Only to wake up with his arm tossed all the way across me, 'casually' reaching Isa. More shouting, more pushing: 'Ahmed! Ahmed! Go back to your side of the bed!'

And thus it went on and on. Sleep was impossible. Opening an eye to keep a check on him every five minutes, I finally saw the light of dawn through the curtains. It showed that his corner of the bed was finally empty. After ascertaining that he wasn't in the bathroom, I locked the room, and we fell into a heavy and much-needed sleep after the totally sleepless night.

We woke up after noon and took a shower, discussing the situation. We were livid and furious at our devilish host. We counted ourselves lucky that he didn't have other men in the house who got together and attacked and raped and did worse to us, but that didn't make up for his well-planned, methodical, well-mannered and soft-spoken all-night assault. As we stepped out of the shower we heard a knocking on the door. This time we were ready to take him head-on and give him a piece of our minds.

As I flung the door open angrily, two young Arab women with beautiful eyes (the rest of their faces were covered) stood there with large silver trays full of food and sweets and mint tea in their hands. They might have been his wife and sister, or maybe they were both his wives.

They walked in with fury blazing from their eyes and placed the trays on the table. We tried explaining what Ahmed had done to us all night, but they understood absolutely no French. We tried English too, which they understood even less. They just glared and walked out, and we realized that they were convinced that we had spent the whole night having wild wanton sex with their husband.

We ate to our hearts' content, since we were starving. Then we picked up our luggage and walked down the hillock back into the little town and headed straight for the bakery.

We were told Ahmed was downstairs in the baking room with his workers. When he saw us it was as though he had seen a pair of ghosts. He turned white (the first time I actually saw someone turning a few shades paler) and froze. We stood at the entrance and started giving him a piece of our minds at the top of our voices. Isa in particular let him have it.

He unfroze and begged us not to reveal his night's exploits in front of his workers, as this would spoil his reputation in town. But we were beyond feeling merciful, and went ahead and exposed him fully, describing his so-called 'hospitality' of the night in detail. He was in tears when we left his bakery, and I don't think he took any more unsuspecting young travellers home after that.

I'm not sure where the third incident took place, but considering there was alcohol involved, it must have been in Tunisia too, as Algeria is forbiddingly strict about its Islamic tenets.

It was up on a hill. We had gone there to visit one of the town's attractions as per my guidebook, a local cemetery with a magnificent panoramic view of the town. The cemetery was wonderfully simple and natural; the graves covered with smooth stones, blending with the arid dry desert earth – none carried names or monuments or plaques. Each one had an earthen water pitcher atop it though, originally filled with water to help the deceased cross the Great Desert. By now many of the pitchers were broken and disintegrating, but each grave carried the vestiges of one nevertheless.

We were the only ones there, and after watching a glorious sunset we walked around the little hamlet nearby, where we came across an unexpected terraced restaurant. It had a jukebox playing lovely Arabic and French music, and the owner was a slightly plump Arab lady wearing a very tight-fitting, short and low-necked shining dress exposing quite a bit of her voluptuous cleavage. She wore blue eyeshadow and bright red lipstick. Puffing on her cigarette, she welcomed us and told us she had lived several years in Paris – which I guess explained her unlikely way of dressing in this North African Muslim country, where she looked more a brothel madam than a restaurant owner.

Besides good French food they also served alcohol, and we ordered our first chilled beers in quite a while. We had just ordered our second one when a very well-dressed, jovial and friendly local man walked in. From the way he greeted and spoke to the lady we knew he was a regular, and he greeted us too. While we were finishing our beers and were about to order our dinner, he came up to our table and started chatting us up. Always happy to meet and talk to locals, I guess we had still not learnt our lesson from the two unpleasant experiences we had had, and we chatted back happily.

'Having your dinner already? Why not have a real drink first, a Scotch whisky? It's on me. I've lived in Marseille, and am always happy to meet people coming from France. Please do me the honour of accepting.' He seemed genuinely friendly and respectable, and although Isa declined, I accepted. With my whisky arrived a glass of French wine for Isa, and this she could not refuse.

The whisky after two mugs of beer, together with his interesting non-stop banter and heady music from the jukebox, coupled with my inexperience with mixing alcohols, went to my head. When he proposed a second whisky I had lost the will to say no, and was treating him like a dear long-lost friend. By the time I finished it, he was proposing a third one. By now I was really flying, and was trying with all my might to refuse. But he was turning unnaturally insistent, and though pretty sozzled, I could make out there was something not so friendly happening here. 'Come on, I hardly get to meet nice interesting people like you from France. Not just the whiskys, but your beers and wine and dinner are on me too. You must accept; it is very hurtful when you refuse someone's hospitality in my country,' I could hear him overriding my refusals through my stupor.

That's when the lady owner came up to our table. Through my daze I could hear her chastising the guy in Arabic. He was trying to argue back with her, but she overpowered him with her sheer presence. She kept interspersing her Arabic with French sentences, so I understood things like, 'No, you will not do this to these people', 'No, they are not that type; I spoke to them, and they are a very nice young couple', 'No, I will not allow you to do it to them'.

I don't know exactly what the 'it' was which he had in store for us, but you and I can take wild guesses. His usual modus operandi seemed to be to get his 'victims' drunk first. And the owner seemed well aware of his ways. She drove him away from our table and served us good wholesome steaks with fries and vegetables which made the alcohol go down considerably. Then she called up a taxi for us, and made the guy pay for everything.

What made her stand up for us that night I do not know, but I realize that we were very lucky to have come across quite a few guardian angels during our travels. It can get pretty dangerous out there, in some countries much more than in others. We made it through the whole trip totally unscathed, but when I think of young European women who have been molested, raped and even famously murdered in my once safe, friendly and hospitable Goa, my heart bleeds for them and their families. And it makes me appreciate yet again how lucky I've been in these and later travels in not-so-safe countries.

Tunisia had its clever thermostatic desert dwellings and beautiful troglodyte houses. Its delicious mint tea and couscous. Its magical oases. Memories of being invited home by a group of youth (all male of course) to a delicious dinner on a rotating community table which we all sat around and partook from. Despite all this, however, the first souvenirs which surface to my mind when I think of Tunisia are those of sexual aggression. This is very sad indeed, especially for a country's image. I ardently hope things have changed there since then.

To Algeria

Entry in my sketchbook on the day we crossed from Tunisia into Algeria. Read on, and you'll know what the drawing is all about.

Algeria was reputed to be the most difficult of the three North African countries we were planning to visit, the last one being Morocco, the most tourist-friendly. We just didn't expect it to be this difficult right from the start.

We had taken a bus from somewhere in Tunisia to Algiers, the capital of Algeria – no more hitch-hiking or accepting 'friendly' invitations for us in this continent, thank you very much. At the border, everyone in the bus (mostly European tourists) was made to get off – and wait. And wait. And wait. Finally we were made to stand in a queue to go through immigration. Going through this tiny step took forever, and if we thought that Tunisian authorities were unfriendly, these guys had invented unfriendliness. After what seemed like a lifetime, and after more waiting in the desert heat, we were made to queue up again – this time for a police check. Which of course took even longer than immigration. After that another hour or more of waiting and queuing for customs – you get the drift. By now we had run out of drinking water, and there was none being provided or sold there. We asked the authorities if we could please have some, but they glared back as though they would throw us into a cell full of scorpions for daring to ask. After almost four hours of crawling through these simple formalities, we were finally on our way to Algiers, where we arrived four hours late, that is at around midnight.

Isa and I had bought our tickets at the last moment, so we had middle seats in the very last row of the bus. We were among the last ones to alight, and by the time we had collected our haversacks and my guitar from the luggage compartment, all the passengers had departed.

That's when I noticed that the small bag I carried around my shoulder was open and felt lighter than usual. Upon checking it I noticed that I had been robbed. My purse and all my money were gone. And worse, so was my passport.

The bus had stopped in a beautiful old French city square which was deserted at this time of night. It was lit with very dim yellow bulbs, and had steps on all sides leading to streets running above it. I knew that, as an Indian citizen, I was doomed without a passport, especially in a country like Algeria. The bus had left, and now Isa and I were the only people in this empty deserted square – the people had all climbed those steps and walked away along the streets above.

Something made me walk around the square and shout out loudly, for anyone within earshot to hear: 'Please! I appeal to the man who has picked my bag. You can keep my money, but do return my passport. I am an Indian citizen, my passport is worthless in the market. Not like an American or British or French passport. It is already very difficult for me to travel around on an Indian passport, and without it I'll be in very, very deep trouble indeed… Please return it! Keep my money, but please return my passport! That's all I ask of you!' All this in my new-found French, of course, because that's the foreign language spoken in North Africa, not English.

Finally Isa said, 'The thief must be far away by now, surely out of hearing. We'll go to the Indian embassy tomorrow and try to solve this problem.' I wasn't sure India even had an embassy in a country like Algeria. And, knowing what things were like in Indian government offices, especially back in 1978, I wasn't looking forward to that experience. I kept walking around the square and shouting out the same things again and again, begging for the return of my passport, while Isa sat in one spot on our luggage.

Suddenly something landed from the darkness with a plop at my feet. Footsteps quickly ran away up on the street above the square. I picked up the object from the footpath. It was my passport – my prized possession was back in my hands! Of course the money wasn't returned. But the advantage of earning as you travel is that you never have a lot of money at once, and you can always recover it and make more as you go. Have guitar, will travel.

We picked up our luggage and, heaving unending sighs of relief, climbed up the steps. Above too we saw that everything was closed. Well, not quite; one solitary cafe owner was in the process of closing down shop in the next block.

We rushed up to him and asked if there was a hotel we could find at that hour and explained our predicament and bad experience in short.

'Was it you I faintly heard shouting some time ago?' he asked.

'Yes,' I said. He fell silent and thought for a while.

'That's a bad experience to go through while travelling, and I'm sorry you had to face it just as you arrived in my country,' he said, and I could see that his nationalistic feelings had been genuinely wounded.

'You will not find any hotel open and accepting guests at this time.' He fell silent again while he finished locking up, and then said, 'But if you wish, you can come and sleep in my house tonight. Only for one night, though. I don't want you to keep this bad memory of my country. I live alone, and I do not have any food at home to offer you. But if you've been robbed of all your money, I offer you breakfast at my cafe tomorrow morning. But only one breakfast, I do hope you understand.'

We had just made up our minds, after our last experience at the restaurant on the hill, never to accept hospitality in North Africa again. But here we were, having to choose between accepting his offer, or sleeping in the square and waking up without our haversacks, tent and guitar … and perhaps waking up dead or raped or both.

Isa and I exchanged a quick look which told each other we trusted this guy. First of all he wasn't trying to entice or charm us into coming. He was offering a choice, and it felt like it was genuinely meant to help us out.

We gratefully accepted. 'I have been robbed of all my money, but Isa has all of hers,' I told him. 'So we would not be requiring your kind generosity of food. But we accept your offer of shelter for the night with deep gratitude.'

And thus it was that, in a matter of minutes of arriving in Algiers, we came across our first thief and our first Good Samaritan. He offered us the carpeted floor of his living room to sleep on, where we spread our sleeping bags. We hadn't eaten a thing after that first harrowing experience at the border; but by now we were so exhausted and so drained by this overdose of experiences in one day that we soon collapsed into a deep sleep. A peaceful, undisturbed sleep.

The next morning he woke us and said, 'I have to leave for my cafe soon. I'm sorry I cannot leave you in my house, I have to lock up and go.'

'But of course!' we said. 'Just give us a few minutes and we'll be ready to leave.'

'Oh, you don't have to rush. Do have a shower. The bus journey must have been dusty and exhausting.'

We gratefully showered and changed our clothes, and were soon ready to follow him to his cafe, where we ordered large doses of North African breakfast dishes and cups of strong coffee.

After paying his bill and profusely thanking him again, we asked him for suggestions for nice but economical hotels, and set out walking in the streets of Algiers, taking in the differences between Tunisia and here.

A song for Goa in Algiers

We found a hotel in the middle of town, housed in a neglected but lovely old colonial building, overlooking a square. They said they had only one room vacant right on top on the fifth floor overlooking the square, which was half price as they had no lift – which suited us fine. But we'd have to wait while it was being cleaned. So we sat in the lobby and I got my guitar out of the case to help me pass the time, while Isa read her book.

I guess the hardships of being in North Africa got to me then, and I started thinking of the day I left Goa. I plucked a pattern on the strings, and it developed into what became 'Little Goa', a song which featured in my first album back home a few years later. I didn't want it to be a sad melancholic song of missing, though, so I reminded myself of the reasons why I had left Goa:

I went away from little Goa
On a warm October afternoon...
But I didn't go away forever
I'll be back someday
I'm just going to have a look-see
At other pretty little ladies
So that I may understand you more.

By the time I finished the basics of the song the room was ready, and Isa and I went up and had a long, much-needed sleep. We woke up in time for dinner and, after a good typical mutton couscous in a little restaurant nearby, returned to the room feeling fresh and reinvigorated.

'I have my periods,' Isa announced with a very mischievous glint in her eyes and a naughty smile on her lips.

'And that makes you smile?' I asked, disappointment in my voice.

'Do you know that North Africans write and read from right to left?' Isa asked enigmatically, ignoring my question. 'Well, there's a lot of things they like to do the other way round.'

My disappointment suddenly flew out the fifth-floor window into the cool Algiers night. 'Are you thinking what I think you're thinking?' I asked excitedly.

'Yes. Tonight, we shall do in Algeria the Algerian way,' she said, slowly turning off the bright light in the room.

And there, in our comfortable double bed by the window overlooking the starry quarter-mooned night sky and rooftops and minarets of Algiers, and with the help of some body lotion, Isa introduced me to the often-forbidden pleasures of sodomy. I had never thought about it and, even if I did, I had never imagined it would feel so good.

The next morning I woke up determined to recover at least some of the money I had lost the night before. So after breakfast I told Isa I was going downstairs into the square to test the busking waters in this strange city.

Even as I placed the guitar case on the floor and took out my guitar, a small crowd gathered around me. 'Ah,' said I, 'I'm going to recuperate my money pretty soon here!'

When I finished my first song, half the little square was already crowded with people surrounding me. But no one clapped, no one smiled, and certainly no one came forward to drop any money into my guitar case. They just gaped with mouths half-open.

I was halfway into my second song, as usual with my eyes closed, when a strong rough arm grabbed my strumming wrist, preventing me from playing.

My eyes jerked open, and I saw it was a cop. He started shouting at me in Arabic. Grabbing my guitar, he yanked it off me and shoved it roughly into the case. I tried explaining to him in French that I had just arrived in his country the night before and had been robbed of all my money, but that if it was illegal to busk in Algeria I was most willing to stop and not do it again.

He shouted back in Arabic what I understood to mean that he spoke no French, and demanded to see my passport. Seeing I was an Indian, he grabbed my left arm while I carried my guitar case in my right, and started dragging me away, I presume to the police station. The crowd around us kept gaping, and parted silently to let us pass. I started seeing visions of being beaten up by Algerian cops, having my guitar smashed (or confiscated, read stolen) by them, and languishing interminably in an Algerian jail for singing.

Suddenly, Isa's voice rang out loud and clear from our fifth-floor window. '*Qu'est-ce vous faites, monsieur? Pourquoi l'emmenez-vous?*' (What are you doing, sir? Why are you taking him away?) Hearing a woman's voice shouting at him in perfect French, the policeman froze and looked up. Seeing Isa's white skin, his rough hand instantly released me, and his tongue suddenly found the French language. '*Je suis désolé madame, mais il n'est pas permis de chanter dans les rues ici!*' (I'm sorry madam, but it is not permitted to sing in the streets here!) His voice had suddenly turned meek, apologetic, servile.

'You can just say so, can't you?' Isa's voice continued chastising him. 'I heard him say he would stop if it's not permitted! He wasn't insisting on doing something illegal!'

'*Non*, madame. You're right, madame.'

To save face in front of the crowd, he turned to me and added, 'Don't do it again,' and disappeared from the square.

The French colonizers had left Algeria in 1962, sixteen years ago. The cop must have been a lad of fifteen at the time, and must have been used to kowtowing, and probably to seeing his father kowtowing, to white-skin right until then. Old habits die hard. It was curious how it took a white-skin to save a brown-skin from being harassed by another brown-skin. Literally. The colours of skin played a very important role in this little drama. Once again I had a very strong guardian angel on my side, this time in the form of

Isa herself, who had luckily walked out of the shower, heard the commotion and stepped up to the window just in time. Or else she might not have heard of me for days. Or weeks. Or ever again, if you go by films about prisons and the police in countries like these.

Once back in the room Isa and I talked things over. These bad trips one after the other, and the lack of sufficient redeeming experiences, made us decide to leave North Africa at the earliest. The very next morning we would leave for Oran, the north-western Algerian city from where one took the shortest boat to Spain. We had found out that the Algeria–Morocco border had been closed anyway, due to some dispute over oil, so we were unable to go to Morocco, the most tourist-friendly country in North Africa, as we had planned to. Breathing European air would do us good.

Algeria: The parting shots

We sight-saw in Algiers the rest of the day, and after good North African meals and another night of Arabian bedroom delights, we woke up feeling a little better disposed towards Algeria. We decided to give it one last shot and visit Ghardaïa before leaving, since we'd come all the way already.

Ghardaïa was beautiful. An ancient city right out of the 1001 Arabian Nights. If we rubbed an old oil lamp found on the street hard enough, Aladdin's genie would certainly pop out. I saw pictures of Ghardaïa online recently, and it's been extremely well preserved; a lot of its buildings and streets have been restored, and the restoration has been done very well. But in 1978 it had been totally untouched for centuries; it was still ancient, some places crumbling and broken, men still moving around on donkeys, and that made its timeless charm priceless.

We were happy that our last experience in North Africa was going to be such a pleasant one, but North Africa had different plans for us. We left for Oran to catch the boat for Spain, but there the police demanded an exorbitant fee from us – just to leave the country. We spent the whole day at the port arguing with them against this totally ridiculous rule which appeared completely arbitrary, and had to spend an extra night in a hotel. When we returned next morning I guess the policemen saw that we truly weren't ready to pay the ransom, and this time they just allowed us to buy our tickets and leave once they had checked our papers.

Goodbye, North Africa, see you again I shall not.

¡Y viva España!

Spain provided a sigh of relief and a freedom which required no explanations.

Ah, it certainly did feel good to breathe European air again! To breathe in freedom from sexual, criminal and police harassment. To return to the present from the Middle or Dark Ages. To be able to hitch-hike and busk and make music again.

The first ride we hitched after we got down from the boat and positioned ourselves was in a Volkswagen Kombi, my dream vehicle for travelling. The people who gave us a ride were French, a father with his little daughter.

'I've seen you in Paris,' he said as we got into the van.

'What?! Where, how, when?' I asked. How could he remember someone he had perhaps crossed in a street?

'Didn't you play at the American Center?' he asked. 'I saw you playing a couple of songs there one hootenanny night, and when they announced that you were from India and your surname was Fernandes, I said you must be from Goa, the ex-Portuguese colony.'

It was a small world indeed!

'And when you were invited to return and do the main hootenanny slot yourself, I returned there with my friends.'

This lift was going to be another one of those 'planned in the stars' thing, because a couple of years from then this man was going to introduce me, in Goa, to the Frenchwoman who would be my wife and the mother of my sons. Once it's written in the stars, you can't escape it. She had been among his group of friends that hootenanny night; but if you didn't get to meet her in Paris, she came to you through a random lift in Spain.

The man's name was Michel Bonan, he was one of France's top commercial photographers with clients like Mercedes Benz, and he gave us his number and address in Paris, saying I must get in touch once I returned there. I promised I would, and I did.

Spain was oh-so beautiful. Little towns with cobbled streets and ancient squares with old stone fountains, old whitewashed houses with colourful flowerpots everywhere: on the windowsills, on veranda grills, fixed to the front walls, even on the footpaths. Friendly honest people, great food, great sangria. And a language so similar to Portuguese, within a couple of days I could understand and make myself understood without too much difficulty.

Somewhere in a camping ground we met a young Spanish couple, Juan and Paquita. Their tent was right next to ours, and she was one noisy lover. That night she moaned – no, I'd say screamed and grunted – rhythmically for at least an hour, putting us right in the mood in our tent, and probably putting the whole camping ground in the mood as well.

The next morning they told us they were heading for a beachside town, where good friends had lent them their empty holiday home. And we were welcome. We gladly accepted. The town itself was beautiful and old, but there was a new housing area by the beach with several huge and luxurious homes obviously belonging to city people who holidayed there during weekends. Now it was the middle of the week, and they were all empty. Juan said he wasn't very sure which one his friend's house was, so he kept entering empty compounds and gardens, walking to the back of the houses, and coming back saying, 'No, not this one.'

Finally he found the one, and said we'd have to use the back door, as that's what his friends had instructed him to do. The house was extremely comfortable and well equipped, and we had a magnificent suite for each couple. Isa and I had a glorious hour-long bath in the king-sized bathtub, soaked in all the bath bubbles and lotions we could find in the well-stocked bathroom.

In the evening Juan and Paquita took some bottles of great wine from the cellar under the kitchen and we had a quiet candlelit party in the living room. Juan opined we ought to keep the shutters shut. 'The light might attract the attention of townspeople, maybe even cops, and it will be unnecessarily time-consuming and inconvenient explaining to them that we're friends of the owners,' he explained, and we totally agreed.

The next day we went into the town, and there Juan and Paquita saw how easy it was for me to make money busking. Within a couple of hours I had a minor fortune in my guitar case, enough to pay for a few days' camping grounds' fees, food, drink and more like museums, exhibitions and travel. I invited them to lunch to thank them for sharing that great accommodation with us.

That evening back in our luxury home they said they were leaving for Madrid the next day, and insisted we come and stay with them when we hit the city.

The next morning before leaving Juan said they were running short of money for the return journey, could they please borrow some? They would return it as soon as we reached Madrid. I said sure, and I lent him whatever I had earned the previous day.

Today it surprises me how naive Isa and I were. Especially Isa, since I was after all new to Europe. Even you readers must have guessed that the luxurious bungalow's owner was no friend or even acquaintance of Juan and Paquita's; they had looked for and broken into the first house with an easy-to-pick kitchen door lock they had found. I realized this when I met and got to know Juan better in Madrid.

Juan and Paquita left next morning, and now Isa and I were on our own once again. Spain continued like a pleasant dream. One of my favourite works for classical guitar was *'Recuerdos de la Alhambra'*, and Alhambra was therefore one of our first stops. Built by a team comprising Muslims, Jews and Christians on top of ruins left behind by the Romans, this palace/fortress is a marvel of beauty and intricacy. Though teeming with tourists, all I heard during our long visit was the plaintive, melancholic guitar piece playing in my brain. The Walkman hadn't been invented yet.

Puerta del Sol, Toledo. Puerta *means 'door' or 'gate'; in this case ancient 'city gates'.*

I had just seen my friend Noel Godin act and sing brilliantly as Don Quixote in the musical *Man of La Mancha* in Bombay before I left, and it was thrilling to now travel around Quixote's region in Spain. Toledo was another historic revelation of its Christian, Muslim and Jewish multicultural past.

When we finally hit Madrid train station, we were sitting on the footpath curb waiting for the bus which would take us towards the camping site. Two gypsy kids around twelve years of age were hovering around us, handsome, with dark skins and black eyes and hair, roughly dressed. I had had lots of warnings about gypsies, especially gypsy kids, and my grip around my guitar case tightened.

They came and sat next to me on the curb. '*Ei hombre*, can I play your guitar?' one of them asked. Despite the warnings, something made me hand it over to him. He picked it up, played an incredibly fast and accurate flamenco salvo of machine gun-like bullets and, without a word, handed me back my guitar with a disdainful look which said, 'Match that if you can!' He probably expected a ragged version of 'Blowin' in the Wind'.

I smiled and nodded my appreciation at him, and played him the superfast section of my guitar–sitar piece. A look of mutual admiration was exchanged, and our bus arrived.

Who hasn't heard of the Spanish bullfights? I had grown up to images of the incredibly-dressed matadors in intricately embroidered tight trousers and jackets, waving a sword and a red cape like graceful ballet dancers, and I'd heard exciting Spanish bullfighting music and songs with two trumpets playing in harmony and guitars strumming furiously, and passionate cries of '*Olè*' interspersing it all. Lately I had heard of movements asking for the banning of this 'sport', denouncing it as cowardly cruelty to animals; and I had heard of movements defending it as a courageous, skilful and graceful duel between man and beast.

I decided to see for myself and make up my own mind, and went one day to the legendary Plaza de Toros de Las Ventas. Bulls were brought out one by one; picadors on horses speared them with colourfully decorated lances which remained stuck in their bodies, making them bleed and weakening them; then the hero, the matador (literally meaning killer), strutted in and wounded the bull some more with his sword during a display of skill at waving the cape and avoiding the bull's charges, and when the bull was finally too weak to even run and charge any more, finished him off with an accurate plunge of his sword into the bull's heart.

I'm sure there have been a few matadors who were legendary in their exploits, but what I saw that day was neither courageous nor graceful. And I read later that the bulls were subjected to intense mental and physical torture for at least two days before the fight. There will never be another bullfight I shall attend, thank you very much.

We finally decided to go meet Juan and Paquita and collect the money I had lent them. The address they'd given us turned out to be a squatters' commune, one of those empty crumbling old buildings simply taken over by homeless, moneyless and mostly jobless youth. Every room had beddings spread out here and there, and there were quite a number of people around. No, Juan wasn't in, but he stayed there most days all right, and usually came in later in the evenings.

We met him the second or third time we tried. He was friendly as always, but a bit surprised to see us, and didn't seem as keen to return the money as he had promised; financial problems, you see – he would try though, maybe we could meet again tomorrow? No, he wasn't living with Paquita; they had got together to undertake that journey, but they weren't a permanent couple, you see.

I don't remember whether I recovered the full sum from him, but he did return at least some of it.

The parting of ways

Here Isa and I parted ways. No, we didn't split up; but now she had to return to work in Paris, and for some reason the French embassy in Madrid wouldn't give me a visa. So Isa left for home, and I got myself a visa for Portugal.

I was going to leave in a couple of days, but before that there was an eventful night with Juan. We were walking around the centre of the city at around midnight or later, when a big police van drew up. A couple of cops jumped out and, without explanation, pushed us into the armoured back of the van. Apparently for no other reason than our long hair and unconventional appearance. I had all my papers in order, and I obviously had no drugs or anything illegal on me; but they didn't even check what we had or didn't.

There were a few more people in the van, mostly creatures of the night. They all seemed cool about being there. So was Juan. But I, who had never been picked up by cops before, was quite shaken. Juan asked me to stand between him and the driver's cabin where the cops were so that he couldn't be seen. He fished out what looked like a card from his inside pocket; the van was dark, lit up only by the passing shop and street lights. Then, tearing it up into four pieces, he started swallowing them.

'What is it?' I whispered.

'My membership card of the anarchist movement,' he whispered back.

At the time I had no clear idea about what the anarchist movement was; when I found out later that it was an armed and violent resistance against the government, involving killings and bombings of policemen and people in authority including ministers, I shivered thinking what Juan – and I, being in his company – would have been subjected to if they had searched us and found the card on him when they picked us up. Torture, beatings, and indefinite or permanent incarceration. Franco was dead, but his fascist legacy still carried on unofficially in Spain.

The van slowly circled around the seedier parts of the city, picking up half a dozen ladies of the night in the red-light district. They protested vociferously as they were being bundled into the van, but once in, were cool and joking and laughing loudly among themselves, as though they were in a familiar city bus on their regular route.

Finally, at about 3 a.m., their quota for the night fulfilled, the cops drove into the police precinct compound. We were made to alight, and were marched into a small waiting room, harshly lit with naked tubelights. The prostitutes shamelessly teased and flirted with the responsive cops. The room had enough chairs for all of us, a large jar of drinking water and a common glass, and a dirty but adequate toilet. The cops locked the door on us and disappeared.

After almost three sleepless hours on those hard uncomfortable chairs, during which the ladies chatted and laughed with all of us as though we were bosom pals, the cops opened the door and reappeared.

And, without any preamble, without any explanation as to why we had been picked up and held the whole night, or why we were now being released, they simply barked, 'Go. Come on now, everybody out.'

We trooped out, waved our goodbyes to each other like old friends, and started walking towards our respective destinations in the breaking light of the Madrid morning.

I was still dazed with lack of sleep and the 'excitement' of the experience. Juan walked coolly, hands in his jeans pockets, whistling merrily. As we passed a sleeping house with milk bottles just delivered on its doorstep, he opened the garden gate, walked in, picked up both bottles and walked out. Opening one he passed it to me, and opening the other took a very long swig.

'Aaaah! I was thirsty!' he exclaimed and, freshly out of a police station, swaggered down the street drinking stolen milk.

There's no dearth of exciting people you can meet when you travel like I did... And, if that guardian angel is well-qualified and efficient, you survive them all.

12

Paris: Mon Péché Mignon

Belgium and the diamond scene

Later that day in Madrid I was woken up by the receptionist of the guest house to answer a phone call which would change my plans considerably. It was from Rajesh Jhaveri, a guy who'd come to meet me backstage in Bombay after the 'farewell' show there with my band Street. He was the son of a diamond merchant, was crazy about music, had studied the sitar, and had dreams of creating the mother of all Indo-Western fusion albums. Would I play guitar on it? I had said sure, but I was leaving for Europe in a couple of weeks, and didn't know when I'd be back.

How had he tracked me down in Spain? He had called my parents in Goa, who had given him Hubert's number in Paris, and luckily I had happened to drop Hubert a postcard with my number in Madrid. Rajesh had recorded the other Indian musicians in Bombay, including Hariprasad Chaurasia, Rais Khan, Shivkumar Sharma, Zakir Hussain and Shamim Ahmed, and jazz musicians/rockers like Louis Banks, Braz Gonsalves and Ranjit Barot. Only I was missing from his list. Rajesh was presently in Antwerp, Belgium (one of the centres of the diamond business in Europe). Would I join him there if he sent me an air ticket?

Sure. When you're footloose and fancy-free, you can leave for Belgium instead of Portugal at the drop of a peseta.

And thus I found myself sharing a hotel room with someone who was the exact opposite of all the characters I'd met in Paris and on the road these last few months. Rajesh might have had a passion for music, but he came after all from a diamond merchant family, and he had the sobriety of mind and the business acumen of one.

I remember the smell of Indian spices permeating everything as this pure Gujarati cooked pure vegetarian food in the room's kitchenette. Europe still hadn't woken up to vegetarianism, and a customer who asked for 'something strictly without meat, fish or eggs' in a restaurant was viewed as a space oddity, or a goat.

After quick visits to one or two of the better recording studios that Antwerp had to offer, we found them thoroughly inadequate, so off we flew to London. This flying from starred hotel to starred hotel certainly differed from hitch-hiking from camping ground to camping ground. Though not half as exciting, a bit of comfort and luxury were welcome after a few months of having been on the road.

London Town

Ah, here I was in a country to which I had been denied entry by a mean-hearted migrant Indian immigration officer just a few months earlier. I found London in general less friendly and more racist towards Indians. I guess it was due to the sheer number of Indians there. Familiarity does breed contempt.

But I was in the city which boasted some of the best studios, musicians and engineers in the world. More than anything else, to me it was the city where The Beatles had recorded their songs and launched their global conquest.

We chose a studio, and I recorded my parts there. The studio receptionist was a beautiful black girl, and I'd never seen such amazing purple eyes before. When I told her so, she said, 'Thank you sweetheart, but they're

ABOVE: Infinite Fusion, the live band with which we performed music from Rajesh Jhaveri's album after I was back in India in 1979, live on stage at Patkar Hall. BELOW: Backstage, looking like a line-up of suspects, left to right: Remo (vocals, guitar and flute); Dinsha Sanjana (keyboards); Taufiq Qureshi (tabla); Miles Perry (bass); Rajesh Jhaveri (sitar); Ranjit Barot (drums); Dallas Smith (saxophone and lyricon).

coloured lenses.' I'd never heard of lenses before, but she looked amazing anyway. The next day she turned up with eyes that looked like a cat's. Meooooww.

Since I was in London I decided to visit the French embassy there and try my luck for a visa. And lucky I was. Surprisingly the embassy was housed in a tiny old English building, and the visa section was manned single-handedly by a very elderly gentleman. Unlike the French embassy people in Madrid, he didn't ask me why I was obtaining so many French visas and spending so much time in France, what I did and how I sustained myself there, and so on. In fact he asked me nothing at all. Just took my passport, stamped a three-month extendable visa on it, and that was that. I made a mental note to return here the next time my French visa ran out.

Of course I also took the opportunity to see the sights of London. London was the theatre capital of Europe, so I saw a couple of plays. But after Paris, the city and the people seemed very dull, colourless and sad to me. The dark brown of the bricks and the grey of the concrete and tarmac and sky were depressing. To say nothing about the rain. Or the food. Or that underlying racism towards Indians I spoke about.

Anyway, after the recording was done and the sights were seen, I headed straight back to my beloved Paris.

I'd never felt truly at home anywhere other than Goa until then. But now I finally understood the expression 'home away from home'. Whenever I returned to Paris from anywhere – whether from other countries or other places in France – I felt I was returning home.

Besides, there's one fundamental truth I reiterated to myself when I returned to Paris that day: I had come to Europe to travel, not to 'try to make it' in music. Or else, London would be the place for me to be, because there was no way I was going to write songs in French. But what can you do when you're in love? I was head over heels in love with Paris. And with France. All I felt for London was an aversion.

I went back to Isa's and Hubert's. It felt great living with a woman. Felt grown up, running a home together. This wasn't just about sexual convenience any more, though that still played a very important role.

My first multitrack recordings

It was around this time that Eric introduced me to his Revox tape recorder. It was a huge grey spool tape machine, and its speciality was that one could record on the left and right stereo channels independently of each other. He said, 'I think you'll be able to make full use of it, so I'm lending it to you. Keep it for as long as you like.'

So now I could record say the main vocal and rhythm guitar simultaneously on the left channel, and while transferring them to the right channel and listening to them on headphones, I could add say the bass guitar – and now I'd have all three on the right channel. Then I could transfer all three back to the left channel while adding say a flute. And thus I could go on and on ad infinitum. Only, the quality of the earlier recordings which were on the layers 'below' would gradually gather hiss, and would keep losing quality.

The whole transfer and addition of the new instrument or voice had to be done in one long take of the whole song; no stopping and punching in was possible. Also, every time I added a track, all the tracks recorded until then were firmly locked on one single mono track; if you recorded something too soft or too loud, no adjustments (neither in volume, nor EQ, FX or

The messy basement in Hubert's apartment which, when Eric lent me his Revox spool tape recorder (centre), acted as my home recording studio.

whatever) were possible later on. So I had to envisage and foresee all that I was going to record later, record each track at more or less the right volume and with the desired (and available) effects, and charge valiantly on. I bought myself a couple of little luxuries: a tape echo machine called Copycat made by WEM, and a few pedals for guitar, as and when I saved money.

I could not have asked for a tougher or stricter introduction into the world of multitrack recording. That is why it was sheer luxury when I got myself my first four-track cassette recorder in Goa a few years later, on which I recorded my first four albums (*Goan Crazy!, Old Goan Gold, Pack That Smack!* and *Bombay City!*) and the music for two films (*Jalwa* and *Trikal*). Seems like a joke today, when one has literally unlimited tracks and plug-in inserts on the computer.

But in 1978, to me luxury dwelt in this two-track Revox spool tape recorder. For the first time, I was listening to all my acoustic guitar songs with arrangements as I envisioned them: electric lead and bass guitars, three voice harmonies, flutes, bongos and tambourines. The tape recorder was set up in the cave beneath our apartment, and I now spent hours and hours there every day and night.

One of the first songs I recorded was 'Little Goa', which I had written in the hotel lobby in Algiers. And also other songs which I haven't re-recorded or released till date, such as 'Cathedrals' (my sister Belinda's favourite song of mine), 'You' (written in Bombay for the girl in Goa who I thought was a snob), and so on.

New friends, a new lifestyle in Paris

This was also the time when I met another batch of friends who would seriously change my lifestyle in Paris. Hubert told me about a girl he had known a couple of years earlier; he said she was still in school, but way, way beyond her years. She made love like a goddess, and was wild in every way.

This description was enough to get my mind and blood racing. She was coming to Paris, and would be staying in our apartment. I was eagerly looking forward to it.

She turned out to be a beauty. That first night after dinner she went to sleep in my bed. Hubert and I stayed up sipping wine and talking. He had a more or less steady girlfriend now, and no, he wasn't interested in resuming a relationship with this girl any more. I turned off the lights an hour later and went to bed myself. When I put an arm around her she woke up, and we made passionate silent love in the darkness, no words exchanged. And promptly fell asleep in each other's arms.

I considered my sister, who was eight years younger than I was, a kid. This girl was nine whole years younger to me, and the fact that she was younger than even my kid sister held a strange fascination. She called me *'playboy des isles'* or playboy from the islands, as I came from the land of beaches and coconut trees. She lived in the mountains in the south of France, and I called her *'playgirl des montagnes'* or playgirl from the mountains. Besides becoming casual lovers, we became good friends, and our friendship lasted until about four years ago when she came to visit me in Porto. Then, although we were no longer lovers, a stupid misunderstanding (on her part) fractured a friendship which had lasted thirty-eight years.

Anyway, through her I met her whole gang of friends, who were all at least five years younger to me. And a couple who were older than I was. Age didn't matter. It was a common way of thinking and style of life which drew us together. We all loved music, art, books and movies, but most of all we loved hanging out together. Our hangouts usually started in the evening and lasted through the whole night.

Like I have repeatedly said, I came from sexually repressed India, and though I'd had quite a few experiences both in India and by now in Europe too, they weren't enough. Nothing is really enough when you're in your twenties. Sex was no taboo here, and certainly not in this group, and no one really went steady one-on-one. Who one met in the (unlocked) bathroom and ended up taking a shower with, or whose bed one ended up in, or who one woke up with the next morning, or who one felt an attraction to during the day, was often a matter of welcome chance. And when new girls (friends of friends) ended up at one of our hangouts, I'm happy to say many gravitated towards me. I was after all the *'Indien exotique'*. Although there were lots of Africans, North African Arabs, Vietnamese and so on in France (those being their ex-colonies), the French had hardly seen any Indians, and things Indian were the rage there due to the hippie movement, though it was gradually coming to an end. By that time I had shaved off my beard, got to wearing and tying my shoulder-length hair in different ways, had pierced one ear in a little earring boutique in Saint-Michel, and was given to wearing clothes like loose colourful Afghan pants disappearing into knee-length leather boots, and shirts which could have been borrowed from my girlfriends. My hippie look was out, and a new, almost androgynous look was in. The look was very avant-garde in Paris – I loved it, and took to it

Summer in the French countryside.

naturally, though I was strictly and fully heterosexual. The girls seemed to find it, and my brown skin and black hair and black eyes, irresistible. Good for me.

That look was to carry on onto my stage (and also offstage) persona when I returned to India. An officer at the Bombay airport, seeing my earring, asked with a very lascivious smile, 'What does that signify?' When I said, 'Oh, it's the latest trend for men in Paris,' he smiled even more broadly and knowingly, saying, *'Haan, haan, main samajh gaya hoon!'* (Oh yes, I've understood!)

Besides the clothes, kajal around the eyes became another regular feature, together with neck chokers, rings, belts, boots. But my jewellery was never made out of gold and precious stones – I can't stand those. It was mostly artistic stuff made out of oxidized silver and leather – and I developed a great attraction for turquoise. I wasn't surprised when someone told me later that it was 'my' stone as per some calculations of the astral kind. But I'm jumping ahead of myself.

These new friendships in no way took away from my friendship with Isa, Hubert and Eric. We're friends to this day – I say that in the present even though Eric died of cancer on his beloved Réunion Island a few years ago. I was shocked and devastated, and I still think of him as living.

I have never wanted to hide any aspect of my life from anyone, especially not from my lovers, and when I talked to Isa about my new friendships and liaisons, she felt she couldn't 'share' me with other girls. So we slowly stopped being lovers, though our friendship stayed as good as ever – which I see as a great personal achievement, because Isa was someone who could never keep good relations with old boyfriends; she always spoke ill of them. When I remarked upon it one day it made her stop and introspect, and perhaps that's the reason why she's still friends with me. Which is wonderful.

One day Hubert asked me, 'How come you're going out with almost every girl you meet? Don't you think it's immature? This is the kind of thing we did when we were teenagers.'

I explained myself to him. 'Hubert, you did it as a teenager. I didn't, and I'm making up for that. And today, here in Europe, I'm using relationships and sex as a way to evolve; to learn non-attachment, non-possessiveness, and the universal nature of life. If I do meet a woman who makes me feel like settling down with her, I'll do it; but right now I feel a universal love and affection for each and every girl I go with, and I'm learning how not to feel jealous and possessive when she feels the same about other guys.'

Hubert understood, and never asked me this question again. Years later he did see me settling down with one woman. And well, what can I say, except that I'm very grateful I had all these beautiful experiences before AIDS hit the world. I felt truly very sorry for the as yet inexperienced youngsters when it did.

One day someone came up with the news that a friend of a friend, who owned a Volkswagen Kombi (that van favoured by nomads and which I loved) was willing to drive us all to the country house of another friend of a friend for the weekend. Excited, all of us (and some friends of friends) took the metro and assembled at this guy's door – only to find out that he'd taken ill. But he didn't mind lending his Kombi to us if one of us knew how to drive.

No one did. I kept silent, but one of them remembered having seen photos of me in my car in Goa.

'Yes, I do know how to drive, but not on the right side of the road! Besides, I don't have a European driving license. And yet besides, I'm a foreigner here, and I don't want trouble with the law.'

My protests fell on deaf ears. I wasn't going to let everybody down due to mere trifles like that, was I? And, before I knew it, I was in the driver's seat. A seat on the wrong side of the car, with gears on the wrong side of the seat – in short, everything I was totally unaccustomed to.

But it was exciting. It was an afternoon in the summer, most Parisians were out of the city on holiday, and the traffic was down to a minimum. The guy who knew the way best sat next to me to give directions. As we neared the exit from Paris I had quite got the hang of it all, when suddenly we saw a group of cops in the distance, stopping random cars for checking.

I saw one of the cops take a step forward on seeing our Kombi, which was incidentally brightly illustrated.

'I'm going to drive away fast!' I said nervously.

'Don't!' shouted the guy at my side. 'Drive straight to the cop and stop there.'

'What?! Right into the lion's mouth?!' I said incredulously.

'Yes! Just do as I say!' His voice was urgent but calm.

The cop was about to raise his hand to signal us to stop, when he was caught by surprise by our vehicle heading straight for him and stopping instead. My co-pilot, who knew the roads like the back of his hand, rolled down his window and, before the cop could speak, asked most innocently and politely: '*Bonjour monsieur*, which road do we take for Noyers-sur-Serein, please?'

The policeman, programmed to do his duty, saluted and gave detailed directions. And, before he had fully realized what had just happened, my friend gave him a bright smile, said '*Merci bien!*', rolled up his window and whispered 'Go quickly!' to me through his smiling teeth.

As soon as we were back on the road, everyone burst into nervous laughter.

'*Merde*, if they had searched us, they would have found my grass!' said someone from the back seat.

'And my hashish!' said someone else.

'And my cocaine!' exclaimed my co-pilot.

'And the first thing he would have asked to see is my driving license, which I don't have, if you remember,' I said.

Hmmmm. My guardian angel was with me in Paris too.

In my early days in Paris, Eric and I had gone to a club (what we call a 'disco' in India). I saw a very beautiful young girl sitting alone. I walked up to her.

'Would you care to dance with me?' I asked.

'If you like,' she answered.

'Oh, it's all right, you don't *have* to,' I said and returned to my seat. I wanted her to dance with me if the feeling was mutual, not just 'if I liked her to'. Little did I know then that *'si tu veux'*, which she had literally translated as 'if you like', is a common French expression commonly used to mean 'Sure!'. The English version sounded pretty disinterested to me.

A year later I met her again in a totally different context, through different friends. Her name was Francine, and she actually remembered me from the club. She even remembered seeing me in the street one day while she was passing by in a bus. That's how rare Indians were in France in those years.

She was more beautiful than ever, and in broad daylight I saw that she was even younger than she had seemed in the club lighting. In fact she had just passed out from school a year or two earlier. We became long-term lovers, and I half-moved into her very cute apartment in one of the most picturesque areas of Paris, on the Quai de Jemmapes, which still wasn't the chic quartier it is today. Barges skilfully negotiated this narrow canal, and ancient locks lowered and raised the water for them to pass under the little Parisian bridges across it, while all traffic patiently stopped. They still did a few years ago when I visited last, and I think they still do. I loved watching these manoeuvres. Her lovely old building was right next door to the legendary Hotel du Nord,

The fabled Hotel du Nord in Paris.

where the classic film by that name had been made in 1938, containing the unforgettable phrase, *'Atmosphère! Atmosphère! Est-ce que j'ai une gueule d'atmosphère?'* She loved sunshine, so I painted a huge colourful sun who wore sunglasses on the wall behind her bed.

I introduced her to all my friends, and she became a happy part of the group, particularly the new bohemian one. Eventually I also introduced her to the wonderful guy who became her husband and the father of her two daughters. We are all good friends until today.

Among this younger group, I noticed that many were fond of speaking ill of their parents. It was almost fashionable to say they didn't get along with them and hardly ever visited them – that they were stupid and *con*. I guess those who did have a loving familial relationship hid it almost as an embarrassment under peer pressure. I also visited a high school once for some reason, and was shocked to learn about students' violence, not only towards each other, but towards their teachers. And I realized that however many things I might love about France, Paris and Europe in general, I was very happy that my Goa and India were still old-fashioned in these ways, and held on to those good old-world family values. And I hoped they always would.

Other than busking

Hearing the recordings I was churning out on his Revox in our cave, Eric decided to send a few to someone he knew who knew someone at the Polydor record company in Paris. 'Don't expect much,' he said. 'I have friends who have been sending them tapes for years, but they evoked no positive response whatsoever. But your songs are good.'

I was thrilled to hear from Polydor shortly. They wanted to hear a better recording of three songs, and were assigning me their studio for the day. Eric was proud of me and drove me there with all the instruments I would need.

No one had done a solo multitrack recording in their studio, and the Polydor engineers and A&R manager were quite kicked. After the Revox, recording on a sixteen-track was a piece of cake, especially with engineers handling the machines and mixing and mastering while I only had to sing and play. I'd never sounded so good, and I completed the three songs in no time at all.

But eventually the fact that my songs were in English, and that I didn't have a live band, didn't go in my favour when the big bosses met to take a decision.

However, the girl Eric knew in Polydor had a very cute plump friend with the most beautiful and kind light blue eyes, she lived close by, and we became lovers for a while. All in all, not a total loss.

Also, through the Polydor demo recordings, a French guitar legend called Christian Boulé – or rather his wife, who managed his band – heard of me. Christian had been second guitarist in The Steve Hillage Band in England. Hillage was recognized as a guitar hero not only in England, but in France too; he had developed a very unique electronic sound out of the electric guitar using multiple echo machines and volume pedals and other stuff, and had opened for Queen before 70,000 people prior to touring successfully on his own. Would I like to join Christian's band, which was called Rock Synergie, as guitarist/flautist/singer and go on an all-France concert tour, opening for Hillage? Sure.

The only two photos I have with Rock Synergie, a band I played with in Paris. LEFT: On stage.
RIGHT: Shooting in a TV studio somewhere in France.

We rehearsed, and then performed for a week at the renowned Campagne-Première in Paris as a warm-up for the tour.

Before we left, Christian's wife came over one morning. I was still in bed. Without much preamble, she took off her boots and slipped under the covers with me. I was taken by surprise; I didn't want a relationship like that with the wife of a musician with whom I was playing. In fact I'd never had anything to do with anyone's wife before, and it didn't seem quite right. But though I had learnt a lot from women in Paris, I hadn't learnt how to say no.

After we made love she surprised me even more by saying she had fallen in love with me, and wanted to leave Christian and move in with me – with her child and all. She was Christian's official manager, and said she would be very good at launching my career. But hey, this was not at all what I wanted, and I told her so.

We left on the tour, one happy family. These were some of France's top rock musicians, and it was a change being in a professional musical set-up after my nomadic life. Huge venues, huge audiences (who mainly came to see superstar Hillage; Christian was just launching his band), our own coach which drove us all over France while Hillage had his separate one, a new city and hotel every second day – the life of a rock 'n' roller on the road.

But after four or five concerts I grew bored, realized I didn't like or enjoy the music all that much, and told Christian's wife that I wanted to leave. She asked if I was lonely, and if bringing along a girlfriend might help. I said yes, and called up Sol, an exotic girl of Chinese–African descent from Réunion Island who lived in Paris; she was happy to join us in the next city.

But after the tour I left the band. Like I said, I hadn't come to Europe to 'try and make it' in music. I've never been good at making contacts and networking to further my career, neither then nor ever in my life. I've been really lucky that things just 'happened' to and for me. We'll come to that later.

After the tour Christian's wife renewed contact, and said Christian wanted to see me and talk to me. Was he going to beat me up or kill me?

I didn't know. This was another situation I'd never been in before. And never since, thankfully. But I knew that mature people talked these things out, especially in the West, and I said sure.

The two of them came over, I served them coffee, and all three of us sat around the table, all acting calm and normal but inwardly pretty tensed and nervous, Christian particularly so.

'So my wife is beautiful, uh?' he started.

'Yes,' I replied.

'She's a great lover, no?'

'Yes,' I repeated.

'She wants to move in with you, with our child and all. Is that what you want?'

'No, that's not at all what I want,' I said, 'and I've told her so. I live a free life, and I really didn't intend to have anything to do with your wife other than friendship.'

Christian was visibly relieved, and he relaxed palpably.

'I'm happy to hear that. These things happen between two people, it's a natural part of life. They've happened to me too. But I'm happy that this isn't going to break up our marriage, because I really love her.'

After the coffee and some friendly chatter, the two of them hugged me and left. I never heard from them again.

I googled Christian Boulé while writing this today, after all these years, and was saddened to know that he died of cancer in 2002. But I was happy to see my name as part of his band on his website, though I had been with them for just a couple of months.

My summer in Paris

Yes, I know – all I'm writing about is Paris now. The thing is that I was falling deeper in love with this city, and with France, every day. I was now seriously thinking of settling there, and visiting Goa and my family as often as possible.

I was trying to think of ways and means of obtaining French nationality. Someone suggested a 'marriage of convenience', i.e. marrying a French woman-friend for the sole purpose of obtaining French nationality. I believe there were women who would do this professionally, for a fee, but of course I wanted nothing of the sort. So I asked my best French woman-friend, Isa, whether she would go through such a marriage with me.

She said, 'If you want to have a real marriage with me, that is, live together as husband and wife, and even make children, yes. But just a marriage for nationality – I'm sorry, but no.'

Though I liked and loved Isa a lot as a friend, I had an aversion to traditional marriage, and my time to have children had most certainly not come; so that option was out. There was no way I was going to trick her (or anyone) into thinking I was marrying her 'for real' while secretly doing it only for the nationality, and then divorcing her as soon as the papers came through.

Since I'd gone hitch-hiking during that first summer, this year I decided to stay put mostly in Paris. And, for the first time, I was able to appreciate this city devoid of crowds and traffic – every Parisian worth his camembert goes on vacation in the summer, taking with him the traffic jams which accompany his daily life in the city throughout the year, on to the highways leading to the south.

A friend lent me a bicycle for the summer, and I rode around everywhere, my long hair flying in the wind, learning the streets like a pro. I truly was beginning to feel like a Parisian, like I belonged here. I was thrilled to see 'my' city in the bright sunshine, to watch the people so relaxed and colourful and smiling, and especially to watch the beautiful Parisian girls wearing skimpier and skimpier clothes as the summer heat increased. I walked in the magnificent gardens like the Bois de Boulogne and Jardin du Luxembourg, admiring the age-old statues (which truly belonged in museums) and fountains again and again. I now busked in the open and warm sunshine instead of in metro corridors, in squares like the Beaubourg (Centre Pompidou), which were full of appreciative tourists in the summer. I made some new friends here, including a beautiful Franco–Spanish girl called Anna, who was into guys as well as girls. Seeing the sun shine until 10 p.m., and watching people sitting at outdoor cafe esplanades, right up till this late and still in shirtsleeves, sipping their digestives, was a veritable miracle of nature, after having seen it get dark by 4 p.m. in the winter.

Wish I had more pics of me busking in various spots and countries, but these are the only two I seem to have; both in Paris.

I was thrilled to see that normal little cinema houses held 'film festivals' of their own. I was reading the biography of Charlie Chaplin, and out of sheer coincidence there was a Chaplin festival going on somewhere, i.e. a week or two of nothing but Chaplin films. So I was able to watch them as I read about them. And then there was a festival of Satyajit Ray films – one hardly had the opportunity to see them in India. Most Indians didn't know his work at all, and didn't really want to – no masala and no song-and-dance routines in them; while in Europe he was and is appreciated, venerated and studied as the master he was. Elsewhere, there was a festival of Ingmar Bergman films, and yet somewhere else one of Federico Fellini films – I devoured them all.

The third cycle

Like all good things, the summer too came to an end. I had come to Europe in autumn two years ago, and as this autumn was beginning, I realized a few things: in the first year, all the changing seasons were a beautiful first-time revelation, and bore the thrill of the unexpected; in the second year, the changing seasons had the beauty and intimacy of the familiar, and made me feel that I knew them well, that I belonged; in the beginning of the third cycle, they were starting to bear signs of routine.

And this routine of autumn settling in, coupled with the certainty of a long winter which would follow, dark, cold and wet, made me realize a few more things.

That, however welcoming, this fair off-white soil wasn't mine; I began to yearn subconsciously for the red soil of Goa. That, however beautiful these trees and flowers and vegetation in general were, I was longing to see coconut trees and rice fields. That, however I might enjoy order and discipline, I was needing to revisit the carefree casualness of 'never do today what you can put off until tomorrow' which so exasperated me sometimes.

These longings were still in my subconscious though; consciously I was still trying to think of ways to stay on in Europe. But difficulties in staying on in France were weighing me down. My French visa had now expired, they weren't extending it any more. That accommodating old gentleman at the French embassy in London had retired.

Ah, why was an Indian passport so difficult to travel and live in the world with? I watched Europeans travelling so freely; having bank accounts and withdrawing money from machines; having cars and homes here, as I had in Goa. And I wished I could too.

I took a daring decision: to stay on in France visa-less, at least for a while longer.

I woke up in a cold sweat a couple of times, after nightmares that the police had found me out during routine identity check-ups, and deported me back to India.

But when I was actually stopped in the metro one day, I was as cool as a cucumber. I don't know from where the idea came to me on the spot, but I just smiled my most friendly smile and started speaking broken French with a very heavy English accent to the very serious cops.

'*Mon passport ... revalidatè ... chez Embassade Indienne...* (My passport ... renewal ... at Indian Embassy...),' I said.

'They must have given you some paper to show while it is being renewed?' they asked, but I pretended I didn't understand, and, with a wide smile, kept repeating, '*Passport ... revalidatè ... Embassade Indienne...*,' softly hitting my open left palm with my right fist like a stamp, as if trying to explain something simple to dummies.

I had really long hair by then, an earring (quite a new phenomenon on men even in Paris), a colourful scarf around my neck, and a very long dark blue winter coat worn with jeans which were in high leather boots. They decided to frisk my pockets, a very normal procedure for the French police, perhaps thinking they might find some illegal smoking substance there.

They felt suspicious when they found a hard little bulk in one of the coat pockets. But when they fished it out and saw it was an unused sugar cube I had absent-mindedly pocketed in some cafe, they found it amusing. They looked at each other and smiled a smile which said, 'He's not into drugs, he's just got a sweet tooth.'

They saluted and apologized for the inconvenience, telling me that the next time I ought to ask the embassy for some temporary document. With a couple of '*Oui monsieur!*', '*Merci monsieur!*'s, and more smiles, I pocketed the sugar cube and walked away casually.

It was only afterwards that the seriousness of what could have happened hit me.

After this incident I took the decision not to risk staying on in France visa-less any more. I would go to Portugal and apply for Portuguese nationality, to which I was entitled as a Goan – even though it was French nationality I really wanted. The European Union hadn't been formed yet, but a Portuguese passport would make it that much easier to settle in France.

To Portugal, my sad battered 'Mãe Pátria'

So I packed up all my earthly belongings in Paris (whatever fitted in a suitcase), took a train to Lisbon, and booked myself into an economical little *pensão* in the centre of the city. I searched for a lawyer who would handle my paperwork to obtain Portuguese nationality, paid him half his fees in advance, asked my parents to procure and mail me the required documents from Goa, and asked the lawyer to start proceedings.

I went around a few record companies and presented them the Polydor recordings from Paris. But of course, if they wanted French songs in France, here they wanted songs in Portuguese.

One of the companies told me they were about to launch a very talented young man from Porto called Rui Veloso, and that I could audition as a musician for his band – the auditions were being held later that month in Lisbon. I took down the address and thought I'd go. (Veloso, incidentally, is a veteran superstar in Portugal today.)

As the day drew closer for the lawyer to complete my documentation, a thought struck me though: once I had Portuguese nationality, I would require a visa to go to Goa! I didn't care about needing a visa to go to India; but there was no way I wanted to be a foreigner in my beloved Goa!

That thought was a cold shower in winter. It woke me up to the fact that Goa was home, and always would be. I didn't want to sever ties with my roots, certainly not with my Goa, and never wanted to be a foreigner there, not even technically.

I called up the lawyer, told him to keep the 50 per cent advance I had paid him, but to stop the proceedings immediately. It was the beginning of December. I started to plan how to get back to Goa by Christmas. I certainly didn't have the money for an air ticket, and I didn't want to ask Father, as I wanted to arrive there and surprise them all.

The richest friend I had in Europe was Michel Bonan in Paris – the commercial photographer. I called him and explained my needs, and said I'd send his money back as soon as I got back to Goa. He said sure, and wired me the money immediately.

I booked a one-way ticket, Lisbon–London–Bombay–Goa, arriving in Goa on 24 December 1979. I couldn't have hoped to arrive home on a better day than Christmas Eve. I'd just walk in on the 24th and surprise the daylights out of them. How I loved springing such surprises! I still do.

Ah, India!

My flight until Bombay went off without a hitch. I remember I felt super excited as we circled over Indian soil, even over once-hated Bombay.

The Indian customs officers eyed my acoustic guitar like vultures eye a corpse. It wasn't even an expensive one, but it was 'foreign', and anything foreign was highly precious and taxable in India then.

I said, 'Sir, I know you will not believe me, but this is the story of this guitar. I had taken my guitar from India – also a foreign Yamaha – when I went, and I was earning my living while travelling by playing it and singing. It was my first time out of India, and I had no idea that one had to declare and get such items stamped on one's passport on departure, so I did not.

'One day that guitar was stolen from my apartment in Paris, and I had lost my bread-earner. So I asked my father to send me money to buy another guitar. This is the one I bought – also a Yamaha, very similar to the one I had taken. It is now pretty worn out too, as I have travelled and played a lot with it.

'But I know you will not believe me – though I have no idea how I'm going to pay the duty, for I haven't come back from abroad with a bundle of money!'

He looked at my faded jeans, hair below my shoulders, faded shirt and truly worn-out suitcase, and he knew I was telling the truth.

He and his colleague exchanged glances and smiled. No, they weren't going to find gold bars or even bottles of scotch to confiscate (read extort) from this passenger.

'Ok,' he said, 'keep your precious guitar. I believe you. You may go through.'

I genuinely didn't expect this, even though I had spoken my heart out to him. Overjoyed, I smiled and thanked him, and floated on air all the way out of the airport into the heavy, smelly Bombay air. And I smiled even more when I remembered the WEM Copycat echo machine and the guitar FX pedals in my suitcase – this he would have certainly found to be futuristic rocket science, and would have charged me for sure. Ah, my guardian angel was returning to Goa with me. Thank goodness no X-ray machines had been installed in Indian airports yet.

Incidentally, the story of the stolen guitar and the new one was absolutely true. The theft took place in Rue de la Collégiale, in the apartment I shared with Hubert. We were sure it was an inside job by one of the several people who visited our apartment (probably a friend of a friend of a friend) who knew that we kept the key under the doormat. Nothing else had been taken, so the guy or girl certainly knew how to play the guitar – or where to sell it. We never did find out who it was, though.

Bad old Indian Airlines

From there I went straight to the Indian Airlines terminal to check into my flight to Goa.

To my dismay, on Christmas Eve the Goa counter was more crowded than a railway platform, with people screaming and shouting. Typically, the flight had been overbooked (which meant the airline employees had assigned our precious seats to last-minute VIPs, or to relatives and friends, or to people who had paid them bribes). Indian Airlines, owned by the Government of India, had a monopoly over the Indian skies, and they treated their non-VIP passengers like dirt. My Goa–Bombay ticket, paid for with precious dollars in Europe, was totally ignored here. Reimbursement? Make an application in triplicate, and you'll be lucky if you get a reply. And there went my plans to arrive home on 24th December!

I called up Meena. She came to the airport like a shining knight in a rickshaw, picked me up and took me straight to a Bombay–Goa bus operator she knew. Unfortunately they were fully booked too, with waiting-list passengers hoping to get a seat. But he suggested we try an ST (state transport) bus, the only hope on Christmas Eve.

ST buses were government-operated. Which meant they were badly maintained, washed and cleaned once in a blue moon, had vomit stains caked and stuck on the outsides, bugs on the seats, and cockroaches and sometimes even rats inside, from the foodstuff that passengers dropped under their seats. Yes, they had a seat.

Thanking Meena and saying goodbye and wishing her a Merry Christmas, I boarded the bus.

Home for Christmas

And thus it was that, after two years and three months of glorious adventuring in Europe and North Africa, yours truly un-gloriously returned home in a dilapidated ST bus.

But nothing mattered. In the taxi from the bus station in Panjim to our house in Miramar, as day was dawning, I was bursting with childlike excitement at the surprise I was going to spring upon my parents and Belinda.

And surprised and overjoyed they were. Mother was in the garden, tending to her beloved cacti. Father was in the dining room, sipping his morning tea. Belinda rushed downstairs as soon as she heard the loud, excited voices.

All four of us were together again, it was Christmas morning, and all was well with the world.

PART III

BACK TO ROOTS

13

A Three-Letter Word: Goa

Home is where your dreams lie

That magical, euphoric feeling when you return to the place you've been dreaming of, to people you've been dreaming about, is indescribable. In fact, strangely enough, besides being fully there, you're also floating somewhere above it all, in excitement and wonder, watching it happen to you.

We had a lovely home breakfast, all of us talking and asking questions at the same time. We had been corresponding regularly throughout these two years and two months, aerogrammes flying between us at their own pace. I'd send them one, and it took ten days to reach them. They'd answer, and that would take another ten days to reach me. That's how long it took to ask a question and receive a reply: twenty days. Today if a WhatsApp message doesn't get answered in twenty seconds, we become impatient.

After breakfast Father and I walked up to the first floor – I was dying to see my bedroom. He climbed the stairs ahead of me, and, for the first time, I had to slow down my step to keep to his pace. I said nothing, but felt a great sense of loss; I guess we all feel it when we see the first signs of ageing in our parents. They aren't supposed to grow old ever. A few lines crossed my mind, and I jotted them down.

1. LOADS

They climb
up the staircase
one behind the other
son and father.

One bears his luggage
the other, his age.

Lines which came to mind the first day I returned home from Europe and saw that Father's step on the staircase had slowed down in front of me. He was far from carrying a walking stick, but it drove the point home better in the illustration. This was the first page in a book of poems I was to publish some time later.

My room looked like they had been expecting me every day of the last two years and two months: everything in its place, and clean as a whistle. I settled in, emptied my suitcase, hung up the huge poster of *The Garden of Earthly Delights* by Bosch which I'd bought in Paris, and revelled in the sounds of the Goan birds – and crows – in the trees outside. And I fell into a grateful, contented sleep until Mother woke me up to my favourite lunch which she had cooked up meanwhile. It was like waking up to my favourite dream.

After lunch I borrowed Father's car. Father always kept two cars; one we called 'the small car', and the other we called 'the big car'. The most popular small car in India at the time was the Fiat Padmini, and among the big cars, the Contessa had just been launched. I hated driving the latter. I took the Fiat and went around Panjim and surprised the hell out of my old gang of friends: Norman Faleiro, Noel Pereira, Joe Araujo, Mahesh Rao, Mustafa Sheikh Kader, and the girls – Neelam and Neeta Sharma, Viki and Isabel Sequeira, Thelma and Lisa Dias, and Bismarque Silveira. And slowly caught up on the new stories, laughs and adventures.

And that old 'all's well with the world' feeling engulfed me again, like it did when I chanced upon Eric and Hubert in Paris. And, though my return to Goa was no matter of chance, it was quite impromptu and unexpected, and took everyone by surprise, myself included.

A life decision

I knew that the time had come for me to become a totally self-reliant man. Though I had paid for all my expenses in Europe these last two years, the trip had been sponsored by Father, in terms of the air ticket and the replacement of the stolen guitar. Now that I had travelled around as I'd wanted to after having completed my studies, the time had come for me to stand on my own two feet. And of course to eventually look after my parents. I was now twenty-six years old.

But I couldn't see myself working as an architect. I thought long and hard, and I finally came to a decision: *I would earn my living on this earth only doing the things I loved doing.*

Once I took that decision, I sat and made a list of things I loved doing. The list was short and simple, and went like this, and in this order:

1. Music
2. Drawing
3. Writing

In music I had more than enough original songs to release an album. I would approach record companies in Bombay. And of course I would do live shows.

In drawing, the most commercial thing I could think of doing at that time, when Goa was just being discovered as a tourist destination, was to design postcards.

And in writing, well, I had many poems I had written right from my college days and through my travels. I would make a selection and publish them as a book.

Would all this work? Would it pay enough? That didn't matter at the time. The main criteria was to do what I loved doing. I was doing these things already, for my own pleasure; now I just had to find a way to earn from them.

The Taj Fort Aguada

Most of my friends had completed their academic courses at the same time as me. During my absence, many of them had started working at Goa's first five-star hotel, the beautiful Taj Fort Aguada Beach Resort. They invited me there for dinner one day, which we had at the circular-shaped Anchor Bar. After dinner the house band put an acoustic guitar in my hands. 'Haven't heard you in years, let's hear some of your new songs!' they said.

And thus started a singing session which grew and grew, until all the guests present were involved as well, singing along and clapping after every song. Someone must have informed the general manager about what was happening, for she came and sat in a corner, watching and listening. When we finally called it a night and were about to leave, she asked if we could talk a while.

The manager was Asha Rishi. She was tall, slender and as beautiful as a model, but she never let her beauty undermine her no-nonsense authority. A woman who's beautiful has to work that much harder at extracting discipline and obedience, especially from men, especially in India.

She offered me a job singing at the hotel. I said, 'Thank you so much, but I'm afraid it would kill my love for music if I were to play in one place every evening…'

'I understand,' she said. 'Maybe you could play just twice a week then?' I was still a bit reluctant. 'We would pay Rs 300 per night, that is for three sets of one hour each per night,' she offered.

I said I would think it over for a while, and call her within three days with a final answer.

Think it over I did. To put those figures into perspective, I must state here that a good salary for receptionists and accountants in Goa was about Rs 800 a month back in 1980, that too offered only by a five-star hotel. Being offered Rs 300 per night to sing eight times a month worked out to Rs 2,400 a month. And that too for just three hours of singing each night, between 8 p.m. and midnight, with breaks, twice a week. I would be a millionaire! And I would be free the rest of the time to do whatever I liked: travel around, write songs, draw, write poetry, or simply do nothing.

I called Mrs Rishi back on the third day and agreed. And I named my other terms as well: I would require hotel porters to carry my instruments from and to my car every night; I would be free to have my dinner in any hotel outlet I chose – and little things like that.

They agreed to it all. Could I start next week? Sure.

After a week, they asked if I could sing three nights a week instead of two. Sure.

Now my monthly earnings went up to Rs 3,600 a month. I was a multimillionaire!

The Amsterdam Balloon Company

One day Edwin Saldanha (who had played with me in The Beat 4 some years ago) called.

'There's a hippie in our guesthouse who wants to sell his Fender amplifier. I thought you might be interested. Are you?'

Was I? 'Yes!' I almost shouted. 'Hold him right there. I'm on my way.'

As I've explained earlier, it was impossible to buy foreign stuff in shops in India at the time. You were lucky if someone was selling a foreign article you wanted. This was a Fender Twin Reverb, *the* guitar amplifier of the time, and an industry standard used until today.

I drove to Edwin's shop and met the 'hippie' – most Goans called most foreigners hippies and used the word 'hippie' to mean 'white man'. It applied even to men in suits and ladies in gowns, as long as they were white. As in: 'The company manager is not Indian, he's a hippie.'

Anyway, thus I met Lucas Amor, a wonderful violinist from Amsterdam, who would go on to be a lifelong friend and occasional musical partner. His Fender Twin Reverb had been fitted with dual-coned JBL speakers, which were better than the original Fender speakers, and was therefore a rare item. He wanted Rs 4,000 for it, a princely sum then, but I knew its value. I promptly paid him the money and took my new baby back home. I set it up in my bedroom, connected the WEM Copycat echo machine and the other pedals I'd bought in Paris, and played my trusted old Höfner guitar through it. Ah, the power and sweetness of the sound!

The amplifier would come in handy at the Taj Fort Aguada, and I wouldn't have to use the hotel's dubious sound system any more. I'd connect my microphone to the reverb channel, and my acoustic Yamaha guitar (with Barcus Berry pickup, also fitted in Paris) to the dry channel, and I'd be completely self-sufficient with a much better sound system of my own.

Lucas said he was part of a group of about a dozen artists who had travelled from Amsterdam to Goa in their own bus. Their group comprised musicians, poets, writers, painters, actors, the works. They put up impromptu shows in every country they passed along the way. They avoided sticking to other westerners, and preferred to meet and mix with locals everywhere. So they had avoided the popular Goan beaches, and discovered a then totally obscure one called Agonda in extreme south Goa. There they and their bus had camped. Why didn't I come and visit?

It wasn't easy finding the Agonda village or beach in those days, before the time of signposts in rural areas; I had to make several enquiries and then go down an almost imperceptible narrow mud road. I marvelled at how these guys had discovered it. And when I saw the bus – a huge, tough old number which looked like it had been built for World War II, but painted a baby sky blue with white clouds all over and the words 'Amsterdams Ballon Gezelschap' running psychedelically along both its sides – I couldn't believe it had negotiated up that road.

It was lovely meeting them all, seeing each one contribute towards their community living in some way or the other. They had rented a big old dilapidated house on the beach, which mainly consisted of one big half-broken-down room with a huge wooden table, surrounded by a wide veranda on three sides. The bus was parked a few metres away on firm non-sandy ground, and they used both the house and the bus for various purposes – work, storage, sleeping, etc.

As night fell Lucas and I played together for the first time, and we discovered there was an instant musical thread which joined his violin and my guitar. They sounded beautiful in that natural paradise without electricity, by the campfire near an ancient banyan tree. After we had dinner, when the campfire was dying, a lovely Dutchwoman who looked like she had distant gypsy blood asked if I wanted to sleep in her 'palace'.

She walked me up a moonlit path towards the dunes on the beach. There she had tied white cotton saris to four bamboo poles she had dug into the sand. The saris were the four walls of her palace. We lay on her bedding after she lit an incense stick or two, and looked at her roof – the whole starlit sky, where the stars and the moon were slowly moving on their nightly errand.

And we made celestial love. Her name was Wilka, and she made love like the dancer she was: with grace, abandon, supple and flexible contortions (which at one time caused her to exclaim 'Oops, wrong hole!' to our great mutual mirth), and with a great affinity for pleasing and taking pleasure.

Ah, these Dutchmen (and women) were my kind of people. I had always regretted that most foreigners who came to Goa stuck to themselves, their contacts with locals being restricted mainly to commerce. Lucas had said they loved mixing with and performing for locals everywhere they passed through – Iran, Afghanistan, Pakistan. I thought: why not put up a show on Miramar Beach, for the people of Panjim?

I explained to them that most Goan people saw all white youth who came here as 'hippies who wasted their lives and their parents' money taking drugs and doing nothing'. I'd love them to see that among these youth there were also talented artists who worked hard at their art.

They loved the idea, and one fine afternoon the big Amsterdam Balloon Company bus landed up on Miramar Beach. I had hand-made and put up big posters at three or four strategic points in the city; these were enough at that time to alert the whole of Panjim about an exceptional happening. The rest of the publicity was word-of-mouth.

I myself had not seen their 'show', and I was mesmerized. They had each dressed in a very colourful and weird costume. There was no stage – it all happened on the sands of the beach, where the audience too was seated or standing. There was so much happening all around ... everything by firelight, tall fire torches dug in the sand ... a poet reciting poetry, a dancer doing slow ballet-like movements to it ... a mime dressed as a crazy astronomer going silently through the audience, catching them by surprise as she sneaked up on them and examined them through a telescope as though *they* were the oddities, and suddenly changing their perimeter of reality from being the observer to being the observed ... actors acting out skits ... clowns and jugglers doing their thing ... a painter painting ... fire-eaters ... and Lucas and I providing the impromptu, inspired music.

All the while, three actors at the periphery slowly built a huge paper balloon. And then built a fire to fill it up with hot air. The balloon slowly started inflating itself into a giant size, drawing the audience's attention. Would it catch fire or wouldn't it? Once fully inflated, the balloon was finally let off into the Miramar night, rising slowly to join the stars, while the music rose to a crescendo and the participants went wild – and so did the audience. The Amsterdam Balloon Company's signature highlight of the show, the grand climax, had been reached.

After the show the Company went to sleep in the bus, and I took Wilka across the beach to my room, at home.

I wondered what my parents would think and say, but they had no objections whatsoever. They had been mesmerized by the unique show too, and welcomed Wilka in the same spirit.

The newspapers carried articles by Panjim stalwarts and respected citizens like Carmo Noronha, Carmo Azavedo and Vasco Alvares: they all praised the show in glowing terms, and even mentioned their misconceptions about hippies. My goal was fulfilled; the Panjim society saw that not all long-haired weirdly-dressed people were useless wastrels.

My yellow submarine

Though Father lent me his car anytime I wanted it, I now wanted to be totally self-sufficient; and not having to borrow a vehicle was a prerequisite to self-locomotion. Of course I could not afford a car, but a two-wheeler would be just perfect in the open, almost traffic-free roads of Goa of the time. 'A Bullet would suit you best. Why don't you get yourself one?' asked some. Of course a motorcycle would have been more macho and manly.

But I wasn't really a motorbike man; I loved cars. All I needed from a two-wheeler was for it to be practically useful to my needs, which I weighed carefully.

I wanted to go exploring my Goa like I had never explored it before. That meant going into the deep interiors, on mud roads and paths, to places where there would be no one to repair a punctured tyre for kilometres around. Therefore that spare tyre which a scooter was fitted with; that space at the feet where I could carry my guitar; and the low fuel consumption, which would allow me to go further into areas without a petrol pump, all made a scooter worth more than all the manliness of image that a Bullet would provide.

Vespa was the good old standard in India, considered the best scooter for decades. But it was said to have unequal weight on the two sides, which made it a bit difficult and sometimes dangerous in tight situations.

There was a new entrant in the market, the relatively unknown Vijay Super. Its lines were more modern, the bike was easier to handle, it consumed less petrol, it came in more exciting colours, and it was cheaper – an easy choice. I picked a bright yellow to go with the Goan sunshine, and that was it. I was independently mobile.

After the car, it was a pleasure to feel Goa's clean air and wind on my face, smelling the rice fields and sea, smelling all kinds of trees as I crossed forests and jungles, hearing all kinds of birds and animals, and, while crossing little villages in the interiors, smelling the rustic but intoxicating food being cooked inside the houses emitting firewood smoke through their thatched or tiled roofs.

No haversack and sleeping bag required here; it was too hot for that. I bought a typical Goan mat made of straw, and a mid-sized bag made of tough jute cloth. I had a carrier fixed to the back of the scooter to which I attached these with a strong rope. And, armed with a map of Goa, a notebook, a sketchbook, a pen and colour pencils, and a flute, besides of course a few clothes, never forgetting a couple of multipurpose lungis, I took off whenever the mood struck me.

Once I had distanced myself from the towns, I avoided the roads shown on the map, and took the narrower, rougher, unmapped ones. They invariably took me to magical places: ancient deserted ruins, virginal clear lakes, deserted beaches of which only the native fishermen knew the names, untouched hills and valleys of nothing but greenery, rivers of clean, slowly flowing waters with untouched mangroves along their banks where you could discern a multitude of thriving life, from birds to the tiniest of crabs … I was seeing and absorbing it all before the onslaught of concrete and construction, plastic and waste, corruption and illegality, which today defiles almost every resisting bastion of Goan nature.

I spent the nights anywhere I could, mainly in verandas of little isolated chapels or temples. Not once was I robbed or even my sleep disturbed. My bag and scooter were always there in the morning. As were, quite often, a dozen curious village kids' faces staring at me and smiling excitedly.

Of course I still used Father's Fiat to go play at the Fort Aguada, as I had to carry my new heavy bulky amplifier; but now I filled up the petrol, which felt great.

Goana postcards

Ok, now that my music was paying, I would start working on my second love, drawing.

After a few casual conversations with my childhood friend Norman Faleiro, it turned out that he too wanted to start something outside the nine-to-five job he held. So we decided to start a partnership. I would design postcards and get them printed and produced to a standard which met with my approval, and he would see to their distribution and sales, which would be up his alley, he being a Commerce graduate.

When the time came to choose a name for our enterprise, the perennial Beatles fan in me thought of 'Mango', the most delicious Goan fruit, since The Beatles had named their company Apple, after Europe's most famous fruit.

Norman broke into a quiet giggle.

'What's wrong?' I asked.

'I'm imagining walking into a serious bookshop manager's office. He would ask "Which company are you from?" and I would have to answer "Mango". If he then asked "What's your address?" I would have to answer "Pineapple". His next question would probably be "And what are you selling, fruit salad?'"

Norman was then staying in a building called Ananás, the Portuguese name for pineapple. I saw his point. We settled on the name Goana Partnership, named after our Goa which we loved so much.

I made enquiries about different methods of printing available in Goa, and found screen printing the most appealing. The quality of local offset printing was awful at the time. Colours ran into each other, putting lips on chins and eyes on foreheads.

I was directed to Mudra Printers. They comprised Prabhu (the boss) and Naresh (the printer) and a couple of helpers in Mala, Panjim. They were extremely helpful and friendly, and introduced me to the world of screen printing. Though it only allowed me to use straight colours without shadings in between, that would have a naive charm of its own.

My postcards would be statements about Goa and what I felt about it. What struck me most when I returned from Europe was how Goa still lived as a universe unto itself. What happened outside its tiny boundaries didn't matter much here. Our two English dailies, *The Navhind Times* and *The Herald*, carried nothing but news of Goa and the incestuous Goan politics, with just one inside page for news from 'the rest of India and the World'.

I took into consideration that the only tourists in Goa at the time were westerners. These belonged to two extreme categories: the hippies on the beaches, and the well-oiled five-star types.

I was more hippie than five-star, even if I did play at the Fort Aguada. But my heart was intrinsically Goan and, now that I had lived abroad, I could see Goa as I'd never seen it before.

The postcards were an instant hit, both in the Goan beach shack restaurants and the flea market, as well as in the bookshops of starred hotels. Norman distributed them intelligently.

We soon branched out into Goana t-shirts, to which I adapted our most popular postcard designs. These were screen-printed by an Englishman who made good-quality t-shirts for the Fort Aguada and other reputed companies in Goa. They sold very well too.

When I say things 'sold very well', I mean they were popular and our stocks easily exhausted themselves, not that the profits were astronomical. Our tourist market was tiny in 1980. You may have figured out by now that I wasn't after big money for its own sake anyway.

Loads

Now came the time for me to let out my third love, writing. Like I said, I had written quite a few poems since the time I was in college. I had recently collected and handwritten them all in one thick notebook, illustrating some of them in pen and crayons. Of course I had also written hundreds of pages of prose in my diaries, but never did I think these might be for public consumption or of public interest.

Until then, my poems and drawings were secrets to be shared with very, very few friends who were really close, and who might have the same sensibilities or inclinations. Charlie, the American girl, had been one of them. But otherwise, although I was regarded as quite a rebel and revolutionary for a Goan, I too suffered from what I shall call 'Goanitis'. It was an affliction which made us hide our lights under bushels not necessarily out of humility, but out of the fear of 'What will people say?' For example, had I dared to send my drawings or poems for publication, editors and readers alike might have said, 'Ha, what does he think he is now, a poet and a painter too? He should be contented that he is appreciated as a musician.' And I guess I had allowed that thought to imprison my poems and drawings within me.

I said once that, unwittingly, Europe had helped me find myself. It had done that by teaching me how to 'let things out'. It changed me from an introvert to a near-extrovert. Singing in the streets had taught me how to grab an audience from among pedestrians who had come out not to listen to me, but to get from point A to point B. I had to make them want to stop at point X in between, listen to me, and give me some money. My stage showmanship and audience-grabbing powers started there: in the streets and metro corridors of Paris.

A line by someone I read somewhere helped a lot too. It went something like: 'The woods would be very silent indeed if only the birds who sang best were to sing.'

I decided to let my woods resound. I didn't have to be 'the best' at drawing and writing. If I had it within me, I'd let it out. And if people liked what they saw and read, they'd go for it. If not, they wouldn't. That was cool. But at least it would all be out there, flying free, and I would have gone through the rigours and pleasures of its birth.

A flower gave off its fragrance, good or bad, without bothering with what people smelling it would think or say. Well, I'd let off mine.

I guess it was in this spirit that I called my book of poems *Loads*. They were living feelings and thoughts, alive and kicking, which I was unloading off my mind and chest. I wanted to illustrate them as I had in my personal notebook. Again, normal printing made this extremely expensive, especially in small quantities. So I was advised to go in for cyclostyling. I was directed to a friendly couple who ran Maureen Printers in Rua de Ourem, Panjim, and they instructed me in the art of cutting the special paper which would act as the template for the pages they would cyclostyle.

This paper was a curious two-layered job which consisted of a soft butter-paper kind of sheet on top, and a thicker carbon paper-like sheet attached beneath it. One had to carefully cut what one wanted printed on the top sheet with a steel pointed pen, whether text or drawing. If you cut it too soft, it wouldn't print. If you cut it too hard, the paper would tear. If you cut the lines too close together, they would merge into a big hole.

After a few torn and wasted sheets of paper, I got the hang of it and cut the whole book.

I knew a book of poems would not be a bestseller in Goa; in fact, that it would hardly sell. But you know its raison d'être: the joy of giving birth and letting it out.

I had also started writing the odd article in Goan newspapers, and a regular column in a monthly magazine called *Goa Today* (it had named itself decades before the national *India Today* came into existence). The latter paid me a monthly stipend, though I forget what it was.

Father's rare outburst

My parents must have seen all of this as strange, and frankly, quite troubling; their one and only son, now a grown man of twenty-seven, not going to a reputed office (preferably his own) dressed in a crisp safari suit (the craze of the impressively dressed professional man and politician of the day, a kind of corporate uniform I held in contempt), looking important and busy, but instead spending time upstairs in his room drawing or writing, going off three nights a week to sing in a hotel, and taking off whenever he fancied to strange places in Goa he spoke about but which they had never heard of.

Now, on some mornings, my mother would push *The Navhind Times* under my nose at breakfast, opened to the classifieds page, with 'Architect Wanted' ads circled in red.

He didn't normally do this, but I remember one night when Father made me cry at the dinner table.

'What are you doing with your life?' he let fly. 'You ought to be working as a respectable architect, not as a hotel musician!'

'But … I'm doing fine for myself doing what I love, earning about Rs 5,000 a month, when most of my friends are earning Rs 1,000!' I said.

'Peanuts!' he argued. 'You graduated as an architect for this? You could and should have been earning much more! Look at Ralino Souza! Look at Sarto Almeida! Besides earning well, they are respected in all of society, not long-haired ear-ringed hippies who spend their days and nights just "doing what they want to"! Your Rs 5,000 a month is peanuts compared to what you could earn as an architect!'

I was hurt to the core, because I loved and was proud of what I was doing. My eyes watered. I could not eat any more. I excused myself and went to my room and tried to sleep.

To keep my parents happy, I decided to work for my childhood hero, architect Lúcio Miranda, who sang old Goan, Portuguese and Latin songs like a god. He was having drinking problems at the time, but he was the only one I could think of working with. I told him I wanted to apprentice with him, without a salary, in the mornings only, and he agreed.

He would leave office mid-morning and not reappear before I left at lunchtime. As you can imagine, this stint couldn't last long, and I gradually stopped going there altogether.

Mother would tell me that, a few years later, when I was earning several lakhs of rupees for each two-hour concert, Father would say to her when they sat in the veranda in the evenings: 'Who guessed that Remo would earn so much out of mere music, no?' with lots of pride and pleasure in his voice. It was he who had installed and encouraged this love of music in me, buying me this instrument and that as a kid, even forming my first groups for me while I was too young to do so. If that love had turned into a burning passion, he had only himself to blame.

I knew that it wasn't meanness or malice which had made him say those things at the dinner table that night. It was the natural instinct of all parents to see their children 'well settled' before they left this world. And to parents generally, 'well settled' means 'earning enough or more than required', not 'doing what you love most'. I'm really glad that he lived to see me earning 'more than I require' – though how much one really requires is of course relative.

I've never seen a rich sparrow with an eight-bedroom nest.

But when I see multibillionaires trying to earn more and more and more, destroying the planet and even their fellow men in the process, I feel sad for them … they are the real paupers of this world, for they shall always want, as they shall never have enough.

Bondo

Before leaving for Europe, I had spent some time in Dr Rajadhyaksha's Eyecare Hospital in Panjim, keeping Father company when he was operated on for cataract. The hospital was right opposite the Club Nacional, and one day I heard energetic music coming from the club; there was an afternoon wedding feast in progress, and I hung out in the veranda of the hospital listening. Out of the whole band, the one who caught my attention was the drummer. He played with total abandon and fire, unlike most Goan band musicians who just played and sang 'correctly' and 'carefully'. He was particularly brilliant with Goan beats. The stage was at the opposite end of the hall from where I stood, and I could not make out who the band was. Upon making some enquiries later, I discovered the drummer was the youngest brother of Timóteo Fernandes, the founder and leader of the legendary Tuna Sparks, which had enthralled Goa with their lively music since my childhood. I had made a mental note to contact the drummer boy when – and if – I returned from Europe.

Now I did. And I learnt that his real name was José, but that everyone in Goa knew him as Bondo, which meant a small and empty coconut – a name usually reserved for kids poor in studies. The way they called out his name when they saw him passing by on the street had a mixture of admiration and derision, especially when they shouted 'Ei Bondea!'

We hit it off from day one. If I was rediscovering the 'real Goa', he was living it. Among other things Goan, we loved sitting in tiny local taverns, especially in villages where the other customers were all local farmers and fishermen, with a kerosene lamp as the sole illumination, and downing a cashew feni or two – rather than in a club or bar in the city. These taverns were still authentic and rustic then. No formica tabletops; in fact no tables at all. The locals stood at the dark old worn wooden counter and downed their little glasses of straight pure feni in one gulp after a hard day's work, with a grimace at the fire lighting up their veins, before going home to their wives and dinner. Bondo and I would take our drinks, topped up with soda or water, and make ourselves comfortable on the tavern's little veranda's stone or mud parapet, or under a coconut or mango tree just outside. We both favoured local beedies over cigarettes. I still do, whenever I do smoke. Ah, the tastes and smells of Goa!

Musically too, we hit it off as though we had always played together. My gut feeling that distant afternoon had been right. We never played a song the same way twice. Our middle names were Improvisation and Fire, and every song became an exciting, unpredictable adventure.

ABOVE: Remo and Bondo, as drawn by the legendary Mário Miranda. RIGHT: Remo at the Jazz Yatra in Bombay, also by Mário. Images courtesy Mário Gallery, www.mariodemiranda.com.

We decided to form a duo: me on amplified acoustic guitar and vocals, he on percussion. I developed a curious kick drum for him, out of a Goan dholak. And we added other curious things to the set, like a baker's cycle horn, bongos instead of toms, and other weird, funny but effective stuff we could think of.

He would continue playing with his dance and wedding band on weekends, of course. But he would play with me at the Fort Aguada thrice a week, all on weekdays (I had intentionally kept my weekends free).

When the question came up of how much Bondo ought to charge the hotel, I said he ought to charge at least half of what they were paying me (which came to Rs 150 a night, more than he was earning with the band), which was a high figure in Goa then.

'*Ché* man Remo, how can I charge so much man?' Bondo was uneasy.

'You deserve it, and they can afford it,' I said. 'If you're feeling nervous about it, I'll drive you to the meeting. I won't come inside, as it will look very unprofessional, me negotiating on your behalf. Besides, you need to learn how to discuss your own deals. I'll wait in the car. But remember,' I firmly repeated for the hundredth time, 'don't go lower than Rs 150 a night.'

'Ok,' said Bondo, and walked into the hotel as though he was reluctantly walking into unavoidable battle.

An hour later he still hadn't returned, and I wondered what was going on. Finally the guest relations manager he was discussing terms with, Roland Righton, walked out of the hotel looking drained, and leaned on my car window with his hand on his tired creased forehead.

'Remo, please come inside and explain to your Bondo!' he said. 'For the sake of clarity in our accounts, I'm offering him the round figure of Rs 2,000 a month for twelve nights, but he's insisting on Rs 150 a night and nothing else! I've been trying to explain to him for the last one hour that what I'm offering him is more than what he's asking for, but he is adamant about his Rs 150!'

I knew then that my new percussionist had the most apt name in the world.

When the time came to name ourselves, my mind was clear; we both had short, two-syllable, memorable names, and they sounded good together.

'We'll call ourselves "Remo & Bondo"!' I said.

'*Ché!* How can I call myself that man? Bondo means an empty coconut!'

'Bondo, even if you officially call yourself José, people will always call you and know you as Bondo in Goa. Most of them call out to you with a lot of affection and respect – though I can hear a bit of amusement and ridicule in some people's voices. Well, let's take this name and make it something to be proud of. A name they will call out *only* with respect and awe from now on. And for that, *you* need to be proud of it yourself to start with.'

I told him stories about how clever people had taken weaknesses and turned them into strengths. How Serge Gainsbourg, who loved to smoke and drink and had no singing voice, had projected himself as an unshaven, hard-drinking chain-smoker and raspily drawled his way through his amazing poetry to become one of France's most famous singers. How he had launched his lover Jane Birkin's career not by hiding or correcting her strong British accent to French, but by accentuating it. How he had used her weak, whispering voice to make it sensuous and sexy. How he had used her flat chest to launch her as an actress in a film he wrote, directed and scored, *Je T'aime Moi Non Plus,* in which she seduces the man she loves, a homosexual truck driver, by dressing up as a short-haired boy and taking off her shirt.

Bondo understood and agreed. And all that I predicted came true. People don't even think of coconuts, empty or full, when they call out his name today. There's only respect, awe and affection for the greatest and most loveable and jovial percussionist in Goa, who until then was hidden in a band. He's one of those guys whose enormous laughter makes you laugh, even if you haven't heard or followed his joke.

We were a hit not only in Fort Aguada, but all over Goa. People came from all over to listen to Remo & Bondo at every show we played, for they could be sure there would be lots of good music, energy, fire, humour and witty repartee with the audience in our performances.

Bondo and I doing the opening duo set before
Indiana hit the stage. Bondo plays bongos here;
now his full drum set was used with Indiana.

Indiana

Soon I wanted to do more than what I was doing with Bondo. Not just the Goan, but the Indian identity in me had been awakened by the two years abroad. I wanted to create my own brand of fusion. Not the one which was already existent, which fused Indian classical with Western jazz – that was more for the intellect. I wanted to create a fusion which would make the body move, which would be high-energy and more 'of the people', where I would fuse our punchy Indian folk with Western rock and Latin.

After enquiries and searching around, we found Lala. Another two-syllable, punchy, memorable name, though his surname was Bharwani. He had no classical training whatsoever, but played the tabla the way Bondo played the drums: with feeling, energy and fire.

'He has a hole in his heart, so he must not exert himself too much,' his worried mother said. She was a widow with three sons, and was very protective of Lala, who did indeed have a heart condition.

There was no stopping Lala though. Heart condition or not, he wasn't going to let anything dampen his high excitement for music. And he said that being asked to play with me and Bondo was the height for him.

'Don't worry, Mrs Bharwani, we are not forming a band for all-night balls and weddings,' I assured his mother. 'We're going to be a concert band, performing for a maximum of two hours with an interval in between. Our rehearsals will be longer though, but they'll take place at home, more relaxed, and with lots of breaks.'

Now we needed a bassist. I asked Lawry Pires, who was also a live wire. He led a dance band of his own, but on being assured that our band would in no way clash with his, he agreed.

I already had a few Indo-Western compositions which we started rehearsing with the band. And as soon as we started playing together, more compositions came into being. We rehearsed in my bedroom in my parents' house in Miramar, but eventually shifted to its big open terrace. The youth among our neighbours, adults now, still remember standing on their terraces and listening to us.

Indiana in concert in 1982. CLOCKWISE FROM TOP: The full band, from left to right: Abel Pereira, Bondo Fernandes, Lala Bharwani and Remo; Abel on bass; Bondo on drums; Lala on tabla.

I decided to have an Indian cobra as our logo. And when the time came to choose a name for the band, well if I could turn Goa into 'Goana' for the postcards, why not India into 'Indiana'? Some might initially think it was an American fixation, but as soon as they saw us in our traditional Indian costumes and heard our music, they would realize Indiana had nothing to do with the American state.

Somehow Lawry didn't last long in our band; I don't remember the reason why, but he was soon replaced by Abel Pereira, the kid brother of Noel Pereira, a close friend from our old gang. His whole family had now moved to south Goa, but Abel had remained in Panjim, where he was studying.

Abel was hard-working, and excellent at catching songs and complicated riffs, which was surprising, as he came from a family of non-musicians as far as I knew. The band was soon cooking better than ever.

Michèle

One of the first things I had done on returning from Europe was to write to Michel Bonan and ask him for his bank details to return the money he had lent me for the air ticket. He asked me not to wire it; he was coming to Goa on holiday soon, and I could return it then.

'I told you I have a good friend from Paris who lives in Goa and has been inviting me there for at least ten years,' he said. 'I never made it. Well now I have two good friends who are inviting me to Goa, Jacques and you, so I've decided to come.'

I was overjoyed. 'Come and stay with us!' I exclaimed. 'I'm sure my parents would love to have you!'

'Ok thanks! I'll stay half the time with you and half with Jacques. But I'm coming with a girlfriend, so there will be two of us; is that ok?'

'Sure!' I said. 'She's most welcome!'

After a few happy days in Miramar, I dropped Michel and his girlfriend at his friend Jacques Lasry's house in Anjuna.

I was now also occasionally playing and singing with the house band at Music House, Anjuna, which called itself The Goa Family Band.

The band consisted of Nafi, a German Yosho follower, whose bass was a real fortress-like wall of sound. He relentlessly and almost percussively ran up and down the scale of every chord on his fretboard, thus making a rhythm guitar redundant in the band. The lead guitarist was another German, a guy called Bendt, and he was excellent too. The drummer was William de Souza, a Goan from Mapusa, whose rock drumming was unheard of in Goa. He was the only Goan then who played almost exclusively with the foreigners (read hippies) on the beach, who played a much higher kind of music than Goan bands did, in that it was mostly brilliant on-the-spot improvisation, while Goan bands copied set structured hits and played them without any creativity of their own.

One evening Music House was having an acoustic concert (not the usual night party), and I decided to play there with Indiana, totally unplugged. The stage was the open veranda of Music House, and the audience sat on straw mats spread out in the garden, with lit candles and incense sticks. All around the periphery of the audience were the chai shops, which comprised local village women sitting on their mats with hissing kerosene stoves on which they made hot tea, and sold biscuits, fruits and cigarettes.

I was happy to see my friend Michel Bonan and his girlfriend there, with Jacques and his then girlfriend Odile, and another French girl I hadn't met but who Michel introduced me to. After our performance I went and sipped chai with them on the straw mat they were occupying. We chatted for a long while, and then they all slowly left. All except, surprisingly, the new girl. Her name was Michèle, and she was blonde and beautiful. We had hardly spoken to each other while the others were there. But now that we were alone she whispered, 'You played the flute so well,' in her soft husky French accent. 'You are Krishna.'

'Hmmm, I've heard many lines before, but never this one... Krishna indeed...' I thought to myself.

Turned out she had been in Michel Bonan's group of friends at my performance at Centre Americain in Paris, the hootenanny night he spoke about when he picked me up hitch-hiking in Spain, remember? I had written: 'He was going to introduce me, in Goa, to the Frenchwoman who would be my wife and the mother of my sons. Once it's written in the stars, you can't escape it.' But of course I didn't know all this then. Stars tend to keep their secrets until the right time.

Michèle and I made a plan to meet again. In fact she was going to a party in Anjuna the very next day, a friend's birthday, why didn't I come along with her? I said I would look forward to that.

I picked her up and we went to the party. When I was dropping her back to Anjuna we went to the beach first, and there we made love for the first time – on the totally safe Goan sands of 1980, under the innocent moon and the stars, the sound of laughing waves in our ears. It was wonderful.

And we made plans to see each other again. And again. And again. She was living at Jacques and Odile's, and soon I too was spending days and nights there.

The house Jacques had rented was a beautiful old Goan structure. One of the few which had never been plastered, neither outside nor within. The golden light which the old laterite stone created indoors during the day was sheer magic. And the moonlight which came in through the open windows in the night, bathing our sensuous and affectionate lovemaking, was sheer magic too.

Michèle had come to India to do her second stint at studying Mohiniyattam. She had stopped by in Goa to spend a week with her good old friends Jacques and Odile before proceeding to the dance ashram in Kerala. But now that we had met, Mohiniyattam and Kerala were totally forgotten.

One day while returning from a drive to Dona Paula I casually said, 'Oh Michèle, I might not be seeing you often in the next two weeks. A German girl I met in Lisbon is coming to Goa for a fortnight, and I'll be spending time with her.'

Since Michèle lived in Anjuna, among people with a hippie mindset, and since she came from Paris where I'd just spent time with friends with a similar mindset, I had presumed she would be cool with what I said.

She jumped off the moving scooter, mercifully landing safely on her feet. 'Sorry, I can't share a man with other women,' she said.

'Oh!' I said, abruptly braking the bike and feeling very disappointed. 'Well, I'm a free spirit and I simply cannot be in a closed one-on-one relationship,' I replied. 'I don't believe in it. So however beautiful our relationship may be, I guess it's not meant to be.'

I had said this to many girls who had wanted an exclusive relationship in the past. Our partings had always been easy, and I had always moved on smoothly. But I was soon to learn that I simply wasn't able to stay away from this woman.

She finally agreed that I drop her back to Anjuna, and climbed back on the scooter. We were very sad-faced when we entered Jacques' house, but we were both adamant about our decisions. I said my goodbyes, telling Jacques and Odile about our split and that I would probably not be returning there any more.

14

The Commitment

Lala loses his virginity

In the middle of my romantic turmoil, a high drama developed. My German friend Ragna had arrived in Goa with a friend of her own, a girl called Annika. My parents agreed that they could stay at our house for a couple of days until they found a place to rent. All three of us stayed in my bedroom; Ragna and I slept in my bed, and Annika on her sleeping bag on the floor.

It was really nice seeing Ragna again. But I surprised myself thinking of Michèle instead.

Ragna and Annika attended a performance of Indiana, and Annika and Lala took a shine to each other. The next day, she and our twenty-five-year-old virgin disappeared. Into thin air.

Lala's brothers frantically called me, saying their mother was at her wits' end. I picked Bondo up and we went straight to Lala's house, all the way admiring him and cheering him for what he'd done.

'Baba, Lala must not go with a girl! Lala must never get married! These things are not good for him! Remember the hole in his heart?' Lala's mother couldn't utter the word 'sex'.

I was silently thinking that there could not be a better way to go than in one magnificent, glorious bang, rather than in a whimper after spending a whole miserable life without sex. But I wisely refrained from telling her that.

I offered to put a quarter-page ad in *The Navhind Times* saying only 'LALA COME HOME!', which appeared the next morning. But tell me, how many couples on a wild escapade do you know who read newspapers?

Ragna and I scanned all the beaches and beach shacks we could think of for a whole day, but there was no sign of them. Curiously, Annika hadn't given Ragna a clue about their plans either.

Lala and Annika finally surfaced when they were good and ready, three days later – Lala smiling like the cat who didn't mind paying for the consequences now that he'd emptied the cream bowl. Heart hole and everything else in perfect shape. In answer to the quarter-page ad or not, Lala came home.

Was Michèle thinking of me?

Life goes on

The season was over, the hot Goan summer had started, and Michèle must have gone back to France. She would probably never come back. Good for me, I could not afford to lose my freedom and, however strong my feelings might be, they would go away.

Meanwhile life went on as usual. I designed more postcards, I wrote more songs. After I had returned to Goa, I had started writing another genre of songs. While until then they had all been about love and relationships, now they were about what I saw around me: the near-imperceptible beginning of the destruction of Goan nature, the first few ugly (and illegal) constructions, the dismal state of the roads, telephones, and government-run institutions. Songs like 'O, Panjim', 'Ode to Graham Bell', 'Paper Caper' and so on saw the light of day. One might call the genre 'sociopolitical satire'. They were hugely popular wherever I sang them, giving vent to people's frustrations through unbridled laughter, taking the stuffing out of ministers' and politicians' fake clean images.

Every time I had a drink too many I'd bore Bondo with the same litany: 'You know Bondo, however many chicks we might meet, there's one, man … just that one, y'know what I mean? Just one that I truly regret… But it was just not meant to be. I can't give myself up to just one woman, man!'

The jazz fest which launched my yatra

Jazz Yatra was this new festival in Bombay created by Niranjan Jhaveri. He brought down jazz greats from the US, Europe and elsewhere, lured by 'exotic India' to come and perform for free or at highly reduced rates. There were rumours and protests that Niranjan had been racist towards the great black jazz musicians and had favoured the white ones as far as hotel allocations, etc. were concerned. A brown man doing that is a hilarious case of the pot calling the kettle black. I don't know how far these rumours were true.

But what was true was that Niranjan hadn't spoken to his late brother Prabhakar for ages. And his brother was the father of Rajesh Jhaveri, who had cut the *Infinite Fusion* album. Now Rajesh wanted us (the Infinite Fusion band) to perform at his uncle Niranjan's festival. I had no idea how he was going to pull this off.

After last-minute tensions where we didn't know whether we were going to be physically thrown off the stage or allowed to perform on it, perform we did. I guess Niranjan simply could not afford to antagonize the Indian classical and jazz heavyweights in our band.

After our performance someone who knew us came up to me and said he had just seen Michèle walking out of the stadium. My brain stopped working. All I could do was run like a madman towards the stadium gates.

There she was, in her electric blue dress and golden hair, walking away from me. I ran after her and caught up with her.

I don't know what I kept blabbering, but I remember almost begging her to come with me. She kept smiling her Mona Lisa smile and giving me reasons why she could not. But she promised to meet me at the Yatra the next day.

She'd meet me! It meant that she hadn't been able to forget me either. And of course I understood that a woman worth her womanliness had to play hard to get for at least one night after I had walked away from her proclaiming I would keep seeing other women.

The next night in my room in Bombay we clearly saw and showed just how much we had missed each other, and how much we meant to each other.

'I can't live without you,' I said. 'All these months have been empty and made no sense.'

'I've been empty too…' she said.

'I had never met a woman who made me feel like giving up my free spirit status, but now I have. I want to stop seeing other women and be with you only.'

'Are you sure you can do that?' she asked.

'I'm not sure…,' I said, 'but I certainly am going to try with all my might.'

The adventures of our ancestral house

The house in Goa which I own and where I live now was built by my ancient ancestors, way before my grandparents and great-grandparents, and remodelled and added to as new generations emerged.

After my grandmother died, and while I was in Paris, Father wrote asking whether I was interested in living there. If I was, he'd buy it together with another brother, and divide the house into two with a wall running down the middle (like many Goan families had done to their sprawling ancestral houses, mutilating them totally). If not, the family had decided to sell it off to a non-family member, for whom the price would be three times higher.

I had told Father that I didn't want the house divided, that I wasn't too sure of returning to live in Goa anyway, so not to buy it especially on my account. Once back in Goa I totally fell in love with the house, but Father had promised to sell it to a German gentleman who was in the cabin next to his on a Bombay–Goa ship voyage recently.

I pleaded with him not to sell it. 'The house means nothing personal to the German, Father,' I said. 'Return his advance, even a little more for the inconvenience, and he will happily find another – there's no dearth of ancestral houses for sale in Goa today.'

*Our ancestral Siolim House. Now, whenever
I shift here from Portugal for about six to seven
months every year, I realize I really had to be
disgusted with the state of affairs in Goa in order
to migrate, even if partially.*

But Father was not to be shaken. 'My promise is my promise,' he said. 'To me it means more than a written agreement. I shall not go back on it.'

The house was sold, and I stopped driving by Siolim – I could not bear to look at it any more. I blocked it out of my mind.

Strangely, after that Father and Mother could not get it out of theirs. 'All of us got married in that house! Children were born there! Weddings held there! It holds so much family history!' Mother bemoaned, and started a novena to St. Jude Thaddeus, the patron saint of lost causes.

Miraculously, Herr Hermann, who had been refusing to sell until then, suddenly agreed. He was an easy-going man who was happy as long as he could sip on beer from morning till night. But he was married to a tough woman from Dehradun, who was convinced that we could not have been driven by sentimentality to buy back the house, but by business plans. She insisted on selling it to us at three times the price they had bought it for.

Father ended up buying back his own house at six times the price he would have paid if he had bought it from the family to start with. By that time he had retired, so it was a serious dig into his life savings.

But at least we got our ancestral house back. Many Goans got rid of theirs like white elephants and, to their great regret later, lost them forever during those years.

I had managed to talk my parents into letting Indiana stay in the house for the monsoon, composing and rehearsing our first songs. Even though electricity was non-existent half the time (we used battery-driven amplifiers), municipal water hardly if ever flowed in the pipes (we preferred using the pure water from the well in the garden), and telephones were still a distant myth in the village (we rode to Mapusa to book a trunk call to Panjim, which could take hours; it was quicker to go there oneself), the house clutched at my heart tighter and tighter, claiming I belonged there.

A home for two in Goa

Michèle and I returned to Goa after the Jazz Yatra, determined to find a house of our own. I wasn't too happy with the lazy, hedonistic lifestyle in

Anjuna – late wake-up, breakfast, lie naked on the beach until sunset, shower, dinner at a restaurant, and then a party somewhere or the other, big or small. Wake up late the next day to start the same routine again. Many of her friends came from well-to-do families in Europe and, though they lived the hippie life, it was hippie deluxe; they all rented huge houses, had a man deliver a block of ice for their ice box every morning (electricity was too weak to make a refrigerator work), had a cleaning lady, a gardener, a cook, the works. I named them 'the aristo-freaks'.

Though to me all that I was doing was anything but work, I saw myself as a working man. I had songs to write, a band to rehearse, a hotel to play at, postcards and t-shirts to design and their printing to supervise, correspondence to write to our concert organizers… No, I had no desire or time to spend the whole day on the beach and party the whole night.

However much I loved my family, the time had come for me to move out of home too. We looked at houses available for rent which were not quite on the beach, but not in a town either – somewhere in between, in the green countryside of Goa. But even though we could perfectly envisage it in our minds, we found no such house that suited us to perfection.

And my mind's eye slowly turned towards Siolim … why, our ancestral house would be just perfect.

'Remo, the people in Siolim know our family since generations! How can you go and live there, unmarried, with a foreign woman?!' Mother asked, shocked, and Father seconded her. 'If you must live together without being married, do it elsewhere; not in our village, not in our ancestral house!'

But after seeing that we genuinely kept searching for the ideal house without success, Father and Mother relented, and agreed that Michèle and I could stay in the house, in the last bedroom before the kitchen section.

When they came to visit one weekend, they saw how well we had kept and decorated the house; how well Michèle cooked; and, most importantly, how loving and friendly she was towards them. And they gradually forgot that we were not married, and started seeing and accepting us as a couple.

Michèle and I during our initial days together. Here on the Goa–Bombay boat.

The last bedroom had been a storeroom in the past, where coconuts and rice and fruits had been stored after harvest. It had old rounded tiles on the roof, and no false ceiling like the front portion of the house did. One night as we went to sleep, Michèle and I heard a soft thump on our mattress. Upon turning on the light, we discovered it was a deadly scorpion. I flicked it on to the floor and killed it with my leather Kolhapuri.

'Scorpions are said to always move around in couples. We must look for another one,' said Michèle breathlessly.

And sure enough, there was the dead one's husband or wife, looking for revenge. After committing the second murder of the night, we eventually fell into an uneasy sleep.

The near-death experience left us shaken. It left Mother and Father shaken too, when they heard about it.

'Please shift immediately to one of the front bedrooms which has a false ceiling,' they said. 'It will be safer. And use one of the poster beds, and make sure it has a mosquito net covering it.'

And thus began our unintentional and gradual sting operation whereby we eventually occupied the whole house. Of course we left the main bedroom, the famous *quarto dos noivos* or 'room of the newly-weds', exclusively for Father and Mother for when they visited. They loved coming to visit during weekends and being spoilt silly by Michèle and me.

My first home studio

I came to know about a new multi-track tape recorder called the TEAC Tascam Portastudio. After the two locked-in tracks Eric's Revox in Paris offered, these four independent tracks, with independent EQ and inserts for FX, would be sheer luxury. I searched for and read all I could about it in those days prior to the internet, and could think and dream of nothing else. This was just what I needed to record and release my own albums.

I had approached record companies in Bombay, and they had all told me that original songs in English by an Indian would never sell here. Give them Hindi disco, the craze of the hour (spearheaded by Biddu and his *Disco Deewane* with the rototoms), and they would sign me on. Disco? No way.

I knew they were wrong, because my 'songs in English' were not American wannabe stuff. They were written and sung in Indian English, about Indian realities, and I was sure there was an eager audience for them. But hey, these were company executives, they wore suits, so they knew more about music than musicians did, right?

Wrong.

I didn't set out to prove them wrong, but – you guessed it – to feed the creative urge. I simply had to start my own studio, since these suits couldn't see what I saw. And now a home studio was possible and affordable, if I could only have the Portastudio and a few complementary gadgets.

But as I've explained several times already, one couldn't just walk into a music shop and buy foreign stuff in India. So Michèle and I hatched a plot.

She and I would pool in the resources together. I'd make a list of the items I required. She would go to Singapore, the tax-free port where she could get them at half the French prices. As a foreigner, she would stand a better chance of bringing them into India.

The ticket to Singapore? Why, she worked as an air hostess for UTA in France, and as such was entitled to free air tickets to anywhere in the globe, even though she now worked for half the year only, by choice, so she could travel the other half.

And she pulled it off. A pretty foreigner with a sweet smile, the customs officers didn't even pick her out for inspection in those pre-X-ray machine days at the Bombay international airport. I was twice as excited when I went to the Goa airport that morning – for I was picking up Michèle as well as my first home studio.

My first home studio: The famous Portastudio is in the foreground. Next to it is a BOSS eight-channel mixer and a guitar synth. To my left is a Korg synthesizer, which came after I had recorded my first two albums. And below it my second drum machine, a Roland 909.

Goan Crazy!

I had to learn how to use the Portastudio on my own. Being a non-technical person, it was rocket science to me, and there was no one I could ask – I was the first one to use such a machine in Goa, and probably in India. I had to go through the lengthy and confusing RTFM method as a friend referred to it – 'Read the F*cking Manual'!

But teach myself I did, and soon recorded my first album, for which Noel Godin suggested the title *Goan Crazy!*. It comprised my new sociopolitical satirical songs about Goa, love songs for Goa and Siolim, and the prophetic and notorious 'Hello, Rajiv Gandhi', which in 1985 would be one of the things which helped catapult me from Goa into the national limelight.

I got a thousand copies of the cassette manufactured in Bombay, and was super-excited to receive the delivery of the first half of the batch in Goa. I tried out the first one – and the tape snapped. I tried the second one – one of the stereo channels was blank. I tried the third one – this time the tape got stuck in the player. On the fourth one I sounded like The Chipmunks on amphetamines. I broke out in a cold sweat.

I refused to pay for and take over the rest of the stock, went back to Bombay and found another cassette duplicator. I was assured by reliable sources that this one was trustworthy.

By the time I returned to Goa, people were congratulating me on the release of my album. What release? I was still getting them duplicated! But the first manufacturer, the crook with the bad quality, had supplied the rejected copies to Radio Mundial near the Panjim ferry jetty. When confronted, Mundial denied any knowledge that the goods were rejected, but agreed to withdraw all stocks.

Ah, the travails of the inexperienced musician who was dealing with the big bad music industry world for the very first time …

The second manufacturer proved to be honest and efficient, and the new batch sounded good. I bought myself a receipt book and went around on my yellow scooter distributing the cassettes to the main music shops and a few other outlets around Goa.

Goan Crazy! soon became the highest-selling cassette Goa had ever known. Goa's main dealer, V.P. Sinari, told me it had even outsold Chris Perry and Lorna, the local Konkani superstars.

I had hand-designed the cover, which I got screen-printed like the postcards, and I enjoyed writing the legend '*All music, lyrics, instruments, voices, recording, mixing and album cover by Remo Fernandes*'. Other than

Paul McCartney's first album after he left The Beatles, a full-fledged album by one man alone was unheard of. And though he had played all the instruments, he hadn't handled the recording and mixing and album cover himself, so there!

Two gentlemen who were to play an important role in my career would lay their hands on this cassette. One was Shyam Benegal, and the other was Gul Anand. Upon hearing it, the former asked me to create the songs for his film *Trikal*, and the latter the theme song for his film *Jalwa*. Gul Anand had been gifted the cassette by Father's good old friend Froilano Machado, whose son Carmelino would marry my sister many years later.

While I was an architecture student in Bombay I didn't even know about the existence of 'art films', which was what serious Indian cinema devoid of masala – which I avoided and still avoid like the plague – was called. So a serious film poster, portraying a tribal woman who truly looked like a tribal woman, i.e. without make-up, lipstick and plucked eyebrows, caught my eye, and I went to watch *Ankur*. And that's how I became infatuated with Shabana Azmi – or rather, with a girl back home who reminded me of her. And became an ardent admirer of director Shyam Benegal. Never did I imagine that he would someday call and ask me to make music for a film of his.

I presented the scratch recording for *Jalwa*, which I had conceptualized as a five-minute improvisation with just one lyrical line, '*Dekho dekho, yeh hai jalwa!*' (since my Hindi was almost non-existent), to Gul Anand in Bombay. I asked for Rs 10,000 for it, which I then felt was a small fortune. He took the cassette to his office to listen to it in private, and returned with a cheque for Rs 11,000. But Shylock wanted several extra pounds of flesh for the extra thousand rupees: he wanted the piece to be extended to fifteen minutes. Fifteen minutes of recorded improvisation! Despite the limitations that my four-track cassette Portastudio imposed, I did it. And thus created a piece which is regarded as a revolutionary classic in modern Indian film music. Until today, the audience doesn't allow me off the stage unless I sing it. Thanks, Gul.

Breaking out of Goa

The next year, 1985, a few things happened which helped launch me at a national level, as I mentioned earlier. It is important that I list them here.

❖ *Jalwa* and *Trikal*: These two films, each one a hit in its own genre (the first in commercial cinema, the second in art cinema), introduced me to a spectrum of cinegoers. I had been writing and singing English songs for a while, but after *Jalwa,* where I played a minuscule spot role, released in 1987, street urchins who cleaned car windscreens at traffic lights in Bombay recognized me. And I realized the power of Hindi films.

❖ Aid Bhopal: The Union Carbide catastrophe had taken place in Bhopal and, in keeping with the Live Aid concert which had just been held in London and Philadelphia, and with our Indian penchant for copying things including charity efforts, a handful of youth in Bombay decided to hold a concert called Aid Bhopal. I had a show in Calcutta the previous day but, on an unplanned transit stop in Bombay, I attended this as a spectator. I don't know how they spotted me in the throng at the stadium, but at the request of the organizers, and in the midst of all the Bombay rock bands and singers, I sang just two songs with a borrowed acoustic guitar, 'Pack That Smack' and 'Ode to Graham Bell', which, with their Indian identity and humour, brought the huge stadium down. Doordarshan covered the long concert and played it over four consecutive Sunday afternoons. And though they showed different participants each week, they decided to feature me and my two songs each and every Sunday. Doordarshan then being the one and only monopolistic TV channel in India, government-owned, one can imagine what being on it for four consecutive Sundays did for my exposure.

❖ 'Hello, Rajiv Gandhi': Rajiv Gandhi was only the prime minister's son when he visited Goa some years ago, but I saw how frantically the Goa Congress government repaired hitherto neglected potholed roads and completed long-pending projects before his arrival, things they wouldn't bother doing for the people. Sanjay Gandhi had been killed in an air crash, and I noticed a reluctant Rajiv being force-groomed into politics by his mother Indira Gandhi so he would take over her (and Sanjay's) mantle.

And I wrote a song called 'Hello, Rajiv Gandhi', where I mentioned all
this and, among other things, invited him to Goa every month, so that our
government would keep it spick and span at least for him, if not for us.

Now, in 1985, rendering my song prophetic, Rajiv Gandhi was visiting
Goa as the prime minister of India, and I was asked by the government
of Goa to perform for him and his wife Sonia at a programme in
Mormugao Port Trust (MPT), Vasco. Knowing me and my penchant
for being outspoken in front of authorities, I was made to promise
I would not sing or say anything to offend him. I promised I wouldn't, and I
didn't. I sang 'Hello, Rajiv Gandhi', which exposed and offended the Goa
government instead.

Rajiv loved the song and had a good laugh, and when I asked on the
microphone if I could offer him my cassette despite the security surrounding
him, he walked up to the stage to collect it.

But one newspaper in Goa, *The Navhind Times*, started persecuting
me each and every day thereafter, the editor Bikram Vohra accusing me of
distorting and insulting Goan culture – of which he knew nothing. Respected
citizens told me they had written letters to the editor defending me, but that
he had failed to publish them. I had seen him systematically destroy the
careers of people who had crossed paths with him or his mine-owning bosses
and their political pals, with similar relentless one-sided daily attacks, and
I decided I had to try and stop him somehow.

I collected some of these newspaper clippings and posted them to
the prime minister. With thousands of letters coming to him every day,
I wondered whether he would even come across mine; imagine my surprise
when a couple of weeks later there was an official envelope with the seal of
the Prime Minister's Office on my doorstep.

The letter was short, sweet and to the point. But it was probably the
very first time that an Indian prime minister had acknowledged the
existence of, leave alone written to, a pop/rock musician. This reinforced
Rajiv's image as a young, forward-thinking prime minister. While Bikram
Vohra's tirade had been restricted to his local Goan daily, the press
from all over the country, comprising reputed newspapers, weeklies and

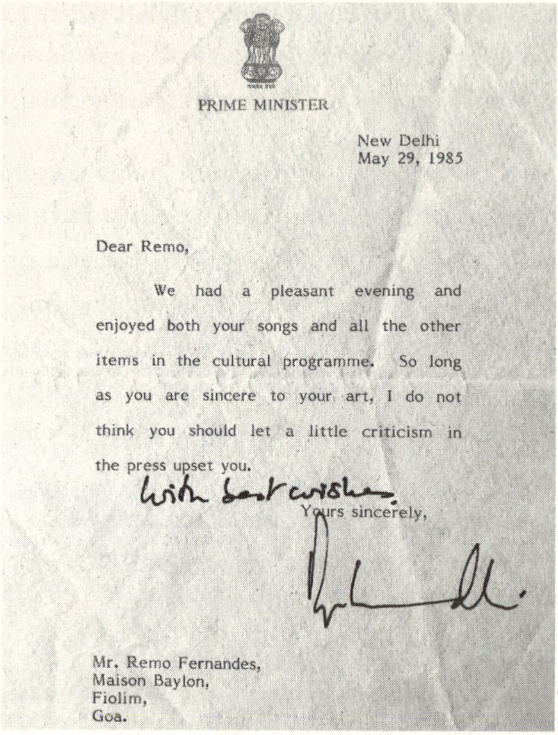

PRIME MINISTER

New Delhi
May 29, 1985

Dear Remo,

We had a pleasant evening and enjoyed both your songs and all the other items in the cultural programme. So long as you are sincere to your art, I do not think you should let a little criticism in the press upset you.

With best wishes,

Yours sincerely,

Mr. Remo Fernandes,
Maison Baylon,
Fiolim,
Goa.

monthlies, wanted to carry Rajiv's letter and my story. So Vohra's attempt to destroy me backfired, and in fact helped boost my fame to a magnitude he never imagined.

Old Goan Gold

There were some old Goan and Portuguese songs I felt nostalgic for. I wanted to buy the records, but they were not available any more. Not in Goa, and apparently not in Portugal either. Frustrated, I thought I'd record them for myself, and for others like me who missed them.

My friend Gyanna Gracias lent me her thick treasure-filled songbook in which, over the years, she had written down the lyrics of most of these old songs and many, many more. I had never thought I would ever compose a mando or a fado, but I ended up doing both, and three of my original compositions found themselves on this album, which was called *Old Goan Gold*. One was '*Panch Vorsam*', which I composed for the film *Trikal*, and for which the brilliant poet Prof. Manohar Rai Sardesai, a man I admired and loved a lot, edited my Konkani. One was 'Soiri', a poem by Prof. Sardesai which featured in a book he offered me, and which I loved at first sight and set to music. And I don't remember when and why I wrote 'Fado Goa', but it must have been during that period of time, driven by the mood that all the old Portuguese songs in this album had put me into.

Goans who tend to see Goa as the beginning and end of the universe (and there are lots of those) still see these first two albums, which were absolutely Goa-centric, as my best.

But then I broadened my vision, and started writing songs which had national and even global relevance.

Let's get married!

Meanwhile, between *Goan Crazy!* and *Old Goan Gold*, Michèle and I got married.

Until now Michèle had been going back to France every six months or so, due to visa restrictions, and also to work at her part-time air hostess's job with UTA. If we were going to start a family, we both felt she should not keep moving every six months, nor fly as an air hostess any more.

Father's birthday was coming up. He had been hinting for some time now that he wanted a grandchild. Mother was too wise to influence us into doing anything, whether marriage or parenthood, but I knew that she obviously wanted the same. We decided to gift Father our decision to get married as his birthday present, and I wrote it out in the form of a very informal birthday card-cum-wedding invitation. We'd marry in court to enable Michèle to obtain an OCI card and thereby live in India, and in church as a gift

DEAREST DAD,

We have decided to get married in the Siolim Church in the near future. Here's your INVITATION!

HAPPY BIRTHDAY!

Michèle & Remo.
22/02/84.

to my parents for having accepted us as husband and wife for the last three or four years.

I cannot describe the joy and happiness which exploded in the house with this news. Father said it was his best birthday present ever. Mother, whose birthday had taken place just ten days earlier, claimed it as her present too.

Michèle and I were as much in love as ever, and our life together in idyllic Siolim was absolutely beautiful. Michèle was soft-spoken, with that sweet soft French accent I love, and had integrated with my Goan friends fabulously, loving and caring for them as for her own.

There was a heavy cyclone in Siolim for two days during the monsoon before our wedding. On the third day the rain stopped, the sun shone, and we decided we'd go for a drive to survey the damage in the village – fallen trees and lamp posts mostly, and we had had no electricity for the full duration of the storm.

We were just driving down our road when a rather inoffensive remark of mine aroused in her the wildest reaction. For the first time in four years, I saw another Michèle and heard her scream.

I didn't know whether to take it as a sign of things to come or not. I had given her enough signs of things to come with my weakness for women, and she had stood and stuck by me. Who was I to judge her for a little outburst? It was only anger; she hadn't been disloyal to me like I had been on several occasions. Maybe all that electricity in the stormy air had caused it.

Michèle was six years older than me. And a divorcee. I was thirty-one, and she was thirty-seven. She was adamant about having children by the time she was forty, and said so in no uncertain terms. There's no way I was going to let her down after she had given me four wonderful years of her life.

You bet I'll be at the chapel on time!

Michèle and I had started off calling each other 'mon amour' (my love). When that felt too long, she invented the shorter form M'amour. And that eventually became M'am. Which, curiously, we still call each other most of the time, even thirteen years after our divorce.

A week or two before the wedding, I panicked. No, it wasn't just panic; it was a doubt I carried deep in my subconscious.

'M'am,' I said, 'I've got to talk to you. I don't think this nature of mine will ever change. I know I love you and only you, there's no two ways about that; but I honestly think I'll never be able to stop seeing other women.' It was a serious concern. 'Do you really think we ought to get married?'

She laughed it off. 'We don't know what might happen tomorrow!' she said. 'Maybe you'll change and won't feel like seeing other women any more. Or maybe I'll change and won't mind you seeing other women.'

That sounded like such a wonderful attitude to take, I immediately relaxed. And I marched ahead towards the wedding with a stronger resolve than ever to be a one-woman man.

It was February, and we fixed the wedding for the next January, on the 13th, a Saturday. That would give us time to prepare all the paperwork required for an inter-nation marriage. I knew that, by virtue of people's superstition, we would have the choice of whoever we wanted for a reception on a 13th: the caterer, the band, the illuminator, even the wedding venues if we so desired. We decided to have it in our house in Siolim. It had a big enough garden in the front to accommodate tables and chairs for all the guests; and a big enough living room (I should call it a hall, or *sala*) to accommodate all the dancers and revellers. There was no built-in stage of course, but I decided to place the band in the veranda between the hall and the garden. That way they would perform for, and in full sight of, the dancers as well as those at their tables.

Father had had the brainwave that Michèle, a Frenchwoman, should dress in the Goan traditional *bastodô*, which no one ever wore any more. Though the traditional ones were in black, burgundy and gold, she decided to make hers in her favourite pink, white and gold. No dark, sad colours for the bride.

Ah well … if she was going traditional Goan, I would go French punky. Electric pink socks, and ankle-length trousers to show them off, an electric pink belt and tie to match them, a black baggy jacket, and a black hat. And of course kajal in my eyes and a blonde streak in my hair.

Lúcio Miranda, who had totally stopped drinking by now, sang like a baritone angel at the chapel, and Emiliano da Cruz played a heart-melting violin. And Bondo, the Best Man, had planned a surprise: a traditional Goan brass band that played just outside the chapel soon after the Mass. City folks had not heard one in centuries, and neither had I; the band put everyone in the mood right from the start with lively Goan *reng-tereng*. Mother had arranged yet another traditional surprise for us: she had dug up the old lady who had carried the traditional old red umbrella with a golden fringe over her and Father at their wedding. Instead of at the main Siolim church a distance away, we had decided to get married in the tiny little old chapel right in front of our house, from where we walked home under her umbrella, followed by a smiling crowd of guests marching to the music of the brass band.

ABOVE: Michèle and I at our wedding, 13 January 1985. BELOW LEFT: Bondo setting an amazing festive mood with a Goan brass band. RIGHT: The same lady who had escorted my parents at their wedding under that same traditional red umbrella, now escorting us.

I'm not saying this because it was *our* wedding, but it was a jolly success. At a time when weddings were serious solemn affairs where hardly anybody dared smile too much before the third drink had been served, ours exuded 'party' right from the word go. Bondo's brass band, and Michèle's and my informality, had seen to it.

If I wondered how our guests from two extreme ends – the 'aristo-freaks' from Anjuna and the Goan society from Panjim – were going to get along, I need not have worried. Bypassing all the popular wedding bands of the time which played the latest commercial pop, I had chosen Emiliano da Cruz, whom many considered passé. His band comprised middle-aged men playing 'old-fashioned' trumpets and saxophones and such. But they played Latin and Goan music like no one else could, and that's the only music I wanted at our wedding – the music I had grown up to. It was a hit with both extremes. Emiliano even broke out into an impromptu fusion piece which lasted almost an hour (there is proof on video), where Bondo fetched his percussions, I fetched my flute, and the people all danced with wild abandon.

I was now a married man. I was thirty-one years old. I used to joke that Jesus had been crucified when he was thirty-three: I had beaten him to it by two years.

15

Pop and Pophood

Pack That Smack!

The drug scene in Goa was becoming bad. While it was mainly restricted to hashish and marijuana (which are natural substances) earlier, now the dreaded chemical killer 'smack', a crude form of heroin, was making inroads. Dealers sold it near college campuses, while the police turned a blind eye. Some, that were ex-students turned addicts, even infiltrated the college canteens. This was the context in which I wrote the songs 'Pack That Smack' and 'Down with Brown'.

After the national exposure I mentioned earlier, the same Bombay record companies that had rejected me before came back with offers. R.V. Pandit, who headed CBS, held very strong anti-drug beliefs for personal reasons. He wanted very much to release and promote my album *Pack That Smack!*, not just as a business proposition, but for the message it conveyed. The two anti-drug songs were now part of an eleven-track album, which included a live recording of the song '*So Wie Du*' as I had performed it in Dresden, East Germany.

CBS was an easy choice for me; a record company which *believed* in my music and crusading lyrics was invaluable, and I signed with them. My albums were now promoted and distributed nationwide, and I didn't have to deliver them on my yellow scooter any more.

Dresden, East Germany

To go back for a minute to the Dresden performance. In 1983 I received a letter from the Indian authorities saying the East German government had invited them to select and send their best pop artist to compete in their International Pop Song Festival to be held in less than a week, where about twenty socialist and communist countries from all over the world would participate – as usual, they sent this to me very late, and without any more details. And one day before I left, they sent me a cassette with three German songs, saying I was to choose one of them to learn and sing; and that the second song should be one from India, which I needed to send to the organizers so the conductor could write the orchestra parts and rehearse with their large festival orchestra which would accompany everyone.

I chose '*So Wie Du*' which I liked best among the German songs – it was peppy and upbeat, had a lovely melody, and suited me perfectly. But how would I learn the German lyrics, a language I knew nothing of, within a few days which included exhausting travelling? And which Indian song could I send them the day before my departure, in pre-internet times? And even if there had been internet, would they have had the time to write down the different parts for the whole orchestra, and most importantly, rehearse it, before my arrival? I decided to play my 'Guitaraag' (the sitar on guitar piece) as the second song. It was mostly instrumental, and I decided to adapt and sing a German lullaby in it, in Indian scale and tone. It would certainly disqualify me or cut marks drastically, since it wasn't technically a song but an instrumental with some sung lines, but I could think of nothing better to do at the last minute. At least I could perform it without the backing of the orchestra, as I would be playing it solo; I ended up performing it with just a synthesizer playing a tanpura-like one-note drone, and a conga replacing the tabla. Hardly any rehearsal was required for this. It was ok, I wasn't going there to win; this was my first opportunity to visit a hard-core communist country after all the cloak-and-dagger spy stories I'd read about them, and I was going to enjoy the experience to the full.

The best artists from the vast communist and socialist world were competing: the USSR, China, countries in South America with their wonderful music that I love, and an amazing singer from Cuba whose plaintive song I still remember. Some came as full bands of five or six members, but all had rehearsed extremely well with the brilliant festival orchestra.

Imagine then my surprise and elation when they announced at the end of the evening, one after the other, that I had won the three main awards: the Press Music Critics Guild's Award (the toughest and most discerning one, I was repeatedly assured: 'Music critics and journalists are the hardest people to please!'), the Loudest Audience Applause Award (measured by computer sensors in the auditorium), and the overall first prize.

On my way back I transited in Delhi. I called up the office of the authority who had selected and sent me to the festival, in order to give them the good news that I had just won three awards for India at the first international pop song contest the country had entered. If I had expected excitement and appreciation, I had to make do with an indifferent 'Ok'. I guess they were all very busy rushing to haphazardly complete other jobs at the eleventh hour.

My son Noah

Michèle was expecting our first baby. Ah, the excitement in the family! The pregnancy, the birth, everything went smooth as can be, and we were extremely grateful for that. I knew that the miracle of birth had been taking place ever since time began, yet I felt as though it had happened for the first time when it finally happened to me. Does everyone feel this way?

I never drove slower or more carefully in my life than while I was taking Michèle and Noah the short distance to my parents' home from the hospital. In the car was the most precious cargo in the world.

Noah had Michèle's skin colour, features like mine, and blonde hair which slowly turned dark brown later, as he grew into a young man. To us, the most beautiful baby in the world.

Before he was born we knew that he was going to be a Pisces and, before we chose a name, we playfully referred to him as 'Kingfish'. I composed 'The Kingfish Lullaby' and recorded it on both sides of a cassette, so it would

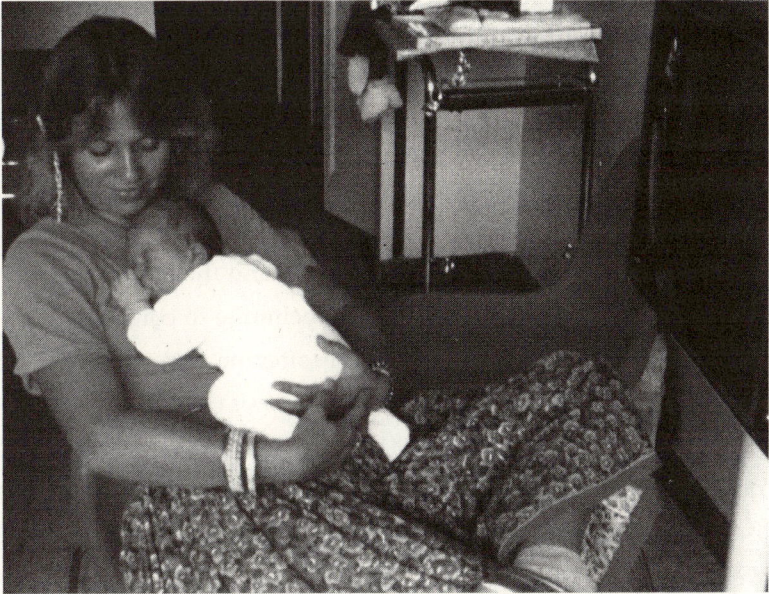

Michèle and Noah

softly play on and on while we fell asleep. The doctor, freshly returned from Germany, allowed, nay, encouraged me to have the tape recorder in the delivery room, where the lullaby played softly throughout; before he pulled the baby out, the doctor had caught the tune and was merrily whistling along. Soon after the birth, I luckily thought of stopping the music and pressing record, so I could have my son's first sounds in this world on tape. I included them in 'Noah's Lullaby', which also featured in the album *Pack That Smack!*.

The album, though carrying hard-hitting tracks against drug dealers and politicians, contained other very family-oriented songs too: 'For Michèle (Don't Let Her Get Away)', which was my firm resolve to change myself and my ways, and '*Mon Amour*', a love song for her.

Bombay City!

With popularity and – let's face it – stardom, came lots of things. Foreign concerts; festivals abroad; awards; money; fame; commercial endorsements such as Shure microphones and Raymond suitings; and temptations.

For the first time in India, CBS and *Bombay Dyeing* brought together the two crazes of the moment, rock music and fashion. And the country's top musicians and most beautiful models embarked on two very successful metro concert tours of the country together.

Something curious was happening now. The other artists were made up of or were being backed by full bands on stage, while I was up there alone, doing a few songs with just my acoustic guitar, and the bulk of my set with my own backing tracks. Yet everyone was beginning to consider me as 'the boss' of the scene. No one wanted to perform after me, and everyone weighed their order of performance according to where I was placed. I remember one particular show at the Rang Bhavan (not part of the Bombay Dyeing tour) where, at the sound check, a whole lot of artists kept shifting my placement around. They were all visibly nervous about their own placements, and I was the only one who was looking at the whole proceedings with amusement, agreeing to be shunted wherever they shunted me. Until, finally, they shunted me to *exactly* the place I wished to be.

Then I put my foot down and said firmly, 'Ok guys, this is it. Now I'm not going to change my order any more.' After the show began, an artist who was an old friend came to ask me whether I would please shift my order yet again so that he could perform before me. I said no to him, and explained that all these changes were affecting my mood, as I psyched myself up for my entry according to the time left to go on stage, and now it would totally dampen my spirits to have to delay my performance.

My performance that night drove the audience wild as usual (I shall try and discuss the reasons why I think I had the power to do that). Soon after that, my old friend went on and was literally booed off stage even before he could complete his set. To be truthful, he sang very old-fashioned songs in a very old-fashioned way. But somehow he blamed me (and my declining to change places yet again) for his poor reception. And he didn't forgive me for it for a long while. I wonder whether he has forgiven me yet.

The reasons for the power of my performances? Well ... there must have been a few. For one, I know I sang and talked *to* the audience as though it was one amalgamated person – on a one-on-one basis. Whereas the other artists sang and talked *at* them. I was myself on stage, with my kajal and outlandish clothes and whatever – I'd be wearing something similar when I went out shopping or sightseeing the next day. Whereas the other artists took on another persona and another accent just to go on stage, and put on pieces of clothing which they would never wear elsewhere, like a bandana or a fancy waistcoat or sunglasses. The audience can smell and sense genuineness. I *moved*, taking the mic off the stand and in my hand, from one end of the stage to the other, right up to the edge slapping high fives with the guys in front; all this not in a choreographed or pre-planned way, but with the genuine excitement of the music causing the locomotion. This excitement naturally transmitted itself to the audience. Can you believe that no one else moved on stage before I did? Even in the heavy rock bands, the height of showmanship was for the vocalist to raise one foot and place it on the monitor speaker in front of him; and for the guitarists, to face each other from up close, with their legs spread apart, holding their guitars parallel to each other – these being poses one saw foreign artists striking in posters and photographs (there was no MTV from which to learn other moves as yet).

Artists started moving and actually talking to the audience after me (albeit mostly with fake American accents). Some actually came up to me in private, in airports and even in airplanes, and said things like, 'Hi Remo, I've learnt a lot from you about how to be on stage! I'm going to copy your idea of dividing the audience into left and right halves and having them compete over which half sings loudest!' (This was an idea that had come to me on the spur of the moment one night, and which I sometimes used after that.)

But while some said these things to me, none ever credited me in public with having influenced their stage showmanship or behaviour. Perhaps some will on the day I die and channels call them up for comments, when they're eighty-plus. We always tend to reserve words of praise for that time, don't we? Human nature.

By that time my album *Bombay City!* had been released, and it turned out to be the highest-selling English album in India. If *Pack That Smack!*

had made the media dub me 'the rocker with a conscience', this one firmly established me as the top pop/rocker in the country. That same year, *Jalwa* was released too. Together, the two hit albums proved to be a two-pronged assault on the two main audiences in India: the westernized English-speaking one, and the colloquial Hindi- and film-music lovers.

I had tried very hard to be a one-woman man for Michèle. But now it was becoming truly too difficult for a man like me to keep his head on his shoulders. Famous actresses, famous politicians' young daughters and daughters-in-law, young journalists who came to my hotel rooms to interview me, singers who came to my studio to record harmonies, fans who came for photographs and autographs – they were not just temptations, but downright provocations. As were the Bombay Dyeing tours with the most beautiful models and beauty queens in the country. I didn't even have to go looking. Things just happened mutually – or else 'things' came looking for me. Sometimes in twos, and sometimes in threesomes. I did try my best to keep my promise to Michèle, but there were times when I failed. And failed miserably.

One thing I've got to stress here is that not once, never ever, did I coerce any girl or woman into anything. That kind of 'conquest' never appealed to me, and I wondered how some men could enjoy it. I guess a brute totally devoid of charm or goodness to attract a woman would resort to force or coercion. Or someone who loves a power trip. Or someone who needs to subjugate and humiliate a woman to turn himself on. I wouldn't know. To me, mutual desire and mutual consent have always been the most pleasant and stimulating turn-ons in the world.

I was honest with Michèle whenever I did fail, and I told her everything. It hurt her, of course, but she preferred knowing. In fact she insisted on knowing. And even if sometimes it took her a few days, she forgave and forgot.

Jonah, my second son

ABOVE: *La famille: Noah, me, Michèle and Jonah.*
RIGHT: *Jonah, a bit grown up.*

On 28 November 1988, our second son was born. I was very keen on having a daughter, but you do turn philosopher when you can't make things go your way: I told myself I would be blessed with two daughters-in-law instead. Michèle said, 'I don't much care about the sex of the child; the main thing is that the child be all right, that he or she be normal. That is blessing enough.' I totally agreed.

Jonah was the cutest kid: curly hair coming down in ringlets, a cherub's face and mouth, good-natured and uncomplicated. It really didn't matter whether he was a boy or a girl. I loved him unconditionally too.

When he was a child he'd hold on tight to Michèle's skirts. When he grew a bit he believed that 'big brother knew best', to the extent of letting Noah assemble his He-Man castle and Lego games while he merely watched, despite me encouraging him to the contrary. It's only when Noah left home to study in Bombay that Jonah gradually gained his full autonomy.

'You're a father of two now,' I told myself. 'If you don't stop being swayed by women at this stage, when will you?' And I resolved – this time really, definitively, seriously – to change my ways. A new Remo was born. Hallelujah!

India, my India...

As my Indian Airlines flight taxied into place at the Delhi airport, I noticed an official white Ambassador car with a red beacon flashing on its roof rushing up to it. 'We must have some VIP on board,' I thought to myself.

As I climbed down the aircraft steps with my handbag, my only luggage, a military man in full livery walked up to me and saluted.

'Welcome to Delhi, Mr Fernandes. My apologies, but due to the delay in the Goa flight, the prime minister asks if you might come directly to his residence, instead of being taken to your hotel first?'

Sure. I changed out of my 'Goa clothes' (Bermuda shorts, t-shirt and crocs) into the more formal clothes I was carrying, in the back seat of the moving car.

When I walked in, the room was already full of the who's who of Indian rock, pop and jazz. I barely had the time to say hi to everyone when Rajiv Gandhi walked in and, with a broad bright smile, opened the meeting.

'It's such a pleasure meeting with you artists after all the politicians and bureaucrats I have to meet all day long!' he greeted us.

Until then, apart from the Dresden festival, India had been officially represented at international events exclusively by classical and traditional folk artists. There was a Festival of India at the USSR coming up, and Rajiv wanted to project a young, vibrant image of India for the first time.

It worked wonders. Everywhere we performed, people were telling us they had no idea that rock and pop and jazz even existed in India. I just loved travelling around that enormous country and, for the first time, I felt like a real rock star, with girls rushing the stage through the curtains at the end of my performances.

The communist countries I visited (first East Germany, then Bulgaria, and then the USSR) were total revelations. It was easier and more popular to travel to capitalist Europe or the US, and I had not expected to ever have an opportunity to see the 'infamous' communist world first-hand. My head was filled with images which the Western world had projected, and I was surprised that no cloak-and-dagger person was following me on the first day.

But ah, I had been assigned a personal interpreter/guide! She was certainly my spy in disguise, assigned to see to it that I didn't go to undesired places a visitor wasn't meant to see… On the third day I decided to test her out.

I said, 'Birgit, I won't need you tomorrow. I'm just going to sightsee on my own.'

I expected her to do a double take and say that wouldn't be advisable, that it was dangerous, that I might get lost, whatever… But all she said was, 'Oh, great! I can take a holiday! Have a great time tomorrow then!'

Was she going to stay home and send the cloak-and-dagger man to trail me all day instead? Nah, I was letting my imagination run too wild. It was my turn to do a double take: 'No, on second thoughts, I think it would be great doing the sightseeing with you. So please do come, Birgit.'

She would point out all the good things about her communist country she could, though. She proudly told me once that their cars were made out of a metal-like substance created out of cardboard which was compressed through a very special process. She wasn't too happy when I asked, 'And what do you make out of the cars in case of accidents, schoolbooks?'

The capitalist countries (mainly the US with its propaganda machinery) gleefully gloated that the prices of TV sets, cars and other such items were exorbitant in the communist world. They were. But that was because they were considered 'luxury items'. What the capitalists failed to point out was that the basic human necessities – housing, electricity, food, water, education, health services – were extremely cheap. While in the capitalist world the exact opposite ruled: unnecessary 'luxury items' were consumer-fed to the masses cheaply, while one had to think twice and thrice before turning up the much-needed heating in winter, before sending children for higher studies, and before going to see a dentist. I know doctors, and even hospitals in Goa who thrived on 'medical tourism', catering to people from the UK and other expensive European countries. They found it cheaper to buy a chartered flight ticket to Goa, turn off the heating in their London flat for two weeks, stay in their chartered hotel on a warm beach with all meals included, drink cheap Indian beer all day, and get new reading glasses and their teeth fixed in Panjim, than to simply stay at home.

The interpreter/guides I was assigned in all the communist countries were young women. And often, after a concert or press conference or a sightseeing tour, they would drop me to my hotel and walk back through Moscow or East Berlin or Sofia alone, well after midnight.

When I asked if it was safe, they were genuinely surprised. 'Of course!' they said in a matter-of-fact way, and off they went. America (and the UK and France and so on) failed to speak about this aspect of the communist world, and about how dangerous – read impossible – cities like New York, London and Paris were for a lone woman walking about at night.

I'm not saying the communist world was ideal. I'm saying it had many wonderful aspects which the capitalist world hid and ignored while highlighting and exaggerating the bad.

I did quite a few concerts for the ICCR too – that's the Indian Council for Cultural Relations. While I guess they reserved offers for concerts in cities like London and Paris for artists who didn't shy away from wielding influence and connections – and which I, who had lived in Europe for a couple of years and not just visited it on some demented quickie 'foreign shopping spree', had no interest in revisiting – I was offered concert tours in countries like (besides the aforementioned communist ones) Kenya, Mozambique, Seychelles, Mauritius, and so on: offers which I devoured hungrily. The ICCR offered honorariums and per diems which were negligible compared to what I was earning in my concerts, but the way I looked at it, I was actually being paid to travel to destinations I would have happily paid to visit!

Some months later Rajiv wanted to promote rock and pop more widely within India, and he called the rock and pop musicians to his residence again to ask for suggestions. A prime minister, or even just an average government authority, who asked for suggestions and advice from the youth was unheard of in India. We suggested television exposure, and he proposed starting a special programme featuring a different artist each week. When the time came to name it, I suggested the tongue-in-cheek *Pop Goes India*. He and

Mani Shankar Iyer saw through it though, and settled on the bland and safe *Pop Time* instead.

With Rajiv Gandhi at his residence.

Modern music was not the only thing Rajiv was encouraging in India. My knowledge of politics and economics is meagre, and was even more so at the time. But I knew that he had big plans to open up the Indian economy, which had hitherto choked under the stranglehold of policies that bordered on the communist. India was a giant just waiting to break free. And I knew that if allowed to go smoothly forward, Rajiv's new modern plans, which he had already started working on, could usher in a golden era for our country.

But all of a sudden, all that remained of those golden plans was a pair of sports shoes on a ground in Sriperumbudur, near Chennai. Rajiv had been blown up by a seventeen-year-old Tamilian girl, a human bomb belonging to the LTTE.

Michèle told me about the assassination as I woke up. I didn't utter a word. Just stayed in bed the whole morning, feeling empty. Then I got up and silently went up to my studio and poured out my feelings into an instrumental piece I named 'The 21st of May'. I also rewrote the lyrics to 'Hello, Rajiv Gandhi' and named the new version 'Goodbye, Rajiv Gandhi'. These featured in an album called *Politicians Don't Know How to Rock 'n' Roll*.

My entire being was mourning and hurting, not just for Rajiv whom I had grown very fond of, but for our country.

Ironically, despite the guitar being my main instrument, I had not been able to use one on any of my albums until now due to the silly reason that I didn't have enough tracks to record on. But now I had graduated from my four-track Portastudio to an eight-track spool Fostex, had just bought a superb anniversary model Jackson electric guitar and, together with my acoustic guitar, finally gave vent to my favourite instrument on this album. Incidentally, this is my son Noah's favourite album of mine.

Pepsi *was* the right choice

In a country like India which offered no awards in pop and rock music, being asked by Pepsi USA to endorse not one but two of their launch ad films in India was like being offered the biggest international recognition one could think of. They were unofficially saying: 'In America we have the world's greatest pop star, Michael Jackson, endorsing our drink. In every country in the world we have chosen their greatest pop star to endorse us. We've chosen you in India, and you know why.'

Today you might say that aerated soft drinks aren't the healthiest things to endorse. And I agree. But I had flatly refused even more lucrative deals to endorse alcohol and cigarettes at the time, saying, 'I might have a drink and smoke sometimes, but I refuse to encourage others, especially the youth, to do so.' Having refused to endorse substances which could turn into serious evils, I found the 'recognition' (more than the money) involved in endorsing this cold drink irresistible. And I don't regret it one bit.

Pepsi wanted me to copy Michael Jackson's song with lyrics in Hindi, but I refused. I said I wanted to compose my own. They indirectly expressed their doubts that an Indian artist could compose good enough pop and rock, but they were willing to give it a listen. They approved my '*Yehi hai* right choice, baby!' without any changes suggested.

In the film I was cast alongside Juhi Chawla, whom I had loved in *Qayamat Se Qayamat Tak*. She didn't seem to be too happy at my friendly, informal wave and 'Hi, Juhi!' when we met; being a Bollywood film star, perhaps she expected more *bhav* (undue respect) from a rock musician, but I saw no difference between the two. During all the days of the shoot, I dreaded the director's shouts for more '*Dhuaan! Dhuaan!*' The artificial smoke which I think was created out of burning coal (no electric smoke machines in India yet) blinded and choked me for three days in a row, and through it I had to emote and sing and dance and play the guitar hero in the jugalbandi bit. The film, 'the longest and most expensive ad film in Indian advertising history', was an incredible hit, though. You can imagine what it did to my career.

Frankly, I found the second film, where they got another music director to copy Ray Charles's 'Ah ha' song, much less exciting, and so did the public. After that, unfortunately, Pepsi went the way of most advertisers in India, and chose to feature lip-syncing film heroes instead of real-life singers and musicians.

'Humma Humma'

I first met A.R. Rahman in the huge empty backstage area of an auditorium in New Delhi where we were both performing for some fundraising concert. He told me that he had a band while in college, and they played my songs like 'Ocean Queen'. I was very pleasantly surprised and flattered, and told him how I had loved his music from the time I'd heard it in a car in Tamil Nadu. He asked if I would like to sing in Tamil and/or Telugu. With a huge amused smile and both eyebrows raised in surprise, I said, 'Why not?'

About a week later he called and asked if I could come to Chennai to record a new film song of his. He started work in the studio pretty early. I'm not a morning singer and, on top of that, the song was very high-pitched for me; but a couple of very strong and piping hot South Indian coffees came to the rescue.

I asked him to run the track while I did some vocal improvisations to slowly open up my throat – he needn't record them. I was more than amused months later when I saw that he hadn't only recorded them, but had kept some of those impromptu lines as part of the final track, including the now famous '*Yaabireh*' and other scatting before the main song begins. The song itself, with its powerful syncopated beat and minimalist bass line, was a pleasure to sing.

After I finished recording the Hindi version of the song, he asked if I would do the Telugu version. I didn't know what I'd let myself in for when I said 'Yes'. If I thought that the pronunciation of some Hindi words was tough for me, Telugu had nuances which my ears could not even discern.

Some months later a TV crew from Delhi flew down to Goa to do an in-depth documentary on me over a few days. I took them around all my old haunts: my first schools, the first stage where I performed as a child of five, and so on. They flew back to Delhi and were completing the editing of the footage when there was a frantic call from the producer-director. Strangely I cannot remember her name or that of her channel, though I can see her lovely, kind face in front of my eyes.

'Remo, you have a blazing hit in the charts! How's it that you didn't speak about it at all during our interview?!'

'Hit? What hit?'

'A song called "*Humma Humma*" you sang for Rahman! It just got released a couple of days ago.'

'Oh! I'd forgotten all about it!'

'What?! How could you have forgotten?'

'Well … you walk into a recording studio, hear a song for the very first time in your life, record it, walk out, and never hear it again for months, so obviously you totally forget it. Until suddenly, without warning, it is released.'

'Yes, I guess you're right … well, you have no idea, safely ensconced as you are in Goa, but it's proving to be a mega hit. Could you please fly to Delhi first thing tomorrow morning so that we can add a chunky bit to the interview about "*Humma Humma*"? Now the documentary would seem totally incomplete and outdated without it.'

'Sure.'

And then one day, suddenly...

We had just gone to bed, and were not yet asleep, when the telephone rang. It was Mother.

'Remo, Father's not feeling too well. Do you think you could come over immediately?'

She had never ever made such a call and such a request before. I didn't even waste time asking for more information. Michèle and I dressed in record time and were out of the door. Luckily we had two excellent live-in maids whom we could blindly trust our children with.

During the forty-five-minute drive to Panjim I was picturing driving Father to the best doctor and hospital as soon as we reached there.

Mother greeted us at the door, but was strangely silent. She led us to the guest room which was on the ground floor next to the dining room, and Father was lying on the bed. Our family doctor, who lived opposite our house, was in the room, in his pyjamas.

'Hi, Pop!' I exclaimed in my usual jolly way of greeting him. I had always used this exaggeratedly modern greeting with him, as it amused us both for the simple reason of being so incongruous. 'Not feeling too well tonight?' And I proceeded to bend down and kiss his cheeks as always. He felt strange and cold.

I looked questioningly at Mother, and her return look said it all. Father was no more.

'What? When?' I blabbered.

'He was already gone when I called you, Remo. I didn't want to give you a shock, didn't want you to drive in that state of mind.'

God, I could have sworn he was resting, or at most sleeping, peacefully. The doctor, who had waited to keep Mother company until we arrived, left after warm words of consolation. I spent time sitting at Father's bedside, holding his hand, caressing his immobile cheeks. Unlike my touch-me-not (but very loving) Mother, he loved tight warm hugs just as I did, and his ideal way of life would have been one big joint family, with all of us under one happy roof.

After a long while I went and sat in the dining room with Mother, where she told me exactly what had happened.

'Your father, who was petrified of hospitals and who called his doctor for every little thing, had a wonderful death: no sickness or illness, no need or cause to call a doctor, and certainly no hospital,' she said. 'He had his customary two drinks of whisky and soda in the evening, his full favourite dinner of fish and mayonnaise, his favourite dessert of caramel custard, and then, as he was lifting his glass of water, satisfied, he suffered a massive heart attack. He placed the glass back on the table and died sitting in his chair. In a state of shock, I held on to him, and screamed for João to run and fetch the doctor, who rushed here. He said Father was already dead when he arrived. The three of us managed to lift him and carry him to the bed.'

Even in that shocked state, I realized that one could hardly have a better death, and I hoped mine would be as good when it came: after a good favourite meal, in the company of the woman of your life, sitting upright in a chair. And, most importantly, after having lived a full and fulfilling life, nothing left undone, with no illness or suffering, at the ripe age of eighty-five.

In the days that follow such an event, one always seems to be half in a dream and half in reality, at least until the funeral, which is the irrefutable closure. Mother informed me that Father had wanted a Goan brass band to play happy mandos and dulpods at his funeral, and I made sure I fulfilled that wish of his, besides making the traditional arrangements with the church and funeral agency. His funeral was crowded, and the church was full, and there were newspaper articles about his life and achievements being published afterwards.

A few simple, humble, unknown men appeared over the next few days, to shake my hand and condole, and to say things like, 'Baba, you don't know me, but when I was young, your father gave me my first job in his soda factory/at Panjim municipality (where he was honorary councillor for a few years)/ at Club Nacional (of which he was president for a few years),' and so on. They warmed up my heart.

A day or two after the funeral, Mother handed me Father's ring. It was a thick gold job with a very prominent hexagonal black onyx stone. I had seen it on Father's hand forever, it was part of him, of who he was. He never ever took it off.

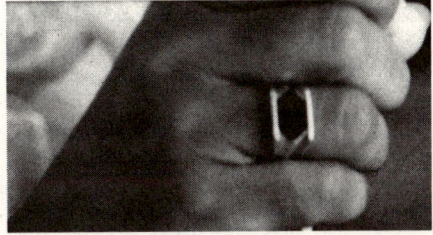

My father's ring.

Putting it on my own finger was much more than just wearing his ring. It felt like I was physically taking on his spirit, his legacy, his responsibility as head of the family. Made me feel how much like him I was in character, and also how much like him I looked physically.

When his first birthday came along after his death, Mother passed a decree: 'No sadness and regrets. Let's celebrate his life, not mourn his death. I'll take us all to dinner at his favourite restaurant.'

A decree with which we all agreed wholeheartedly; this has now become a family tradition, which I hope my children will carry on in my case too.

The band that grew organically

I was the first to perform to backing tracks in India. To the uninitiated: backing tracks are recordings of the accompanying music to your song minus your voice, and you sing live on top of it. Something like today's karaoke, without the screen and the lyrics. I used to announce from the stage that I felt justified in using them because I had played each and every instrument on those tracks, that the compositions and lyrics were all mine, and that I was therefore playing with myself, which I loved doing.

There's nothing like playing with a live band, though. One can improvise and do a song differently every night; one can speed up or slow down a song on different days, according to the human heartbeat and feel; and of course there's the excitement of human interaction with various musicians on stage, which is indescribable. But at the time concerts featured several artists, which meant that setting up and sound-checking a band in between two acts would mean simply too much of a break in the show with equipment being carried on and off stage, being connected and disconnected, mics and monitors being fixed in place, and unpleasant sounds of 'Check mic 1', 'Check mic 2', etc. taking up at least half an hour of the audience's patience – and an artist's mood. And, let's face it, most sound engineers just weren't experienced enough to conduct these on-the-spot sound checks efficiently, so the band ended up sounding horrible.

With backing tracks (each song on a separate cassette, so the sound man could change the order and play any song I called for from the stage), my sound check took all of ten minutes, and was done way before the show. And my tracks always sounded impeccable. I had no hassles, no one to depend upon, no rehearsals to conduct, nothing – I could just walk on and off stage anywhere, anytime.

I also did some songs on acoustic guitar, without backing tracks, and after a while decided to travel with an excellent tabla player called Dharmendra Hirve, or Dharma. He was from Mapusa and a gem of a human being. He accompanied me on tracks like 'Guitaraag', 'The Flute Song', Goan folk songs, and such. To add some high metallic sound to our music I asked him to tie ghungroos on his wrists.

After a couple of years of this I decided it would sound much fuller if our duo had a bassist. Victor Alvares had just returned after a few years' stint in Delhi. He was, together with Karl Peters, one of the best bassists in the whole country. And another gem of a human being.

Vocals, guitar/flute, bass and tablas – the trio now sounded full. And my troupe was still down to a minimum, with easy-to-mix instruments.

But now I was beginning to do full concerts on my own, as the only artist featured – or sometimes with a lesser-known artist as the opening act. So now I could perform with a full band at last. I would have all the time for our sound check before the show, with the stage and the sound-mixer settings all to myself.

A bass warranted a full drum kit. I knew this was the most difficult instrument for Indian sound engineers to mix on stage, so I chose a drummer who used an electronic kit reputed to have a very natural acoustic sound: Glenn de Costa with his V drums.

Well, now that we had drums, why not a synth to play all the additional sounds and parts I heard in my head? Enter Selwyn Pereira on keyboards, yet another gem of a guy with a crazy sense of mischievous humour. He and Victor formed a comic team which kept the band in splits during flights, airport waits, in hotel rooms, everywhere.

The Microwave Papadums

I wanted a name which would embody old India and the modern West, with a good dose of fun, because that's what our music was about. Around that time my sister Belinda, who was now a professor of French in two universities in Portugal, returned home on one of her three or four visits per year. And, over dinner, told me she roasted papads in her microwave oven there. These ovens were not available in India yet, and even in the West were still considered a high-tech luxury symbol, while our papads were part of a cultural tradition. Now there was the combination I was looking for! I jumped up from the dining table, went into my office and jotted down the name.

I wondered how the band would take to being called papadums, whether microwaved or not. At the next rehearsal I tentatively put forth the proposal to them. After laughing for five minutes, they all agreed. So 'Remo & The Microwave Papadums' we were.

Why papadums and not papads, which is what we call the savouries in Goa? Because papadums sounded punchier. And funnier.

'*Pyaar To Hona Hi Tha*'

I'd recorded a few film songs in between, such as '*Huiya Ho*' and '*Shinga-Linga*' which I composed, directed, produced and sang for the film *Khamoshi* in 1996, and the title song of the film *Aflatoon* for music directors Dilip and Sameer Sen in 1997. All of them moderate hits, I would say. Then in 1998 I received a call from music directors Jatin–Lalit to record a new song of theirs called 'Pyaar To Hona Hi Tha', which would be a duet with a new singer in the Bombay circuit, Jaspinder Narula, who had come down from Canada.

Jaspinder was the easy-to-get-along-with talkative type, and I hit it off well with her right from the start. I saw she was a great fan of Whitney Houston; that was obvious from the Houston-style lines she incorporated in this song. Besides which, she was an awesome singer on her own. I truly had great fun singing this duet with her, and I'm glad we recorded it together instead of dubbing our parts separately on different days, as this way we were able to push and raise each other to higher levels, live and on the spot, as the recording of the song progressed.

While Jatin was the quiet, serious type, Lalit and I hit it off well too. The song was pretty different from the highly danceable high-energy ones I was normally being asked to sing. But though it was a beautiful, melodic love song, it had an energy all its own, besides the energy Jaspinder and I infused into it, not usually heard in romantic ballads. I truly enjoyed this three-way collaboration between Jaspinder, Jatin–Lalit and me that evening, and I remember going back to my hotel and falling asleep feeling happy after a job well done.

I only wish they hadn't physically lifted the flamenco guitar introduction played by Paco de Lucía in 'Have You Ever Really Loved a Woman' by Bryan Adams, and placed it at the beginning of 'Pyaar To Hona Hi Tha'. This song didn't need that little bit of plagiarization at all – it was a born mega hit on its own.

Again, I forgot all about it, until it was released and proved to be another song I'm strongly identified with, one of those I am not allowed to leave a stage without singing.

When the fact that my Goan Catholic pronunciation in Hindi had made me sing 'taa' instead of 'tha' made amused news throughout the country, Lalit confessed that he and the lyric writer had intentionally conspired not to correct me and to ignore the lapse in the studio that evening, as they 'found it cute'.

I guess Sonu Nigam didn't, as he tried to ridicule me for it in a Hindi I couldn't quite follow, at a press conference we were both giving prior to some concert. Insecurity makes people do strange things, even highly successful people.

O, Meri Munni

While jamming and trying out new grooves with this full band, I wrote many songs like 'Indian Lady' and 'Keep on Moving', and completed others like 'O, Meri Munni' and 'The Flute Song'. Soon we had enough material for a full album, and the band was sounding really tight.

At a time when everyone was using sequencers and synthesizers in their recordings, and even rock bands with drummers were using drum machines in the studio, I had a very ambitious and daring idea: I would record this album live, no sequencers. And that too, in my home studio.

The recording set-up was elaborate, with the drummer playing downstairs in my office, while the rest of us played upstairs in the studio. I played the guitar and flute and sang live with the band, while handling the multitrack levels and recording simultaneously.

I upgraded my studio to a forty-eight-channel Mackie mixer and forty-eight-track audio recording on four synced ADAT machines, each with eight tracks, plus a Roland eight-track digital machine which controlled all the others for this recording. The sequencing had already been upgraded to Cubase with an unlimited number of tracks running on Mac, but we weren't using any on these recordings. In the end we had a brilliant 'live in studio' album.

I cannot refrain from telling you a couple of incidents which made me write 'O, Meri Munni'.

The first one took place after a party at my friends Frank and Geeta Simões's house in Goa. We all got up to make a prolonged exit from the living room to the veranda, with extended goodbyes and plans for future meetings. The youngsters who had been hanging out in another room marched out into the living room and then out to the veranda too. One of them, a young miniskirted girl of about thirteen from Delhi or Mumbai, introduced herself and cornered me in the living room and kept me there chatting about my latest album until everyone had walked out of the room. Then she stood on the tips of her toes, put her arms around my neck, hugged me tight, and kissed me – on the mouth.

The other was at a girls' school in Jamshedpur. We had performed a fundraiser for them the previous evening, organized by my good friend Probal Mukherjee. The principal, Sister Flaviana, insisted we drop by for a little entertainment put up by the girls the next morning. It was delightful, and as Michèle and I sat facing Sister Flaviana in her office enjoying high tea later, I could see the school playgrounds through the windows behind her desk. There, schoolgirls were looking into the office and smiling, and some were blowing kisses at me – all this in full view of Michèle. All I could do was to keep a straight face and not laugh. As we were leaving Sister Flaviana's office, a bunch of them had gathered at her door for autographs. The boldest among them asked the principal, 'Sister, can I kiss him?' Taken by surprise, Sister Flaviana answered, 'Yes, why not?' And there, in front of her principal and my wife, the schoolgirl kissed me – again, straight on the mouth.

Me, Michèle, my friend Probal Mukherjee and Sister Flaviana.

We would never have had the guts to ask for such permissions, leave alone to kiss someone, and that too on the mouth, during my schooldays in Don Bosco. These incidents made me realize that while I had been busy becoming an adult and getting married and having kids, there had been a kind of sexual revolution taking place in India. But I felt sad for the kids, because it had come too late; they now had another deadly thing to worry about, not just unwanted pregnancy.

The song is advice, given in fun, to a young girl of thirteen, to stop trying to shorten her school skirt and tighten her school blouse; to stop wanting to go to discos and come home late; to stop wearing lipstick and make-up and driving guys crazy. And to stay home and play with her Barbie doll for a while longer.

Frankly, I'd be the last one to advise *anyone* against sex. But now the dreaded and incurable AIDS had burst into the world, and it was so easy for unaware youth with hormones raging, growing up in a country which was just discovering a degree of sexual freedom, to fall prey to it. And, just as I'd written songs warning youth against drugs, communalism, corruption and other poisons, I felt like warning them against careless immature sex too.

The beat was qawwali, which had never been used in a modern pop song. I devised a simple drumbeat which syncopated with and accentuated it perfectly. So did the bass line, which was reggae-like. And, I guess since almost every household in India, especially in the north, had a little daughter whom they called by the affectionate pet name Munni, which means a sweet little girl, the song and video spread like wildfire.

My greatest professional regrets

Sony had just launched in India, and an Englishman from Sony London called Richard Deniskamp had come to Bombay to set it up. Since I was the top-selling pop and rock artist in India, he wanted my new album to be released by Sony. He heard *Munni* and loved it; and offered me Rs 1 crore in royalty advances for it. An unheard of sum for an album in 1998, when companies offered advances of a couple of lakhs, if at all. I agreed.

He also heard *Bombay City!*, and wanted to take it and propose it to Sony London. The song had attracted the attention of several foreign companies when I had performed it in Tokyo, including London's BMG Publishing, who wanted to sign it. It truly had international potential.

Often during interviews one is asked what one's greatest regrets are. I've always skirted around that question. But here I shall list and name them for the first time in my life.

I told Richard Deniskamp, 'Oh no, the recording of *Bombay City!* is not good enough to be presented in England.' But I was being modest, and I didn't think he would take me seriously. I thought he would present it to Sony London anyway, and that the first thing they would do is re-record it in London with brilliant studio musicians.

A great, great regret. *Bombay City!* was just crying for a company like Sony to launch and promote it worldwide the way Richard intended to.

After Vijay Singh was appointed the head of Sony India and Richard had returned to London, Singh called to carry on with the signing of the *Munni* album. But he said, 'You know Remo, Richard didn't know the market in India well, and I believe he made you the very unfeasible offer of Rs 1 crore. The realistic figure we can offer you is Rs 50 lakhs.'

I was livid. I felt Singh was going back on the Englishman's word, even though deep down I knew that Singh's figure was indeed more reasonable.

I made the mistake of trying to go over his head, and called Richard in London directly, complaining about it. Richard said, 'Oh, I'm sorry about that, Remo, but Singh is now the head of Sony India, and I'm afraid he knows the market there much better than I do. I'm sure what he's offering you is indeed a realistic figure for India.'

'Hmmm! And by the way, have you presented *Bombay City!* to Sony London?' I asked.

He was taken aback. 'Oh, I'm so sorry, I didn't realize yours was an Indian "No", which actually meant "Yes"!' he said.

That's the moment when I should have swallowed my pride and agreed that they were both right. I should have accepted that mine had indeed been a hypocritical 'No', and should have asked him to please go ahead and present

Bombay City! in London. And it was the right time to call Singh and agree that he was right too, and to accept Rs 50 lakhs as royalty advances on the album.

But I allowed my ego to rule my mind. *They are going back on their word! How dare they, don't they know I am the top cat in the pop/rock scene here? I'll show them; I'll release the album through another company (every company in India would be happy to have me), and it will be the biggest hit India will see this year!*

All the top companies in India did indeed call me for the album, including Amitabh Bachchan's ABCL, who also wanted me to do a duet with Amitabh in his next film. But ABCL and Amitabh had just begun to flounder at the time, so I politely refused. Bachchan ended up doing a duet with Daler Mehndi instead, which I don't think did anything for Mehndi.

Magnasound called me too, and Shashi Gopal the CEO flew down to Goa to hear the album. He totally loved it, and said, 'Remo, I'm very keen on signing on this album, but the future of Indian pop is Hindi. It's got to be in Hindi.' And I think he offered me a Rs 6 lakh advance on royalty.

Like a fool, I settled on Rs 6 lakhs instead of Rs 50 lakhs, due to my misguided ego at the time. Cut my nose to spite my face. It's not just the royalty advance which would have been bigger with Sony. I don't remember which pop album they launched first in India, but their promotion and publicity were stupendous. Even though my album went on to sell extremely well, I was just imagining how much more Sony's clout would have done to it…

And, I'm certain that if Sony London had launched *Bombay City!* in the UK and the world, you would be reading the autobiography of a truly international star right now.

Yes, these two are perhaps the greatest professional regrets of my career.

But regrets bring out the philosopher in us, to help make us feel better about the bad choices we make. And that philosopher tells me, 'Well, maybe international stardom would have made you an addict of cocaine, alcohol and worse, and you would have died of an overdose long ago. Or maybe you would have been drawn into a sex scenario of such epic proportions that you would have died of AIDS. Or maybe your private plane would have crashed in a snowstorm in the Swiss Alps.'

I argue back, saying, 'Well, it wouldn't have hurt being half the legend Morrisson or Mercury or Holly are.'

One can't change one's past. But one can change one's stupid ego. I do hope I have changed mine, at least to some extent.

As it turned out, I never got from the album sales the money which I felt it deserved, even though *Munni* was one of the highest-selling – if not *the* highest-selling – pop album in India that year. If huge international record companies could shortchange superstars like George Michael and others in the West, making them take recourse to high-profile court battles which record companies often lost, one can imagine what was happening in India. After some years Gopal moved to Dubai permanently, and *Munni* was released by a dubious record company called Bayshore, allegedly owned by his brother-in-law Madhav. They of course never paid me a rupee either. I wrote to Gopal for more than a year, and he never answered. When I finally sent a registered letter saying that if I did not hear from him within fifteen days all the rights to *O, Meri Munni* would revert to me, he quickly wrote back denying all knowledge of the Bayshore company, also denying that he owed me any money. Now, ironically, I came to know that Magnasound had sold its whole catalogue to … Sony! I didn't see a single rupee from that deal either.

Two shady covers of O, Meri Munni, *for which I saw no payment whatsoever.*

Symphonic Chants

The world was approaching its new millennium. Everyone was going crazy with preparations (mostly commercial), as though it meant that the earth or humanity itself was going to turn 2,000 years old, not that we had reached at that attractive number simply because of the year a section of humanity decided to begin counting time. People who believed in Jesus, as well as those who hated Christianity, all forgot just why they were writing down this date, and were ready to welcome the year with the three lovely round zeroes.

There were lots of disaster theories doing the rounds all over the planet about what the world's computers might or might not do at midnight on 31 December 1999. Well, as long as the White House and Kremlin computers didn't unintentionally launch missiles at each other at the stroke of the new year without the help of their crazy presidents, we would be ok.

I on my part decided I'd had enough of my pop- and rock-star image. As the new millennium approached, I felt it would be a good time to shed it, and move into the more serious, mature music I'd wanted to do for a long time. Enough of the 'Munni' and 'Jalwa' tags. Every album of mine until now had contained one serious peaceful piece of this new music I wanted to create. I invariably squeezed it right at the end of the albums, so that the more poppy and rocky people could skip that piece without missing any of their favourites.

I had fallen in love with two of the mantras our friendly neighbourhood temple woke me up with at 4 a.m. on choice mornings: the '*Gayatri Mantra*' and '*Jai Jagdish Hare*'. They were beautiful, repetitive and trance-like. On those mornings I would lie on my pillow half-asleep and wish that the pieces would never end – and they didn't.

I decided to record these two not the way they were, but with the feelings they infused in me. Each mantra was going to be half a CD's duration, or one whole side of a cassette. In order to depart from my pop/rock image with no possibility of return, I did a photo shoot with a goatee beard.

My serious attempt at growing a goatee to shed my pop/rock star image and get into more serious music.

And I decided on Times Music as the right record company for this changeover. Besides owning the record company, the Times Group was the most powerful and extensive media house in the country: newspapers, magazines, TV channels, the works. I explained to them exactly what I wanted done, and gave them an article I wrote about this more mature phase I was entering as an artist and a person. They agreed to everything. The recording was completed, and I gave them the master.

Imagine my surprise when *The Times of India* carried a very prominent article about my new peaceful mantra album – with a photo from my *O, Meri Munni* cover with the tramlines hairstyle and a rock guitar pose! And they titled the article 'Remo's New Jalwa'. Precisely the two images I had wished to shed.

I immediately sought out the head honcho of the *Times* and explained to him the gaffe which had been committed. 'People who like my Munni and Jalwa kind of music will not want to listen to my mantras; and those who love mantras will not want to hear them by an electric guitar-wielding rock musician. Please instruct your media people to right the wrong immediately, or else this album is going to be a huge waste!'

'Well, sorry about that, Remo. Do give us another serious album like this one, and we'll correct your image with it.'

Really? A fresh article the way I wanted it would take them forty-eight hours to write and publish. Whereas another album would take me at least a year to conceive and record.

Was it inefficiency, or pure lethargy in their style of working? Had the record company simply put an impersonal journalist on the job, who did it without listening to the album or reading the article I had painstakingly written? The most powerful media house and record company in the country had miserably failed to effect the maturing of image I had so badly sought.

Other record companies were also 'vampiring' on the blood of artists by not paying royalties. I guess like other artists I too could have contented myself with the huge number of well-paid shows which the record promotions were bringing in, turning a blind eye to the fact that the record companies were cheating me. But I simply couldn't bring myself to ignore and live with this injustice.

So I decided to never sign my music and my soul to a record company again. I would record my own stuff, produce my own videos, and give the finished product to my listeners for free from now on. Why should a crooked corporate middleman make money by cheating me and charging my fans?

Mother Teresa

The day after one of my concerts in Calcutta, my return flight to Bombay/ Goa was cancelled – a common occurrence then. I wondered what I ought to do with the extra day in the city, whose sights I had already seen during my earlier visits, when it suddenly struck me that this was the home of Mother Teresa. Ah, I would go and visit one of her Homes.

My driver took me to the Home for abandoned children. I was amazed to see the cleanliness and care accorded to each and every baby, all in white cradles in neat rows.

Even while I was there, a bell rang, and two young nuns ran out. 'We have a basket in an opening in the compound wall, where mothers come and place unwanted infants,' a nun explained with a smile. 'Next to it is a rope attached to a bell, which they ring to alert us, before quickly disappearing.'

While saying goodbye, I asked perfunctorily, 'Of course it wouldn't be possible to see Mother Teresa herself, would it?'

'Why not?' the nun said. 'Go at 3 p.m. to Mother House, ring the bell outside the gate, and ask to see her. Here's the address.'

I felt strange going back to my five-star hotel for lunch in between. At 3 p.m. sharp I was at Mother House's old wooden gate, pulling the string attached to a bell. A nun opened it.

'Sister, I'm just a musician, I'm from Goa, and I have no serious work with Mother Teresa; I don't wish to waste her time; but may I see her for just three minutes, for no good reason?' I asked awkwardly.

'Certainly. Do step in,' the nun said, opening the gate wider.

I entered the courtyard. In front of me stood an old white building with a rickety old wooden staircase running straight from the ground to the first floor. In a few minutes, a seventy-plus-year-young tiny lady came skipping down its steps and clasped my hands in hers, looking deep into my eyes.

'So you are from Goa?' she asked.

'Yes, Mother,' I managed to speak despite this inexplicable joy choking me. I kissed her hands. They felt warm, comfortable, soft and radiant. I thought of Vovó. An idea came to me at that very moment.

'Yes, Mother. And I'd like to compose a song for you. And all the royalties from that song will be my little contribution towards your work. I would like your permission and your blessing. I know that one minute in your presence will give me all the inspiration I need.'

Her eyes twinkled.

'Very good, son. Go ahead and do it. But remember, do it with love. With love for Jesus.'

I must confess that I am incapable of feeling love for any one particular messiah or god or religion exclusively. I would create the song with love for Mother Teresa; with love for the Great Love in her heart.

I don't think I had ever written more than one song in a day. But while on my flight back to Goa the next day, I wrote four – music, lyrics and all. This 'one song' idea had expanded unintentionally.

I went home and started recording them, simultaneously looking for singers to sing the parts. The four songs I had written were to be sung by the Pope, the Mother Superior of Loretto Convent in Calcutta, a character I invented whom I called The Slum Bum, and Mother Teresa herself.

On a visit back to Calcutta I met Mother Teresa again, and asked for her permission to sing for the inmates in her Homes. It had become a habit of mine, whenever I performed at a charity event anywhere, to insist that the organizers also arrange for me to sing for the inmates themselves (be it in old-age homes, leprosy hospitals, orphanages, whatever), besides at their fancy fundraising dinners in five-star hotels. It was my feeling that the destitute often received enough cheques from unseen benefactors, of course extremely necessary and useful, but not enough personal attention, love and entertainment.

Mother Teresa happily gave her permission in her own writing, and asked one Sister Shanti to write down other details and addresses. I have kept both these papers and more as priceless relics from a living saint. Her canonization means nothing to me; in my mind, no one has the power to bestow sainthood like a college degree. To me she was a saint already during her lifetime.

LEFT: A little note written in Mother Teresa's hand, instructing the heads of her various Homes to allow me to sing for the inmates. RIGHT: A note written by Sister Shanti at Mother Teresa's request.

After singing at all these Homes I went back to Mother House towards the end of the evening and met Mother Teresa again. I told her I had written her a song, and asked if I could sing it to her. She gathered all her nuns in the courtyard, and there I sang 'She Can See' to her personally, and to them all.

'It is not I who sees, my son,' said Mother Teresa softly when it ended. 'It is Jesus. And then I just go wherever He points me.'

I included this little monologue at the end of the final recording of this song recently. But at that time, somehow, the singers in Goa just weren't working out to my satisfaction. They had no theatrical experience whatsoever – and this element was essential to these songs, as they portrayed different characters and told a story.

So I kept this project aside temporarily, thinking I'd record with theatre friends from Bombay as and when the occasion arose.

But I was entering a very busy stage in my career, which was to become many times busier still. And before I knew it, twenty-seven years were to go by before I resumed work on these songs. And Mother Teresa would also have passed away by then.

16

A Mouthful of Hell

The worst year of my life

Munni was my first pop album in Hindi, and it was the greatest hit I'd ever had, clearly demonstrating that English wasn't the language of India. It immediately translated into a vastly increased number of live shows. We were now flying from one gig to the next without having time to return home in between, and I had to add 'Laundry' to the services to be provided in the hotels where we stayed. Money of course was pouring in. My band members all bought cars; those who already had them bought new ones.

One of the shows we did was at IIT Kanpur. On the way from Goa to Lucknow, I missed the Goa–Mumbai flight. As per our strict rules, if anyone missed a flight, the others never waited; we needed to minimize the number of tickets required on the next flight, which might be full. I took the next one and caught up with them in Mumbai, and we flew together to Lucknow, where cars were waiting to take us to Kanpur.

There's nothing like performing for students on their campus, and the show absolutely rocked. Every band member outdid himself – it was that kind of a night. Later, the professor who had corresponded with me came to my room and said I was the only artist who had performed at the IIT festival during his tenure who had insisted on the full payment being made by cheque.

'We are an educational institution, we have no black money!' he said. 'Yet every artist asks for about 50 per cent to be paid in cash, and we are obliged to withdraw cash showing this fake expenditure and that, just to be able to pay them.'

I sympathized with him.

'It was so refreshing having you. Last year we had a renowned classical pandit,' he continued, 'who insisted on 75 per cent in cash. And he insisted on a bottle of Black Label. He drank half of it before going on stage, the other half on stage, sang for just half an hour and went off.'

I went to sleep feeling very righteous that night. The next afternoon we were flying to Mumbai, where we were performing the day after at an event in the Oberoi Towers Hotel.

As a rule, the band always left for the airport before me, as they needed to check in all the instruments. That day as I left for my car, I crossed them in the lobby.

'You guys still here?! How come?'

'We went shopping and were a bit delayed...' they said sheepishly.

'Ok, don't waste any more time now guys, the airport's in Lucknow, it's quite a drive.' So saying I got into my car and left.

Once in the aircraft, I looked out for them through my window, and didn't see them boarding until take-off. Well, they'd have to get seats on a flight tomorrow, and there would be fresh funny stories to hear.

I reached Mumbai, checked into the Oberoi, and was about to fall asleep when the operator put a call through despite my Do Not Disturb instructions. It was the professor from Kanpur. Ah, he was surely calling to say the band was back on campus, and would join me tomorrow. But no. Without any preamble or softening of words, and in a shaking voice, he said:

'Remo, there has been a terrible accident on the highway. Your band's car. Your band is dead.'

'I ... I beg your pardon?!' I stammered. I could hear students' voices instructing the professor in the background. He came back on the line.

'Ah … no, there is one survivor. I'm not sure about his name. I shall let you know in the morning.'

I don't have to tell you what state of mind that phone call threw me into. These guys weren't casual hired musicians; they were my musical family, and had been with me for years and years – the first, Dharma, for twelve.

In a stupor, I called the travel desk and booked myself on the first flight back to Lucknow, called the professor and asked him to please have me picked up.

I could not sleep a wink of course, but in that daze I had the presence of mind to email the promoters of the next day's show, as well as about ten other shows which were already confirmed with advances, telling them what had happened, and that they would be reimbursed the full amount as soon as I returned to Goa.

Before the break of dawn I was in a car on the way back to the airport. I had to inform the boys' families. I didn't want to inform the parents directly, aged or otherwise, as it might cause them shock and even heart attacks. I felt like I might suffer one at any moment myself. Somehow, the only sibling's number I had was Selwyn's younger brother's. When I called and woke him up, I realized that the news was so terrible, it wasn't possible to soften or sugar-coat it. I was as blunt and direct as the professor had been with me.

After this I could not make another one of these calls, so I asked Michèle, whom I had already informed before anyone else, to please convey the news to the rest of the families as best as she could.

A car from IIT awaited me in Lucknow with a couple of students, one of them the official students' representative. He told me the whole story. The students were so excited with the concert, they wanted to travel with the band, and wanted them to split into two cars to make place. But the band preferred to travel together. If not, at least half of them would have still been alive, though three students would then have been dead.

The band had left for the airport late because of their shopping spree. As they got into their car, Dharma had received a phone call at the reception from his pregnant wife, so he went back to speak to her. The poor thing blamed herself for making that call thereafter, saying that if she hadn't, the accident would have passed them by in those few minutes. After that the driver had stopped to fill petrol – something Indian drivers invariably do *after* picking up their passengers instead of before. And then, as they crossed a bridge over the Ganges, they had stopped to pray, buy flowers and toss them into the holy river.

With all that, they were running late, and had urged the driver to drive faster. At one time there was a huge truck coming slowly from the opposite direction. Suddenly, a bus impatiently overtook the truck at full speed, coming head on against the band's car. The bus was empty of passengers, probably going back to Kanpur for some repairs, and the driver had been flying. It was an ancient government transport bus, built like a tank, which only suffered a minor dent. The band's car, a Tata Sumo, though a solid car in itself, was rendered a wreck.

'There are hutments all along the Lucknow–Kanpur highway; the hut dwellers live there specifically for the purpose of looting the baggage of vehicles which suffer accidents, which happen on almost a daily basis,' the student rep said. I had seen wreckages all along the highway, including an overturned truck whose load of gravel had spread over half the highway's width. It had been lying there dangerously for a week now. 'The dwellers descended upon the band's car and started making off with their instruments and luggage. We didn't know whether to go help the band or save their belongings,' he continued.

Human vultures. That is what India bred with its forced poverty especially in states like Uttar Pradesh, while its choice citizens (read politicians and their cronies) stashed away the state's trillions in Swiss bank accounts. I couldn't believe that one of the country's premier educational institutions, the IIT, was at one end of this killer highway, and that some of the country's best and most precious brains precariously drove up and down it to deliver guest lectures there.

'The accident happened in Unnao, sir,' said the student rep. 'We rushed them to the Unnao hospital, where they were declared "Dead on Arrival". All except Santana Carvalho, the drummer. He is in a coma and being treated at the Regency Hospital, the best in Kanpur. May I ask you to please stop and identify the bodies in Unnao?'

It wasn't going to be pleasant looking into the dead faces of my companions, but I would do everything I could in order to spare their families these horrible ordeals. I had seen enough films where a person is taken into a cold refrigerated morgue where bodies are pulled out in steel drawers, sheets lowered from their faces, and the person identifies them and breaks down. I braved myself for just such a scene.

But I wasn't ready for what I saw. As our car drove into the hospital complex and to the morgue building, I saw four bodies fully covered in white cloth laid out on the footpath near the entrance door. On the footpath! And I realized that I wasn't in Goa. I was in a strange, primitive place. I didn't know it then, but things like permissions to take the bodies home, the formalities to be carried out for that exercise, and so on and so forth were going to be nightmarish here.

'Why are the bodies on the footpath?!' I asked the students incredulously.

'That is unfortunately the custom here, sir,' said the rep disapprovingly; he was obviously not from here either. 'Even if a family member dies, the first thing they do is take the body and lay it outside the house, on the footpath if they have no garden. And from there straight to the crematorium. A dead body in the house is considered impure, a bad omen.'

A morgue assistant was now pulling aside the cloths from the faces, and took down their names as I recited them.

'Dharmendra Hirve ... Selwyn Pereira ... Victor Alvares ... Sunil Redkar...' It was surreal. I was used to announcing their names from the stage, to thunderous applause. Their faces were untouched, and looked absolutely normal. One small consolation.

From there we drove back to Kanpur, and I was installed in the same guest room on the campus which I had occupied under such happier circumstances until a few hours ago. Somehow through this daze I remember that it had huge fat lizards in the bathroom, who stared back unafraid, without running away from you. I had learnt to shower while talking to them. They were practically my only company now.

The whole campus was silent as a tomb. I came to know later that the faculty had forbidden all students from approaching the guest house or interacting with me. Even the professor who dealt with me must have come to meet me but once or twice, briefly, during the whole ordeal which lasted about three or four days – I had lost count of time.

Michèle called and asked if I wanted her to take the next flight and come to be with me in this difficult time. In retrospect how I wish I had said yes. But I was thinking of the families – though I didn't know then that some of them had already turned against me in their great need to find someone to blame.

'No M'amour, I'll manage everything on my own, I'll take care of all this,' I told her. I felt guilty though I wasn't at fault, and I was punishing myself. 'You please stay put in Goa, to relay news and information and to comfort the families if possible.'

I got news that the Pereira family was going to send two of Selwyn's cousins to Kanpur, in order to help me. I was happy, as everything seemed to be 'not possible' here, and I was going mad all alone – firstly with this grief and my state of shock, and secondly with the difficulties I was facing getting anything done at all. To take the bodies to Goa, they would need to be embalmed, or the airlines would not take them. All right. Where could I have them embalmed? Sorry, no embalming services were available in Kanpur or even in Lucknow. What?! Yes. The closest place was Delhi. Take four dead bodies on an eight-hour road journey to Delhi? All right, I could start getting that arranged. For that, I would need to get them out of the Unnao morgue. Could I have permission to get them out please? No.

In the middle of all this the two cousins arrived, and after condoling with them and seeing that they were comfortable in the room allotted to them in the campus guest house, I was happy I was going to finally have some help.

The first thing they asked me was: 'How is it that you were not in the same car with the band?'

I could feel the immediate palpitations which this question caused. Until then I had been grieving, in a state of shock, trying bravely to handle this whole thing by myself. With this question I came to know that there was something else I would have to deal with here: nightmarish unjustified accusations. And I guessed the question did not come from them alone, it came from the family back in Goa. I was dying to scream out my answer:

'Selwyn has been playing with me for eight years, and if you truly cared about how we travelled, you should have found out long ago! But none of you saw it fit to even attend one of our shows, though I always gave the band free passes for the Goa gigs! We always took separate cars, because we usually stayed in different places: me in a five-star, and they in a four-star hotel. Do you and your employees share the same cabin? Does a bank manager sit in the main hall with the staff? But if I flew, they flew! If I took the road, they took the road! And if I took a train, they did too! Would you have felt happier if I had died with them? Are you upset that I am alive? If my car had crashed and I alone had died, would you have asked your cousin and the band why they were not in my car?'

But I said nothing. I understood they were grieving. And some people are unable to grieve unless they can blame someone. But if I was already shattered, that one question drove me beyond my limit. I have no idea how I found the strength to carry on. How could anyone, besides perhaps the drivers and the authorities responsible for traffic control and the state of roads, be blamed for a road accident?

The professor called my room and told me that some kind of Catholic community leader from Kanpur wanted to visit me. Oh no ... the last thing

I needed was having someone come and pray over me and make a big fuss, and put on an egocentric show about being some kind of representative of God on Earth. But he was already on the way to my room, so I decided to receive and get rid of him in a few minutes.

Allan Noronha, or Chhotebhai. If not for him, and for Mimi Dias-Menezes who contacted him, the bodies would have never reached back home to Goa.

He walked in. A tall big man, in a simple long white cotton kurta and trousers, and a thick rosary around his neck. But there were no prayers. There was no talk of god. His name was Allan Noronha, and he was known as Chhotebhai. His great-grandfather had come to Kanpur in 1858 from Aldona, Goa, by bullock cart, as a photographer. He and his subsequent generations had prospered well. Among the many honorary official posts Chhotebhai held was national president of the All India Catholic Union. He condoled with me on my terrible loss, told me he had been contacted by Mimi Dias-Menezes from Goa, also a prominent member of the All India Catholic Union, who had asked him to help me out. He came straight to the point.

'The bureaucracy in this place can be nightmarish. Do you need help?'

In those few seconds I understood that this was a man for whom prayer was action, not mere words. I told him of my difficulties in taking the bodies back to Goa.

'I'll try and see what I can do. Leave it in my hands.'

My guardian angel had arrived in the form of Chhotebhai. The bodies going back to Goa started to seem a possibility now that he was on the scene.

The only person from the whole campus who came to see me and offer moral support and strength was the professor's wife, Madhumita. She said, 'I'm ashamed of the faculty's behaviour. The only thing they are concerned with is that there was no student involved in the accident. Once that was ascertained, they lost all interest in the case, and instructed all students not to involve themselves with this at all, but to concentrate on their classes and studies. This part of the campus has been declared totally out of bounds to them all.'

Television crews had heard what had happened by now and were relaying the news, and the main channels and newspapers had sent down their crews from Delhi to interview me. I avoided them like the plague, as the last thing I wished to do was to make a public spectacle of my grief and the tragedy which surrounded me. Besides, I knew I would end up cursing the UP government for allowing such killer driving on these highways, while ministers' cars were safe, preceded and followed by guard vehicles which cleared all traffic in their path. This was not the time to antagonize the UP bureaucracy.

Getting the four large wooden boxes with the bodies on to the flight seemed to be another huge hurdle – mountains of permissions, paperwork, etc. I had the brainwave of calling Gen. Mathew Mammen of the Indian Army. He and his charming wife had become family friends while he was posted in Goa. He was now posted in Delhi.

'Don't worry, Remo,' he said with typical military efficiency after I apprised him of the full situation. 'There will be army officers at the Kanpur airport who will see to it that the coffins are loaded on your Mumbai flight. In Mumbai there will be no time to pass them through the normal channels, so there will be army officers on the tarmac who will transfer them directly from this aircraft to the one going to Goa.'

I didn't know how to thank him. I just knew that I could count on his military word 100 per cent.

That night we were at Chhotebhai's house, awaiting the arrival of the bodies after they had been embalmed in Delhi. It was a huge handsome colonial house with a large compound. It had seen better days, and now contained very sparse antique furniture, the worse for wear. That told me plenty about my benefactor. He came from an old well-to-do family, but had spent most of what he had in helping others, not in building up or maintaining his wealth. A true man of lofty, godly principles.

Noronha Bhawan, Kanpur, in its glory days.

But the beautiful ancestral house was demolished in 2002, at the insistence of other family members, to make way for the city's first mall. 'That is life!' Chhotebhai said.

Meanwhile, I continued avoiding the TV and the press, who were trying to get into his house.

The bodies arrived and were laid out on the floor of the wide veranda, covered in the mandatory white cloth. White candles were lit beside them, white flowers were laid around them, and the old colonial house itself being white, the whole scene looked peaceful, serene. Chhotebhai's friend Father Benedict Pereira blessed the bodies, while Mr Vinaybhai, the president of the Gandhi Peace Foundation, said the Hindu prayers.

One had to identify them again for the embalmment guys before they left. Eager to test the so-called usefulness of the cousins, who until then had only served to ask me why I wasn't among the dead, I requested them to please carry out the identification this time. Reacting as though I had asked them to look into the faces of scary ghosts, they refused with horror showing in their eyes.

Earlier that evening I had tested them too. I said, 'Ok, now that all arrangements for the coffins to be taken to Goa are done, you guys go ahead with them. I'm staying back in Kanpur to be with my drummer who is in a coma.'

Again, they had reacted as though I had asked them to climb Mount Everest. 'No, no, how will we be able to do that? You please come along with us! You must!'

These guys were absolutely useless. Far from them helping me, I had ended up looking after them like children, besides looking after everything else.

I went up to my loving friends of up to twelve years, lifted the cloths, and looked into their faces to identify them once again. The embalmment had changed them some. But now I knew they were at peace at last.

They were going home.

As we neared the campus gate that night I managed to spy a tenacious lady TV reporter and her crew still waiting for me in the shadows behind some trees. I hurriedly told the driver to drive ahead and take me in by the back gate. And I escaped the last of the reporters in Kanpur.

Bringing them home

I can just imagine what it would have been like for the families if I had arrived back defeated by the hurdles, without the bodies; if not for my guardian angels who made it possible...

All the families had come to the airport to take their sons' bodies home, and mine had come to take me. Some of those accusing eyes were making me feel guilty for being alive at every turn.

I was a wreck. With sorrow, with sadness, with shock, and with lack of sleep and food – I just had not been able to eat these last few days. The doctor at the campus in Kanpur had insisted on checking me, and, alarmed, told me that my blood pressure was dangerously high, and that I ought to get myself seen to and start medication as soon as I reached Goa. That seemed like the least of my concerns.

Curiously, two of my dead band members were Hindu, and two were Catholic. The two Hindu cremations took place on the very day we arrived back in Goa, so I went straight to their houses from the airport.

Sunil Redkar

Sunil lived just down the road from me. His aged widowed mother was sitting on the floor in a corner of the first room of their little house, in a silent daze. I hugged her in tears. 'I'm sorry…' I said. 'I'm sorry I was not able to bring back your son alive this time…'

She hugged me back real tight. 'Baba, my son is gone! But now I have another son! You are my son!'

I was overwhelmed. Never in my wildest dreams had I imagined such a reaction. We hugged and cried for the longest time.

Michèle and I proceeded to the crematorium, which in our village is in a coconut grove by the river. From there one can see the bay where the river meets the sea. As is usual in a crematorium, the scene was quite formal and quiet and serene, and the villagers shook my hand with looks and words of sorrow and consolation as they walked away.

It surprises me to think during how many days afterwards I forgot that Sunil was gone, and kept calling out his name loudly in the house, where I was used to having him around all day long. Normally the maids would say 'Sunil is not here, he has gone out to get this or the other'. But the total silence which greeted my calls would finally send a signal to my brain that something was amiss, and I would remember that he was no more, and fall silent like the rest of the household. Michèle and the maids must have felt their skins creep, hearing me call out loudly to a dead man.

Sunil had first come under my radar when I had needed a couple of village boys to hold up reflectors during a video shoot. He was one of them, and I was impressed by his seriousness and dedication to this simple task. So I asked him to work as my personal assistant in my home office. Soon I asked him to accompany me to shows as my stage assistant. He came from a humble background, spoke no English, but took very good care of my instruments and costumes. Like everyone else, he enjoyed flying around the country and abroad and staying in four-star hotels with the band. His mother had told me how their family's luck had opened up after Sunil started bringing in his monthly salary for the work in the office, plus the payment per show.

Dharmendra Hirve

From the Siolim crematorium, our driver took Michèle and me straight to my tabla player's house; Dharmendra had been with me the longest, for twelve wonderful years. The Hirves were important cloth merchants in the Mapusa market, and their house was overflowing with the citizenry of the town, with people spilling out on to the footpath. I entered the crowded house and hugged his shattered father, crying, 'I'm sorry, Mr Hirve … I was not able to bring your son home safe this time…'

His younger brother, a sitar player in his own right, came and held me by my shoulders and said in a very loud voice, for everyone inside the house as well as on the footpath outside to hear through the open window:

'Remo, don't say you are sorry! You are not at fault here! You have been taking him for shows for twelve years, and he always returned safe and happy and with wonderful stories! Thanks to you he travelled the country and the world! Didn't you bring him back safe from the US, Europe, Africa, the Gulf, and everywhere? This is destiny, and none of us can avoid or change it! Please remember, you don't have to feel guilty *at all*! *This is not your fault!*'

I hugged him back gratefully and sobbed into his shoulder, while he sobbed into mine. The whole family was responsive and loving towards me, just as Sunil's had been. The Hindu tradition of recognizing and accepting fate without needing to find someone to blame revealed itself to me in all its deep wisdom and infinite spirituality.

From the Mapusa crematorium we drove back home. On the way, and for many weeks after that, I was paranoid on the road. I would see every person we passed – pedestrian, cyclist, motorcyclist, car driver – as a dead man. I knew exactly how his face would look after embalming. I could see that embalmed face right there, lying on the road. And I kept urging our driver to drive slowly and carefully, though he always did.

And there is something very curious that I felt. I'm not sure the reader will truly grasp it. I felt that I was in the realm of the dead. I was physically in this world, but in reality I was 'living' there. It was a real, existent, populated world, and I was living there.

Selwyn Pereira

The next day we drove to Selwyn Pereira's funeral. On the way there I received a phone call. It was from someone who portrayed himself as a 'social activist' from Chimbel, the same village as Selwyn. He had studied law, but was rumoured to have taken to extortion as he was very bad at his profession. Some years earlier he had force-invited me to dinner in London, had got drunk and slipped off his chair under the table; I had to pay for the dinner, and then drop him in a taxi to his home which he could not find.

'Remo, you're on your way to the funeral, right? I'll wait for you at the church front door. From there I shall escort you straight to the altar, from where you please speak a few words about Selwyn,' he said.

'How can I do that? I myself am shattered, not in a state to speak in public. Besides, his two cousins who came to Kanpur made it clear they thought I ought to have been dead as well. If his family were to ask me to speak, of course I would; but I'm not at all sure they would like it.'

'It is his father who has requested you to speak, Remo! I am calling on his behalf.'

'Oh … in that case of course I somehow must and will do it,' I said.

But something made me feel uneasy. Would Selwyn's dad really make such a request at such a time? Something didn't seem right. So I decided to call him up.

'Mr Pereira, I'm sorry to disturb you today, but I just received a call from so-and-so saying you have requested me to speak a few words about Selwyn from the altar at the Mass. I wanted to confirm the same with you.'

'Ah, no, Remo, I have not. In fact I have not spoken to this person at all in quite a while,' he said. 'But of course if you want to speak in church you're most welcome…'

'I'm not in a state to speak in public, Mr Pereira!' I said.

'Of course, I can imagine. Strange that the man should make that call to you…'

I was shocked. And I was livid. I called the 'activist' right back, trembling with anger at such a traumatic time, and shouted at him in disbelief:

'How dare you use an occasion like this for your own self-glorification? Would escorting me up to the altar in front of the gathering give you that much self-importance today?'

'No, no, it's the truth, Sewlyn's father has asked you!'

'I have just spoken to Selwyn's father, you liar, you have been exposed! I cannot believe that you would use someone's death and funeral to further your dirty games! You should be ashamed of yourself!'

He fell silent, and I hung up.

The church, of course, was overflowing. People made way for Michèle and me to get in. I was shedding tears at the drop of a hat for the last few days. I simply couldn't control them. I was hoping my dark glasses were shielding them somewhat.

After the Mass was over I walked up to the coffin like many others for a last adieu, as I would then have to rush to Victor's, and hugged Selwyn's father. He hugged me back warmly and, without a word, we cried on each other's shoulders for a while.

This was the photograph which some reporter present clicked, and which appeared on the newspapers the next morning: of me, with a week's unshaven beard and in a shattered state of mind, condoling with Selwyn's father, who was also in a similar state.

On seeing my photo in the press, some people possessing the worst of the Goan mindset remarked that I was seeking publicity out of the incident. If they only knew how much trouble I had taken to avoid the national publicity in Kanpur and Delhi.

Victor Alvares

From there we drove to Victor's house in South Goa, from where the funeral procession hadn't left yet. I think the two families had timed their funerals in such a way that those who wished could attend both. The house was full and overflowing and silent. As in other places, people parted at the door to let Michèle and me enter. As we stepped into the house, a female voice screamed from the other end of the hall, where the altar and the coffin were placed:

'Why is he coming here? He has killed our brother! Why is he coming here?'

I could not believe my ears, and my already shattered mind received yet another terrible blow. A woman in black near the altar was glaring at me with devilish eyes and doing the screaming. As I froze to the spot, I felt the hands of two men and one lady in black hold mine and gently pull me and Michèle into a side room which was empty.

'We're very sorry about that, Remo. We are Victor's brothers and sister, and we have the highest regard for you, just as he did,' they said.

If I had been devastated by the attack of a few seconds ago, I felt extremely assuaged and grateful at being protected by these three siblings of my friend. I could recognize Victor's features in them all.

'That was our other sister screaming; please do not mind her. She lives in London. She has always been known to behave that way,' they added. 'We'll take her away. Please do come to the coffin to say your farewell to Victor.'

So saying, the two brothers went and forced the sister who had screamed to go into the house, and the other sister took us up to the coffin. There we tried to pray in peace.

But such an ugly scene at a funeral, aimed at a man who was already at the end of his physical and mental capabilities due to his inability to eat or sleep properly, high blood pressure and undeserved guilt, but without whom there wouldn't have been a body to bury, can be devastating.

17

The Healing

The aftermath

Now that I had safely handed all my friends back to their families and prayed for them at their cremations and burials, Michèle insisted on taking me to a doctor. Yes, my blood pressure was dangerously high, and I was immediately put on medication.

At home, every little thing would make me burst into tears unexpectedly. Memories, thoughts, sounds. Whether I was in the middle of narrating something to someone, or someone was narrating something to me. The opening of a marker pen would bring back the odour of embalming. I could not bear to listen to music – anything to do with music would remind me of my friends.

One day soon after the funeral, two of Selwyn's siblings came to collect his luggage, which had been brought from the airport to Siolim. Michèle said she'd see them. Chhotebhai had thoughtfully and securely tied tiny red ribbons to the handles of whatever suitcases had been salvaged, in order to help us identify them.

All the luggage had been kept in our guest room, and from our room I could hear their voices. After a while Selwyn's brother's and particularly the sister's voices rose in volume, and sounded unfriendly and accusatory. Michèle seemed to be trying to calm them down and explain things to them.

After they left she told me they had been looking for yet another suitcase, which they claimed was missing. She had been trying to explain to them that whatever had arrived at the airport was there in that room, shut and locked as it was. She had even showed them all the luggage tags.

But they had left grumbling about a missing suitcase.

A week later there was a call for me. It was a concert promoter from Mumbai, asking whether I was free to perform the week after. I was aghast.

'Haven't you heard the news? Don't you know that my whole band has just died?' I asked incredulously.

'Yes, but that was last week, wasn't it? You mean you haven't put together more musicians yet?' I was livid.

'Are you human or what, man? Do you have any feelings whatsoever? Please never call me for a show again!' I said and slammed the phone down.

But as I sat there, I realized that in Mumbai my fellow artists would have indeed got together other 'orchestra musicians', and it would be business as usual within a week, all in the name of 'professionalism', 'keeping commitments' and 'not letting concert promoters down'.

I also learnt that back in Goa my band members' families themselves had reopened and restarted their businesses after a week.

There were many such calls in the following days and weeks. I wasn't even taking them any more; Michèle was dealing with them, until word finally spread that I wasn't doing any shows, and the calls gradually reduced and eventually stopped.

My band wasn't just a bunch of 'filmi orchestra' musicians hired by my manager to back me. I didn't even have a manager, I kept things personal. I had handpicked them over the years, and they were more than a band – they were my second family. They were my musical family. They were my brothers-in-music.

And I didn't ever want to form a band or perform again.

Ever.

A month can be forever

I woke up crying every night, my pillow soaked in tears and my face choking into it. It was only after hugs and comforting words from Michèle that I'd finally fall into a troubled sleep again.

I decided I would give a monetary compensation to my departed band members' families. Most of them didn't need it, and I worried they might see my offer as an insult. Sunil's family could certainly use it though, and I could not give money to just one or two families and not the others.

My lawyer and chartered accountant both tried to convince me that I was not at all required by law to compensate them, as they didn't fall into the category of 'regularly employed contracted workers' or something of the sort. But my wish had nothing to do with legalities; it was a wish, pure and simple.

After some thought, I settled on the amount of Rs 3,00,000 for each of the four families who had lost a son. And Rs 1,00,000 to Santana Carvalho after he got out of hospital.

To put these figures into perspective today, I consulted inflation graphs by experts. The money of the year 2000 was worth 3.56 times more in 2020. That is, giving Rs 3,00,000 in 2000 was the same as giving Rs 10,68,000 to each family today.

I remember being at Wendell Rodricks's house for dinner that same year. Our common friend, a mine owner and perhaps the richest man in Goa, had undergone a somewhat similar experience: a Brazilian player in his football team had died on the field due to a grievous injury sustained during a game. He told us all how he had given the grieving Brazilian widow Rs 3,00,000 as compensation.

I remember thinking, 'Well, if the richest man in Goa has given Rs 3,00,000 as compensation, the same figure that I, a mere musician, have given for each band member, then I have been adequately generous.' But I told no one what I had given, or even that I had given any compensation at all. Not at that dinner, not to anyone from the press and media, not ever.

No one refused the compensation, incidentally, and no one saw it as an embarrassment. Neither the well-to-do nor the needy. And why should they? Sunil's family, the neediest, was also the most grateful.

The more attentive readers among you might remember that somewhere in the beginning of this book I had written: 'A motto Mother drummed into my head was "Never let the left hand know what the right hand gives". It stayed embedded in my mind very deep, and would cause me some pain decades later.'

The pain it caused me now was that some newspaper in Goa published an article painting Sunil's mother as a poor, helpless widow lying all alone without any monetary or moral help whatsoever – thus insinuating that I had not helped them at all. All this in the 'normal procedure' of the Goan press, who print what they want to without bothering to verify their facts with a simple phone call. But not even being painted as a heartless man could make me talk about the compensation I had given, or about the fact that Sunil's family and I had become good friends and visited each other regularly since the accident. If they had bothered to enquire with the mother, she would have told them that, thanks to my compensation, the unmarried daughter had done a beautician course and started a beauty salon at home, that she now had a dowry, and that his younger brother's higher education had been taken care of.

Do excuse me, dearest Mother, but following lofty ideals can be a waste, especially today when the world is filled with tiny pathetic minds and gossipmongers who occupy the undeserving posts of journalists and editors. In this book, finally, I have broken my silence.

Santana in a coma

I had offered for Santana's cousin and his fiancée, who were more like his siblings, to go and stay with him in Kanpur, and I had regular reassuring news that he was recovering well and fast.

Being the newest addition to the band, Santana had been given the most uncomfortable seat in the Sumo by the other band members; that is, he was sitting precariously at the back, in the luggage compartment, on top of shaky suitcases. Which, ironically, was what saved his life, and his life alone.

He was not crushed in between the seats like every other person in the car. (The driver, Kanhaiyalal, a young man from Kanpur who left behind a young widow and child, had died too.) Santana had been flung out of the vehicle by the impact, through the rear door which had burst open. He had banged his head on the tarmac, which had put him in a coma. But he was the sole survivor.

A psychiatrist for me

My nightly pillow-wetting continued. And so did my bouts of uncontrolled crying during the day. I continued seeing dead versions of everyone I crossed on the road. In short, I was a useless wreck.

Finally Michèle and I agreed that I ought to see a psychiatrist. She chose one from the recommendations she received, and we saw him at his consulting room in Miramar.

'How and what are you feeling, Remo?' he asked.

I told him all. I must have talked for about half an hour. With unavoidable bouts of crying of course. To his credit, I must say he listened without interruption.

At the end of it all, this is what he had to say:

'Remo, remember something.' He adopted this very serious professional look, voice and pose. 'Life is a game of cricket.' He must have been a fan of the game. 'Along the way, some of us are bowled out. And some of us keep batting.'

That's it. And he gave me a prescription of mind-numbing pills.

I started feeling worse than ever. If earlier I woke up crying naturally, now I woke up crying like a zonked zombie.

Getting away from hell

Michèle came up with a plan. I needed a change of scene. Waking up daily in Goa, seeing the look in people's eyes which were either accusing or pitying, was taking its toll on me.

'You have to be here until the one month's Mass, so just have strength and courage until then,' she said. 'But soon after that let's take the kids and go to France. I think you need the change very, very badly, and I believe it will do you a whole lot of good.'

I agreed. She handled everything, and booked the tickets for the very day after the one month's Mass.

A few days before the Mass, I received a call from Selwyn's father.

'Remo, I have been thinking,' he said. 'I have calmed down considerably now, and for the first time I have been thinking about what *you* must have gone through. I have been putting myself in your place, and imagining what I would go through if, on one of my frequent business trips, my staff members who usually accompany me had to die in an accident. I would be crushed. And yes, their families would probably blame me unjustly. So I want to apologize for whatever my family might have put you through. And I want to thank you for all that you did to bring Selwyn and the others back to Goa. It must not have been easy, especially in your shocked and shattered state. Thank you, and god bless you.'

Of course, that got me crying. Meanness and kindness both got me crying in an instant.

'Thank you, Mr Pereira,' I said. 'It was truly nice of you to realize these things, but even grander of you to make this call and say so. God bless you too.'

Somehow I made it to, and through, the month's Masses and pujas, and visited all the four families. And on the next day we were gone.

Landing in Paris

Our flight was via London. The transit in London was extended because of bad weather. It was a bad storm, and we could see it raging through the airport's huge glass walls. Finally, after more than a couple of hours' delay, we got the all-clear signal and took off.

By the time we started our descent into Paris it was stormy there too. The wind buffeted the plane left and right, and the heavy rain made it impossible for us to see the runway. This seemed more like the Goan monsoon than European rain. The tension was palpable in the plane, even among the air hostesses. I couldn't help thinking: 'Is this a retribution for the death of my band members? Am I and my family destined to die now?'

The plane bumped hard, slid and skidded as it landed, but finally slowed to a steady straight run. We had made it safely.

Michèle's sister Jeanine had come to pick us up from Le Havre. While driving us home she voiced my dark thoughts without mincing words: 'The weather was so bad, I didn't know whether your plane was going to land intact or not. For a moment there I wondered whether this had something supernatural to do with the accident y'all were leaving behind in India, whether you were all destined to die here while landing.'

At least I wasn't the only one who was thinking overtime.

When we reached home, Michèle's favourite speciality by Jeanine, *lapin à la moutarde*, was awaiting us. As was a nice bottle of red – or two. My sons were happy to see their cousin, and the house was resounding with the kids' laughter. Michèle's and Jeanine's happy banter was the first 'normal' conversation I was hearing in ages; no one was whispering in hushed tones anywhere around me.

And when I opened my eyes next morning, I realized that was the first night in a whole month I had slept without waking up crying midway. I heaved a gigantic sigh of relief, I felt the joy of coming back to life… I had left that realm of the dead at last.

The first thing I did when I got out of bed was to take those damn pills and throw them into the dustbin with a vengeance. Howzzattt!

I felt gradually more and more alive as the days went by. We spent Christmas and New Year in France. By the time we returned to Goa I was pretty much rejuvenated, and not in a mood to take any nonsense from anyone who spoke falsities about facts surrounding the accident. But fortunately for them, by now no one was talking or writing much about it any more. Or I would've let them have a piece of my mind, in the press or otherwise.

Back in Goa and in the studio

Santana was discharged from hospital and returned home. I gave him his compensation. With a part of it he purchased the latest Roland Octapad, as his old one had been robbed by the human vultures.

A few days later, he called to tell me I ought to form a new band. 'No, Santana, I just don't feel like going through it all again. It was tough enough finding the right guys one time – I don't think I'll find them again,' I said.

But Santana was in the mood to talk about the accident. And among the other things he told me, there was an eye-opener.

'Selwyn had composed a song, had it translated into Hindi, and was going to stop over in Mumbai to make his first music video. He was carrying US$10,000 in cash for that purpose,' he said. 'I heard the family was looking for that suitcase, but it must have been one of those stolen by the hutment dwellers on the Kanpur–Lucknow highway. There must have been some celebration in those huts that night.'

Unknown to anyone even within the house itself, for a year before the accident I had been recording a 'secret' album which would be called *India Beyond*. How did I keep it secret, if my studio wasn't 100 per cent soundproof? I hated working in a sealed room, with perforated acoustic sheets on the walls and roof, and with artificial lighting through the day and night. My studio was in a quiet village, and I took advantage of that fact and had normal walls, a sloping wooden roof, and three large glass windows which looked out to coconut trees and a red tiled roof and the sky. By playing this music very, very softly, and by singing every song very, very softly, which suited this music just fine, I was able to keep it a total secret.

The album was a dream coming true. I had always told myself, as well as journalists who asked me 'what I saw myself doing in the future', that I had another kind of music in me (besides the 'Munnis' and the 'Jalwas') which I was waiting to let out – a more serious, more 'musical' music. Its time had come in 1999 and I had started recording it, waiting to disclose and release it in the new millennium. Why did I record it in secret? I don't know;

but I didn't want any outside influences or interferences, not even in the form of appreciation. It just had to be mine alone, done by myself, for myself. At least while I created it. Somewhat like a writer writing a book, I guess.

I've always looked at 'making music' as something that has two distinct phases. One is the actual creation of it. A song normally starts with something which I've named the 'seed' – it's an idea which comes into the head uninvited, whether while driving, in the silence of a plane or in a noisy airport, sometimes strangely even while working on another song, or while taking a shower or sitting on the potty. I started carrying a dictaphone everywhere before mobile phones with recording facilities were invented, because it is very easy to forget a seed before you've played it in your mind a few times. A seed can be a melody line, a lyrical line, or a new drum groove or bass line. Or it could be something not yet musical at all, just an idea for a topic for a song, triggered off by something you've read in the newspaper that morning. It might have come to your head yesterday or a year ago. But it's something which has hooked you and hasn't left your subconscious, something you know you've just got to take from your own head into your solitary studio and have fun working upon, beefing it up, hearing it for the first time in the real world of sound waves in the air. Building up the basic feel on the drum machine, and hearing it grow and take shape, as you add the bass, a basic chords instrument like a piano, organ or guitar; then humming or singing the rough tentative vocals to which you've started to write lyrics, slowly getting more intricate ideas for detailed arrangements and harmonies. And then finally, when the lyrics are more or less complete, starting on the final and fair tracks, adding more icing on the cake, changing a note here or a word there. Until you declare the song complete, and mix it down and master it. Of course the next day you make a new mix which you name the Final Mix. And the day after, or that very night, another one called the Fin Final Mix. And then the Fin Fin Final Mix. Until you kick yourself and force yourself to let go.

The other phase of 'making music' is actually performing it on stage, finally taking it out of your solitary studio and placing it in front of hundreds or thousands of people, a spotlight shining bright on you; infusing it with 'live' excitement, with improvisations which depart without warning and out of sheer excitement from the studio version. Some of these improvisations become a permanent part and parcel of the song thereafter; some change at every performance.

I know artists who are great on stage, but leave the first phase to an army made up of a lyric writer, a music composer, an arranger, and a recording and mixing engineer, and only come into the studio and sing the song after the army has finished creating it. Or those who are brilliant in the studio and create a masterpiece, but cannot really put it across on stage without an elaborate light show, dozens of dancers, giant screens, a huge orchestra, and so on.

I've always counted myself extremely lucky for loving and enjoying both these phases like a junkie reportedly enjoys a fix. Ah, the highs of being in a studio and on a stage... These are two of the places on earth where I live. Or come alive. Plain and simple.

Anyway, back to *India Beyond*. Now that it was finally complete, I had played a song or two from it to the band at the Mumbai airport on the way to Kanpur. They were blown away, and I had promised to play them the full album when we returned to Goa.

During that month of mourning and hybernation, I played it for Michèle. She was amazed. 'When did you create and record this? It's so beautiful! And totally different from what you've done till now. It must have taken you months, but we didn't hear a single thing in the house!'

When we returned from France after my convalescence, I knew I had to add another song or two to the album, dedicated to my band; the seeds were germinating in my mind already.

It hurt me physically – going up to the studio, turning the system on, touching my guitar or flute or keyboard or any musical instrument whatsoever, even trying to hum a tune caused a pain in my chest and stomach. I had never known that sadness and sorrow could give one physical pain besides mental and emotional trauma.

But I pushed and forced myself. And my pain and grief poured out in the form of a song called 'A Fishbowl Called Life', and a shehnai-driven instrumental called 'The Empty Stage'. They served as therapy, as a release, as a cure. If going to France had rid me of my nightly bouts of crying, recording these songs freed me from the pain in my chest and stomach which music had been giving me.

And now my album was fully ready. And it truly was the most beautiful album I had created until now.

A band? Concerts? Never again!

Santana kept on calling at least once a month or so.

'You cannot remain holed up like this! You were born for the stage, and you have to form a new band!'

I was used to his calls now, and I would repeat the same thing every time in different words: 'That band took twelve years to form, Santana. I'm not about to spend years looking for new guys now. No, no more bands and concerts for me. But thanks a lot for your concern!'

And I'd be rid of him for another month or so.

Almost a year later, he made his monthly call, his twelfth one. I was busy at that moment and, thinking I'd finally found the perfect excuse to get rid of this insistence for good, said, 'Ok, you find the musicians then. Because I cannot.'

Of course I didn't tell him I had not even tried. Or that I was sure he would never ever succeed.

Imagine my surprise when he called me a week later. 'I've found the perfect keyboard player and the perfect dholak player! I just have to find a bassist! When can I bring these two over for an audition?'

Oh no … he had gone ahead and found some guys. I had put myself in a situation, and would now have to listen to them… Well, before he found a bassist, I'd politely audition these two for half an hour, get rid of them tactfully, and categorically tell Santana not to look for any more musicians. I grudgingly fixed the 'audition' for the coming week.

Santana knew my methods, which I had picked up at the Dresden festival in East Germany. 'If the rehearsal is at 10 a.m., it doesn't mean you arrive at 10 a.m.; it means we start rehearsing our first song at 10 a.m. Which means you arrive at 9.30, set up your instruments and mics, and are ready to play by 10 a.m. sharp.'

'Ok,' I said patiently at 10 a.m., 'let's try out "*O, Meri Munni*". I'll show you the chords and try to teach it to you as we go along.'

I gave the count: 'A-one … a-two … a-one, two, three, four…' and the three of them exploded into a tight, synchronized sound as one.

I couldn't believe my ears. Apart from a little fine-tuning, I didn't need to show them a single chord or teach them a single line or break. They knew the whole song.

Well – this was my most famous song at the moment, it was in Hindi, and they probably played it in their 'film orchestra'. So no wonder they knew it. As they knew my film songs like '*Pyaar To Hona Hi Tha*' and '*Humma Humma*'.

Well, now I'd try out my English songs, which they surely wouldn't know, which would give me the perfect opportunity to say it was a no go.

But they knew 'Bombay City', 'Ocean Queen', 'Indian Lady', 'Keep On Moving', 'The Flute Song', and even my original versions of Goan folk songs such as '*Maya Ya*' and '*Maria Pita Che*' from Daman. I simply could not believe my ears.

'How's that you guys know all my songs by heart?!' I asked. Santana could teach them beats, but he certainly wasn't capable of showing them chords and melodic lines.

They answered sheepishly, 'Sir, we're your fans, sir. We listen to your CDs, we know all your songs.'

'Sir'?! God, did they think this was a 'film orchestra'?! I simply had to put a stop to this 'sir' stuff. But … why was I even thinking that far ahead?

Well, the band seemed almost ready to perform in public. One week of rehearsals would kick them into perfect shape. And they seemed like good and pleasant guys all right.

'But do you know any good bass guitarist who is free, who's not playing with any band at the moment? The last thing I want to do is to break up an existing band,' I said.

All three of them came up with the same name: Rocky Lazarus.

'He's an all-rounder,' they said. 'He plays with beat groups, rock groups, film orchestras; he plays lead guitar, rhythm guitar, bass guitar, whatever is required of him. I'm sure he'll do a good job, sir.'

'Ok, first of all, stop calling me "sir". The name is Remo. This is a rock band, not a bloody government office. Does anyone have Rocky's mobile number?'

'Yes, sir.' All of them had it.

In my personal experience, even those who were dying to join me would play just a little hard-to-get at the beginning. 'Audition? Hmmm, maybe not today, but I can come tomorrow' – that kind of thing. My old band members had done the same too.

The first thing Rocky asked me when I called him was, 'Should I come right now?'

'How about soon after lunch? The rest of the band is ready to eat and continue,' I said.

'Done. I'll be there at 2.30 p.m.,' he said.

Before the rest of the guys dispersed for lunch I got to know them a little better. Mukesh Ghatwal, the keyboardist, was indeed into 'film orchestras', but very keen to learn other forms of music; would I point out some good rock, pop, reggae, and especially Latin to him? Of course I would. And I could somehow see that he would soon pick up the right feel for them.

The dholak player, Munna Chari, happened to be the guy who had auditioned some time ago for the same position. He hadn't passed the test then, but I recalled that in my studio he had played and recorded a mean qawwali beat at that time, on which I had composed and built up a song – which, after his name, I had called 'O, Meri Munni', and written it about a nubile schoolgirl. Coincidence of coincidences. It was as though this guy was destined to be in my band somehow – and was alive, which he would not be today if he had joined me then.

I had a special soft corner and respect for all-round musicians (false humility aside, because I am one too), and when Rocky came over after lunch and proved to be more than capable of handling the bass, it suddenly struck me that my intended 'half-hour audition and dumping' had turned into a regular, serious, very enjoyable six-hour rehearsal. And that, by the end of it, not only did I have a complete new band, but 75 per cent of our repertoire in place.

I confirmed them all and welcomed them to The Microwave Papadums. No, they had no superstitious objections whatsoever to the band carrying on with the same name.

After we had fixed the next rehearsal date and they had all left, I went up to my studio and sat alone in silence, looking at the evening sky and coconut trees through the double-glass window in front of my chair. I shook my head and almost pinched myself. So that was it?! I actually had a new band? Formed in the course of one single day? While I had taken twelve long years to grow my old one organically?

And there and then, like an irrefutable certainty, it hit me right between the eyes: my old departed band had put this one together for me. In one stroke, as only they could from their vantage point. And I saw all four of their faces up in the sky, smiling and winking at me from between the clouds.

And tears welled up in my eyes for the first time since I had left for Paris almost a year ago. But these were not tears of sadness and depression. These were tears of joy, of communion, of gratitude.

The old band's last debt

We had started rehearsing towards end-October. By the beginning of November I had signed up to perform on New Year's Eve 2001 in Bangalore – it was going to be the first performance with the new band. The price agreed upon was Rs 13,00,000.

The new 'Remo & The Microwave Papadums'.
LEFT TO RIGHT: Remo, Rocky Lazarus (bass), Mukesh Ghatwal (keyboards), Munna
Chari (dholak), Santana Carvalho (drums).

LEFT TO RIGHT: Remo, Munna, Rocky, Santana, Mukesh.

Hold on – that figure seemed familiar somehow. Ah! It was the exact figure which I had given as compensation to the four families of the expired band members plus Santana. Anyone would say my old band was paying me back.

It was a gig for a prominent builder who was building a new township just outside Bangalore city. It was meant to be a free concert for the buyers and prospective buyers of plots in this hitherto remote spot, and their families and guests. The concert was supposed to start at 7 p.m., and go on until 9 p.m. I wasn't going to be away from my family on New Year's Eve, so I travelled with Michèle and the kids.

That evening there was such an unseasonal storm, the event management company weren't even able to take us to the venue for the sound check. The stage itself had been fully erected and covered, but the rest of the venue was totally open green virgin land, with no temporary roofing provided whatsoever. The sound and lighting men had set up their systems but were not able to connect them for fear of short circuits and electric shocks in the rain. We were requested to stay put in our hotel rooms and await further news.

The rain finally abated around 9 p.m., and that's when we were picked up from our hotels.

By the time we reached the venue the sound and lights had been connected, and we were asked to please start performing straightaway, as the audience had been waiting for long already. We went straight up on stage, I said hello to the audience, apologized for the delay, joked about the storm, and worked them up. They were fully drenched but surprisingly in the highest of spirits, like wet school kids, super-excited that the show was starting at last. I asked the engineers to adjust the sound levels while the first song progressed, and, on the spot, I invented a song called 'Sound Check'. I started scatting on these two words, slowly building them up into a vocal percussive rhythm. When my mic sounded fine, I took the scat into the words 'electric guitar'. Reynold's was one of the best sound systems in the country, and their engineer, Mike, knew our band and our sound like the back of his palm. When he had adjusted the sound and level of the electric guitar, I scatted on the word 'drums', and the drummer came in, then 'bass', and so on and so forth until, by the end of this impromptu song, all the instruments and mics had joined in and been perfectly adjusted. And then, without further ado, we launched straight into 'O, Meri Munni'.

The audience went wild and burst into a frenzied explosion of clapping, dancing and singing. By the time we reached the middle of the song I could see the security people having a tough time trying to keep the excited audience from climbing on the stage. By the time I finished singing another verse, they had overtaken security. They were up on the stage, all over the stage, with more climbing up, going crazy, trying to dance with us, trying to hug us. I could smell alcohol on their breath – I should have known that's how they had dealt with four hours of waiting in the rain, and now they were more than ready to rock 'n' roll.

I felt arms grabbing me from all around. Some people were kissing my cheeks. I could not sing or play guitar, but it didn't seem to matter to them. I remember thinking, 'Thank god they're happy and they love us; but such love could inadvertently kill. A mob like this, if angry, could be lethal.' I looked around at my band and saw them receiving their generous doses of hugs and kisses and dance steps too.

At that point, in the face of the chaos, I felt the strong arms of the event management guys and security holding and pulling me, while other arms pried loose the strangleholds of audience members whose arms were now tightly and dangerously wound around my neck and everywhere. Within a minute or two I had been taken off the stage, and no one seemed to have even noticed. They were all busy dancing and making merry. Mike saw that my band members were stopping to play one by one, so he had the presence of mind to put on the O, Meri Munni CD – and no one even noticed the difference, as it had been recorded live anyway.

The four guys who had got me off the stage took me straight to a waiting car whose engine was running. 'Where are my wife and kids?' I kept shouting, refusing to go without them. They were in the car already. The guys opened the door and almost pushed me in, shouting at the driver, 'Go! Now! Straight to the hotel! Don't stop anywhere! Go!'

'But my band! My band! Where's my band?' I shouted. 'I'm not leaving without them! I want to see them leaving in their cars first!' No, I wasn't going to relive that nightmare again. No way.

'Go, please! We are already taking care of them! They will be at the hotel with you! Now go!'

The car shot off. I could see the audience in the distance, dancing in a frenzy, filling up the whole stage and the ground, totally oblivious to the fact that there was nobody singing or playing any more. The CD was on, the CD was loud, the sound was thumping and deafening, they were happy. But I could not see my band.

All the way back to the hotel I tried to reach them on their mobiles, to no avail. My blood was frozen. If the dangerous landing in Paris in that storm seemed to be a supernatural retribution of sorts, this one was certainly it.

'We've paid back your money. We don't owe you a thing any more. But no one is going to take our places.'

'But you're the ones who formed this band for me within one short day! Why did you, then?!'

Eerie silence.

Back in the hotel, I still could not get through to a single mobile. The luxury five-star hotel room started to feel like the IIT Kanpur guest house.

There was an ominous-sounding knock on the door. Not the door bell, a knock. Dreading the worst, I opened it.

Mukesh stood there smiling, the rest of the band smiling behind him. They were always either smiling or laughing.

And then I turned fifty

A whole two years or more had passed since the accident, full of concerts and travels and lovely things.

I know that attaining sixty years of age is a milestone of special significance in the Indian tradition, but I found something unique in the number fifty. And I wanted to do something very memorable on that birthday. Throw the biggest party I had ever thrown, in a five-star hotel or some exotic venue? Naaaah ... none of that appealed to me at all.

I asked myself what I would be happiest doing on that day. And my answer was, I would be happiest on stage, making music. So I decided to throw a free concert of Remo & The Microwave Papadums for the people of Goa. This idea excited me no end.

As the days went by this idea grew: why not regroup my first band, The Beat 4, as well? Brilliant! All the members agreed, and Tony Godinho, the drummer who now lived in Qatar, offered to fly down for the event at his own expense. He insisted on coming straight from the airport to a rehearsal, super-excited about The Beat 4 reunion which he'd been proposing and looking forward to for years, and that night he suffered a heart attack; he had to spend that whole week, including the day of the concert, in a hospital ICU.

ABOVE: The Beat 4 (minus one) taking a bow after performing at the '50' concert. LEFT TO RIGHT: Nandinho Lobato Faria (bass), Remo, and Caetano Abreu (rhythm). Missing is Tony Godinho (drums). BELOW: Jamming with Tony Godinho unexpectedly during my concert in Qatar some time earlier.

Then the plan got more and more ambitious; why not The Savages too, with whom I'd played in Bombay? They too agreed: I managed to procure sponsored tickets for them, and their stay was generously taken care of by Anju Timblo, a great singer-guitarist and music lover herself, at her Cidade de Goa five-star hotel in Dona Paula.

The Savages. LEFT TO RIGHT: Ralph Paes (bass); Bashir Sheikh (drums, insert); Prabhakar Mundkur (keyboards); Remo (lead).

The Indiana members were all in Goa. Abel was unable to play, though, but at least I had Bondo and Lala, and with the help of Rocky on bass and Mukesh on keyboards, we played a few of our tracks from those times.

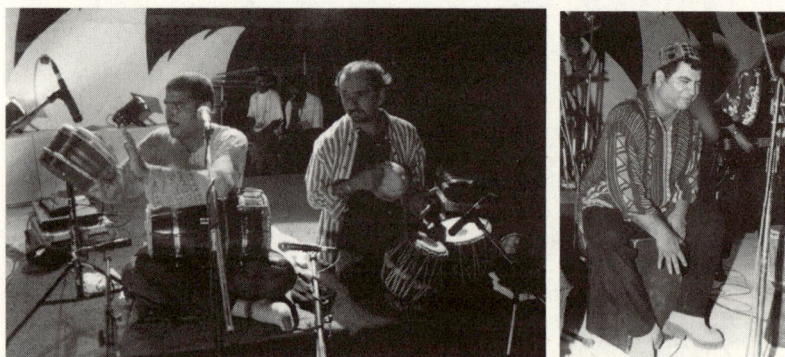

Munna and Lala Bharwani (right), and Bondo (extreme right).

I chose the Campal Grounds, between Panjim and Miramar, as the venue. My friend Felix Remedios of the excellent Reynold's Sound, Bangalore, agreed to do the sound and lights at no cost, sending his fleet of trucks to Goa with the equipment. Goan newspapers *The Navhind Times* and *The Herald* gave generous free space for publicity. Pradeep Guha, the president of the Times Group, Mumbai, gave free front-page headline space in the popular supplement of *The Times of India*, 'The Mumbai Times', publishing a huge collage of my past photographs together with a lovely write-up.

In addition to my past bands, I asked two Goan acts which I loved and considered classics to perform, and they readily agreed too: Lúcio Miranda, the singing architect, and The Valadares Sisters, the wonderful harmony group. The latter had not performed in decades, declining to regroup for international presidents and prime ministers and royalty. I was particularly touched when they agreed to come together for me. Eloy Gomes, their founder and the eldest sister Ruth's husband, had passed away, so I took over his role of guitarist. Lúcio agreed on the spot too, and came in a wheelchair, still recovering from the devastating road accident he had been involved in in Bangalore recently.

LEFT: *Lúcio Miranda (performing sitting on a chair, after his road accident).*
RIGHT: *The Valadares Sisters: Jacinta, Ruth and Lucia Valadares, who regrouped after decades.*

I asked Brian Tellis, my favourite MC from Mumbai, to compere the show, and he did. I asked Colin Curry, who now lived in Goa, to help organize it, and he did.

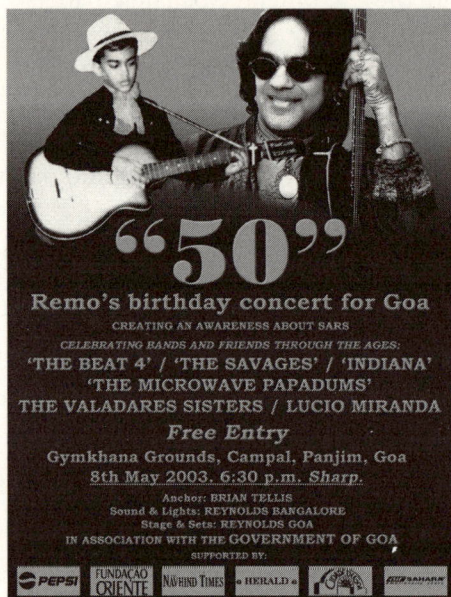

The poster for my 50th birthday free concert for Goa.

One can imagine the kind of concert it was. A free evening featuring all these near-legendary bands and artists... It was goodwill, smiles, love and music. All four hours of it. People of all ages, three or four generations together. Loads and loads of them.

A part of the audience.

I was on stage with every single band and artist, and had been rehearsing with all of them for weeks, morning and evening, sometimes with three acts in a day, besides masterminding the whole thing.

Playing with (clockwise from top) The Beat 4, Indiana and The Savages at the 50th birthday concert.

Yet I had an energy that had no bounds, and I could have gone on all night long. As in fact I did, dancing at the after-party we had for close friends and family.

Energy, excitement and a sense of happy fulfilment spilling over at the intimate after-party.

It was the happiest birthday I ever spent as an adult. And the knowledge that Mother was there, sitting in the audience as my very special guest, added to it. It was the last time she was to see me on stage. I missed Father, the man responsible for my music, very much that night.

The last bow, with everyone who participated and my immediate family.

18

More Goodbyes

Mother's heart

After the tragic experiences concerning my bandmates there were no others that had to do with the band; the rough seas under the ship smoothened out, at least as far as my professional and musical life were concerned. Shows began coming in again, though not as many as before, firstly because I was in no mood to make another album of commercial hits like *Munni*, which is what brings live gigs pouring in, not this serious new music I was into now; and secondly, because word had gone around that I had not been taking on shows for more than a year.

However, tragedy seemed to begin striking my personal life. Since childhood, I had always been told I was born with a silver spoon in my mouth. And until now I had lived my life with that silver spoon safely in place – things coming true simply because I wished them, successes falling into my lap without me trying too hard. But now my life and my world seemed to be crumbling. Whatever could go wrong, went wrong. However hard I tried to make it go right, it still went wrong.

Mother had had her first heart attack a few years earlier. Belinda and I had rushed her to Mumbai, got her admitted and tested at the Jaslok Hospital, where we were told that we had to rush her to the US *immediately*, or get her operated in Mumbai, also immediately. Nervous and full of stress, I had luckily called up R.V. Pandit, CEO of CBS Records, my record company at the time. A good friend of his, heart specialist Dr Sid Bhansali from New Orleans, happened to be in town; Pandit would get him to examine Mother. He did, and Bhansali said, 'Don't even think of touching her with a scalpel. Just give her this tiny little white pill once a day, every day for the rest of her life, and she'll be fine.'

And so she was! Mother had no heart problem whatsoever for five years thereafter. For this I'll be forever indebted and grateful to Pandit and Bhansali.

When the song is over

On another front, my marriage was going downhill. If you remember, I had made a serious resolution to change myself, that I would now be a new person. And indeed I was: I became a strictly one-woman man, dedicating myself to my family and my work.

But now Michèle found other reasons that made her unhappy and angry, including our beautiful Siolim home, which she said depressed her because it was an old Portuguese colonial-style house, just the thing that renders it a priceless treasure.

There were scenes very often, and we weren't sharing anything that a married couple was supposed to share. I stuck on for the sake of the children – I believed that, at least until the younger one turned eighteen, they needed both a mother and a father. And I'll be the first to say that Michèle was an excellent mother. And I daresay I was a great father too. I gave them the best I could; and not only in terms of material things and education, I also spent time with them and inculcated values in them.

Michèle and I and our two sons had a 'meeting' once, sitting around a table, having a friendly and honest discussion about our situation. And Jonah said to us, 'You two just aren't able to make it work. I've seen you both trying very hard, for years, but it isn't really working, is it? Instead of living together miserably like this, why don't you separate and live happily? Why don't you divorce?'

It had come from a son, and that too from the younger one, who had now turned eighteen and reached an age and a level of maturity to not only accept but propose such a solution himself. The elder one, Noah, had already expressed similar sentiments earlier.

I'm afraid very few divorces are carried out maturely and without altercations. I know they make for juicy tittle-tattle, but that's not what this book is about. Suffice it to say that after Michèle filed for divorce without warning, and after three years of a dragging legal nightmare which wasn't getting her what she wanted in terms of half the house my father built, half the house my grandfather built, besides of course half of my own worldly possessions (which I was very willing to give), there was a phone call offering to settle out of court.

But before that some curious things happened: a camp was formed, in which some people who I had thought were close friends (including Mina, whom I had considered my second mother, and also Noel Godin, whom I considered my best friend ever, to a great extent) showed just how 'close' they were not, practically cutting off all communication with me. It hurt at first, but applying the old philosophical dictum 'good riddance to bad rubbish' helped me get over it.

Michèle tried very hard to influence our kids too, and it was most hurtful to hear our seven-year-old parrot her indoctrination almost verbatim by saying 'Don't try to buy our love with your money, Papa!' when I took them out to buy a new pair of ordinary school shoes one day.

Michèle spent those court-battle years under my roof, fighting a cold war, sitting opposite me at the dining table, 'talking' only through lawyers. One can imagine the stress and tension that permeated the household during that time. Luckily, until today, I have a saviour and refuge: my recording studio. Once I'm in there, I suspect I could peacefully keep creating music even if the house were to slowly collapse around me.

My Independence Day

India attained its independence from the British on 15 August 1947. I attained mine from the French on 20 August 2007. Freedom from the nightmare we'd gone through seemed indeed like a liberation.

And I took a solemn vow: never again would I get into a one-on-one relationship. They weren't meant for me, and I should never have tried to change my intrinsic nature and get married in the first place.

The second thing I did was to build a swimming pool in our back garden, mainly for my personal exercise and for my sons' and their friends' enjoyment. If I'd built one earlier, the ten or more spoilt dogs (two of our own and eight or more strays Michèle insisted on having in the house much against my wishes) would have been in it, and I outside. I burnt the mattresses and cushions from the divans and chairs in the TV lounge which were filthy and crawling with ticks from the strays who had been allowed to sit and sleep on them. I also rearranged and repainted the house to my liking.

Life became very peaceful and idyllic. It comprised swimming in my new pool ... yoga ... my music, my band, my concerts, my recordings ... my artwork and occasional writings ... reading my favourite books, watching my favourite films in a totally refurbished and clean TV lounge ... travelling ... sometimes meeting and going out with girlfriends without the compulsion to hide like a criminal ... solitude, peace, and lack of daily tensions in my life. And the company of my sons every second week, and whenever else they felt like it, which, to my great happiness, was very often indeed.

After Michèle left, I found an old paper on which the following words, or words to that effect, had been written. It had a date on top, which was a little before our marriage.

I hate him. I can't stand his smile and sweet words. But I've crossed the age of forty, where am I going to find another man in a hurry to make children with? So I guess it will have to be him. The Goa divorce law, still based on the Portuguese, is on my side; the wife here is entitled to half of everything the husband owns. So yes, I guess I'll marry him, at least for now.

It chills a man's blood to learn that his marriage had been doomed since before it had even taken place.

Mother's passing

Mother belonged to the old school where 'divorce' was the ugliest word in the dictionary. She had begged Michèle not to go in for one, but to opt for separation. And to insist on my providing her with another house, and paying for a life she was used to here at home, instead: with four maids, a car, driver, gardener, and all expenses paid – all of which I had readily agreed to.

However the divorce was filed anyway, and it affected Mother very severely. Unknown to me, she started forgetting to take those daily little white pills for her heart. And, a few weeks later, had a terrible stroke. A stroke which incapacitated her, affected her speech and her powers of recognition, and greatly limited her movements.

A person who loved reading, who lived for her garden and her collection of rare cacti which won prizes every year, who loved doing things around the house all day long, in short who loved being active, was suddenly half turned into a vegetable.

A picture of Mother before she passed.

Belinda and I took turns staying with Mother every alternate week and looking after her. After a happy weekend together at Belinda's house, we were driving Mother back home when she suddenly suffered her sixth heart attack. We drove her straight to the hospital, but the attack proved to be her last. It happened two days before my birthday.

Among Christian families in Goa, a person is normally buried two days after their death, after the mandatory post-mortem at the morgue and the arrangements with the church and funerary agency. I decided to stick to this age-old custom, and buried Mother on my birthday, the very day she had brought me into this world fifty-two years ago.

There are some things a son can never ever forget – and harm caused to his mother tops that list. But time heals. The unpleasant memory has returned on writing this book, but I know it will fade away again.

Orphans

I found myself calling up my sister more often now. Several times a day. When I travelled for a show, I would call her from the airport before taking off. And from the other airport after landing. Just to say Hi.

It took me a long while to realize that that's how often I used to call Mother. I was now substituting Belinda for her, and that wouldn't do; Belinda had her own life and other things to do than play mother to me. So I minimized my calls to her.

But somehow Mother's passing had brought us closer together. And if I didn't call her, she called me. We were now two orphans, we were each other's closest family from our respective pre-marriage times, when our family consisted of just our two parents and the two of us.

I had always loved both my parents equally, and I had never had any issues with either of them. And yet, today, I miss Mother more often than I do Father. She is the one I feel like telling things to first, showing things to first. And I almost feel jealous to know that, as a man and a father, I will always play second fiddle to my sons' mother. But I guess that is a law of nature that no one can change. Or could it be that daughters feel closer to their fathers? I shall never know.

Parents are irreplaceable, and they always shall be. As a sixty-eight-year-old man today, I know that there is a child in me who misses and will miss them always.

'Luiza'

Some time after Mother's passing, I started pouring out my feelings in a song. But I could not get further than the first four lines; it wasn't an easy song to write. How does one put such loss into words? I certainly did not want it to sound banal or clichéd.

A few years later the tune and lyrics progressed a little further, and then stalled again.

Finally, sixteen years after Mother's passing, in the middle of giving finishing touches to the line edits of this book, it fell into place in August 2021, and I completed all the lyrics and music. I recorded it, and then made my very first music video shot in Porto. Some of my musician friends who have known me forever have told me that it's my most beautiful song ever.

It means a lot to me.

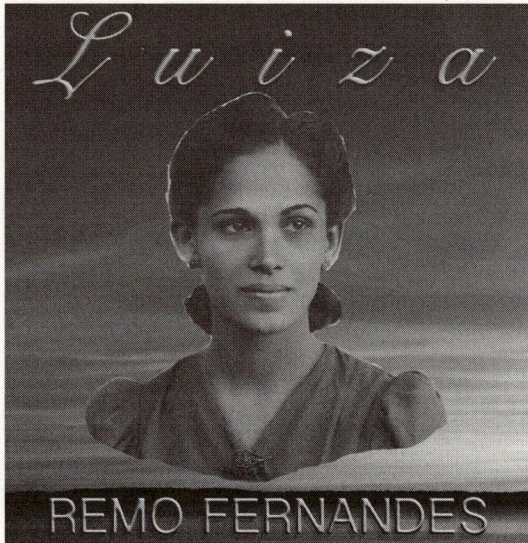

Playing with god

Meanwhile, the outside world kept turning, as it always does.

For me, it resumed its rotations when Jethro Tull's Dubai concert promoter called out of the blue one day in 2005, saying Ian Anderson was intending to collaborate and perform with a contemporary Indian artist; would I be interested? I said yes – as though there was anything else I could or would have said – and that was that. An impossible dream which I hadn't even dared to dream was on its way to coming true.

During the holidays in the '70s my friends and I lazed and hung out the whole day, listening to and playing music most of the time. One of the main bands we listened to was Jethro Tull – *Aqualung* and *Thick as a Brick* being our favourite albums. If some clairvoyant were to tell me then that one day I'd play with Ian Anderson, I'd have told him to take two aspirins and lie down until the hallucination went away.

I was initially told we would jam on one of my songs, 'The Flute Song', and would I please send it to Ian Anderson on MP3. I did, and now here I was, exchanging emails with the man. He wrote back saying he wanted to hear more of my music. I was thrilled and flattered. I sent him four more songs, out of which he selected three to be performed live, with Jethro Tull backing me.

Jethro Tull backing *me*?! God, this dream was becoming more and more surreal; I was sure to wake up with a rather nasty bump on the head soon.

Several emails later, during which we discussed song tempos and flute keys, I received one from Ian saying that Jethro Tull were now busy rehearsing '*Maria Pita Che*', 'Bombay City', '*O, Meri Munni*' and 'The Flute Song'. I tried to imagine the sound of my songs filling a rehearsal room somewhere in England.

The big day came. Ian and I met in Dubai. I shook hands with the legend, looking into his fifty-six-year-old face and recreating in my mind the twenty-something young man who faced the world standing on one foot, colourful tights disappearing like a second skin into knee-high boots, tail coat and long fuzzy hair flying wild, fidgety hands clasping a huge silver flute to his mouth. I regained speech finally, felt the warmth and friendliness beneath his notorious eccentricity, and we headed for the press conference with our concert promoter driving us with one hand while screaming into his cell phone in the other. Ian and I exchanged glances and a resigned smile which said we'd keep conversation for later.

At the conference hall we caught up with Sivamani, India's ace percussionist, who was going to jam with us as well. Eyeing Siva's trademark bandana, Ian turned to me and said in a mock stage whisper loud enough for Siva to catch, 'Never trust a man who wears his wife's knickers on his head.' He then proceeded to wear one himself at the concert. Throughout the press conference Ian's weird version of Scottish humour was very much in evidence, especially when he sailed forth on a detailed account of his prostate problems, much to the journalists' mixed embarrassment and amusement. We ribbed one another, had fun, and then picked up our instruments for the television crews present – and that was the first time I played the flute with god.

LEFT: At the press conference with Ian Anderson. RIGHT: Backstage during the show.

We then had a quiet lunch together, just Ian and I. And I was able to hear him hold forth about 'everything I ever wanted to know about the world rock scene in the '70s and '80s, but didn't know who to ask'. I listened while he talked about his life, his music, the drug and alcohol scenes (given his freaked out and often trippy lyrics, I was surprised to learn from him that he had never partaken of either drugs or alcohol), his painting which he wanted to resume one day, his four trips to Goa, his adventures with vindaloo, and his friends Bob Dylan, The Beatles, Eric Clapton, Pink Floyd. Later in the car on my way to shopping in town I noted the conversation down while it was still fresh in my memory.

The next day our respective bands arrived: Jethro Tull, and The Microwave Papadums. We had a marathon rehearsal from 12 noon till 7 p.m., with just a half-hour coffee break in between. During almost the entire evening we did nothing but rehearse my songs. It turned out that three Jethro Tull members (Martin Barre, guitars; Andrew Giddings, keyboards; and Jonathan Noyce, bass) lived in totally different corners of England, while one (Doane Perry, drums) lived in the US. They had received MP3 files of my songs from Ian but had only worked on them individually until now. However, as they sat at their instruments it became clear that they'd each done their homework thoroughly. Out came the pages on which they'd noted down the arrangements, and the riffs and the chords were all perfectly in place. And they reconfirmed my belief that the higher you look into the echelons of professional success, the harder you see people work. Those who you think do not need preparation are those who prepare the most.

I'd heard from everyone that Ian could be quite eccentric and difficult to work with. He himself told me that his band could be quite difficult as well – they had put down their instruments and walked out of a rehearsal with a respected Indian ustad the year before. But we hit it off famously, and here they were, urging me to go on and on rehearsing, as they wanted to learn the finer aspects of the arrangements to my songs. These international superstars didn't have to do this, but they came up and told me they really enjoyed playing 'my catchy music with its exotic rhythms'. And I was grateful they went out of their way to make me feel at ease and at home.

In the last half hour we ran through the four Tull songs on which I was going to jam, and we ended the evening exhausted but happily satisfied.

The next day we were to run through all my songs during the sound check. But as it often happens when the show itself is going to be good, the sound check started going all wrong. My electric guitar was giving out a hum which no one could trace; the source was discovered to be an earthing problem with the mixer, but not before a considerable lapse of time. We then had a bomb scare, and everyone dispersed back to the hotel, where Ian and I had a quiet cup of coffee in the lobby coffee shop. The 'bomb scare' turned out to be a routine security check. When we finally started the sound check we hardly had much time left, but Ian was as good as his word: we went through all of my songs without exceptions or shortcuts.

Came showtime. Was I nervous? Yes, I was: something which hardly ever happened to me. I was nervous about my guitars' tuning, my stage placements, my costumes, the order of my songs and stage entries... The audience had come to listen to Tull, would they boo me off the stage? These and other such 'pleasant' pre-show musings floated around in my head.

And then they called out my name, I climbed up those steps, and that was it. No more space for nervousness. As soon as I announced that I was from Goa, there was a loud roar of approval from the multinational audience, and that set the ball rolling. They were soon singing 'Maya Ya', clapping their hands, dancing in the aisles; the ice was melted, the party had started. I was home.

Then Ian Anderson and Jethro Tull joined me on stage. Even though I was totally engrossed in the music, I was fully aware that I was living out one of the most historic moments of my life. I wanted the night to never end. It still hasn't.

Almost exactly a month later, Ian once again kept his word and sent me a CD with the digital recording of the live concert. I spent a whole lazy sunny Goan Sunday afternoon listening to the hard proof that it wasn't all a dream after all.

João

After Mother passed, I brought our old caretaker João, who was now alone in my parents' house in Miramar, to live with me in Siolim. Rather than write afresh about him, I shall reproduce something I wrote the day he passed away, in August 2012. He was a very important part of our family's lives.

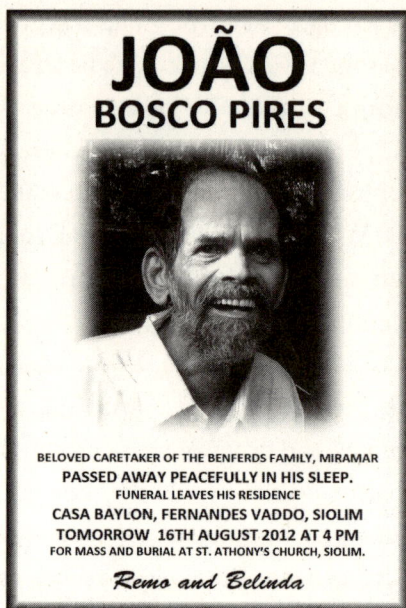

JOÃO
BOSCO PIRES

BELOVED CARETAKER OF THE BENFERDS FAMILY, MIRAMAR
PASSED AWAY PEACEFULLY IN HIS SLEEP.
FUNERAL LEAVES HIS RESIDENCE
CASA BAYLON, FERNANDES VADDO, SIOLIM
TOMORROW 16TH AUGUST 2012 AT 4 PM
FOR MASS AND BURIAL AT ST. ATHONY'S CHURCH, SIOLIM.

Remo and Belinda

João passed away peacefully in his sleep at 4.15 a.m. on 14 August 2012. Without illness, not even a cold. I always thought he was a young man who looked old. Now I know that he was an old man who looked young. And yesterday it was confirmed that he was eighty-five.

It was 1963. I was ten years old. To the happy house which we rented from Eugénio de Melo on Rua Heliodóro Salgado, one morning came a humble elderly lady (who would then be described as a '*mulher de pano*') accompanied by a young boy who looked a few years older to me; he was slightly built, wore short pants, and had a friendly toothy smile. The lady asked for my mother, and the two women huddled together in serious hushed discussion for a very long time. Then the elderly lady hugged the boy, left him behind with us, and walked away. That's how João came into our lives and stayed for precisely half a century.

Years later, my mother narrated the gist of the lady's talk that day. It turned out she lived not too far from our house and was often in need of charity. She had said, 'Bai, this is my son, and he is a bit of a simpleton. He was being looked after by the priests in Don Bosco, but they are not in a position to keep him there any longer. He is not very strong mentally or physically, so he can't get a job anywhere. I am advancing in age and not keeping well. When I pass away there will be no one to look after him. He will be out in the streets with only the option of a life in the marketplace or near the ferry boat. He will not last long there. Would you please take him in and look after him for me? He may not be of much practical use to you, but he is a good boy.'

I realize now that the 'young boy' who was brought to our home that day was a grown man of thirty-five. Who didn't look a day over fifteen, though in a slightly curious way.

When we moved to Miramar a few years later, I remember that João had two chores. To fetch milk from the milk booth down the road in the morning. And to walk the dogs on the beach at the other end of the road in the evening. Both chores which he loved and couldn't be talked out of doing, as they provided what he prized most in life: human contact and *gozalio* (talk, chit-chat, shooting the breeze), both in the milk booth queue, and on the beach. And they satisfied his unconditional love for animals, whom he adored. My mother always defended him against all criticism and funny comments, saying, 'João may be simple. But can you find such honesty, loyalty and commitment today? Even at your high fancy modern salaries? I would trust him with unweighed gold powder. João is priceless.'

He lived a happy, carefree, healthy life in spite of being a bachelor, or probably because he was one. He had countless friends and well-wishers from every walk of life (my friends and my parents' friends, doctors, lawyers, chartered accountants, musicians, actors, all asked 'How is João?' when they saw me, usually before asking how I was), and he had not a single enemy. And there was no one he ever did or wished ill.

All this is much more than I can say for myself.

When younger he never missed a temple or church or mosque feast in distant corners of Goa, from where he always returned with pockets full of food – for the dogs. He never missed a 'matka' bet, his countless day trips to the *gaddo* for beedies, and of course his happy evening trips to his favourite Miramar tavern, on whose terrace he graced a table of half a dozen or so old cronies who missed him badly on the rare occasions when he couldn't make it. He returned from these excursions often in the mood to sing jolly songs, and sometimes in the mood to quarrel with the maid.

After both my parents passed away, he did not wish to be uprooted from Miramar. The action was all there: his friends, the never-ending stream of people he greeted and talked to at our garden gate – they had been a part of his life for years. So I hired a maid to look after him, cook for him, and clean the house and garden.

All seemed to go perfectly, until I made an unannounced trip there one evening, and discovered the maid lying in a stupor in her room which was strewn with empty bottles. She was an alcoholic, and had been cooking extremely pungent food to her own liking, which João's delicate stomach could not take. She had forced him to gradually withdraw all the money from the bank account my mother had built up for him, and had taken it all. And she had threatened and frightened him into silence. I took a few quick decisions on the spot: within a couple of hours I had fired the maid, hired pickup trucks and coolies to clear out all the antique furniture and crockery, locked up the house, and headed home to Siolim with João.

In the beginning, village life was too quiet for the Miramar boy. 'Inga zaddam chodd!' (Too many trees here!) was his verdict. But he eventually settled in, enjoyed the peace and quiet, made friends with the immediate neighbours and everyone who came over, and soon got used to the affectionate attention and joking chatter, motherly care and wonderful food cooked by Sandhya and Vonita, my maids.

In the years he spent here, I religiously poured him a small caju feni in the evenings. He didn't want a large peg any more, he said it made his legs unsteady. Sometimes we shared a drink together, listening to old Konkani cantaram (songs) and talking about the old days. He had an uncanny memory for people, and incidents I myself couldn't remember. He wasn't good at recalling names, but had his own for everyone: foddó dotor (bald doctor), motteli bai (fat madam), haddió bab (bearded sir), dantró padri (big-toothed priest, even though his own were much bigger!), and so on. These were not names he gave in mockery or in malice. They were innocent descriptions, like a child's. On some of those bonding evenings of ours he would sing, invariably starting with 'Heróis do Mar', the Portuguese national anthem, followed by the hymns he had learnt at Don Bosco during the Portuguese days. In the last two years, of his own volition, he totally stopped drinking. And curiously, a few months later, so did I.

João loved music, and had a fabulous ear and taste for it. After I auditioned a new musician for my band, he would come up in the evening and tell me what he thought of him. And his opinion invariably coincided with mine. He had a weakness for good drummers and percussionists. Though he couldn't walk very steadily of

The old rocker fooling around with my sunglasses.

late, during our rehearsals he would dance where he thought we could not see him, to the great amusement of the maids.

João had no concept of time or age. He would sometimes ask me, 'Baba, how old do you think I am, about a hundred and fifty?' I would say, '*Na re* João, you must be a hundred and twenty-five only.' And then I'd say he was actually eighteen, to which he'd laugh; and end the conversation by telling him he was a few years older to me – which I really believed he was.

Old age didn't creep up on him. In November 2011 it suddenly ambushed him. And overnight he was old. Really old. Sometimes when he sat down he couldn't get up again without help. Sometimes while standing he would lean like the Tower of Pisa, sideways or backwards, giving us all a fright. That's when I first started suspecting he wasn't just a few years older than me. He started keeping me up nights, calling out and wanting to be picked up from bed, walked around, and laid back in bed, which he wet. And after a while he wanted to be picked up again. So I hired him a full-time professional nurse. He kept her up the same way, and after three nights she disappeared. So I got him another; this one survived two nights.

When I finally timidly asked whether he would like to go to a home for the aged, I thought he would protest vehemently. But to my great surprise, he smiled and said, 'Yes, when can I go, today?' He spent the last eight months at the Candolim Home for the Aged, where he miraculously stopped his night-time demands overnight. I guess he had become a bit of a spoilt brat at home, pampered by the maids whom he quite often bullied, throwing his seniority around: 'Hanv adló tempachó! Portuguez tempachó!' (I am from the Good Old Days! From the Portuguese Days!) At home he was the seniormost citizen, the only old man, and he tended to overplay that role. I think being with other men his age and above embarrassed him into behaving like them, and into being more self-sufficient. Wonder of wonders, he even stopped wetting his bed.

In the Home he found companions who had all the time in the world to indulge in his favourite activity: gozalio, chit-chat. They also played cards, watched TV and listened to music. They were given a glass of port wine in the evenings, and – to João's great delight – beedies. There were a few who read The Herald front to back every day, and then narrated the news to the others. Their favourite characters, whose exploits they followed avidly, were of course Babush and Churchill (maverick ministers in the government of Goa).

Whenever we (my sister, my sons, their girlfriends, my friends, my maids, etc.) visited we were always happy to find him, and the other inmates, spotlessly clean and smiling at any time of day – which is much more than one can say for many other homes for the aged out here, especially those run by ill-tempered frustrated nuns. And fussy though he was here at our home, he always complimented the food in his new home to me, even in private, out of the warden's hearing. The other inmates grew fond of him, and I saw the more able ones being protective when his walk was unsteady.

In the last few weeks he turned too weak and stiff to get out of bed. The nurses wheeled him around in a wheelchair a couple of times a day. The in-house doctor, as well as my own who examined him, said there was absolutely no illness which they could detect in him or treat him for. No diabetes, no high or low blood pressure, no nothing. Perfect health. It was plain old age, which had so suddenly pounced on him a few months earlier, and which was now slowly hugging him closer and closer. All they could prescribe were tonics with supplementary vitamins, but these couldn't help João much. I knew conversation didn't mean much to him any more, so the last time I went I just took my guitar and softly sang him his favourite songs at his bedside. He murmured along to 'Heróis do Mar' and his feet moved in time under the bedcover to all the rest.

One way to describe him may be as a simpleton. But another way would be as a pure soul. Someone who, perhaps thanks to that very 'simplicity', was naturally incapable of pretence, jealousy, arrogance, vanity, intrigue, greed, hatred, and maybe even lust – though he had an infinite capacity for love. I think that just about eliminates most of the mortal sins. A soul free of all that *has* to be in heaven, there's no doubt about it. It is souls like mine that I'm worried about.

João was even incapable of lying. All one had to do was repeat the question a little louder the second time, and the truth would come tumbling out. *'João, kitleo biddio vodlai re aiz?' 'Donuch bab.' 'Kitleo? Sarkó saang!' 'Hé ... hé ... dhá vodlom dhá...'* ('João, how many beedies did you smoke today?' 'Only two, sir.' 'I beg your pardon? Tell me the truth!' 'Well ... well... I smoked ten.') He would finish a bundle of twenty beedies in two days, but I never denied him his little pleasure. After all, like President Clinton of the US, João too didn't inhale. And I took a cue from Mother Teresa, who went out of her way to buy beedies for her old inmates.

I know João is doing much more than resting in peace. João is partying up there. I am certain he is already busy making a whole lot of new friends, and meeting a lot of the old ones. And making St. Peter's eyes water with beedi smoke.

João (extreme right) dancing at my birthday party in 2010.

Socio-politics and celluloid

That same year, in 2012, representatives of the Election Commission of India from Delhi flew down to Goa and asked me to be their brand ambassador, and to urge the youth of Goa to vote, as there had been a terrible decline in voters aged between eighteen and twenty-one. In short, Indian youth were frustrated and disillusioned, and saw voting as a totally futile exercise. I wholeheartedly agreed to do this for the Commission, as I still believed that voting was the answer, and I went beyond what they asked of me. Besides designing and creating their giant billboards, I wrote a song called 'Vote: Tit for Tat', made a video of it, and actually went around Goa addressing people in public meetings.

One of the billboards erected all over Goa.

That year Goa saw the highest voter turnout in the eighteen- to twenty-one-year group, and a toppling of its corrupt government of the time. Though the previous one had not been any less corrupt, the people heartily applauded this change. But just a week or so after the elections, the fresh new faces the youth had voted to power sold themselves to the 'other' corrupt party, thus bringing them back to power.

The youth now became more frustrated than ever, and swore never to vote again. And I swore never to urge them to vote again. Most of our candidates were nothing but political prostitutes.

Around this time, I worked in three Indian films. One was Bejoy Nambiar's *David*, for which I did a Hindi version of '*Maria Pita Che*' and appeared singing it on a beach in Mangalore which passed off for Goa – it was sad to accept the fact that Goan beaches just didn't have that clean old empty look that was required in this film any more. This was going to be the lead song and video which would launch the much-awaited film. But at the last moment, Bejoy decided to launch it with another song, '*Mast Kalandar*' – a huge mistake, since another brilliant version of this song had just been a huge hit very recently, and the public yawned and said, 'What, not again!' Bejoy's launch went almost unnoticed, and sadly, so did his film. Whereas I know for sure that the kick-ass version of '*Maria Pita Che*' I had produced for the film would have been a nationwide superhit, which the original Damanese version was wherever we had performed it live for years. Bejoy tried my song next, but by then the film had already been deemed a flop, and the public had lost interest. He certainly shot himself in the foot with that bad decision.

The other two were films in which, for the first time in my life, I was asked to work purely as an actor, with no music to make or songs to sing – which thrilled me no end. One was *Ek Villain* where I played the senior mafia don who adopts and trains the hero/villain into a life of crime. I loved my role here, which I believe was fashioned after a rather notorious Goan minister. But a lot of it was edited out of the film together with other footage, as director Mohit Suri had overshot and made the film an hour too long.

And the other was *Bombay Velvet*, where I had the short role of a Portuguese gentleman music teacher who takes a girl-child singing prodigy under his wing. He also exploits the little girl sexually, until she grows into a young woman and escapes him. I was thrilled to be seriously taken aside and told by a director like Anurag Kashyap, 'You should act more often. You are a natural, and really have it in you.'

I was surprised to have shed real tears (without the aid of glycerine) while shooting a scene where the music teacher punishes the little girl too severely and then repents.

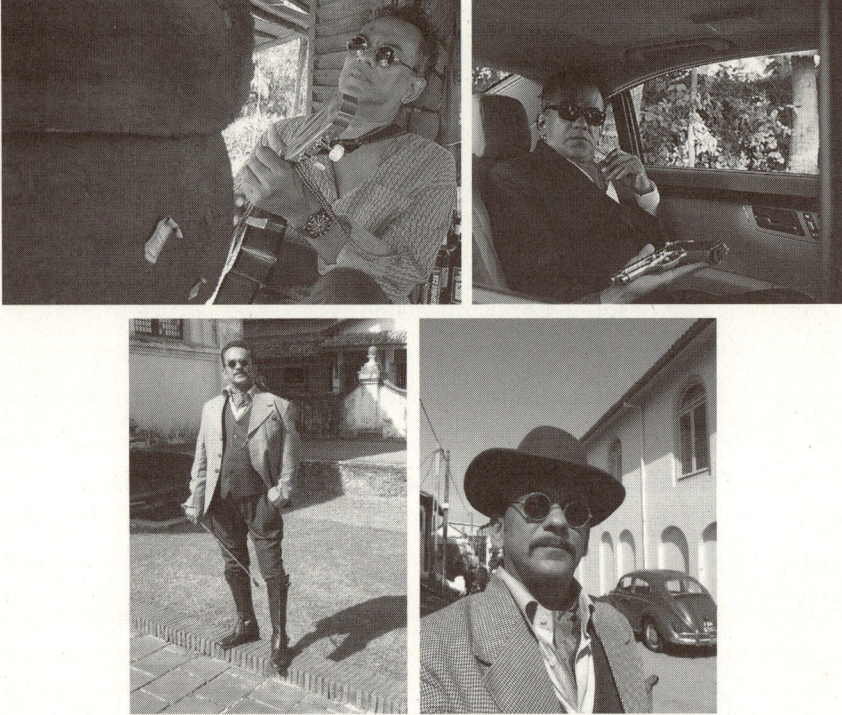

TOP LEFT: A shack singer in David. *TOP RIGHT: A don in* Ek Villain.
BOTTOM: A Portuguese gentleman music teacher in Bombay Velvet.

Seeing myself on Bollywood's silver screens, and my albums and films on huge billboards in the city where I had once been a perennially broke, largely unknown student made me feel that, in some way, I had conquered it. But although I loved the experience of acting, it wasn't really one of my passions. Besides, I found it difficult to memorize lines and say them with natural emotions in a language I wasn't well versed in. And how many Indian films are there which require a character to speak in English, Portuguese, French or Konkani?

The Goana postcards which I drew and designed around 1980. I had taken the decision
that I would earn my living doing only the things I loved: music, drawing and writing.

I always loved drawing my fantasies. When I turned six or seven, my life's ambition was to be a cowboy – The Lone Ranger, Kit Carson, whoever. Capitão Trovão (Captain Thunder) and Dick Daring were just two of my other dozen heroes.

Caros amigos.
Dignai-vos assinar
este autógrafo para
que, quando velho e
alquebrado, me lembre
sempre de vós, ao
recorrer neste livrinho,
Vosso amigo sincero,
Remo.

DEAR REMO

Some loves three
Some loves two
I love one
that is you

From your

Friend

Zita

Queridinho Remo
Desejo-te um dias
muito feliz na vida
vida e que sempre Deus
te acompanhe
Tua amiguinha
Maria
do Carmo
12-9-62

My dearest Remo
To see you big,
good and the
pride of your dear
Ma + Dad would
be my greatest wish.
Be sure always of
my prayers.
Yours affect.ly Ic. Lobo
Panjim 7. 3. 1965.   J. B.

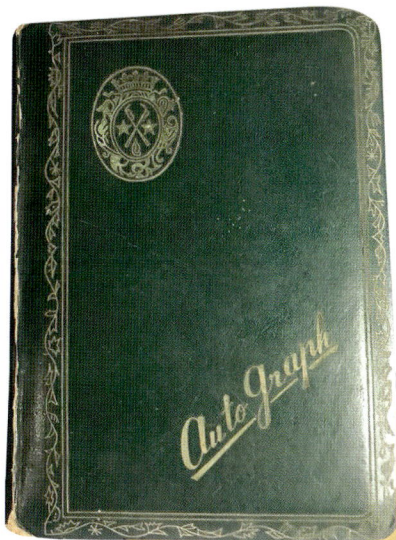

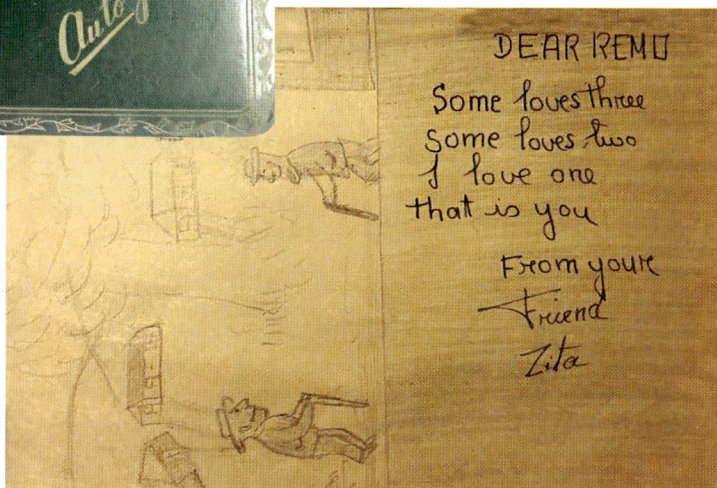

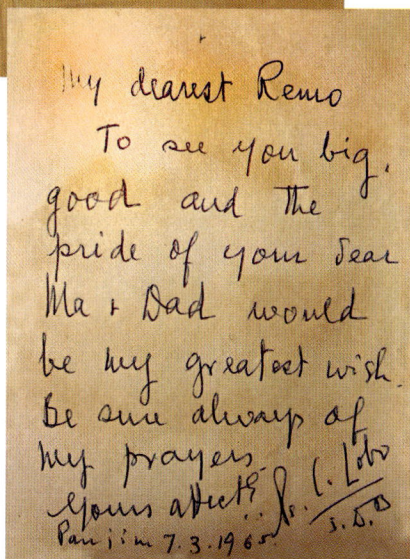

My old autograph book, with some pages inscribed by friends, and a teacher.

Subiaco Temple, nr. Tivoli
OCT '74.

Cafe And Arena, Verona, Italy, 3 Aug '77

The Forum, Rome, 26 June '76

Pisa, 6 June '76

Rooftops seen from my window, Paris '78

Travels change one's life.
My sketches from Rajasthan, Rome,
Venice, Tunis, Toledo, Paris, Pisa,
Siena, Cordoba...

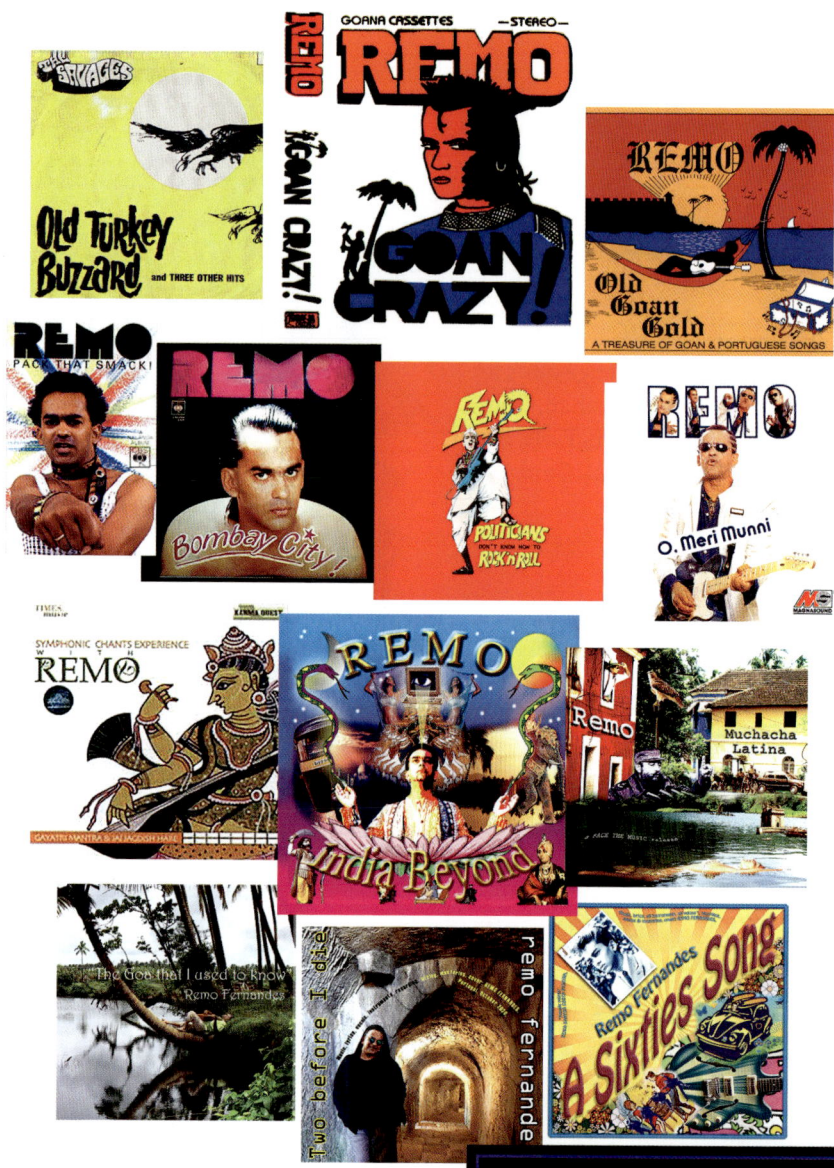

My album covers (including the one on Mother Teresa) along with the covers of some of my recent singles in the fourth row.

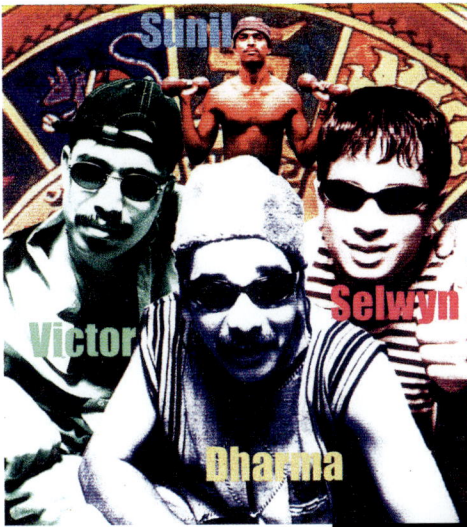

The original Microwave Papadums, my brothers-in-music of up to twelve years, who died in a horrible car crash after a brilliant concert in IIT Kanpur.

The new Papadums.

The Microwave Papadums at my 50th birthday free concert for Goa in 2003.

Music, the highest high.
(Photo courtesy Prasad Pankar.)

Playing with god: On stage with Ian Anderson and Jethro Tull.

'Remo & Bondo' clicked for Friendship Day. We would seldom do the expected.
(Photo courtesy *The Times of India*.)

At my beloved ancestral home sweet home in Siolim, Goa.

With my sons Noah and Jonah
in happier times.

With my boxer Mohammed Ali:
all tongues.

With Zenia, the love of my life...

...After we exchanged our self-written vows in May 2018; her favourite photo of us, on her birthday in May 2019; and at our favourite quiet stretch by the Douro river in May 2021.

PART IV

AFTER ALL

19

Portugal

Belinda triggers off a return to roots

My kid sister had always been shy and timid; it was almost as though she chose to live in my shadow. But of late she had started to show great autonomy. Like when she decided to take up a scholarship and do her PhD research on her chosen topic, 'Goan Writers in French', at the Sorbonne in Paris. Like when, fed up of the politics she encountered as reader and head of the department of French in Goa University upon her return from France, she quietly applied for and bagged not one but two lecturing jobs in different universities in Portugal, packed her bags, and left. And felt a joy teaching in Portugal which she had not experienced until then.

She returned to Goa on holidays at least four times a year, always loaded with presents for her two nephews – my sons. When a few years later she suddenly realized she was in love with Carmelino, whom she had known for years as a good friend, she took an equally spontaneous decision: she quit her jobs in Portugal, gave up her apartment, sold her car, returned to Goa, and they had a wedding to be remembered in Carmelino's family's ancestral *solar* in Nagoa, sanctified in their beautiful family chapel. By then Father had passed away. My parents and Carmelino's had been very good friends for decades, and Father would have celebrated this union most joyously, so it was particularly sad that he couldn't be around to see it happen. The couple had taken the decision to marry totally on their own, without any help or influence from the parents whatsoever.

A year and a half after their marriage, Daniel came along – the cutest child with the cutest eyebrows and eyelashes, inherited from his father. And my first direct nephew.

Belinda took up the post of director at the Alliance Française in Goa. But soon she was tired of the petty politics played out by some of its trustees – petty politics is the 'national sport' of Goa, and even the French who settle here are soon enamoured with it, while those with petty dispositions practise it like champions. So of course, in her usual style, Belinda dumped her job overnight and now enjoyed spending time at home with her new piano.

She had always loved singing and playing the guitar and the piano – but only at home, and only before a few people she knew really well. After she and Carmelino got married, on one of their frequent evenings out at some restaurant or the other in Goa, he, with the help of the performing band that evening, managed to coax and bully her into going up on stage and singing a song. I know her; her hands must have been cold and damp with sweat as she approached that mic in front of an audience. But once she started singing, with the backing of a live band for the very first time, the bug bit her and didn't let go. She looked forward to such jams henceforth, and it didn't take much to get her up on stage any more. I used to tease her that now one had to struggle to get her off it.

Soon she was talking about forming a band of her own. I offered her the use of my musicians whenever we weren't busy with shows or rehearsals ourselves – depending, of course, on their acceptance. Mukesh was very happy to be playing Latin music at last – Belinda's favourite kind of music – and so was Munna. 'Belinda & The Tropicanos' were soon a popular band in Goa, playing at all the major festivals and shows.

Belinda decided to record a CD of her own, and I was amazed at her selections: Brazilian and Latin songs which were obscure and unknown in Goa, but real gems, done in her own way. And a couple of original compositions of her own as well, with lyrics by Carmelino. I really enjoyed adding my little bits, like a flute here or a guitar there or an arrangement elsewhere, to the music on this beautiful CD, which was splendidly arranged by Mukesh.

In 2011, fourteen years after she had last left the country, Belinda bought an apartment in Portugal. Not to relocate for good, but to spend a few months there every year. The first time she and Carmelino went to furnish it and spend a couple of months there, I went along.

Once she was back in Portugal, Belinda soon fell in love with the furniture from the southern region of Alentejo, with the beautiful paintings of colourful flowers it bore on every pastel-coloured chair, table, cupboard and bed, which made it look like it belonged in a children's fairy tale; and soon she painted every piece of furniture in her own apartment in the Alentejo style. I had to warn Carmelino not to sit still for too long while she was on a spree, or he might end up with flowers on his forehead.

When I needed a haircut in Portugal Belinda offered to attempt giving me one. I was ready to be the scapegoat; if it didn't work out I would simply trim it all down to a crew cut, or even shave it off altogether. But the haircut was amazing. When Zenia came into my life and needed a haircut, I suggested Belinda. Zenia wasn't too sure but decided to give it a go.

'Where did you learn how to cut hair, Belinda?' she asked cautiously.

'On my dog, a long-haired Saint Bernard,' Belinda answered innocently.

Initially shaken, Zenia however braced herself and ventured forth. And then declared she hadn't had a better haircut in ages.

These were some of Belinda's multiple and varied talents, besides cooking like a boss, devising different crochet styles, and generally blowing my mind with all these things I'm simply no good at. Yes, I was rediscovering my kid sister indeed.

I have explained that, due to our eight years' difference in age, Belinda and I hadn't spent much time together during our childhood. How much can a boy of twelve, for example, have to converse about with a little girl of four? Or a young man of eighteen with a kid sister of ten? Besides, we had been mostly apart. I had been studying architecture for five years in Bombay while she schooled in Goa; I spent over two years in Europe while she went to college in Goa and in Bombay; when I returned to Goa and moved to Siolim, it was her turn to leave for France to study at the Sorbonne; then she was off to teach French in different universities in Portugal. When she got married she moved to Vasco and I lived in Siolim, while our parents and the house we grew up in was in Panjim. Afterwards, she bought a plot of land near my house in Siolim, on a hillside overlooking the Siolim Bay and its spectacular sunsets, and there she built a house with a gigantic roofed veranda which operated as living area, party area, dining area and kitchen. That, our parents' passing away and Portugal brought us closer, geographically as well as socially, and we started to spend more time together as a family – or rather, as the last two remnants of a family that was tiny to start with.

And the more I got to know Belinda, the more I came to respect her uprightness and honesty, and the deep and loyal bond we share. As the saying goes, I would trust her with my life. And I learnt to respect her temper, on the rare occasions when she lost it – though, mercifully, hardly ever at me.

Like I said, when Belinda and Carmelino decided to furnish their newly-acquired apartment in Portugal, I went along too. And this time I saw and felt the country like I had never done before. Portugal itself had changed since I had seen it last; no longer reeling under a just-concluded revolution, as it was when I had last visited it in the '70s, it was now quite adjusted to being free of a dictatorial fascist regime, and to being a democracy. The country had recently joined the European Union, which was aiding it greatly in rising to its full economic potential. The people were as simple and warm as always, though. And now we were in Porto, a smaller and therefore friendlier city than Lisbon. Yes, I love smaller cities. And I loved Portugal this time.

I had changed too. I was no longer a youth in my twenties, in love with my then beloved Paris. On my subsequent visits, I found that Parisians and the French in general had turned more and more racist. I suspect the French were always inherently racist, but tried to hide it as it wasn't 'proper' to be so; but the recent terrorist explosions in Paris had given them a validation and official permission to let their racism out in the open at last.

In the superb *boulangerie* four whole blocks away where I walked to on some mornings when I felt like an exceptional baguette and croissants, ignoring the half-dozen other *boulangeries* on the way, there was a young employee one day who served the two or three white people behind me before even looking my way. The next time I went there ready to denounce him to his boss, the boss was there, and she turned out to be a wonderful, cheerful, friendly lady without a racist tooth in her mouth. And, wonder of wonders, in her presence, the young employee was all obsequiousness and servitude, the shameless hypocrite. The mood that sunny morning was so good, in the streets of Paris and in the *boulangerie*, that I didn't want to mar it with my complaint; so I picked up my baguette, croissant and pain au chocolat and, after a friendly chat with the owner about Goa and India, during which the employee tried to eavesdrop nervously, I strolled back home to enjoy a wonderful breakfast in a state of mind free of petty strife.

I won't go into the other incidents of racism I encountered, like the cop checking passports at the airport door who was abrupt with me but not with the white passengers; the people in the queue behind me who voiced their impatience as I took a little longer to validate my Indian card in the ATM; the rude conductor in the train from Lyon to Paris … These and other incidents had already made me feel uneasy and unhappy about France that year, especially as I was stopping there after having spent two glorious months travelling around in Brazil, one of the least racist countries in the world, compared to which the racism in France could be cut with a blunt knife. Where was the friendly Paris I knew earlier, which found Indians fascinating and irresistible?

I decided there and then that I would never again return to France. My old friends were very disappointed and tried hard to talk me out of it, but I told them I wasn't going to bring my good money into a country which was going to insult me – I didn't need to.

One of them went so far as to buy me an air ticket to spend some days with her in her apartment in St. Tropez about four years ago. I expected this little seaside town, made famous by Brigitte Bardot and home to personalities like Giorgio Armani, Elton John, Beyoncé and other international celebrities, to be the most snobbish and racist of all, but I couldn't quite say no after she'd sent me the ticket. I had the most pleasant surprise of all: St. Tropez turned out to be one of the coolest, friendliest, most relaxed places I've visited.

On Vasco da Gama's reverse trail

I was disillusioned with the way Goa was going, and I guess I was subconsciously searching for a place where I could find the simple things I had grown up with as a child: cleanliness, respect for nature, discipline and grace on the roads and in queues and in all spheres of life; a government that worked for the country and for the people; no blatant corruption; and above all, a populace that was respectful, polite, kind, helpful and honest towards each other. I realize I had used these qualities to describe the Goa I grew up in in the opening chapters of this book. I was now coming full circle. I had travelled through half the countries in the world thanks to my profession, and I could see clearly that I was rediscovering all of these intangible but priceless treasures in Porto, together with an unexpected sensation of coming back to my roots.

By the time we returned to Goa, I started seriously thinking of getting myself an apartment in Porto, to spend say three or four months a year there. I had never left Goa for better prospects, neither financial nor professional – not even to go to Mumbai, the showbiz capital of India, which I'm sure would have yielded me at least ten times more money and fame. But now that the beauty of Goa I had stayed back for was fast disappearing – not just the natural beauty being smothered under greedy ugly concrete, but also the people's honesty, warmth, friendliness and hospitality – I surprised myself thinking that I could gladly leave it for a few months every year.

In Portugal, I had found 'the Goa that might have been' if it had only developed the right way: restrictions protecting Mother Nature with

A few pictures from the dozens taken during my very first trip to Porto and during a road trip around and about it, which almost took us into Spain.

firmness; historic monuments and beautiful ancient villages carefully preserved and restored; perfect roads leading everywhere; electricity, water, internet, cable TV and other services that didn't break down even once in years; and not just a judiciary that made laws, but also an enforcement that saw to it that everyone followed them. A place where you could walk into a government office and, half an hour later, walk out with everything you had come for, without the rarest possibility of someone asking for a bribe or harassing you.

Also, I had reached a stage in life which made such a move easy. Both my parents had passed away, so there was no longer an aged Mother or Father I didn't want to stay away from for months. My sons had both flown the nest: Noah had completed his multimedia course in Singapore and now worked there, and Jonah was studying underwater cinematography in Thailand. And I no longer had a wife who would have insisted on me buying a place in France instead. No, no more ties binding me down or holding me back. My live shows too had diminished considerably for reasons explained earlier; and I could always fly back for those.

I was going to make Vasco da Gama's journey, from Portugal to Goa, in reverse. And in much greater comfort than in his caravel.

The nationality that I was born into

Portugal had never cancelled Goans' Portuguese nationalities from its records, for the simple reason that Goans, unlike say the Brazilians or the Angolans, had never revolted against Portuguese occupation or fought to drive them out; they decreed that the *satiagras* who fought for Goa's liberation movement had come mainly from Goa's neighbouring states. Therefore Portugal saw and recognized all Goans born in Goa before 1961, and their descendants, as being entitled to Portuguese nationality. And do so till today.

I contacted the same lawyer whose work on my Portuguese nationality I had interrupted back in 1979. Luckily he still had my papers, and said very little was left to turn me into a full-fledged Portuguese national. I asked him to please go ahead and complete the procedure, after all these years.

It was curious how the flag I had drawn as a child in my school drawing books continued to arouse emotion – not as a matter of political affiliation, but as an emotion one feels on eating mother's cooking after decades.

Also, seeing the very Portuguese language written all around me, even the simple and common 'ATENÇÃO' (Attention) or 'PERIGO' (Danger) on signboards near railway lines or high-voltage electrical installations, thrilled me and brought back childhood memories of Goa. I wasn't opting for the nationality of a strange new country like the US or Canada or the UK – I was returning to the nationality, language, country and flag of my childhood, those I had held as my own until the tender age of eight.

When I was a hitch-hiker in Europe in the '70s, I had marvelled at people who travelled so easily with their European passports, without requiring visas for most countries; at how they used a plastic card to walk into an ATM and withdraw their money whenever and wherever they needed it; at how they could own cars and get driving licenses there; and even at how they could go to their own homes and apartments at the end of the day. Well, now I would have all these things, and it felt like a long-cherished dream coming true.

Making the Porto dream come true

A couple of years went by before Belinda, Carmelino and I returned to Portugal. In Goa I had looked at Porto property ads. There was one apartment I had seen, close to Belinda's, which I fell in love with at first sight. But of course I wasn't going to buy it without visiting it personally, and seeing many others.

When I saw the apartment in person, I loved it even more, and yes, it was still for sale. Portugal was going through another economic crisis, and there were lots of premises everywhere with 'For Sale' signs and no takers. I visited at least ten to twelve others, though, and then ended up buying this first one. And I've never regretted it once. Its large sunny living and dining room, the curved wall with four windows, the three balconies in different directions; its distance from yet proximity to the more crowded and congested but gorgeous ancient central Porto and my favourite spot there, the Douro river bank and the Ribeira; the good people of this area which until recently was known for its rural *quintas* or farms; the fact that it was now mostly residential, yet contained all the facilities one required within a five-minute drive – all made this an ideal place to live in: it had the convenience of a city without being in the thick of it, still maintaining some greenery and farmland.

The Porto apartment as I began to furnish it. I tried to keep it minimalistic; I bought almost everything from IKEA and an innovative Portuguese boutique called O Gato Preto. After the red mud of Goa and having children and pets which didn't permit any light-coloured furnishings, I went to town on the colour white.

I went to the Loja do Cidadão (literally translated, 'The Citizen's Shop or Store', but in fact your one-stop point for most things official) and smoothly obtained my Portuguese identity card and passport. I went to the Indian embassy in Lisbon, gave in my Indian passport and applied for an OCI (Overseas Citizen of India) card, which entitled me to almost everything that Indian nationality did. I searched the net for a used car (it was the first time I was going to officially drive in Europe, in a left-hand drive environment, and most importantly by learning and strictly observing all international traffic rules; until I got used to all of that, I didn't want to risk even a scratch on a brand-new car), and found a magnificently maintained powerful BMW X3. I opened a bank account and acquired debit and credit cards.

Now I had all those things that I had marvelled at in Europe thirty-five years ago.

I like giving names to my cars, and I called this one The Black Prince.
LEFT: The day I bought it. RIGHT: On a lone road trip down to Alcoutim, south Portugal.

I surprised myself because not once did I try to 'make it' in music in Portugal. I had had enough of it, and was enjoying being a 'normal' citizen, unrecognized by anyone except by the rare Indian in a supermarket or in the street, in a country where one didn't need to be famous and influential in order to be served and treated as one should be.

I devoted my time to driving around and discovering my new country, from the north to the south, from the east to the west. And the more I saw of it, the more I loved it. It was marvellous how a tiny nation could contain such varied beautiful scenery and nature, historic cities and castles and forts and villages. And everywhere, a people that were mostly friendly and helpful, and non-judgemental of skin colour, origins or religion.

Although I didn't try to form a band or even to perform solo anywhere, never would I stop making and creating music. So, as planned, I immediately converted one of the three bedrooms in the house into my home recording studio – better equipped, and better acoustically treated, than the one I had in Goa. It also doubled as my study.

The odd recordings I made here turned out to be chilled out, peaceful pieces of music. And although I soon had enough for a whole album, which I tentatively referred to as 'The Porto Album', I wasn't going to try and present it to record companies, neither in Portugal nor anywhere else. Like I said, I guess I'd really had enough of that rat-race life – chase, chase, look over your shoulder to see whether someone is cheating you or stealing your ideas, and keep on chasing. I had quit it while I was still a well-known artist in India, and there was no way I was going to restart from scratch as an unknown here. I was making music for my own personal pleasure now.

My recordings here were sporadic and disjointed, though. They didn't seem to follow any particular direction, except that they all shared a contented, peaceful vibe.

On a trip to Goa in 2018, after a few years of having lived in Portugal for almost six months every year, I was to complete and record a song I had been writing about leaving my beloved Goa. And that was when 'The Goa That I Used to Know' took shape. Jonah provided the concept for the music video (me locking up the Siolim house), and shot it beautifully too; and Zenia appeared and gracefully danced in it.

The inspiring back pain attack

A year or so after moving to Porto, I suffered a severe attack of back pain. This pain had originated during my early stint at the Taj Fort Aguada in Goa, when I was bending to lift up my heavy amplifier and someone had called out to me from behind. I had lifted it and turned around simultaneously, and felt a searing pain in my back, the kind I had never felt before.

Over the years, the pain recurred once in a while. Though I tried all kinds of treatments possible, from allopathic doctors and orthopaedists to acupuncture and acupressure and normal yoga classes, it is only when a good friend called Sharmila Joshi introduced me to a wonderful teacher of Iyengar Yoga called Zubin Zarthoshtimanesh in Mumbai that I experienced a relief from these attacks, which didn't recur then for years.

In the three weeks that I now spent in bed in Porto, reading a mountain of books and listening to music, I entertained a dark thought: *This damn pain recurred even while religiously practising Iyengar Yoga with the wooden blocks and belts I've carried everywhere since then… What if it gets worse with the years? What if I am never able to sit up in my recording studio again?*

And that led me to another thought: *The music for Mother Teresa which I'd started twenty-seven years ago! And that autobiography which I'd started six years ago! They would remain forever incomplete!*

These thoughts led me to a happy decision: *I will make two covenants with myself: I shall make the Mother Teresa music, and my autobiography, my life goals. And, as soon as I am out of bed, I'm going to restart work on them both. And this time I won't stop until they are complete.*

As soon as I was free from the back pain, my good neighbour Senhor António Silva took me to one of the best orthopaedic doctors and surgeons in Porto. 'Your Iyengar Yoga exercises are wonderful,' the good doctor said, 'but your back muscles are lax and weak. Together with yoga, I suggest you join a gym. I'll prescribe the exercises you ought to do. Avoid others. And get yourself a good personal trainer for the first three months.'

The Mother Teresa Project: from four songs to twenty-eight tracks!

The gym on three days of the week, and yoga on the other three, did wonders. I now had what I felt was the perfect combination: strength and flexibility. And, as soon as I felt the two, I hit the studio and started re-recording the first song of the Teresa project, 'Take Me to Calcutta'. It was wonderful how very much better it sounded with the latest instruments and recording facilities I had today, twenty-seven whole years later.

The song which followed was another one of those I had written then on that Calcutta–Goa flight, 'Welcome, My Child', sung by the Mother Superior of Loreto Convent. The first one seamlessly flowed into the other story-wise, so I made them fuse together audio-wise too – Teresa taking a boat from Europe with its horn blowing, and landing into the din of India's streets.

After that I had meant to record the two other songs I had written in 1987; but something strange happened that morning. I felt a compulsion to write a fresh new song, one which would follow 'Welcome, My Child' in a narrative timeline. Now that Mother Superior had welcomed young Teresa, she was going to show her around the convent, inadvertently highlighting its comforts as compared to the slums, which Teresa accidentally glimpses through a window. So a brand-new song was born: 'The World Within/Without'.

And thus it went on – the compulsion to continue this as a complete linear narration in music, not just a bunch of disjointed songs. Whenever I completed a new song, on that very night, or latest in the shower the next morning, I had the topic, the main lyrics, and the melody ready in my head for the next song. I would just go straight to the studio after breakfast and start recording it.

On and on, song after song. I simply could not help it. Never in my life had I written and recorded so many songs one after the other, practically without a day's break. The story unfolded effortlessly, after all the books I had read and the research I had done on Mother Teresa twenty-seven years ago, and I loved that this project was allowing me to compose music in all the different styles I loved (from western classical to folk to rock to Latin to Indian folk and Indo-Western fusion), according to the various characters and situations involved. I was in musical heaven.

Maggots

People in the limelight are often targeted by the jealous, the incapable, the mediocre, the frustrated, the mean- and evil-minded of this world. They try to feed upon your blood, wishing they could be you, suppressing the unbearable thought that they will never be as good. Or they simply try to inch into your limelight, hoping that by attacking you they will find some of your prominence reflected upon themselves.

But history has never been kind to such people. One only remembers that the luminaries (whether it was Shakespeare, Einstein, The Beatles or even

Mother Teresa) all had their critics, detractors and attackers – but no one bothers to remember the detractors' names. History just smirks and laughs them into oblivion.

Whether they are extortionist lawyers whose victims have retaliated with swords or ink; or extortionist grown women who pose as minors but have no birth certificates; lying priests and bishops; fat, short, crooked cops who think themselves tall, slim film heroes; newspaper publishers and editors who are caught on hidden cameras blackmailing gamblers for 'protection money'; or their myriad insignificant cowardly chamchas who shout in glee in the melee – they're all the same: maggots.

They have never got a cent out of me in extortion or bribe, and here they will not get their moment of fame by being mentioned by name, either.

My love life post-divorce

What am I doing writing about country shifts, saints and maggots, when I'm sure you were waiting for a detailed and juicy account of a super-hectic post-divorce love-and-sex life?

I'm sorry to disappoint, but it wasn't hectic at all. As I had said earlier, I never really ran after women; they usually happened to come to me, mainly due to my profession. As I had also said earlier, my live shows had now happily diminished. Which meant that the occasions for these 'situations' were much less.

Of course, I enjoyed the occasional visits from lovers who had turned into friends. But these visits didn't last longer than three days at a time, or a couple of weeks if they were a long way away abroad.

But even these lost their lustre after some years. And I found myself subconsciously looking for a more permanent companion – but with whom I would always maintain the 'I'm a free spirit and so are you' status.

There were a few of these tentative relationships, but I'm not going to name or describe them all. Suffice it to say that none lasted even a whole year. The shortest one lasted two months, with a blonde blue-eyed artist from Finland. Her beauty and grace reminded me of Mother when young, though that's not at all the reason why I felt attracted to her; I don't have a mother fixation. She even flew down to be with me when I received the Padma Shri award from the president of India Abdul Kalam in Delhi in 2007, but we broke off soon thereafter. The longest relationship lasted for eight months, and it was with a dark Bengali beauty who lived in Europe. I was equally serious about the others. One has to be, if envisaging and considering a more steady and permanent relationship, even as free spirits. However, none went up to the point of cohabitation; every time we got to know each other better, differences cropped up, which proved to be insurmountable, at least for me. Some of the women remained good friends for life, though, and I know I can count on them for anything anytime. And I (and they) know they can count on me the same way.

Whatever relationships I did write about, I would like to assure the reader that I did not mention them in order to boast about my 'sexual conquests'. In fact, for each one that I've mentioned in the book, I've left out at least ten, if not more. And that's not written as a boast either. I've only written about the ones which did indeed help form my character – yes, believe it or not, even the one-night stands were very formative, as were the threesomes, which I don't think I have written about at all. Besides, sex is rightly credited with spiritual attributes if approached in the right way – but I shall not presume to sermonize you about that.

That period in my life helped me fulfil, and therefore get rid of, many fantasies and desires; and definitely helped me reach where I now had, with a satisfied and satiated feeling of 'been there, done that'. And more confident that I was perhaps ready to enter into a one-on-one relationship again with a much more mature approach than the one with which I approached my marriage itself, all those years ago.

Most important was the realization, which came rather late in life, that perhaps I had been too demanding of perfection in my past relationships: that perfection was the last thing I ought to expect, for the simple reason that I'm not perfect either. Ah, sometimes one takes a whole lifetime to learn the simple truths of life.

Zenia

A little after I started work on the Mother Teresa music project, a young woman put a 'Like' on one of my posts, which was a little poem I'd written accompanied by a photo I'd clicked late one evening of the seagulls on the ramparts of the old defensive wall, Muralha Fernandina, near the Dom Luís Bridge in Ribeira. Her name was Zenia Santos Costa Pereira.

I found her triple-barrelled surname amusing and intriguing. If a Goan, she would certainly be from the south, proud of her so-called higher caste and eager to show it, thought I disdainfully.

But then I clicked on her profile. The first photo I saw was of her leaning into a Christmas tree. It mesmerized me – though it didn't even show her too clearly. I almost wrote to Santa Claus saying I wanted that girl for Christmas. And then I saw more and more of

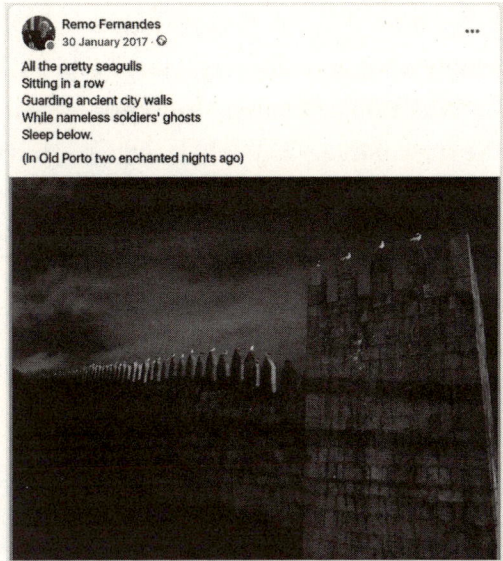

Remo Fernandes
30 January 2017

All the pretty seagulls
Sitting in a row
Guarding ancient city walls
While nameless soldiers' ghosts
Sleep below.

(In Old Porto two enchanted nights ago)

The first photograph I saw of Zenia's, and wished she was on my Christmas tree.

her photos. Whether it was the inner light which shone through her eyes, or simply her physical beauty, I just could not have enough of looking at her.

We became friends on Facebook, exchanged a couple of messages about the state of things in our beloved Goa, and that was it. Though she seemed friendly enough, there was no way I was going to pursue this. She appeared to be much, much younger to me, and I had no intention of being a dirty old man who chased a girl half his age. Like the fabled 'silent admirer', I would appreciate her from afar, without ever telling her about it, just gazing at the pictures she posted on her Facebook page. A very Hindi-filmi attitude, I know. But that would be it.

Probably the second photograph of Zenia that I saw.
It only went to reinforce what I felt on seeing the first one.

Teresa & the Slum Bum

My Mother Teresa project kept growing and flowering. It was now gaining the proportions of an opera, with multiple characters playing and singing the different parts, so I decided to start getting at least the main songs in the right pitch for the singers I was yet to look for.

The most important and numerous songs were of course to be sung by Mother Teresa herself, and I had to finalize this role. The ideal voice I envisioned for it was one like Yvonne Elliman's, who had sung the part of Mary Magdalene in the original Broadway production as well as in the film version of *Jesus Christ Superstar*; gentle and kind, yet firm and strongly emotive. But I knew no one with such a voice, at least not in Goa, where I intended to record most parts.

I thought of Ella Castellino from Mumbai. Though her voice was far from the one I visualized for Mother Teresa, I knew her theatrical capability to adapt. Besides, she had sung harmonies on my *O, Meri Munni* album, and I had been comfortable working with her. I told her it was a fully charitable project without pay. She readily agreed, gave me her lowest and highest vocal notes, and I went on with the project, recording her songs in her key.

The opera music was now exactly half-complete. On a trip to Goa, I flew Ella down from Mumbai and recorded those of her songs which were ready to be recorded. This was a project from which I was going to donate every single paisa, cent and penny earned to 'the poorest of the poor', without even making deductions to recover whatever I had spent. And I was going to look for artists who would participate in it in the same spirit – as their contribution towards the destitute of this world.

However, since Ella had to leave behind her own assignments of jingles in Mumbai to come to record for my project, and since she had the biggest number of songs to sing, I decided to pay her a token amount, besides of course providing her with the air tickets and surface transportation. She said she did not require accommodation, as she would stay at her sister's in Goa.

When she finished recording half her songs, she agreed she would return to record the rest in the coming month of November. And I made the mistake of advancing her half the amount.

I also recorded a few other artists in Goa during that trip: the children of St. Xavier's School in Siolim, who represented the first slum children Mother Teresa taught when she moved out of the convent, in a song called 'Happy Happy Song'; my dear old friend Noel Godin who now lived in Goa and who sang the part of young Teresa's father in 'Take Me to Calcutta'; my son Jonah in 'Give, Mother, Give'; and a few others. I had already recorded Belinda, in the role of young Teresa's mother, in Porto. Until then I had sung all the voices in all the songs as guide tracks, but now the different singers for different characters were beginning to make the opera come alive.

Upon returning to Porto, it was back to my happy routine in my solitary apartment: cooking my own food (whatever few dishes I was in the process of learning) or bringing home take-away from a *churrasqueira* (very popular Portuguese restaurants), doing the dishes, working out at the gym three days a week, doing my yoga at home the other three days of the week, and feverishly composing and recording the rest of the time, every day of the week and even on weekends. I couldn't believe this was going on at such a pace. Half an opera written, composed and recorded by one single man in six months? And the other half on the way to being completed in the next six? Where was all this inspiration and creativity coming from? From me? But I had never written, composed and recorded music at this rate before…

And I kept gazing at Zenia's photos.

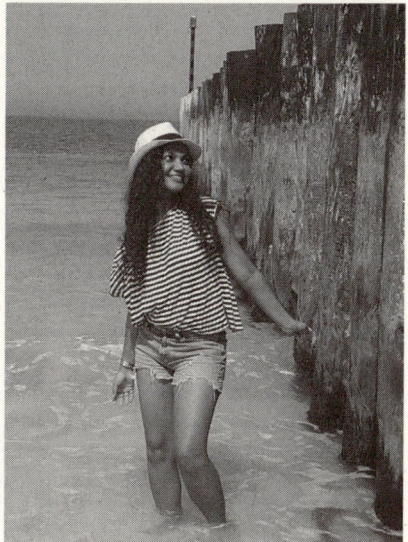

She was young, she was beautiful, she was from Verna in south Goa, and she presently worked and lived in Dubai. Gazing at photos and physical beauty was one thing, but I was more than mature enough to know that physical beauty was far from the most important factor in a relationship – though it certainly helped, if the other factors were right to start with.

Sometimes I wondered what she might be like as a person. But whatever qualities I might have envisaged, spiritual-mindedness somehow wasn't one. Until one day she posted a three-stanza poem she'd written, of which these are a few lines:

> Just as I felt the sun was scorching,
> I saw a woman work effortlessly in the heat.
> Just as I felt my blanket wasn't warm enough,
> I saw a man cuddle up in the rain in the street.
> What should I learn from this, my God?
>
> Just as I thought my basket was heavy
> A woman carrying a load offered me a hand.
> Just as I began to forget your existence
> In your own way my faith you gently fanned.
> This I learn from you, my God.

Not Shakespearean perhaps, but it showed me a side of her I simply could not resist. And, whether she was half or quarter my age, my strong resolution to stay away from her collapsed, and I now felt a compulsion to write to her that very moment.

'God, Zenia, through your other posts I've seen that you're intelligent, artistic, creative, beautiful and sexy ... and now through this one I see that, to top it all, you're spiritual too. If I were younger I would've seriously courted you for sure.'

I patted myself on the back for my clever diplomacy. I had not stuck my neck out; that phrase 'if I were younger' was my genius safety valve. I awaited her response feverishly.

'Awww! Thanks, Remo. I'm not as young as you think. And age is just a number. This is so special to me. I've always admired you, since I was a little girl.'

I was blown away.

I must disclose here that at this point I was pursuing another very important relationship. What I call important relationships were very few and far between in my life. They normally took months or even years to come by – one didn't and couldn't go looking for them. So I could not understand why these two were happening one on top of the other.

Still strengthened (and protected) by my 'we're both free spirits' theory and clause in every tentative relationship, I pursued my communication with Zenia, despite the other one being very much in my life at that moment. I felt I just *had* to get to know this woman before I committed myself to the other seriously. There had to be a higher reason why this was happening, which I could not quite fathom. No, I didn't hide one from the other – deceit certainly wasn't the way I functioned.

From that moment on Zenia and I exchanged messages, and our exchanges grew more frequent by the hour. In a couple of days we felt like we had known each other forever. She was based in Dubai; she had not been to Europe before. So by the end of that week I had invited her to spend a few days in Porto, offering to show her around Portugal, which I was dying to see with her and through her eyes. She said 'Done!', accepting on the spot, which I greatly appreciated – she bypassed the coy fuss which one has to submit to with many Indian women, however 'modern'.

She said later that she would normally never have accepted such an invitation from a stranger; but that I was no stranger, because she had gazed at my *Bombay City!* cassette cover fascinatedly as a child of nine, hiding it protectively when someone walked into the room. Ah, the unexpected advantages of being a rock star.

She had also seen me singing informally to the patients of the leprosy hospital in Goa when she was thirteen, where her aunt, a nurse, had especially taken her that day. And later again when she worked as a Kingfisher Airlines air hostess, and then as ground staff (when she opted to remain anchored in Goa), on a day she had escorted me to the aircraft; we had chatted about my album *Old Goan Gold*, and she had mentioned that she too had sung earlier on a CD by a Goan musician. I believe I had then asked her to 'come and jam up in my studio sometime'. But that had been the wolf in me talking;

I didn't remember that meeting at all when I now saw her on Facebook. I was glad she hadn't accepted the invitation to my lair back then.

I went to pick her up at the Porto airport in the morning, but didn't know her flight had already arrived ahead of time. And, as I positioned myself facing the arrival gate, she came quietly and hugged me from the back. We half turned around and stood glued to each other for interminable minutes, in silence, without moving a millimetre, without even seeing each other, as our faces were buried in each other, just 'feeling each other's vibrations' as one would say in the '70s, and feeling an inexplicable comfort and sense of belonging in our first hug. After the longest time we slowly broke away, she with a soft burst of happy laughter, me with the longest sigh, and we walked hand in hand to the parking lot.

Those nine days together were sublime. Since I hadn't yet heard her speak, the most valuable things I now discovered about Zenia were that a) she didn't have a fake 'foreign accent' so commonly affected by Goans in the Gulf, and b) her triple-barrelled surname wasn't at all indicative of caste or class consciousness, leave alone snobbishness. To me, both these qualities if present would have been totally fatal to our relationship.

The first selfies Zenia and I ever clicked, on 1 May 2017. Difficult to believe we'd just met for the very first time a few hours earlier when I picked her up at the airport; our immediate level of comfort and fond intimacy were incredibly natural.

The nine days were loaded with drives into vineyards and the countryside, to Sameiro and Guimarães, walks in fascinating old Porto, lying in bed at all hours of the day, a blues festival at Palácio de Cristal, and an unforgettable night at the best fado house in Porto on her birthday, which she had decided to spend with me.

On the day before she left she said, 'I'm ready to leave Dubai to be with you. If you want me to join you just let me know. I see ourselves becoming one of those couples who aren't able to do without each other every moment of the day very, very soon.'

I thought she was crazy. However, I wasn't equipped with her women's instant intuition. The cautious, ponderous Taurus in me took much longer, but I finally came to this same conclusion almost a year later.

WhatsApp-calling does not work in Dubai. I have many friends who bemoan this predicament – it is blocked by the UAE government itself. But somehow, Zenia and I were able to connect any time we wanted to. Not only through audio, but video calls too. Every day, several times a day. Whether I was in Porto or in Goa. Call it coincidence, the power of love, magic, whatever.

But soon after she went away we had a serious misunderstanding. I blocked her, and we broke off all communication for a whole month. After that I cooled down, and decided I didn't want to meet her somewhere and pass her by as a stranger; there was no reason why we couldn't at least be civil and friendly. I wrote to her and told her this.

Zenia happened to be in Venice with three girlfriends, about to embark on a South European cruise she had told me about. She said she had missed me terribly while walking around beautiful Venice, and that she had cried tears of joy when she read my message. We were transported right back to our beautiful nine days together in Porto. We got back to messaging and speaking on video calls several times a day, as she took me along virtually on her cruise, on phone and video cam. I was going to Goa after the cruise, to record singers for the rest of the opera which was now nearing completion.

I decided to pass by Dubai, stopping there for just a night and a day, to see her again.

Zenia booked me into a hotel near her home. I couldn't stay with her, as she was sharing her apartment. And she couldn't stay with me at the hotel, as unmarried couples can get into deep trouble for such things in Gulf countries.

It was her turn to come and pick me up at the airport. It was in the taxi on the way to my hotel, when we held hands and she rested her head on my shoulder, and I mine on her head, that I realized I was deeply in love with her. And suddenly it didn't matter that we weren't going to spend that night together. There flashed a clear realization that we were going to spend a whole lot of days and nights together in the future.

How could Mother Teresa let me down this way?

Working on the Mother Teresa songs had always had a touch of the surreal, right from twenty-seven years ago when I uncharacteristically wrote four whole songs (lyrics and music) during a two-and-a-half-hour flight from Calcutta after meeting her, to the twenty-seven songs I now had written seamlessly without a break since I resumed work on the project. I didn't even know how long a modern opera was supposed to be. I avoided timing mine as I worked on it, as I didn't want to go paranoid if it was working out to be too long or too short; I just let it flow according to the story till I finished telling it.

And then I looked at the duration of operas like *Jesus Christ Superstar*, *The Greatest Showman*, and so on – they were all two hours long, give or take a few minutes. And that's when, with slight trepidation (yet a strange calm feeling that everything would be all right), I calculated the duration of my twenty-seven songs.

Perfect! They were one hour and fifty-seven minutes long. Which left me about three minutes for an overture, which I then composed and recorded without timing it as I went along; and which turned out to be three minutes and thirty-one seconds long.

Not bad for the first opera and overture I had ever written, that too purely on intuition.

I couldn't believe it when Ella Castellino started stalling about coming down as she had promised to record the other half of her Mother Teresa songs. I reminded her of her commitment, and told her that she was the only one who had already been partly paid, the only one who had been provided with air tickets, and that all this loss of money was food, medicines and clothes directly taken away from the 'poorest of the poor' – but to no avail whatsoever. As a professional, she knew very well that not recording the rest of a normal album (pop, rock, jazz, whatever) was fine, one could always have different singers on it. But leaving an opera or musical midway, especially when singing the main part, was catastrophic. Yet she declined to come, quoting flimsy reasons, and to add insult to injury, totally ignored all my requests to reimburse the money already advanced to her.

I told her that she was doing such an ugly thing to a genuine charitable project, I would have to make the fact known to the public. I'm fulfilling my promise by writing about it here.

That night while on the phone to Zenia I could not hide my feeling of dejection. How could Mother Teresa let my project down this way, when magic had seen it through until now? I had auditioned two or three other well-known singers in Goa after Ella's desertion; though good, they didn't quite suit the part. Neither did Ella really, as I mentioned earlier, but she had that theatrical professional chutzpah which carried her through.

'I would not have suggested someone related to me if I didn't hear such sadness and despair in your voice,' Zenia said, 'but I have this cousin whose singing I really like. I'm sending you a link to a cover song she's posted on YouTube. Do see if she might suit your needs.'

I couldn't believe my ears: this was exactly the kind of voice I was looking for from the beginning! Remember the 'gentle and kind, yet firm and strongly emotive' voice of Mary Magdalene in *Jesus Christ Superstar* I spoke of? This girl had it.

Sorry I doubted you, Mother Teresa. I should have known you would not let me down. That, even while seeming to do so, you would be leading me to better things.

Me, thinking such thoughts? Nah, I wasn't religious. But this was beyond religion.

The singer's name was Fleur Dias. Contact was established, she came for an audition, and showed me all that I needed to know: that not only did she have the right voice, but that she could catch a totally unknown tune on the spot and make it her own, and that she would be able to emote just as I would need her to, and add a thing or two of her own in the bargain.

Fleur was studying dentistry. Although her final exams were coming up soon, she agreed to record all the songs at a stretch, moving between her daily classes in Bambolim during the day and recording at my studio in Siolim from evening until late into the night, only to be dropped back at Bambolim early the next morning. She completed all her songs in record time, and the character of Mother Teresa finally sounded authentic. And terrific.

After saving my life (well, my MT Project, as I shall call it for short) by suggesting her cousin Fleur for the part, Zenia flew down from Dubai to be with me in Goa the next long weekend, which was two weekends after we'd met in Dubai. She took to Siolim like a fish takes to water. And she came down for three or four more weekends after that, about once every fortnight, always refusing to let me pay or even share in her air tickets. We just couldn't stay away from each other. We spent Christmas and New Year together, and it felt great having a woman to decorate the house with – someone who was becoming a part of me and my life. She resurrected a huge old traditional bamboo Christmas star I had in the storeroom by cleaning and papering it; a real tomboy, she climbed up ladders and hung the other stars on trees and beams; she helped in making the crib.

We saw we loved the same things: drives and walks in nature rather than visits to clubs and malls; simple but good restaurants rather than the fancy ones; the same kind of films and the same kind of music. Even our tempers matched – we both loved a good fight. But the wonderful thing about her was that, unlike me, she made up very easily, quickly and lovingly.

In the meanwhile, the magic surrounding the MT Project continued working. I got the right singers for every part in Goa itself; all the Indian characters, several British ones, an Italian for the Pope, an American for the US presidential medal, and so on and so forth. Very talented, albeit mostly unknown, artists from all over the world visit Goa, and I was lucky to find them all just as required. And in a few months all the thirty-five characters in my opera were fully recorded and safely on a hard disc and on two back-up discs.

20

Here and Now

More Zenia

On the way back to Porto with all the complete recordings for the MT Project under my belt, I decided to spend a night in Dubai again. Zenia had now moved out of her shared apartment and had one of her own, so we could stay together.

She had refused to cook for me in Porto and in Goa until now, saying she didn't know how to cook food without chillies (I can't stand chillies), or that the kitchen in Goa belonged to my maids and she couldn't 'intrude'. 'She's making excuses,' thought I, 'she doesn't really know how to cook.'

It's not that I was a macho man looking for a woman to cook for me. I wanted a woman to cook *with* me. I easily qualified as the world's best dishwasher and was very happy to take on that job too, which I found quite meditative.

But here in Dubai Zenia cooked me lunch. Two of the three dishes were so salty, I thought she'd fetched and used water from the Dead Sea.

Back in Porto, I plunged into the completion of the MT Project, sorting out and transferring all the right takes of the voices I had recorded in Goa into my Porto system.

I like to keep mixing a song as I keep recording it, so the final mixing didn't take all that long. I found and engaged a superb mastering engineer in the best studio in Lisbon. I designed the album cover, posters and ads. I found the right organization to deposit the copyrights of the opera with. I made short promotional videos.

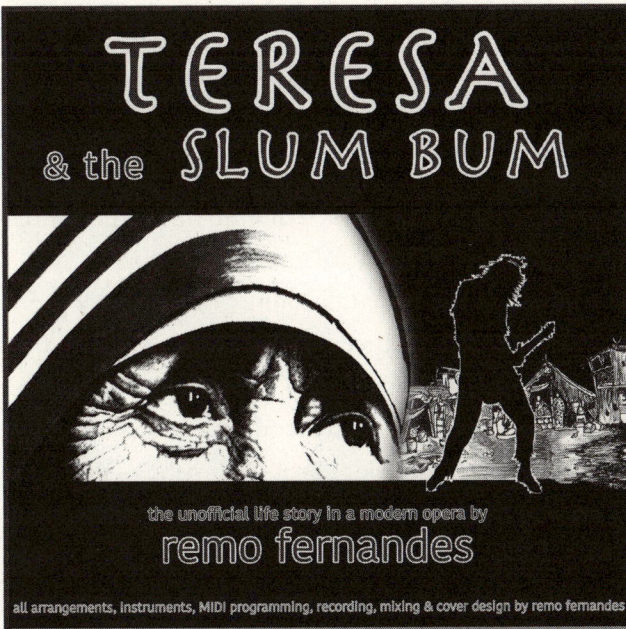

The cover I designed and executed for Teresa & the Slum Bum.

While all this was going on, I could hear the prophetic words Zenia had spoken at the end of those first nine days in Porto: 'I see ourselves not being able to do without each other every moment of the day very, very soon.' They were coming true for me.

And I remembered the rest of what she had said too: 'I'm ready to leave Dubai to be with you. If you want me to join you just let me know.'

It's not that I couldn't live without her; I didn't *want* to. It didn't make sense living apart, when we felt so good and complete together; it seemed like the silliest thing to do. Like living a half-life.

Here I told the girl with whom I was pursuing a serious relationship before I came across Zenia that I had made up my mind. And I must say a huge word of praise to her for the graceful and mature way in which she took it. She will always remain one of my very best friends for life.

Then I picked up the phone, braced myself for a lifetime of salt, and called Zenia and invited her to please move in with me in Porto.

True to her word, she said 'Done', and started the procedure: resigning from her job, giving up her rented apartment before the term was over, buying another set of luggage to carry all her belongings in, and so on. She was a woman who, unlike me, once she decided about something, went ahead without looking back.

Her move was going to take about a month. But as the date came closer, I started having the jitters. What was I getting *her* into?

I couldn't offer her the fairy-tale things which every girl dreams of: I didn't believe in marriage, neither civil nor religious; I didn't want to have any more children (she had none); and I was twenty-five years older to her. Meanwhile, what I was asking her to do required much more of her, including going against her mother's and elder brother's wishes – we had seen on her last visit to Goa that they weren't happy about our relationship at all.

And besides, I hadn't had a one-on-one live-in relationship in eleven years. Would I be capable of one? Seeing each other for a few days at a stretch was one thing, but living together 24/7 quite another. If things didn't work out, I'd feel awful for having made her go through all this for nothing. And, honestly, I was scared myself, of making a commitment for life once again.

I called Zenia and tried to explain all the thoughts running through my mind. She said she understood. So, would she consider a one-year trial kind of thing, to test out the waters, so to say? Renewable every year?

To my great relief, she said 'Yes'. And after a pause she added, 'You know, this makes me feel much lighter. I didn't have any doubts about wanting to come, but this one-year thing we've just agreed upon has eased my mind a lot.'

Zenia and I on 1 May 2018, soon after we read our
vows to each other, just before we moved in together.

The day before Zenia arrived I drove to Lisbon and spent the night in a lovely old hotel with a huge garden near the airport. Her flight was landing in the morning, and I didn't want to reach the airport after her this time. At home in Porto before leaving, I had made, marinated and refrigerated dinner (baked salmon with vegetables, my *pièce de résistance*), and kept it all ready for the oven; had put a bottle of our favourite Portuguese fruity white wine, Grandjó, to chill; and had instructed my maid to pick up and make a beautiful vase or two out of the red roses I had pre-ordered from the florist down the road.

When we drove into Porto, we went straight to the Rio Tinto church's tree-lined courtyard, which was quiet and deserted. And there, as planned, we read out the vows we had written for each other – our feelings, our pledges, our promises. And that was, for us, our wedding. We felt that no other man or woman, whether religious or governmental, had the authority or power to validate our love. That was a matter between Zenia and Remo, and Zenia and Remo alone.

Flowers for Zenia on day one in Porto: 1 May 2018.

The maid had made more than a vase; she had used the flowers and petals to decorate the dining table, the bed, and the bedside tables. My salmon never looked or tasted so good. For that night, I had made a playlist of my favourite soft, romantic classical pieces, starting with Schubert's 'Ave Maria' by Callas, Offenbach's 'Barcarolle', Beethoven's 'Moonlight Sonata', going on for a couple of hours and ending with Ravel's 'Boléro'.

I put it on softly on the stereo as we went to bed with scented candles lit on the bedside tables. Zenia loved it all, and said I couldn't have made her arrival into her new home more memorable.

'Un ménage à deux' after eleven years

This relationship seemed so easy-going and comfortable since day one, I felt as though going to sleep, waking up, and spending the whole day with Zenia was the most natural thing in the world.

And the next day onwards, she started cooking. Some of the greatest non-pungent food I had eaten in years.

I was flabbergasted. 'You can cook?!' I blurted out.

'Of course! Why ever did you think I couldn't?' she asked with a mischievous glint in her eye.

'Well, because you never cooked in Porto or Siolim until now, always giving some silly excuse or the other; and because your hyper-salty dishes in Dubai almost killed me,' I said. 'Why did you do that?!'

She laughed. 'Well, for one, I didn't want you to choose to be with me because of my cooking,' she said. 'And I felt you wanted to evaluate my culinary skills, and I perform badly under such scrutiny. And I genuinely wasn't used to cooking without chillies. About the salt, well … I knew you liked more salt than I do, but I was excited and nervous that you were arriving that day, and overdid it…'

'God! You might have lost me, and I you, if I were the type of guy who judged a woman merely by her cooking and other housekeeping talents!' I said with a shiver running down my spine.

'Yes,' she said. 'But I wanted you to choose me for myself, not for my cooking. And you did just that, my love, even though you were convinced I couldn't cook! I just love cooking, and now I shall happily cook you the best dishes I can.'

I sat there quietly smiling to myself, remembering a childhood fairy tale where the prince had willingly married a very good-hearted but very ugly princess to honour some pledge or the other. But the bride was merely testing him, and transformed into her real self on the wedding night: the most beautiful woman in the world.

'But this is great chilli-less cooking!' I said. 'You said you could only cook with chillies!'

'I did. But when I knew I was coming to you, I asked my mother for her recipes, and I've been trying them out during this last month in Dubai,' Zenia said. 'Actually we don't eat pungent food at home in Goa either, but I'm afraid I had got used to chillies with friends along the way.'

I smiled to myself some more, giving thanks for my good luck.

In a few days a song formed in my mind: 'The Zen Song', perhaps the most beautiful love song I've ever written. I recorded it very quietly in my studio, using only headphones and out of Zenia's hearing, and surprised her by playing it on her birthday at midnight in the beautiful ancient boutique *solar* in Minho where I'd booked ourselves for a couple of nights for the occasion. These lines in particular said it all:

> For once my heart ruled
> Over my mind and
> I'm glad that my heart was right.
>
> For once my mind gave
> In to my heart and
> I'm glad that my mind was wrong.
>
> What have I done to deserve a woman like you
> I must've done something good like a novice I knew
> I thought my validity for happiness had expired
> Until you came along and showed me love and fire.

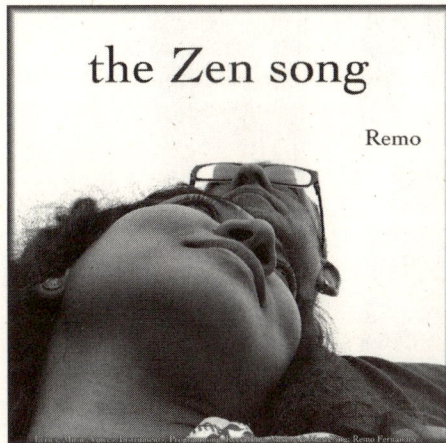

Cover of 'The Zen Song' which I wrote and recorded a few days after we moved in together. The photo was a selfie I had clicked while watching a sunset on a hill in Goa.

A year and a half went by oh so beautifully; Zenia was discovering the beauties of the Portuguese countryside with childlike glee, loving its food, walking through ancient historic villages and castles with awe, finding the vineyards romantic, enjoying the hills and valleys after eight years in the flat desert; we made road trips to all corners of Portugal, enjoyed classical and jazz concerts at the Casa da Música; Zenia cooked more and more of my favourite dishes, discovering and experimenting with new ones from the net and TV shows, and doing an amazing job of them.

She was very interested in my work as well, and helped greatly, whether in the post-production of the MT Project or other recordings and projects.

I was not allowed into the kitchen any more, not even to cook my two-and-a-half masterpieces; she took them over and cooked them better. However, I fought for my rights and forced my way to the sink to wash the dishes at least once a day. When she slept late I greeted her with great-smelling coffee. And sometimes with goodies from a wonderful French patisserie.

Good morning, sunshine!

Incidentally, after a year we went back to the church courtyard to renew our vows. And both of us had one and one thing only to say: that we wanted them extended. Indefinitely.

Two great friendships; two great disappointments

Somehow this narration wouldn't be complete if I didn't include two unpleasant stories which surfaced in my mind.

After my first sojourn and travels in Paris and Europe, I guess Eric Sida never expected me to return. After all he and Hubert had never returned, and never planned to return, to Goa.

When I married a Frenchwoman in Goa and returned on the first of my several trips to France with Michèle to visit her family, he must have been caught by surprise. And while we lounged in his living room, he casually told me that he had deposited my 'Guitaraag' piece, with my original Indian-style tuning and all, as his own composition and creation at France's copyright association, SACEM. They had finally accepted him as a member on the merits of this piece. I just smiled and said 'Oh I see!', and spoke about it no more, continuing our friendship just as before.

And when I went to Dubai for the first time and visited my favourite cousin whom I loved so much since childhood, and who had now settled there, he took me to the souk and introduced me to an Indian cassette dealer who sold pirated Bollywood soundtracks and other Indian hits. 'I sold him your first cassette to pirate,' he said matter-of-factly, 'and he made copies and sold quite a number of them from this shop.' Again, I just smiled and said 'Oh I see!', and spoke about it no more, continuing our friendship just as before.

Neither of these guys had to tell me what they'd done – I would have never ever found out on my own. What made them volunteer to confess, unasked? What they had done were not only breaches of friendship and trust, they were also crimes in the eyes of the law. I guess a guilty conscience does not let you forgive yourself.

Eric Sida, sadly, is no more, bless his soul. My cousin, alas, went on with his brother to do other surreptitious things, as well as to sell an ancestral house to which my sister and I had equal rights without asking for our signatures, which were legally mandatory, and which we would have most happily given in goodwill – we luckily have been blessed with more than enough from our own side of the family. So that can only mean they forged our signatures, though totally unnecessarily. And here finally I drew the line, politely declining their invitations to dinners when they came down to Goa thereafter. Maybe they find it easy to be hypocrites over vindaloo. I do not.

A long unexpected sojourn in Goa

In 2019, just before I started serious work to find an international agent for the promotion of the MT Project, Zenia and I took a much-needed break in Goa, as I'd been working on it non-stop for three years. We would start by landing unexpectedly for Jonah's birthday in end-November and surprising him, we thought, and then stay on for Christmas, New Year, and hopefully taste some mangoes from our garden, and also some *urraca* in March, which was the first distillation of caju feni. Mixed with fresh lime, sugar, water and ice, it was my favourite Goan tall drink, especially in the sweltering Goan summer.

All this went off beautifully until the Covid-19 pandemic broke out worldwide around March 2020. Before we knew it Italy was reeling under it, Spain to a lesser degree, and Portugal to a lesser degree still. Flights were being disrupted and lockdowns being declared everywhere. There was talk of masks and sanitizers, which were either not yet available or already out of stock in pharmacies and shops everywhere. We were reading about and watching empty shelves in supermarkets in the US and Europe, and about desperate people hoarding up on – toilet paper! If only together with the yoga exercises stolen from India Jane Fonda had introduced our toilet hygiene habits to the West, they needn't have had all those squabbles and fights over paper rolls as long as they had plain water, soap and a (preferably) left hand.

We decided that we couldn't think of a better place to be locked down in than Goa. Firstly because Goa was 100 per cent Covid-free. But also because our old ancestral family house which I love is a colonial number dating back a few hundred years, and has a large garden in the front, a much bigger one at the back with lawns, vegetable patches, fruit trees (mango, jackfruit, papaya, banana and others), a swimming pool and a mini-basketball court, and an open-to-sky courtyard right in the middle of the house. It also has three large halls, six bedrooms, my studio and office, besides the kitchen and service rooms and self-sufficient staff quarters, a large veranda in the front, and a breakfast/lunch table on the paved area under the chikoo tree at the back. I didn't describe all that to boast, but to show that it's impossible to feel cooped up in a house like that, locked down or not. Add large extended rice fields with backwater streams just behind the house, where we went for walks or jogs during spectacular sunsets, and it was difficult to remember that the rest of the world was suffering from a pandemic.

The Siolim house: The first and last photos are of the TV room and my recording studio respectively. The ones in between are of the back garden with the pool, which is a constant part of our daily lives.

Back to the book

As we prepared for our most unexpected but welcome extended sojourn in Goa, I realized that the lockdown was the perfect opportunity to resume work on this book. It was curious that no sooner than I had completed my other covenant with myself, *Teresa & the Slum Bum*, I was going to plunge into this second and last one, simply because the right time presented, nay, forced itself upon me.

I had written three chapters of my autobiography in 2009 and just embarked on the fourth one when I 'took a little break' which had lasted eleven years. Now, as I had done when I resumed work on the MT Project, I pledged to myself I would not stop until I completed it.

Would I be able to continue it in the same vein? Apparently I was, because when I sent the first five or six chapters to the very able literary agent I was fortunate to sign with, she couldn't make out or believe there had been such a gap in between.

And write intensely I did, recording four new songs during this time as well for good measure, including 'When Will You Learn, Man?' right at the beginning of the pandemic.

WHEN WILL YOU LEARN, MAN?

Lyrics & Music by Remo Fernandes.
Siolim, Goa, 3 April 2020

They say when this is over
We'll all have learnt our lesson
They say when this is over
Our selfishness will lessen

But hey, what have we learnt from World War I
(We're killing each other)
And whatever have we learnt from World War II
(We're killing other species)
And from the Black Plague, and the Spanish Flu
(We're killing our planet)

We're pirates out at sea (We're the virus)
Out on a killing spree (The real virus)
Ready to go right into World War III.

Chorus

When will you learn, man
It's only love, love, love
That will save your clan
When will you learn, man
It's only love, love, love
Not your greedy power plan.

Before this pandemic
We cried 'Ghanti! Immigrant! Caste! Religion! Outsider!'
After this pandemic
We shall cry 'Ghanti! Immigrant! Caste! Religion! Outsider!'

But right now we can't blame any of these (No more blame game)
Right now we're down on your knees (Now we're tame tame)
Right now we dare not even sneeze (What a shame shame)
So we transfer our hate
To the Chinese.

Chorus

When will you learn, man
It's only love, love, love
That will save your clan
When will you learn, man
It's only love, love, love
Not your diabolical plan.

Not your money
Not your power
Not your greed
Not your hate
That might save your clan.

The End

Even as Goa was 100 per cent Covid-free, the people concerned, in all their wisdom, decided to open its borders to the heavily infected neighbouring states, without enforcing proper safety measures. And Miss Corona thus made her grand entry into what was perhaps the last uninfected paradise in India.

Now Zenia and I felt we would be safer with the rules and arrangements in place and in force in Portugal, so when flights resumed, we did a Covid test and flew back to Porto. We had been in Goa for nine whole months in a row, without a gym to go to, and eating delicious Goan food to our hearts' and stomachs' content.

In Porto I resumed writing, and recorded three new songs too: 'Two Before I Die', 'A Sixties' Song', and 'Keep the Faith', a second song about the pandemic.

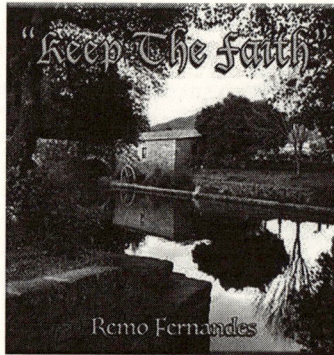

I sit, I think, I write,
My story of longing
Of long ago
I try to fit a lifetime
In a hundred and fifty thousand words
Blow by blow.
Keep the faith,
Keep the faith…

Our favourite drive and walk in Porto, where we always find beauty and peace.

And today, on 15 January 2021, I finally completed writing this last chapter.

Epilogue

And soon after the book was completed, the Covid situation suddenly turned alarming in Portugal and other parts of Europe. Zenia and I just about managed to 'escape' back to Goa before flights out of Portugal were totally discontinued temporarily. Then, as the second wave of the pandemic hit India, we felt it was safer to go back to Portugal again, and we did.

Although we're both fully vaccinated now, we do hope we won't need to play this game of hide-and-seek with Covid for much longer.

If wishes neighed

I wish I could have had the space to write more about some other concerts which were landmarks to me, simply because they involved performing with people who were my superstar heroes while I was a student.

Meeting and performing with Ian Anderson and Jethro Tull was the mother of them all – this I have written about. I'm in touch with Ian even today, and he helped a lot in getting some key people interested in *Teresa & the Slum Bum*, writing a marvellous few lines about it in 2019: 'Remo has a passion for musical excellence. His new project builds on his many previous years of creativity, exploring the genres and telling the tale in rich and poignant terms. Varied and detailed music plus the lyrical depth we might hope for when tackling such a subject of universal truths, love and tragedy.'

And I had only to ask for Ian to give me the most generous of endorsements for this book.

I wish there was space to write about some other concerts too. Like about performing on stage with Robert Plant and Jimmy Page of Led Zeppelin and Roger Taylor of Queen – even though they just lip-synced through Zeppelin's 'Rock and Roll' at the Channel [V] Awards in Mumbai. Performances with Indian artists like Trilok Gurtu, Zakir Hussain and A.R. Rahman. Performing and recording with some of the greats in Mauritius and Jamaica. Receiving visits in Siolim from people like Dave Stewart of Eurythmics and others.

But somehow I approached this book as a reminiscence of my personal life, rather than a detailed recounting of my professional one.

I also wish there had been space to write much, much more about the good years with my ex-wife Michèle. About my sons Noah and Jonah; about my sister Belinda, and her husband Carmelino and son Daniel. About the wonderful decades of my friendship with Noel Godin, who has been a part of my life almost throughout, as my host, guru, adviser, confidante and partner in gluttony. About my childhood friend Xipru in my grandmother's village of Parrá, who showed me birds' nests and snake holes; schoolday friends: John d'Mello (I still call him Johnny Cool); Zitá, Toninho (deceased), Laurinha and Nandinha Nogar, siblings all; Roy Andrade, who loved to play Tull songs, and who is now a successful doctor and surgeon in Santos, Brazil; Didier (deceased), and Eugénio de Melo and Winnie d'Costa (deceased), in Panjim; Norman Faleiro, Joe Araujo, these last two whose friendships may have started during the schooldays but lasted way beyond; college-day friends Neelam and Neeta Sharma, Devika (Viki) and Isabel Sequeira, Thelma and Lisa Dias, Mustafa Sheikh Kader, Mahesh Rao, Noel Pereira, Bismark Silveira (deceased), all in Goa; Mumbai college-day friends Sujata Singh from Nagaland, Poonsak Hootrapavanon from Thailand who sadly committed suicide, and Satya Prakash from Fiji whom I can't trace. I wish I could write more about my other friends in Paris: Sophie Lepreux, Bertrand Henry, Marie and William Altman, Yves Coatanroch. Eric Sida – who died of cancer some years ago; Hubert de Remusat and I are very much in touch, and we visit each other in Paris and Porto. About my friend in Panjim, Jacinta Valadares, who's like a sister, and her twin Lucia; Mark Fernandes (great cheater at carrom and table tennis) and Elvis Carvalho in Siolim, both good friends who also worked as my PAs for a while; my very distant cousin but more than that an invaluable friend, Big Man Alex Fernandes in Mumbai; Roger Drego, who besides being the greatest sound man of India is also a wonderful friend; Senti Toy from Nagaland; my wonderful next-door neighbours in Siolim, Wilfred and Malvina Fernandes and their daughter Wilma, whom I watched growing from a newborn to a college girl; Sai Panandikar, aka Mr Ponytail, poet, writer and much more, who has written so many brilliant Konkani lyrics and translations for my songs; Shyam Banerjee in Delhi who has transliterated so many of my songs into Hindi, including the full *O, Meri Munni* album; Vatsala Kaul, also in Delhi, who introduced me to Shyam Banerjee; and many, many others.

A special word of thanks to Amitav Ghosh, whom I first met after I couldn't help writing him a fan letter when I read his *The Hungry Tide*; he became a good friend, and wrote a lovely endorsement for this book. He also introduced me to Hemali Sodhi, my super-able literary agent; I would also like to thank Udayan Mitra, executive publisher at HarperCollins, who painstakingly and very ably edited this autobiography. A big thank you also to Dahlia Sen Oberoi, my very efficient, prompt, considerate and lovely literary lawyer.

I wish I had more space to write about my pursuit of the 'state of mind' I had accidentally stumbled upon during that college tour; about how it came to me accidentally twice more in my life over the decades, until I saw clearly that meditation was the key to it; and about finally pursuing meditation seriously, but being too lazy to practise it regularly.

Yes, I wish I had more space to write, but I'm grateful that Udayan and HarperCollins have gracefully accepted that this book be this long already, which is much longer than usual, and that too without compromising on the size of the font or the number of photos.

For the precious photos from the past I have Mother to thank. I have watched her, over the years, religiously build up our family albums with her own hands, at a time when one had to accurately stick four 'corners' to hold photos of different sizes on each thick black album page: one album for Mother and Father, one for Belinda, and one for me. If not for her, these nostalgic treasures would have long been lost or destroyed.

After all…

The completion of *Teresa & the Slum Bum*, Zenia, and the completion of this book happened almost together, if you can look at a span of three years as but a moment in a sixty-eight-year-long life, the way astrologers and geologists see millennia as a mere wink of the eye.

Will I reach the end of my life as someone whose popular music became a hit, but whose best but serious work, from *India Beyond* to *Teresa & the Slum Bum*, remained obscure and unknown, due greatly to the fact that he was born in the wrong country with the wrong record companies for such music?

Or will *Teresa & the Slum Bum* be produced into a successful stage opera or film, and will this book be noticed and well-loved, and will my literary agent and publishers then ask for a Part Two?

Whatever happens, I cannot tell you the amazing time I had creating *Teresa & the Slum Bum*, the magical sensation of feeling Mother Teresa's hand on my shoulder every step of the way. And discovering something new about me: that I could write an opera after all.

And I cannot tell you the amazing time I had writing this autobiography. Going through your whole life is therapeutic – something I would prescribe for everyone. Even if you're not famous, and even if you're not a 'writer', write your story as well as you can remember it, even if just for yourself. It will put your life into perspective. It made me discover a second new thing about me: that I could structure and write something as lengthy as a book after all.

And lastly, I cannot tell you how amazing it is to have found Zenia and having her as my life companion, as the love of my life, at a time when I thought I'd never find love again. She made me discover a third new thing about me: that I could turn voluntarily, willingly and happily monogamous after all.

REMO
A Soundtrack for the Autobiography

Listed below are some of Remo's songs mentioned in the book. We have put together a playlist called '**REMO: A Soundtrack for the Autobiography**' which is available on Spotify. The playlist features all the singles, and at least one track from each album. Some of the earlier songs are being freshly recorded and digitized at the moment, and may not be on the playlist to start with, but we plan to make these available soon. The playlist would of course be modified and expanded from time to time.

This list does not include any of Remo's film songs.

These songs and albums are also available at online music stores and on streaming services.

Song	Mentioned in
• *'Shivole, Sonar Khetti'*	Chapter 3
• *'Minha Mãezinha Querida'*	Chapter 3
• 'Till I Die'	Chapter 5
• 'Dreamland'	Chapter 5
• 'Love at First Sight'	Chapter 6
• 'Ode to the Messiah'	Chapter 7
• 'Nightmare City'	Chapter 7

A list of Remo's albums

- *Goan Crazy!* (1984)
- *Old Goan Gold* (1985)
- *Pack That Smack!* (1986)
- *Bombay City!* (1987)
- *Politicians Don't Know How to Rock 'n' Roll* (1992)
- *O, Meri Munni* (1998)
- *Symphonic Chants* (2002)
- *India Beyond* (2002)
- *Muchacha Latina* (2007)
- *Teresa & the Slum Bum* (2019)

About the Author

Remo Fernandes was born in Goa and grew up there in the 1950s and 1960s. He studied architecture in Bombay, busked and hitch-hiked his way through Europe and North Africa as a young man, and returned to Goa in his mid-twenties, with a resolve to pursue only the things he loved: music, art and writing.

His success with his first home-produced albums led to widespread fame and stardom. His chartbusting film songs and his albums were landmark hits for a generation of listeners. His innovative musical journey continues to this day: he recently composed and recorded a full-fledged opera on Mother Teresa.

Now in his early seventies, Remo divides his time between his ancestral home in Siolim, Goa, and Porto in Portugal.